PLANNING AND MEASUREMENT IN YOUR ORGANIZATION OF THE FUTURE

PLANNING AND MEASUREMENT IN YOUR ORGANIZATION OF THE FUTURE

BY D. SCOTT SINK, Ph. D., P.E. & THOMAS C. TUTTLE, Ph. D.

With contributions from Seung-Il Shin, Paul Rossler, Garry Coleman, Tony Pineda, and Sanchoy Das.

Industrial Engineering and Management Press
P.O. Box 6150, Norcross, Georgia 30091-6150
404/449-0460

Library of Congress Cataloging-in-Publication Data

Sink, D. Scott.
  Planning and measurement in your organization of the future/by
D. Scott Sink & Thomas C. Tuttle; with contributions from Seung-il
Shin ... [et al.]
          p.   cm.
  Bibliography: p.
  ISBN 0-89806-090-7: $46.25
  1. Industrial productivity--Measurement.   2. Performance
standards.   3. Corporate planning.   4. Management.   I. Tuttle,
Thomas C.   II. Title.
HD56.25.S56   1989
658.4'012--dc20   89-2228
                                                             CIP

© 1989 Institute of Industrial Engineers. All Rights Reserved.
Industrial Engineering and Management Press
P. O. Box 6150
Norcross, Georgia 30091-6150

Printed in the United States of America.

92 91 90 89   4 3 2 1

ISBN 0-89806-090-7

Quantity discounts available.

To those who have lived a life of "paying forward" rather than trying to only "pay back" and as a result have had great influence on our lives and this book.

Our Parents
Our Wives and Families
Our Teachers

CONTENTS

PREFACE

The thesis of this book is that your organization, regardless of its type or size, has faced and/or will face challenges unequalled in its history and evolution. A global economy, rapidly advancing and increasingly complex technology, more demanding and enlightened customers and employees, dynamic internal and external environments, as well as increasing uncertainty and risk are just a few of the factors that have combined to cause the task of leading and managing to be ever more complex and challenging.

Our goal in writing this book was to go beyond *In Search of Excellence, Passion for Excellence, Managing in Turbulent Times, Megatrends, The Two-Minute Warning, Out of the Crisis, Change Masters,* and *Total Quality Management.* We have integrated what we have learned over the past twelve years from managing quality, productivity, and quality of work life research and development centers at major universities (Sink at Ohio State University, Oklahoma State University, and Virginia Tech, and Tuttle at the University of Maryland). Our research, development, teaching, consulting, and practical experiences are reflected in our views presented in this book. The systems, approaches, techniques, models, and processes we present are being used successfully in a wide variety of organizations. We chose to prescribe solutions rather than to describe the problems and/or opportunities. We have been trained and continue to develop ourselves in a multidisciplinary fashion, and we don't think that performance management can be accomplished successfully without this kind of thinking. You will not respond successfully to the challenges you face unless your strategy is comprehensive and well-integrated. Quality and productivity management is like a complex holographic image; it has many complex faces that when viewed from different angles all look unique. From one angle we see inventory management (JIT, MRP, etc.); from another quality management (TQM, SPC, Quality Circles, etc.); and from yet another gainsharing, automation, job enrichment, or organizational design. We hire consultants and buy programs to "fix the faces" of the hologram rather than to "fix the hologram." It's only when we address the system and integrate and coordinate our initiatives that we see progress and achieve continual improvement.

The title of this book reveals a bias. The bias is that there are two very critical faces to the quality and productivity management hologram: planning and measurement. This bias is not based upon casual preference, but rather upon what we believe literature and experience suggests is the best place to start an effort to revitalize your organization. We firmly believe that unless your organization successfully establishes strategically driven planning for performance improvement and measurement systems, none of the other interventions (SPC, automation, gainsharing, etc.) will be effective.

We devote this entire book to helping you understand how to develop improved planning for performance improvement systems and more effective measurement systems to help you improve performance. These tactics are couched in a broader philosophy of what the "Organization of the Future" will need to be in order to survive. We offer a road map to help you move your organization from "where it is" to "where it needs to be." This road map is neither easy nor straightforward; it is challenging and difficult. You will need three to five years to begin to feel the transformation, and the journey toward the Organization of the Future is a never-ending one. Often the decision to begin must be based on faith. We are convinced that those organizations that do not begin this journey may find themselves in the pages of American industrial history.

Your new competition is now performing significantly better than you are! This book can help you do something about that. But you must decide to begin the journey!

There are many who claim to have the solution, the "quick fix" to your challenges. We do not wish to be counted among that group. Our road map for change is a difficult and challenging one that must be supported by the continued personal involvement of top management, and requires the understanding, commitment, and involvement of everyone in the organization. The approach we outline will take a minimum of three to five years to establish the process and control variances. The responses to your challenges that we detail in this book are not quick fixes.

D. Scott Sink
Blacksburg, Virginia
Thomas C. Tuttle
College Park, Maryland

ACKNOWLEDGEMENTS

We have been working on this book longer than we would both like to admit. Tackling a project of this magnitude while trying to run organizations like the VPC and the Maryland Center for Quality and Productivity is next to impossible. Without the support of the following individuals our efforts would have fallen short.

First and foremost our wives, Bea and Judy, and our families are to be thanked for putting up with the effects writing has on personal time. They have been patient, understanding, and supportive.

Second, Seung-il Shin, an associate of the VPC, did an outstanding job as project manager for this effort. We wrote this book on a Macintosh computer, providing hard copies and disks to Industrial Engineering and Management Press. Mr. Shin coordinated all the logistics of layout, figure and table development, as well as editing between the authors and IIE. Anyone who has ever written a book knows the importance of this coordination and project management support. Thank you Mr. Shin!

Third, a number of other associates at the VPC have made contributions and merit special recognition: Paul Rossler, Measurement and Gainsharing; Garry Coleman, Planning; Tony Pineda, Planning and TFPMM; Sanchoy Das, SPerfC; and other graduate students in VPC. They contributed write-ups on specific measurement and planning techniques. We appreciate their continuing contributions to our efforts. Thanks are due to Jennifer Garman, Brenda Neidigh, and Andrew Harris for typing various sections of the manuscript.

Fourth, we would like to recognize the role that our clients/customers have had in the development of this book. We both have had the opportunity to work with a tremendous number and variety of organizations over the past twelve years, including: the Navy; the Air Force; Baltimore Gas and Electric; San Diego Gas and Electric; Virginia Fibre Corporation; Virginia Department of Transportation; Norfolk Naval Shipyard; Naval Sea Support Center-Atlantic; Naval Ordnance Station - Indian Head; Naval Air Depot - San Diego; RHODIA, Brazil; Rhone Poulenc, US and France; Veterans Administration; Internal Revenue Service; Department of Defense - Defense Systems Management College; Specification Advocate General & Productivity Principal - Navy; SYSCON; Honeywell; LTV-Aircraft Products Group; Orc-Ida Foods; NASA - Marshall Space Flight Center and Goddard Space Flight Center; Los Alamos National Laboratories; Naval Aircraft Maintenance Office (NAMO); Institute of Industrial Engineers; and Virginia Tech College of Engineering.

Other organizations that have contributed to our learning include: Delmarva Power and Light; Washington Gas Light Co.; Potomac Electric Power Company; Grumman Corporation; Maryland Department of Economic and Employment Development; the General Services Administration, Department of Health and Human Services; Department of Transportation; Environmental Protection Agency; Air Force Human Resources Laboratory; and American Public Power Association.

We learn something new from every customer and have worked hard to incorporate that knowledge into this book. Special thanks to: Mr. Shoni Dhir, LTV; Mr. Gerry Hoffmann, Navy; Mr. Lowell Oder, SYSCON; Capt. Cal Colvin, NAMO; Dr. Dom Monetta and Mr. Michael Shapiro, NOS-IH; Capt. Tom O'Connor, NADEP-NI; Capt. Dennis Kruse, NAVSESS; Mr. Bob

Turner, NAVSEACENLANT; Capt. "Skip" McGinley, NNSY; Dr. Paul Torgerson, VPI & SU; Dean Pam Kurstedt, VPI & SU; IIE staff; Mssrs. Edson Musa, Andre´ Alckmin, and Paulo Berringer, RHODIA; Mr. Dick Engwall, Westinghouse; Mr. Dave Acker, DSMC; Mr. Glen Peters, Honeywell; and Mr. Phil Monroe, DEMCON. Other individuals who have contributed to the ideas presented here include colleagues at the Maryland Center for Quality and Productivity (MCQP): Mr. David Ross; Mr. Ollie Amundson; and Mr. Robert Wilkinson, now with Baltimore Gas and Electric Co. Another Maryland colleague who deserves recognition is Dr. Anil Gupta, who helped us recognize the links between measurement and business strategy. Appreciation is expressed to Dr. William Alley and Dr. Charles Weaver of the Air Force Human Resource Laboratory (AFHRL) for their support and critical comments with respect to the measurement concepts. Finally, another source of ideas and a friendly critic who deserves recognition is Dr. John Kelly of the American Public Power Association.

These individuals have made specific and significant contributions to our knowledge and hence to this book. However, any failure to communicate or weaknesses in the methodology lie solely with the authors.

Dr. Kenneth Kiser has been a colleague of mine (Sink) and a co-presenter of my three-day short course for over seven years. He has made significant contributions to my ability to clearly communicate these concepts. Dr. Harold Kurstedt has been a proactive colleague for me here at Virginia Tech; I thank him formally for his contributions to my work.

Finally, the Institute of Industrial Engineers deserves acknowledgement for their willingness to encourage this effort. Their support of my three-day short course since 1981 has provided the testing ground for new ideas and concepts. Industrial Engineering and Management Press staff have taken our manuscript and converted it to the product you see now. Our thanks for their efforts to produce a quality product and to ensure that it is marketed effectively.

1. THE CHALLENGE: NEW COMPETITION IN A GLOBAL ECONOMY

INTRODUCTION

This is a book about the measurement and improvement of organizational performance. It is a cliche, but nonetheless true, that today's organizations exist in an increasingly competitive and complex world. Performance measurement can help or hinder an organization's ability to compete, depending on how measurement systems are developed and utilized. This book is about how measurement can help your organization compete in the decades ahead. We will take the mystery out of measurement for you.

Managers, staff, and employees must view measurement as a natural and necessary part of their jobs and their role in the organization. The primary goals of managers (in the future all persons in an organization will be referred to as employees and managers) in all areas and at all levels in the organization should be twofold:

1. Perform, get the job done; and
2. Continuously strive to improve performance (their own, their group's, the system's, the organization's).

This rather expanded, simplified view of the role and responsibility of an employee is necessary to meet the challenges of The New Competition. It is consistent with the philosophies being espoused by the leading authors, consultants, and experts in the areas of productivity and quality management (i.e., Deming, Juran, Ishikawa, Reich, Peters, Kanter, Naisbitt). The essence of management is that one cannot manage that which one cannot measure. The best measurement systems are a blend of the objective with the subjective, quantitative with qualitative, intuitive with explicit, hard with soft, and judgment with decision rules or even artificial intelligence. The primary yet most neglected role of measurement is to improve. Why measure? Measure to improve. Measure to provide your management team with new insights into why the system performs the way it does, where it can be improved, and when the system is in control or out of control.

There are other reasons for measuring performance of an organization system—whether it be an activity, work group, firm, section, plant, branch, directorate, or function—that we will discuss. In this book we have a bias: that far and away the most important reason for measuring performance is to improve performance. This philosophy at first sounds so obvious and simple; you might assume that no one would measure for any other reason. Yet what we find in practice is that managers at all levels and in all kinds of organizations fall into the traps of :

1. Measuring A while hoping for B. We measure the easy things, the most pressing things, the wrong things; we hope for quality while measuring and controlling only production schedules.
2. Measuring to control in such a way as to make improvement more difficult. We focus

on control of excess, creating a compliance mentality rather than an improvement orientation.
3. Measuring to find those who have performed poorly in order to punish them while ignoring the good performers.

In Chapter 1, we will examine in more detail why measurement of performance has become and will continue to be so salient an issue in the face of The New Competition. At the outset we need to let you know what we mean by performance. The performance of an organizational system is a function of a complex interrelationship between seven criteria. The seven performance criteria are:

1. Effectiveness;
2. Efficiency;
3. Quality;
4. Productivity;
5. Quality of work life;
6. Innovation; and
7. Profitability (for profit centers) or budgetability (for cost centers and non-profit organizations).

We will define each of these criteria in Chapter 5. In Chapter 1, we also will discuss briefly The New Competition: What will it take for an organization to be competitive and survive in the 1990s? What role will measurement play in the process of maintaining competitiveness? We will present several interesting examples depicting how The New Competition is performing. We want to leave you with three messages in Chapter 1:

1. You must begin to put more focus on measurement that supports and enhance improvement, and we must strive to improve the quality of the design of measurement and evaluation systems.
2. There are strong forces causing your organization to need to change in a more proactive fashion, and you must understand these forces in order to respond successfully to them.
3. The needed response is one that addresses systematically and in an integrated fashion multiple dimensions of your organization's management process.

Let's begin by examining the forces and factors that are or should be causing your organization to re-examine its culture, its management systems, and its measurement systems.

THE NEW COMPETITION

Ask the key decision makers (people in pivotal positions of power) in your organization three basic questions:

1. What does our organization need to look like in the next two to five years in order for us to compete, survive, grow, and continue to succeed?
2. What do we have to do next year and in the next two to five years to become that vision of the Organization of the Future?
3. What roadblocks, obstacles, or hurdles exist or will exist to prevent us from becoming our vision of the Organization of the Future?

Assume that you asked the questions and obtained answers using a structured process that created excellent dialogue among these key decision makers. Further, assume that the process you utilized created consensus; visions of the Organization of the Future; goals to be accomplished over the next two to five years and the next year; and roadblocks to be dealt with and/or removed. Suppose that these key decision makers held the enlightened belief that you have to change the management process to change the culture; not the reverse. Suppose that a critical mass of these key decision makers (KDMs), particularly the most powerful KDM, were "intrapreneurs" and supported intrapreneuring. We believe you can use your imagination to envision what this organization would begin to do, to look like, and how it would begin to perform.

Let us share what our imaginations conjured up. The organization would begin to move responsibility and accountability for planning, problem solving, and decision making to the lowest appropriate levels. It would begin to move from management processes focusing on control to those focusing on commitment. The people in the organization would begin to *feel* much differently each day. There would be a spirit of calculated risk taking and openness regarding new ideas. There would be a strong sense of responsibility and accountability for constant attention to performance improvement. The organization would support, encourage, and reward structured efforts to improve performance in all areas. No one would be caught saying, "but I just work here." There would be no programs, just processes, ways of doing business. In five years the organization would have become The New Competition. This is not a fairy tale; no more so than the visions that were created in *In Search of Excellence*, *Passion for Excellence*, *The One Minute Manager*, *Change Masters*, *Reinventing the Corporation*, *The New Competition*, *The Zero -Sum Solution*, *Innovation*, or *American Spirit: Visions of a New Corporate Culture*. The major difference between these excellent, recent books and the one you're reading is in the level of detail and focus on "how to." The authors of these previous landmark works focused on providing philosophy, case examples, theory, concepts, and war stories. Their writing was interesting and captivating. However, they did not tell us the whole story. They did not tell us about technique and approach. They told us what The New Competition is doing, but they did not tell us how they are doing it.

The New Competition is critically examining what organizations do and how they do it, how people are rewarded, what technology and control systems are employed, how they plan, how they solve problems, how they make decisions, how they implement, how they communicate and coordinate, what measurement and evaluation systems are used and how they are used, and, most importantly, how they constantly strive to improve performance at all levels and in all areas of the organization. The New Competition is creating shared visions of the future because it knows that without them it cannot create ownership and commitment to the plans and actions necessary to stay competitive. The New Competition respects and understands the role that advanced technology will play in the Organization of the Future. However, it also understands that all performance improvement ultimately requires behavior change and behavior support. So The New Competition has a mature and sophisticated understanding of how to build and develop effective and efficient sociotechnical systems. Of course, The New Competition is an organization or group of organizations just like yours, filled with people. Do the people in your organization think, feel, and behave differently than those in The New Competition? If so, this book can help you and your organization.

Many forces and factors are causing organizations in the United States to critically examine themselves. There is a sense of a New Competition emerging that exhibits the characteristics we mentioned. For many types of organizations, such as those in utilities, transportation, communications, health care, and the government, the notion of competition is just now becoming a reality.

Many American industries and firms from 1950 to the mid-1960s did not have to face the kind of stiff worldwide competition that is now prevalent. Strategies for success are quite different in a no- or low-competition business environment than they are in a highly competitive one. The past thirty-five years in the United States have been marked by lethargy, a sense of complacency, and arrogance in the mind and behavior of many managers.

There is still a widespread belief that maintaining the *status quo* is sufficient for success and survival in the 1980s and 1990s. This belief is at the heart of the organizational culture problems rampant in American organizations. Empire building, not empire slashing, is the game to play. Productivity and quality improvement are buzzwords; if we wait it out management will forget about these programs just like they lost interest in the others. Productivity and quality improvement simply means that the organization (top management) wins and I lose. "Don't rock the boat." "Don't fix it if it ain't broke." "Maintain the *status quo*." These are the apparent beliefs that exist within most American organizations today. It is clear to us that these beliefs are inconsistent with the beliefs that must exist in your Organization of the Future.

With this brief introduction to The New Competition and the Organization of the Future, we would like to now highlight several examples of how well The New Competition is performing and responses your organization must take to survive as an Organization of the Future.

Performance Levels of the New Competition

Your New Competition is performing better than you are! And your New Competition is getting better every day. Their rate of performance improvement is anywhere from twice as fast as yours to almost infinitely faster than yours. They have a plan, strategies, tactics, are constantly learning and practicing new techniques, and are focusing on effective implementation with a passion. They have a culture that supports and encourages effective implementation and innovation. They are shoving the responsibility and accountability for planning, problem solving, and decision making to the lowest appropriate levels. They are going to dominate their marketplaces. They are going to drive you out of business and capture your market share.

Some of you believe these statements—you may even have taken them personally. You have faced The New Competition and know we are right. Some of you in government, academia, education (particularly higher education), health care, utilities, and traditionally successful firms, absolutely believe we are wrong. We suspect that most employees down inside your organizations, regardless of your type of business, feel the statements are invalid.

The New Competition is a reality. We will share three interesting and revealing examples of how well The New Competition is performing. These cases do not represent a comprehensive set of businesses or industries, so it is unlikely your organization will be represented. However, we believe that it is valid to assume that the levels of performance achieved by the three organizations discussed are representative of your competition now or in the future. If we do not present an example of New Competition performance from your business or industry, please feel free to provide us with one, and we will consider adding the example to future updates with appropriate recognition for your contribution. This book has been designed as a "living" book, to be updated at times.

Musashi Semi-Conductor Works (Davidson 1982)

Musashi Semi-Conductor Works began a performance improvement process in 1971 that was specifically focused on implementing a "small group activity" process. Table 1-1 depicts data regarding the specific performance improvement process.

Table 1-1.
Small Group Activity at Musashi Semiconductor

Year	Activities
1971	Began Small Group Activity process implementation
1971-1975	Enlightenment period, built infrastructure, understanding and support
1977	First improvement proposal received
1978	26,543 proposals submitted
1979	47,347 proposals submitted
1980	112,022 proposals submitted 98,347 proposals implemented (87.8%)

Source: Davidson 1982

The specific intent of this intervention appears to be improving performance via a structured, participative management process. We will not detail the case example since Davidson did an excellent job with that in a *Sloan Management Review* article. However, we do encourage you to read this case, and we wish to make several summary observations.

1. A significant period of time (approximately five years) was spent laying the foundation for the process. It is unlikely that many American organizations would devote this amount of time and effort to design and develop a performance improvement intervention. Our experience suggests that most American organizations spend little or no time designing their management process improvement interventions. We have a tendency to search for "quick fixes" (Kilman 1984) and to act before thinking or planning. We do not develop quality "grand strategies" in our efforts to improve performance. ("Grand strategy" is a term we learned from William T. Morris, which has been used elsewhere for similar applications. It is simply a strategically thought through plan, encompassing two to five years, that is documented in a specific fashion and communicated effectively to all levels of employees.) Several examples of recently developed "grand strategies" are shown in Figures 4-7, 4-10, and 4-11.

2. The small group activity process was developed in a top-down fashion. The "enlightenment" period provided support at all levels of management through education, involvement, and improved understanding of the process. A proper infrastructure was developed to ensure the success and survivability of the process when full-scale implementation took place. Without this enlightenment period, we suspect that there is no way any organization could achieve the level of involvement found in this example. If the foundation had not been laid and an infrastructure built, we know that no organization could have made decisions on 112,000 proposals for performance improvement, let alone implement 87.8 percent of those proposals.

3. Design criteria and design considerations for the small group activity process at Musashi appear to be significantly different than those for a typical American employee involvement program. We believe that the design strategies for employee involvement processes in this case are vastly superior to those employed in the United States. As an example, in the United States we tend to view quality circles, performance action teams, small group activity, semi-autonomous

5

work groups, and autonomous work groups as alternatives. The Japanese appear to know that these are simply different stages of evolution as organizations move from manager-led to self-management enroute to becoming the Organization of the Future (Hackman 1986).

4. The level of performance achieved by this small group activity process is significantly higher (by orders of magnitude) than any form of employee involvement that we are aware of in the United States. Table 1-2 draws a comparison. It is inconceivable that, in its present form and with current management processes, an American organization would demonstrate the design skills, patience, persistence, consistency, commitment, and continuity needed to implement a process as did Musashi. In four years of presenting this case example to literally hundreds of managers we have not found one manager or one company that can compete with the level of performance achieved in employee involvement by Musashi. Our question is: If they can do it, why can't we? The answer is: We can, but not without a commitment to practice concepts presented in this book.

Table 1-2.
Japanese Small Group Activity Performance Compared to Typical U.S. Quality-Circle Performance

Comparison	Japanese Small-Group Activity	U.S. Quality Circles
Development time	5 years	< 5 months
Scope of involvement (definition of employee)	Everyone	Line supervisors, blue-collar workers, and clerical staff
Focus of improvement	Performance	Quality
Proposals developed per work group per year	100 - 600	1 - 10
Proposals completed per month per group	30 - 50	< 1
Percent of completed proposals implemented	80 - 90	10 - 50
Evaluation criteria	Constant improvement, implementation, total involvement, quality	Benefit-to-cost ratios (short-term) from 3:1 to 6:1

Source: Davidson 1982

5. The word "employee" at Musashi evidently means everybody from the president down. In a typical American form of employee involvement, "employee" usually means anybody but management. Participative management doesn't achieve its potential if it isn't designed, developed, and implemented in a top-down fashion. Management must have an appropriate role in implementing participative management techniques, since management must accept and "own" the need to change.

6. Musashi's small group activity process clearly focused on performance (all seven dimensions), not just quality, efficiency, or productivity. American improvement strategies tend to focus on those aspects of performance that are being talked about in the latest, trendy books or seminars, or on those aspects that top management appears to be hot about this week. We do not have a strategic, well-balanced perspective regarding performance improvement. Much of this is due to extremely deficient measurement and evaluation systems.

7. Finally, Musashi's small group activity was very clearly viewed as a process, not a program. To our knowledge, the process is still in existence sixteen years later. In the United States we have a product-cycle mentality with respect to our performance improvement interventions. In America's consumer-oriented economy we have learned that products have births, they mature, and they die. We have allowed that product-cycle mentality to invade our management process designs, and as a result, we have programs instead of processes. We have programs for productivity and quality improvement that have life cycles of about three to five years at the most. This phenomenon is extremely dysfunctional and dangerous, single-handedly presenting a tremendous obstacle to your company becoming the Organization of the Future. We must design processes that continually improve and evolve.

This is our first glimpse of what The New Competition is doing and how they are performing. Admittedly, we don't know the whole story about how well Musashi performed then or now. However, in one important area, participative management, we see a superior design, excellent execution, and outstanding performance over a sustained time period. We suspect and can extrapolate without too much hesitation that Musashi is a better company because of this process. It is not difficult to imagine all the small, nagging common causes and special causes (Deming 1986) of low system performance that have been proactively identified and dealt with in this process. We also suspect that Musashi did not just start with theory and design accordingly, but that transitional leaders (Bass 1985) intuitively sensed an urgency to change the way they did business and developed response mechanisms that they believed would help them become an Organization of the Future. That is what the performance management process presented in this book is all about. We believe that improvement-oriented measurement played a critical role in what Musashi achieved and will continue to do so in the Organization of the Future. Before we take a look at the performance management process, let's examine two more examples that will help us better understand the performance levels being achieved by The New Competition.

Quasar Television Plant (Ossola 1982)

This well-publicized case, in which Matsushita Electric Industrial acquired the Quasar Television plant from Motorola, provides an excellent case study of what can be accomplished. In 1974, the Quasar plant in Franklin Park, Illinois was experiencing a 140 percent in-process rejection rate, high warranty costs, absenteeism in the neighborhood of 10 to 12 percent, and test rejects of 2.6 percent. The plant was in dire trouble. By 1982, Matsushita had reduced in-process rejection rates at the plant to 5 to 7 percent, lowered warranty costs, significantly reduced absenteeism to 2.25 percent and test rejects to 0.32 percent, decreased field rework by 90 percent, and increased labor productivity by 30 percent. Profitability improved while the same sales price was maintained.

According to Dennis Ossola, director of operations for Matsushita, these levels were achieved with the same work force, but with several basic changes in operations:

- Product engineering—26 percent fewer parts;
- Automated assembly;
- Cooperation between design and manufacturing;
- Operator training;
- Quality control/reliability engineering;
- Simplified management systems; and
- Management team attitude.

Achieving Acceptable Performance Level (APL) took six to eight years of concentration on the basics. "It wasn't hard to go from a 140 percent in-process rejection rate to 10 to 12 percent," said Ossola. "We just went back to basics." But, he added, "Going from 10 to 12 percent down to 1 to 2 percent—the corporate goal—will require the full effective involvement of the work force."

The message is that you are not out of the starting gate unless you audit, evaluate, and strengthen certain basic functions: Are you effective? Are you efficient? Are the primary functions in your organizational systems effective, efficient, and producing a quality product or service?

If you look at the various management tools and techniques touted as the solution to performance improvement, going back to basics doesn't look slick or sexy. However, there are no quick fixes. Slapping the latest and greatest management tool on top of a poor quality management process doesn't work. Do not ignore the basics unless you and your management team are willing to risk longer-term ineffectiveness and inefficiency in the performance management effort. There is a lot of performance improvement to be gained, as Matsushita proved, simply by concentrating on some reasonably fundamental issues.

Air-Conditioner Manufacturers (Garvin 1986)

Garvin investigated quality problems, policies, and attitudes in the United States and Japan. The study drew on surveys of first-line supervisors in the room air-conditioning industry to compare practices and attitudes concerning quality in the two countries. It discussed two central issues:

1. The changing mix of problems with quality as quality improves; and
2. The relationships between management commitment to quality, work force commitment to quality, pressure to produce goods of high quality, and quality performance. The results of this study are shown in Tables 1-3 and 1-4.

These findings have several important implications. First, they confirm the widely held belief that high levels of quality performance are accompanied by organizational commitment to that goal; without a management and work force committed to quality, little is likely to happen. Second, Japanese quality practices have evolved over time and considerable progress has been made in solving quality problems. Not only do the perceptions of the mix of quality problems differ in the two countries, the framework for thinking about quality appears to differ as well. Last, there is a wide gap in performance between the average of the *best* U.S. plants and the *average* Japanese manufacturer. If the best U.S. plants are comparing their performance to themselves or to the better U.S. plants, they are going to go out of business. Again, there is a New Competition that is performing better than we are and improving every day.

Table 1-3.
U.S. and Japanese Manufacturers
of Air Conditioners

Ratings	Internal Failure	External Failure
Japanese Manufacturers	0.95	0.6
Best U.S. Plants	9.00	7.2
Better U.S. Plants	26.00	10.5
Fair U.S. Plants	63.50	9.8
Poor U.S. Plants	135.00	22.9

Source: Garvin 1986

Table 1-4.
Attitudes and Policies on Quality in the U.S. and Japan

Dimensions of the Quality Management Process / Manufacturers	United States	Japan
Framework for thinking about quality	Focus on task and activities	Focus on the production process in its entirety
Causes of quality problem	Attributed to internal factors: such as workmanship, process design and maintenance	Attributed to external factors such as incoming parts and materials and product design
Attitudes toward quality	Emphasis on meeting production schedules	Emphasis on producing high quality products
Policies on quality	Rely on formal evaluations against rework, scrap, and goals	Rely more heavily on statements of company philosophy and worker commitment

Source: Garvin 1986

Performance Levels of the New Competition Are Superior

These three case examples highlight for us the superior levels of performance of The New Competition. We believe the levels of performance demonstrated in these cases are becoming the rule and not the exception among global competitors. These levels of performance are becoming the standards by which competitiveness is being defined and measured in your new marketplaces.

In 1986, President Reagan signed Executive Order No. 12552 calling for a 20 percent improvement in productivity in all federal government organizations by 1992. This commendable act has developed a sense of urgency among some government organizations to take action. However, we believe that it would have been more appropriate to call for an improvement in performance (effectiveness, efficiency, quality, productivity, quality of work life, innovation, and budget management). Unfortunately, many have simply translated the president's order in terms of cost cutting. This may be the appropriate response in some areas, but in others a single-minded focus on cutting costs may come at the expense of effectiveness and quality. When we take a narrow view of performance we most often get narrow responses. The president clearly wanted improved performance and simply used the term productivity to convey his goals. However, the Office of Management and Budget (OMB) and other agencies that translate executive orders into required actions must be more precise and clear as to the desired outcomes. Recent efforts in the area of Total Quality Management (TQM) are addressing the broader performance issues.

The second point we want to make about this executive order and its relationship to The New Competition is that a 20 percent improvement in productivity, as we have seen from the examples just provided, is not enough. Our sights are set too low. What is the percentage difference in performance of the Musashi small group activity process and a typical American quality circle program? What was the percent improvement in performance at the Quasar television plant? What is the percent difference in performance of the average Japanese air-conditioner plant and the average performance of even the best U.S. air-conditioner plant? Simple arithmetic reveals that we are looking at orders of magnitude differences in levels of performance, not 20 percent over a five-year period. When the target of 20 percent was picked, we suspect someone sat down and looked at the average rate of productivity growth (partial factor labor) for the United States for the past twenty years or so and figured that a 4 percent noncompounded gain per year would be good. As we have said, looking at past performance improvement gains of typical American organizations is a dangerous strategy when determining expected or needed levels of performance improvement. A U.S. air-conditioner manufacturer with an internal failure rate of 4 percent might be rather complacent unless it compared its level of performance to The New Competition. The difference between a 5 percent internal failure rate and a 0.5 percent internal failure rate is ten times.

If you are comparing your current performance levels with historical performance levels in your organization or within your industry, you might be in serious trouble. And you are very likely in serious trouble if you are comparing your performance levels to your closest U.S. competitor, or if you are evaluating your current performance levels based upon standards set by your industrial engineers or negotiated with your union, or by any other traditional means.

You must know who your New Competition is and how well it is performing in order to compete on those terms in an increasingly global economy. American managers, at all levels, have antiquated perceptions of what levels of performance improvement it will take to be competitive. We have spent countless hours with American management teams who became angry and defensive when we tried to explain that their productivity improvement efforts were not good enough. Our intent wasn't to demotivate, to downplay their progress, or to make them angry. We simply wanted to challenge them to realize that their sights might be set too low in relation to The New Competition. A 4 percent per year performance improvement gain or target is not good enough to be considered a world-class economy, government, or company.

RESPONSES TO THE CHALLENGES POSED BY THE NEW COMPETITION:
Critical Areas Needing Development In Your Organization

These three case examples we have just reviewed should, at the minimum, cause your management team to question how they evaluate measures of performance and what they consider to be standards of excellence. Our contention is that measurement systems in organizations in the United States and elsewhere are poorly designed. It is difficult, if not impossible, to effectively manage something that isn't measured properly. You cannot manage something you cannot measure. This axiom has been true since the beginning of man's attempt to control his environment, to create, to improve his quality of life, and to organize effort. As systems grow more complex so must the measurement systems designed to improve and control. These case examples highlighted specific performance measures for: a participatory performance improvement process (small group activity at Musashi); a management process changeover resulting from an acquisition (the Quasar TV plant); and quality management effort comparisons between Japanese air conditioner manufacturers and American counterparts. Clearly, other measures are needed to convey the total performance picture for the specific performance-improvement intervention, plant, or organization. However, even these partial measures provide us with a glimpse of the performance levels that we believe are being achieved by your New Competition. Even these incomplete glimpses create an uneasiness on our part and challenge many management teams who have visions of what the 1990s and beyond hold in terms of competitive pressures.

A comprehensive awareness that maintaining the *status quo* is not sufficient for survival and success in the future is a critical first step for any performance-improvement effort. However, awareness is only a part of the strategy that must be adopted and effectively implemented by your organization. How can we respond to the challenges posed by The New Competition? How can we create a new vision of our organization? What will our Organization of the Future look like? How can we begin to move toward this new vision of the Organization of the Future? What dimensions of our organization will we have to concentrate on in order for us to begin to respond to this New Competition? These questions and others will be specifically addressed in this book. It is the latter question, the issue of dimensions of your organization that need to be focused on, that we want to briefly turn attention to in this section.

Areas Needing Development as Your Organization Strives to Respond to The New Competition

The selected and suggested references at the end of this chapter represent a fairly comprehensive list of works by visionaries/futurists on the subject of organization, performance, and competition. If you were to carefully study the visions presented by these leading authors in the field, some common threads would appear. In general, we hear all the leading experts suggesting that, fundamentally, it is the management process that is awry in the United States. It is the management process that actually creates and sustains the competitive edge. Whether the management process is conceptualized as the seven S's (strategy, structure, systems, staff, style, skills, shared values) (Pascale and Athos 1981) or rather traditionally as planning, organizing, leading, controlling, and adapting, we gather a strong sense from these experts that it is this process that is at the heart of the challenge and the appropriate responses. Recently several macro-level studies and high-level conferences have addressed strategic responses necessary to help make America competitive again. We will look at two such activities: the report of the President's Commission on Industrial Competitiveness and the report from the NASA Symposium on Quality and Productivity. After this strategic and macro look at the challenge and appropriate responses, we will focus more narrowly on specific dimensions of the management process in your organization that may need overhauling as you strive to become the Organization of the Future.

The President's Commission on Industrial Competitiveness (1985)

In late 1983 and early 1984, President Reagan formed a high-level commission to study and make recommendations to improve the nation's ability to compete. John A. Young, president and chief executive officer of the Hewlett-Packard Company, chaired the commission made up of thirty-one prestigious and diversely experienced persons. In January of 1985, they presented a two-volume report summarizing their findings and making their recommendations. In a sense President Reagan had asked this commission to define and describe the challenge and, perhaps more importantly from a macro and strategic view, to outline the response. In this respect their task was no different than ours in this chapter and not really much different than the task you face in your organization. The general conclusion from the President's Commission was that "America's ability to compete in world markets must be improved, that we should view the challenge as immediate, and that the positive effects of the recommendations we make will be felt far into the future." The report goes on to make recommendations in four areas that the commission believed determine present and future competitiveness—technology, capital resources, human resources, and international trade. The outline of the report will give you a feel for the type of logic employed in their final report:

1. Competitiveness: The Quiet Challenge
2. The New Global Economy Makes Competitiveness Vital
3. Warning Signals We Should Heed
4. Improving America's Ability to Compete
   - Create, apply and protect new technology
   - Increase the supply of productive capital
   - Develop a more skilled, flexible, and motivated work force
   - Make trade a national priority
5. Responding to the Agenda of Competitiveness

Summary of Commission Recommendations

There was strong agreement that the new global economy makes competitiveness vital. Essentially, the global economy redefines the standards by which competitiveness is operationally defined. We attempted to demonstrate this in the last section where we described examples of how The New Competition is performing. "The United States is losing its ability to compete in world markets," wrote the report's authors. "We are still the world's strongest economy. However, the question we must answer is where we will be tomorrow, not just where we stand today." The commission's report supports their conclusions with ample statistics. We will not replicate the data here.

If we are to compete effectively in the future, we must build on our strengths and minimize our weaknesses. Though an exhaustive list of all the factors affecting our competitiveness would include just about every aspect of our economy, four major areas stand out: technology, capital resources, human resources, and the environment in which we conduct international trade. Once the challenge was defined, the commission turned its attention to responses, as we will. The commission was broken down into five groups:

1. The Strategy Group which focused on
   - The definition of competitiveness and how it is measured
   - The current position of the U.S. today
   - The determinants of future U.S. industrial competitiveness
   - The roles that should be played by management, labor, government, and private citizens

2. The Research, Development, and Manufacturing Group;
3. The Capital Resources Group;
4. The Human Resources Group; and
5. The International Trade and Marketing Group.

Volume II of the final commission report contains specific recommendations from each of the groups. The commission itself submitted thirty-two recommendations and eighty-nine action items along with its final report. An executive summary of those recommendations and action items is as follows:

1. To unleash our full competitive potential, leaders in industry must:
   - Take a new look at the opportunities of world trade and the new competitors we face;
   - Establish world leadership in the commercialization of both product and manufacturing technology;
   - Raise our level of investment in productive assets and in the development of our work force; and
   - Seek new ways of creating a sense of shared purpose within their organizations.

2. Individuals in the private sector must recognize their own stakes in competitive renewal and:
   - Equip themselves with the skills required in the workplace of the future;
   - Adapt a more flexible attitude toward changing markets and technologies; and
   - Work together — both labor and management — to strengthen the competitive performance of their own firms.

3. Government must take the lead in those areas where its resources and responsibilities can be best applied. Our public leaders and policy must:
   Make competitiveness a national priority and communicate the urgency of improving our ability to compete;
   - Encourage dialogue and consensus building among leaders in industry, labor, government, and academia whose expertise and cooperation are needed to improve our competitive performance;
   - Provide a stable macroeconomic environment that nurtures economic growth;
   - Provide an environment conducive to prompt commercialization and strong protection of technology;
   - Reform fiscal and monetary policy and tax laws to lower the cost of capital for U.S. firms and encourage investment;
   - Enhance the ability of our educational institutions to prepare and train our people thoroughly;
   - Change U.S. domestic and trade laws that hinder the ability of U.S. firms to compete;
   - Conduct trade negotiations to improve the free flow and fairness of world trade; and
   - Ensure that our human and capital resources can respond to changing markets and technologies in ways that are competitive, equitable, and humane.

The commission concluded its summary report, Volume I, with the following statement:

The goal is clear and within reach: We must perform up to our potential. Americans enjoy tackling new problems. One lies before us now. To meet the challenge of competitiveness, we require only a new vision and a new resolve. We must acknowledge the reality of a new global economy—an economic era that has come quietly, without fanfare. And just as we explored a vast and unknown American frontier, we must chart a course into this new territory and claim it for the generations to come.

This summary of over a year's worth of hard work by politically astute and intelligent leaders in our country is as valid for the nation as it is for your organization. We encourage you to acquire a copy of this report from the U.S. Government Printing Office, Washington, D.C. 20402, and to study its findings in relationship to the challenges and appropriate responses posed for your organization by the global economy and The New Competition.

Report from NASA Symposium on Quality and Productivity (1984)

The National Aeronautics and Space Administration (NASA) has been and continues to be a leader on many strategic fronts in this country. In 1984, and again in 1987, NASA sponsored the most successful quality and productivity conferences in this country's history. Where the President's Commission on Industrial Competitiveness tended to focus on a strategic and national agenda for improvement, the NASA symposium focused on strategic corporate issues that must be addressed to become world-class organizations. We would like to review highlights of the final report from the Symposium on Quality and Productivity held in September 1984.

David Braunstein, then director of NASA productivity programs, makes a number of very critical points in his foreword to the report that we would like to share with you. An underlying conclusion of the symposium was that large, maturing organizations have a particular challenge to maintain high levels of quality and productivity and guard against "hardening of the arteries."

"Without overt management action to continually renew and respark its drive, these organizations would eventually go out of business," wrote Braunstein. "Competitive pressures from abroad have crystallized these issues for many U.S. industries. For those who have not been directly challenged in the marketplace, the lessons learned are readily translatable into management imperatives." He goes on to say that the report contains no "magic" formula for success or "quick fixes" for poor quality or low productivity growth. The report reinforces most of the major points we will make early in this book. It stresses commitment to long-term strategies and a balancing with short-term bottom line results. It presents key underlying principles, in the form of themes, that when implemented can lead to continuous improvements in quality and performance. We will present these principles/themes and briefly discuss how they can help an organization regenerate its vitality and competitiveness. We will compare and contrast the nine themes identified in the NASA final report with principles and themes identified by Naisbitt and Aburdene (1985), Deming (1986), Ouchi (1984), Peters and Watermann (1982), Peters and Austin (1985), Hackman (1986), Lawler (1986), and Kilmann (1984).

"A new worldwide standard of quality has evolved and we cannot ignore its impact on our competitive position in the global marketplace," said Braunstein. "We must look at our management practices and determine what makes the difference between success or failure." The major findings of the 1984 Symposium on Quality and Productivity sponsored by NASA, organized into the nine themes listed in Table 1-5, encompass a set of recommended actions and management practices that have been shown to contribute to high quality and productivity.

These nine themes are then elaborated upon in the NASA final report through use of excerpts from key speakers from the conference. For each theme, there are a number of specific recommendations that are made. As you can see, the scope and unit of analysis for these nine themes is slightly different from that of the President's Commission on Industrial Competitive-

14

TABLE 1-5.
Nine Major Themes for Improving Productivity and Quality
as Derived from the NASA Symposium
on Quality and Productivity in 1984

THEME 1: Challenge for the competitive edge - responding to competitive pressures. Eighty percent of our products in this nation are now challenged in the marketplace by foreign competition, compared to 20 percent ten years ago. Management needs to create an awareness of the challenge to all employees and generate pressure for improvement.

THEME 2: Make a management commitment to quality and productivity - leading from the top. Demonstrated commitment must be perceived by employees as genuine and long-range. Quality and productivity must be understood as more than buzzwords. All managers and employees must be responsible and accountable for continuous quality and productivity improvement.

THEME 3: Mesh goals and responsibilities - opening two-way communications. Management must communicate the goals and objectives of the organization. Philosophy and principles should be clearly articulated so as to guide behaviors. Government, industry, and labor unions need to be less adversarial.

THEME 4: Make innovation rewarding - encouraging innovation and risk-taking. Innovation is a key to organizational survival in a fast changing economy. Create an environment that supports and rewards innovation.

THEME 5: Build dedication, pride, and team effort - promoting participative management. Successful organizations obtain performance from individuals that goes beyond just what is expected. Management of participation can help to create a culture and set of behaviors that reflect commitment and involvement in those things that make organizations truly excellent.

THEME 6: Uncork individual talent - controlling bureaucracy. Mature organizations tend to become preoccupied with controls and checks that are narrowly focused, parochial, and inflexible. This results in overregulation of activity, discourages initiative, and slows down responsiveness to changing conditions. Pushing responsibility to the lowest levels of an organization is the best way to make entrepreneurship a reality.

THEME 7: Modernize for survival - encouraging new technology. Modernization involving new equipment and techniques, although often difficult to justify in the short run, must be done to maintain long term viability.

THEME 8: Maximize human capital - developing strategies to improve education and training. At the national and the corporate level, we have fallen behind in our commitment to and execution of training and development of our work force for the organization of the future.

THEME 9: Improve quality and productivity practices - building a quality ethic. Continuous improvement goals are needed and must have the total commitment from management. Quality and productivity improvement must become integral parts of everyone's job.

Source: NASA 1984

ness. However, it should be apparent, and will be when you read these reports more carefully, that significant commonality exists between them. The NASA report also outlines the challenge and then, as we have mentioned, defines a set of responses. We encourage you to obtain a copy of this report also from the National Aeronautics and Space Administration, Director of Productivity Programs, Washington D.C. 20546.

Several well-respected authors, researchers, and academicians also have taken a strategic look at the challenges facing America and organizations in our country. They have developed their own impressions of what the challenges are and what the appropriate responses should be. Table 1-6 summarizes responses that are being called for by these persons, and we encourage you to compare and contrast them with the responses called for by the President's Commission on Industrial Competitiveness and the NASA Symposium on Quality and Productivity.

In compiling this table and reading the literature from which these responses were produced, it became apparent that each of these authors, as well as the commission and the persons summarizing the NASA symposium, is really focusing on the same thing: how to communicate the nature of the challenge and their perceptions of what appropriate and effective responses

Table 1-6.a
Critical Dimensions to Become the Organization of the Future

Drucker (1954) 7 Key Result Areas	Peters & Waterman (1982) 8 Common Attributes
• Customer satisfaction • Employee performance • Innovation • Management development • Internal productivity • Social responsibility • Operating budget	• A bias for action • Close to the customer • Autonomy and entrepreneurship • Productivity through people • Hands-on, value-driven • Stick to the knitting • Simple form, lean staff • Simultaneous loose-tight property
Pascale & Athos (1981) 7 S Model	Kilmann (1984) 5 Tracks
• Structure • Systems • Strategy • Style • Staff • Skills • Shared Values	• The culture track • The management skills track • The team-building track • The strategy-structure track • The reward system track

Hackman (1986) 5 Conditions
• The overall direction for the work is clear and engaging • The structure of the performing unit fosters competent performance, through the design of the task, the composition of the unit, and through sent expectations regarding the management of performance processes • The organizational context supports competent work through the reward, education, and information systems • Expert coaching and consultation are available and are provided at appropriate times • Material resources are adequate and available

Table 1-6.b
Critical Dimensions to Become the Organization of the Future

Naisbitt & Aburdene (1985) 10 Considerations	Deming (1986) 14 Points
• The best and the brightest people will gravitate toward those corporations that foster personal growth • The manager's new role is that of coach, teacher, and mentor • The best people want ownership - psychic and literal --in a company; the best companies are providing it • Companies will increasingly turn to third-party contractors, shifting from hired labor to contract labor • Authoritarian management is yielding to a networking, people style of management • Entrepreneurship within the corporation - intrapreneurship - is creating new products and new markets and revitalizing companies inside and out • Quality will be paramount • Institution and creativity are challenging the "it's all in the numbers" business school philosophy • Large corporations are emulating the positive and productive qualities of small business • The dawn of the information economy	• Create constancy of purpose for improvement of product and service • Adopt the new philosophy • Cease dependence on inspection to achieve quality • End the practice of awarding business on the basis of price tag alone. Instead, minimize total cost by working with a single supplier • Improve constantly and forever every process for planning, production, and service • Institute training on the job • Adopt and institute leadership • Drive out fear • Break down barriers between staff areas • Eliminate slogans, exhortations, and targets for the work force • Eliminate numerical quotas for the work force and numerical goals for management • Remove barriers that rob people of pride of workmanship. Elimate the annual rating or merit system • Institute a vigorous system of education and self-improvement for everyone

Lawler
(1986)   21 Tips

• Need for congruence among the different parts of an organization
• Beliefs about people involved in participative support
• Moving information, power, and knowledge downward in the organization
• Assumptions should be developed by members of the organization
• Flat structure
• Grouping approach toward organizational units that feel responsible for a particular product or customer
• Monitor performance of competitors
• Involve individually enriched jobs or teams in job design
• Task forces and problem-solving and group-process training
• Availability of inexpensive computing
• Decentralized information systems open to all members of the organization; comprehensive performance feedback
• Goal and standards should be participatively set
• Physical layout of organizations should be equalitarian
• High-involvement organizations should have small locations
• Different reward systems
• Personnel policies should fit the local work force
• Stability of employment
• Recruitment policies
• High level of training
• Vision of the future
• Leadership should promote and support self-motivation

would be. Of course, we all view the world differently and will describe problems, opportunities, and solutions differently based upon our experience, knowledge base, and beliefs about cause and effect. The people we have sourced to give you a feel for the challenge collectively have a tremendous amount of experience and wisdom. They also all speak, to some extent, different languages based upon their present positions and their previous background.

The next section of this chapter is my attempt to translate these views in terms that a manager can understand and develop into strategies and tactics. The areas I have identified as needing attention and development for the Organization of the Future do not necessarily represent the consensus views of my co-author. We agree that there is a significant challenge ahead for American organizations; that The New Competition is setting new standards of excellence; and that responses to these challenges and The New Competition will focus on the issues addressed by the President's Commission on Industrial Competitiveness, the NASA symposium, and the perceptions of the leading authors listed. However, the crystallization of one taxonomy to depict specific areas for concentration has proven to be an elusive goal. As such, the next section represents my concepts on four basic dimensions of the organization that need to be redesigned and improved. These subsystems of the overall management process are the tangible processes that management can design, redesign, manipulate, and control. Much of the literature deals with the response to challenges and The New Competition at a level of language and thinking that is, in our opinion, too abstract. We have to translate the thirty-two recommendations of the president's commission and nine themes from the NASA symposium into specific actions that can be taken to improve the quality of management systems and processes that cause and control the level of performance of individuals, groups, and organizations. We will talk about these management systems and processes in the next section. We will also discuss how your interventions on these management systems and processes can be effectively and efficiently made in the context of the Performance Management Process.

MANAGEMENT SYSTEMS AND PROCESSES THAT REQUIRE ATTENTION AND DEVELOPMENT

We believe four areas of performance improvement must be focused upon in order to successfully respond to the challenges posed by your New Competition. The four areas are: (1) performance improvement planning; (2) performance measurement and evaluation; (3) performance improvement and control; and (4) cultural support systems. We believe these highlighted areas of attention and development must be carefully redesigned in your organizations. Improving your performance in these four areas is, in our opinion, necessary but not necessarily sufficient for your survival and success in the next ten years. Changing environments (internal and external) and technologies dictate that the management process in your organization be redesigned. These four areas represent the places to start. They are the leverage points in your organizations. Starting with these four systems will have a tremendous ripple effect to other areas of your company's management systems. We will only briefly discuss each of these four areas in this chapter, as each is covered in detail later.

Performance Improvement Planning

The term "strategic planning" conjures up many different notions and reactions on the part of managers. We believe that most managers' concepts of strategic planning are myopic. Strategic planning, as practiced by most American organizations:

- Is formal and bureaucratic;
- Focuses on the plan (the product) and ignores the process;

- Is budget driven (the budget drives the plan);
- Involves only top management and their consultants;
- Is overly influenced by marketing, business acquisition, and finance considerations;
- Is myopic and short-sighted because of limited involvement and participation and unrealistic expectations for quick, easy gains; and
- Is therefore often detached from many pragmatic operational realities.

If you ask a manager to show you the organization's strategic plan, you will usually see capital investment plans, facilities plans, and business plans (i.e., products, markets, technology, and capital). You will almost never find significant attention paid to designs for improving management systems and management processes. Plans for how the organization intends to sponsor and promote continuous performance improvement are rare. Managers involved in strategic planning can almost always tell you the steps in the planning process but can almost never tell you how the steps are accomplished. Again, there is a focus on the product and neglect of process. The process by which we plan is just as important as the plan itself.

Effective strategic planning in the Organization of the Future will have to:

- Involve more people in the organization;
- Be structured but less formal;
- Focus on the plan (product) and the process;
- Drive the budget;
- Develop better balance between marketing, finance, and operations;
- Lengthen planning horizons; and
- More effectively link action planning and effective implementation.

Figure 1-1 depicts various planning horizon emphases at various levels in the organization. In the past, it was assumed that the people at the top *think*, the people in the middle *control*, and the people at the bottom *perform*. The environment, technological changes, employee demographics, and competition dictate a dramatic change in these assumptions. As indicated in Figure 1-1, the Organization of the Future will require that people at all levels of the organization think, control, and perform. Planning for continuous performance improvement must be a major responsibility and accountability for every employee in the Organization of the Future.

We have had difficulty communicating the distinction between conventional strategic planning and what we mean by performance improvement planning. Dr. James Bontadelli, manager of Corporate Industrial Engineering at Tennessee Valley Authority, has helped us clarify the concept by developing Figure 1-2.

The Strategic Planning Interface shown in Figure 1-2 highlights the importance of viewing performance improvement planning as an integral part of business planning. It is intended to highlight the fact that performance improvement planning is *not* done in most organizations. We have *not* seen evidence that performance improvement planning is being done in our past ten years of research and consulting. We reiterate that the underlying belief in most organizations is that maintaining the *status quo* is sufficient for survival and success in the future. There are not effective cultures in most organizations to cause proactive search for and implementation of continuous improvements in performance.

In Chapter 4, we will outline and detail a performance improvement planning process that we have been developing and testing for the past five years. The focus of the performance improvement planning process is on involving all levels of management in strategic planning. The process was designed to involve, in a structured and participative fashion, all levels of manage-

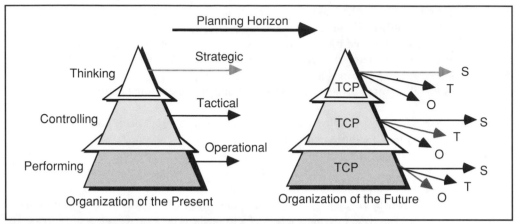

Figure 1-1. Transition from the Organization of the Present to The Organization of the Future

ment in translating strategy into action. The process interfaces with conventional strategic planning by using the "business plan" as the foundation upon which the performance improvement plan is developed. Strategy is developed, business plans are written, and performance improvement plans are generated, which then leads into the budget development process.

Strategic planning, in the traditional sense and as it is now practiced, is extremely deficient in design relative to the needs of your Organization of the Future. The incorporation of the performance improvement planning process described in Chapter 4 will substantially improve the quality and effectiveness of your planning efforts. It will require considerable effort on the part of the management team in your organization to develop and integrate this process. However, it may be the single most important performance improvement intervention your organization will make in the next five years. You will need to work hard with management in order to get them to understand the role that performance improvement planning plays in the strategic planning process. If your strategic planning process is new, poorly designed, not working well, or nonexistent, improving your system or beginning a planning system with just the performance improvement planning process is an excellent initial step.

The Organization of the Future vision development and communication is a natural product of the performance improvement planning process. Early steps in the performance improvement planning process focus on Organizational Systems Analysis (OSA). Guiding principles, values, beliefs, superordinate goals, and vision development are critical points of development in OSA. Because the planning process is so pervasive in terms of who is involved, the communication of visions and other critical foundation issues relative to strategic plans occurs rather naturally as a result of the structured participative process.

Whether the clarity of and communication of the Organization of the Future vision occur as a result of the performance improvement planning process or other activities is irrelevant. What is important is that shared visions are developed and communicated. A misconception persists among non-situational advocates of participative management that visions should be participatively developed. We believe that this assumption disregards the important difference between transitional/transformational leadership and transactional leadership (Bass 1985).

Vision development is an art. It requires wisdom, judgment, and experience. It is not a widely developed skill. In planning, as with problem solving and decision making, it is important to know when to exhibit authoritative/decisive/autocratic, consultative, participative, and/or delegative leadership and management behaviors. Situational leadership and management with

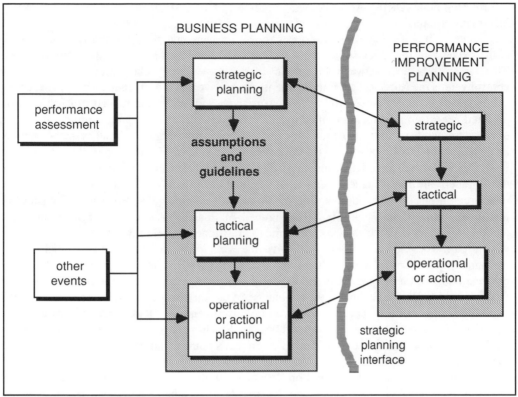

Figure 1-2. Strategic Planning Interface

respect to planning, problem solving, and decision making is critical to becoming the Organization of the Future. As your organization makes the transition from a control-oriented, manager-led organization to a commitment-oriented, self-managed organization, considerable discretion will be required in terms of knowing which types of management and leadership styles and behaviors to exhibit for specific elements of planning, problem solving, and decision making (Blanchard 1982; Hershey 1982; Hackman 1986; Lawler 1986; Sink and Swim 1985).

Performance Measurement and Evaluation

Measurement and evaluation systems in most American organizations are in need of major overhauls. We have tended not to view measurement and evaluation, except for selected systems (i.e., accounting, finance, process control), as an evolving design process. Measurement systems have not been linked to strategy. People and management teams managing systems have not been involved in the design and development of measurement systems. We have generally not engineered, in a human factors or management systems sense, our measurement systems. Measurement systems tend to focus on control only, leaving a huge gap in systems developed to support improvement. Performance is misunderstood; therefore, performance measurement is not done properly. Unit of analysis is not understood; therefore, we have measurement systems improperly designed for specific organizational systems (i.e., a plant, firm, section, branch, department, corporation, center). The purposes and audiences for measurement and evaluation are not clarified prior to design and utilization; therefore, we have the right measures going to the wrong people for the wrong purposes. Our measurement systems have made us data rich and information poor (DRIP). As a television commercial suggests, we are "drowning in a sea of information (data)."

Our approach or view of measurement is that measurement for control is over-emphasized at the expense of measurement systems designed and developed to help support improvement. There is an imbalance between the amount of effort and energy going into measurement for control versus measurement for improvement. We believe that most managers and management teams spend 90 to 95 percent of their measurement and evaluation-related time on control-oriented versus improvement-oriented focus. We collect, process, evaluate, provide, store, and retrieve tremendous amounts of data for other people, other organizational systems (units of analysis), and purposes other than improvement of the systems we are responsible for.

We will use an aircraft instrument panel as a conceptual analogy to illustrate the design and development of improved measurement and evaluation systems and to take the mystery out of measurement. Consider the evolution of the aircraft instrument/control panel. Envision the instrument panel of the Wright flyer (see Figure 1-3). Imagine the evolution of that information and control panel over the years as it became the instrument panel of the Boeing 757. Consider the design and development process entailed in the evolution of each and every instrument (measurement system). Envision the early test pilots coming back from a trip explaining to the design engineer, human factors engineer, and the aeronautical engineer what happened on the last test flight. Test pilot David E. Sink to the engineers: "You can't believe what happened up there! I had no warning; nothing appeared wrong on my instruments. If it hadn't been for my ability to intuitively react to the situation, I wouldn't be here. You guys have got to improve the instrument panel. Find a way to warn the pilot. Tell us when that's going to happen and help us decide what to do when it does."

This scenario could go on and on. It was certainly commonplace in the early years of aviation and is not uncommon today. The systems are more complex now, the improvements less dramatic, perhaps, and more incremental. But the process of designing and developing the measurement and evaluation systems for pilots is continuing.

The design and development of measurement and evaluation systems in your organization for your managers and management teams is analogous to what happened between pilots (managers and management teams) and engineers (management support system "engineers") in the early years of aviation. Our progress with the design and development of management support systems will be more rapid than for aircraft instrument panels partially because we have learned from those other fields and partially because we are at a different starting point relative to technology. However, the design and development process will be similar in that it will be a simultaneously systematic process, along with a lot of trial and error and intuition and skill application.

Every one of your managers and management teams and employees is a pilot in a sense. They are managing (flying) a complex system. They need data and information in order to solve problems, plan, and make decisions. How that data and information is stored, retrieved, and portrayed will determine the extent to which your measurement systems really support the management process. Good measurement and evaluation systems and management support systems don't just happen. They evolve as a result of planned, systematic, conscious efforts to improve their quality. The instrument panels, scoreboards, and information systems your supervisors, managers, management teams, and employees have — the quality of those systems — are no less important than the quality of the instruments and controls necessary for, let's say the Boeing 757 pilot. You wouldn't want to fly in a plane that had one instrument telling the pilot "We're OK or We're NOT OK." And yet, you are willing to "take a ride" with organizations that essentially have the same type of logic built into their information systems; companies that say

Photos courtesy of the Smithsonian Institute, Washington, D.C.

Figure 3-1. The Wright Flyer

"We made money this quarter — we're OK" or "We didn't make money this quarter, we better cut costs — we're NOT OK.

We need to enter a new era in the area of measurement and evaluation systems design and development. We are going to have to be more professional in the design, redesign, and development of the management support systems for our managers, management teams, and employees. Management Systems Analysis (MSA) can help you design and develop performance control panels for your Organization of the Future by taking the mystery out of measurement.

Management Systems Analysis can help your organization design, redesign, and develop your management support systems and your measurement and evaluation systems. Kurstedt (1985) has developed a management system model that serves as the conceptual foundation for MSA.

The design of measurement and evaluation systems often does not start with an understanding of the organizational system being managed and measured. The first step of the MSA involves completing an Organization Systems Analysis (OSA) that includes an Input-Output Analysis (IOA). This is a necessary precondition for improving the quality of the measurement systems for a given organizational system. (Again, an organizational system is a generic word used to define a work group, plant, department, division, function, corporation or firm, section, or branch.) You cannot measure that which you do not understand or cannot operationally define. The second step of the MSA focuses on those actions or interventions that the management team (manager, supervisors, employees, and support functions) can make to the system to improve its performance. This is an early step because we are trying to improve the quality of measures and measurement systems that will support improvement — constant improvement. Too many organizations start by asking "what can we measure," instead of "what can we do to improve and then what do we need to measure to support improvement and to motivate continued improvement." The MSA is designed to sequence the thought process correctly.

Step 3 of the MSA focuses on what information is necessary to support the improvement interventions or to tell us whether the improvement interventions have had an impact. The designers and engineers of these management support systems will need to consider the cognitive style of the decision makers and problem solvers as they develop portrayal systems. How we present information is often as important as the information we give in terms of effective use of that information. Step 4 focuses on the data that is needed from the system in order to create support information. Data accessibility, storage, retrieval, cost, availability, and creativity are all issues to be addressed by the designers and developers of your improved measurement and evaluation systems. The final sequence of the MSA, Step 5, entails identifying or developing tools that will allow you to convert data into information. This may involve designing new information systems, buying new software, creating artificially intelligent systems, developing new software, or developing new applications for existing tools. Notice that the tool selection or development comes last. Too many organizations buy the tool and then force the application. This almost ensures that effective implementation will suffer or not occur.

This has been a quick overview of the MSA. It will be revisited in more detail later when we depict forms and describe processes. The point to be made now is that improving the quality of measurement and evaluation systems cannot occur without a structured process. The MSA is not the only approach to take. However, we find from experience that it is pragmatic and can be applied with modifications appropriate for the specific situation, organizational system, and application.

Visibility systems development and information sharing are critical to the effective execution of measurement and evaluation systems development. As we walk through factories, offices, and other workplaces, we look for scoreboards and instrument panels—information systems that tell people how they are doing in their system and how their system is doing in relationship to the larger system. What we find is either no scoreboards or poorly designed scoreboards. We find bulletin boards with information developed by management for management, or by a programmer for a programmer; not information developed for the employees or for the management teams. The portrayal of information is such that it neither conveys the needed information or makes the management team want to use it. The quality of information sharing and information shared is generally very low. The Organization of the Future will have more carefully thought through how to improve the interface to the people managing and improving the performance of the system so as to support their decision making and problem solving. Visibility systems and quality information sharing will be critical issues in the development of improved measurement and evaluation systems.

Continual improvement and evolution are terms we hear a lot about today. It is the theme of many of the leading experts we mentioned earlier. If our organizations need to adapt and focus on continual improvement, then our measurement and evaluation systems must do likewise. Many of our measurement systems are antiquated. They are not the focus of continuing development. We design them and then forget them. Our accounting systems, our performance appraisal systems, our measures of the financial health of the firm, and our work measurement systems are in desperate need of redesign and improvement. We need to expand the comprehensiveness of what we are measuring, upgrade the tools and techniques we are using to measure, and improve the effectiveness with which we use specific tools and techniques, such as performance appraisal and management by objectives (MBO). You get what you inspect, not what you expect; you get what you measure because that is what you reveal as what you think is important. Your measurement systems tell the people in your organization what you will reward, sanction, or punish. Only the adoption of the same continual improvement orientation that Deming calls for in quality management in the area of measurement and evaluation systems development will support your organization's move in the direction of the Organization of the Future.

Performance Improvement and Control

Improving performance (effectiveness, efficiency, quality, productivity, quality of work life, innovation, and profitability/budgetability) is the bottom line. Every activity that takes place in your organization should be clearly directed toward two goals:

1. Get the job done; and
2. Constantly improve performance.

You need every organizational system and individual in your organization to clearly understand what "get the job done" means and how it relates to the organizational system performance. This understanding must exist in terms to which each organizational system and individual can personally relate. Constant improvement of performance must be translated into real terms. The management process, measurement system, reward system, and overall culture must clearly support the operational meaning of constant improvement. Constant improvement must be coordinated and controlled. As an example, people often confuse participative management with management of participation. Participation in performance improvement and control can only succeed if there is systematic coordination and control. Participative management doesn't reap benefits if it just means getting people in a room and then expecting magic to occur (see Figure 1-4).

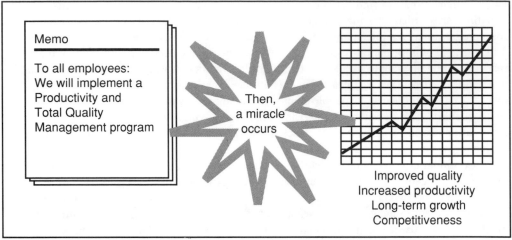

Figure 1-4. Productivity and Quality Have Become Illusions

There are many ways to improve performance. Table 1-7 lists examples. Unless your performance-improvement interventions/tactics are thought through in a systematic and integrated fashion, you will not obtain the full potential of your efforts. Some interventions are compatible with one another and will even create synergistic results. Other interventions and techniques will be incompatible and will actually cause lower performance. These issues have to be thought through. This is not happening in the United States. We have "islands of performance improvement" that are not integrated.

Table 1-7.
Performance   Improvement   Techniques

• Nominal Group Technique	• Process Flow Analysis
• Input/Output Analysis	• Visibility Room
• RIART	• Human Factors Engineering
• Job Design/Redesign	• Gainsharing (Inter-Company)
• Organizational Design	• Gainsharing (Intra-Company)
• Total Quality Management	• Compensation Management Design
• Just-In-Time	• Selection/Placement
• CEDAC	

Strategically speaking, there are important leverage points in your organization relative to performance improvement. There are specific resources, functions, and types of interventions that will have greater payoff for you. There is the issue of stages of evolution, or maturity, to consider. Certain interventions may be too sophisticated or complex at the beginning, or certain interventions may have sequentially interdependent earlier steps that have to be accomplished prior to their implementation. Gainsharing is an example of an intervention that we feel cannot be successfully made without significant ground laying. From our experience, performance improvement should begin by responding to the following issues:

1. Where are your cost drivers? What are your leverage points?
2. Is your selection, placement, and management of the human resource a quality process?
3. Do you have a "grand strategy" for performance improvement for the next two to five years?
4. Do you understand and do you incorporate considerations relative to the balance between structure, technology, environment, and management systems?
5. Where are your areas of lowest performance? Where are the areas of least accountability? Least customer orientation?
6. What are the operations with the oldest equipment, methods, tenured people, and most reactive?
7. What are the newest operations, with which we have the least experience? What operations have most recently emerged from their start-up period?
8. What are the areas with the most rapidly growing costs?
9. What are the operations that involve the most money, the highest number of people, and the highest volume of output?
10. What are the operations that have been least profitable, have the slowest growth rate, or have the highest incidence of foul-ups?
11. What are the operations that have been longest spared the attention of those interested in productivity improvement?
12. Do you have the system to let people tell you areas for performance improvement?

Perhaps most importantly, we believe that the management process drives all performance improvement. If that management process is a quality one, then performance improvement occurs naturally as a part of normal business practice. Unfortunately, most management processes we have seen need significant improvement — major overhauls in some cases and minor adjustments in others. The performance management process we will discuss in the next chapter is an example of the type of management process that we believe needs to be developed in order to successfully respond to The New Competition and become an Organization of the Future.

Learning how to successfully evolve from a manager-led, control-oriented organization to a self-managed, commitment-oriented organization will be a critical factor in the improvement and control of performance in your organization. The change in roles, responsibilities, and accountabilities that will accompany this evolution will be critical. Creating a management process and management skills that will allow for information and power sharing will be essential. These concepts are more than just words; they are reality for many organizations. As you struggle to become an Organization of the Future, these words will take on deep meaning.

In summary, performance improvement is more than just flexible manufacturing cells, just-in-time systems, total quality control, quality circles, autonomous work groups, new organizational structures, office automation, or value engineering. Lasting performance improvement goes beyond the quick fix. Lasting performance improvement comes about because a management team thinks through a strategy that responds to what effective measurement systems, intuition, and judgment must be addressed. An integrated, well-designed strategy that incorporates new techniques along with a focus on more effective utilization of existing techniques ensures lasting performance improvement. Lasting performance improvement occurs when a management team begins to understand that management is a process. The quality of the management process dictates and determines the levels of performance the organization and its organizational systems will achieve. We must manage the management process to ensure that we are constantly improving and moving toward the Organization of the Future.

Cultural Support Systems

In l984, words such as values, beliefs, culture, and principles were thought to be extremely "warm and fuzzy," non-pragmatic, theoretical concepts of little or no value to a "real world" productivity and quality effort. In l987, these concepts became critical buzzwords in the productivity and quality arena. At the heart of this change has been the realization that no matter how good the performance improvement technique and intervention is, in the absence of a supportive culture, it will be less successful and probably even fail. We have seen organizations spend millions of dollars on technological improvements only to have them fail to achieve expected results. We have seen organizations begin huge productivity improvement campaigns and programs only to have them fizzle out after two or three years. Researchers have studied this phenomenon, and the emerging literature appears to be focusing on this thing called cultural support systems.

Guiding principles are where most companies appear to start when they examine and try to improve their cultural support systems. What principles appear to be actually guiding the behaviors in your organization? Playing a "man from Mars" role is helpful in opening up and being honestly introspective about this question (Sink 1987). This exercise often creates interesting lists of actual perceived principles such as:

- Defer decision making until the boss returns.
- Don't take any risks.
- Don't rock the boat.
- Just do your job as described to you when you came here.
- Let the boss make all the decisions and solve all the problems. He is the one paid to do those things.
- If you get your jobs done, don't ask for more work—just keep looking busy.
- We're paid to come at eight and leave at five—no more and no less.
- If you come up with a good idea, don't tell anyone until you get it written down as a suggestion, or somebody else might get credit for it.
- Those at the top think best; otherwise, why would they be at the top?
- We aren't paid for problem solving, but just for doing the job.
- Managers plan, employees do.
- Quality is the responsibility of the quality control department.
- Productivity is the responsibility of the productivity director.
- Measurement is primarily used for control and evaluation.
- Don't share information, since the employees will use it against us.
- Don't share information because it will make us vulnerable and we will lose power.
- Power is finite; therefore, we must play zero-sum games (I win, they lose; they win, I lose).
- If productivity increases, the organization will win and we will lose.

We could go on with this list of actual principles that appear to be guiding the behaviors of American managers and employees. By now, the point is obvious. Actual perceived guiding principles often differ substantially from our intended and desired guiding principles. Most organizations have not thought through explicitly the principles upon which they wish behaviors to be guided or based. The typical assumption is that the principles do exist and they are intuitively obvious. To assume that principles can be left implicit and be effective is increasingly being questioned and proven invalid. Deming started us thinking when he published his fourteen points upon which a quality management program should be built. Many organizations have now picked up on that concept and have begun to manage their cultural support systems by explicating their guiding principles.

Continuously developing the skills of the management team is a critical operational step that must be taken in order to manage cultural support systems. Culture can be defined as the "pattern of basic assumptions—invented, discovered, or developed by a given group as it learns to cope with its problems of external adaptation and internal integration—that has worked well enough to be considered valid and, therefore, to be taught to new members as the correct way to perceive, think, and feel in relation to those problems" (Schein 1985). Schein goes on to say that the "only thing of real importance that leaders do is to create and manage culture." The basic dimensions of culture are:

1. Observed behavioral regularities;
2. The norms;
3. The dominant values espoused;
4. The philosophy guiding policy and practice;
5. The rules and the "ropes" of the games for getting along and ahead; and
6. The feeling or climate conveyed by physical layout and personal interactions (Schein 1985).

We believe that the behaviors of the management team and dominant leader(s) create and shape this thing called culture. The management team's skill at managing and adapting culture will strongly influence the levels of performance achieved. Skills for conflict management, group process management, planning, problem solving, designing, decision making, measurement, and motivation for the management team must continuously be developed lest the culture stagnate. We have stagnated cultures in many, if not most, American organizations. They are stagnated because our leaders and management teams have not continuously developed their management skills.

Paradigm "busting" is almost always required to change cultures. A paradigm is formally defined as a pattern, example, or model. Paradigms are accepted, common, standard, traditional ways of looking at things, collecting information, processing information, making decisions, and solving problems. Thomas S. Kuhn used the concept of paradigms to discuss and evaluate the process by which scientific revolutions do or do not, as the case may be, take place (Kuhn 1970). In an excellent film developed by Joel Barker, the notion of paradigms is utilized to investigate the nature of innovation (Barker 1986). Barker suggests that becoming an Organization of the Future will require some examination of paradigms. His summary points at the end of the film are as follows:

- Paradigms are common.
- Paradigms are useful.
- Paradigm paralysis is a terminal disease of certainty.
- People who create new paradigms seem to be outsiders with no investment in old paradigms and, therefore, lose nothing in creating new paradigms.
- You have to be courageous to select new paradigms.
- You can choose to change your paradigms.

We suggest that some paradigm busting will be necessary as you begin to think through how to become an Organization of the Future. Accepted ways of thinking about compensation, problem solving, decision making, planning, measurement, structure, leadership, and the management process in general will have to be questioned. Resistance to change will have to be met head-on and tackled effectively. Managing cultural support systems will require significant amounts of paradigm busting and a critical mass of paradigm busters.

Finally, congruence between plans, planning process, measurement and evaluation systems, guiding principles, and reward systems will be required in order for your organization to become the Organization of the Future. It is an incongruence between these systems that is causing current low levels of competitiveness. The environment has changed, and we have responded by changing structures, staffing, and technology, but we still see performance problems. The lack of an integrated, systematically thought through strategy has caused our improvement interventions to be less effective and efficient than they should have been. It's sort of like squeezing a jellyfish. If you push one finger in, it just causes the jellyfish to squeeze out between another pair of fingers. It would take a concerted effort by all the fingers to get the jellyfish to come out the top of your hands. So it is with your organization; pushing on one variable may be more than offset by an interdependent reaction from some other dimension of performance. Only a congruence between the major strategic variables in your organization will create sustained, systematic progress.

CLOSURE

Deming has said that everybody doing their very best isn't enough (Deming l986). We must know what to do, have or develop the skills to do it, and be willing to pay the price. The development of a culture that expects, encourages, and supports a constant improvement process is a necessary element to the performance management process. Your quality, productivity and/or general improvement efforts must address the issues raised in this chapter in order to succeed in the longer term. This chapter has focused on providing you with a glimpse of what your New Competition may look like and how they are performing. Effective responses to the challenges presented by your New Competition are obviously critical. This book has been designed to help you and your management team develop continuing successful responses to competitive pressures created by your New Competition. It synthesizes over ten years of study into successful responses to increasing competitive pressures. The theme of the book is the role of measurement in the Organization of the Future. However, the context within which this theme is addressed is the performance management process of the 1980s, 1990s, and beyond. One cannot look at measurement in the absence of an understanding of how it relates to the broader issue of proactive performance management. The focus of the next chapter is the performance management process as we believe it will be practiced in the Organization of the Future. The performance management process we describe well may be the process employed by your New Competition!

REFERENCES AND SUGGESTED READINGS

Barker, J. A. 1986. *Discovering The Future: The Business Of Paradigms (Film)*. Filmedia, Inc. Minneapolis, Minnesota.

Bass, B. M. 1985. *Leadership and Performance Beyond Expectations*. The Free Press. New York.

Blanchard, K., and S. Johnson. 1982. *The One Minute Manager*. Morrow. New York.

Davidson, W. H. Spring 1982. Small group activity at Musashi Semiconductor Works. *Sloan Management Review*. Sloan Management Review Association. Cambridge, Massachusetts. 3-14.

Deming, W. E. 1986. *Out of the Crisis*. MIT Press. Cambridge, Massachusetts.

Drucker, P. F. 1980. *Managing in Turbulent Times*. Harper & Row. New York.

Foster, R. 1986. *Innovation*. Summit Books. New York.

Garvin, D. A. December 1986. Quality problems, policies, and attitudes in the U. S. and Japan: An exploratory story. *Academy of Management Journal*. Mississippi State University. Mississippi State. 29:653-674.

Hackman, J. R. 1986. The psychology of self-management in organizations. *Psychology and Work: Productivity, Change and Employment*. Edited by Pallack, M. S., and R. O.Perloff. American Psychological Association. Washington, D. C.

Hershey, P., and K. Blanchard. 1982. *Management of Organizational Behavior* (Fourth Ed.). Prentice-Hall, Inc. Englewood Cliffs, New Jersey.

Kanter, R. M. 1983. *The Change Masters*. Simon and Schuster. New York.

Kaplan, R. S. 1982. *Advanced Management Accounting*. Prentice-Hall, Inc. Englewood Cliffs, New Jersey.

Kilmann, R. H. 1984. *Beyond the Quick Fix*. Jossey-Bass, Inc. San Francisco, California.

Kottler, P., L. Fahey, and S. Jatusripitak. 1985. *The New Competition*. Prentice-Hall, Inc. Englewood Cliffs, New Jersey.

Kuhn, T. S. 1970. *The Structure of Scientific Revolutions*. University of Chicago Press. Chicago, Illinois.

Kurstedt, H. A. 1985. A series of articles describing the management system model. Management Systems Laboratories. Blacksburg, Virginia.

Lawler, E. E. III. 1986. *High- Involvement Management*. Jossey-Bass, Inc. San Francisco, California.

Miller, L. 1984. *American Spirit: Visions of a New Corporate Culture*. Morrow. New York.

Morris, W. T. 1975. *Work and Your Future: Living Poorer, Working Harder*. Reston Publishing Co. Reston, Virginia.

_____. 1979. *Implementation Strategies for Industrial Engineers*. Grid. Columbus, Ohio.

Naisbitt, J., and B. Aburdeme. 1985. *Reinventing the Corporation*. Warner Books. New York.

NASA. 1984. A framework for action: Improving quality and productivity in government and industry. *Report from NASA Symposium on Quality and Productivity*.

Ossola, D. 1982. Two views of quality results: Factory view. From a presentation made at the 1982 U. S. Productivity Center Network meeting. Utah State University, March. New York.

Ouchi, W. 1981. *Theory Z*. Addison-Wesley. Phillippines.

_____. 1984. *The M-Form Society*. Addison-Wesley. Reading, Massachusetts.

Pascale, R. T., and A. G. Athos. 1981. *The Art of Japanese Management*. Simon and Schuster. New York.

Peters, T. J., and R. H. Waterman. 1982. *In Search of Excellence: Lessons From America's Best-Run Companies*. Harper & Row. New York.

_____, and N. Austin. 1985. *A Passion for Excellence*. Random House. New York.

Porter, M. 1980. *Competitive Strategy: Techniques for Analyzing Industries and Competitors*. The Free Press. New York.

_____. 1985. *Competitive Advantage Creating and Sustaining Superior Performance*. The Free Press. New York.

_____, R. E. Caves, A. M. Spence, and J. T. Scott. 1987. *Competition in the Open Economy*. Harvard University Press. Cambridge, Massachusetts.

Schein, E. H. 1985. *Organizational Culture and Leadership*. Jossey-Bass, Inc. San Francisco, California.

Schonberger, R. J. 1986. *World Class Manufacturing: The Lessons of Simplicity Applied*. The Free Press. New York.

Sink, D. S. 1980, 1983, 1984, 1986, 1987. *The Essentials of Performance, Productivity, and Quality Management*. Short Course Notebook. LINPRIM, Inc. Blacksburg, Virginia.

_____, and L. K. Swim. 1984. Participative problem solving techniques: When are they appropriate? *Fall Industrial Engineering Conference Proceedings*. Institute of Industrial Engineers. Norcross, Georgia.

_____, L. Shetzer, and D. Marion. 1986. Performance action teams: A case study. *National Productivity Review*. Summer. 233-251.

_____. 1987. Guiding principles: The foundation of successful efforts to better manage productivity and quality. *Integrated Systems Conference Proceedings*. Institute of Industrial Engineers. Norcross, Georgia.

Thompson, J. D. 1967. *Organizations in Action*. McGraw-Hill. New York.

Thurow, L. C. 1985. *The Zero-Sum Solution*. Simon and Schuster. New York.

_____. (Ed.). 1985. *The Management Challenge: Japanese Views*. MIT Press. Cambridge, Massachu-
  setts.
Toffler, A. 1980. *The Third Wave*. Bantam. New York.

2. THE RESPONSE: THE PERFORMANCE MANAGEMENT QUESTION

We have attempted to more clearly define and describe the challenges you will face in the coming years. As we indicated, some of you are already in the thick of heated and fierce competition and may believe we understated the competitive challenge. Others, from previously protected, regulated, favored, or fortunate businesses and industries, are beginning just now to shape a better understanding of The New Competition and what their organizations will have to do to effectively respond. And there are some readers from governmental organizations (state, local, and federal), universities, school systems, and currently protected, regulated, favored, or fortunate businesses that probably challenge our view of the world and the challenges, opportunities, and problems. We perhaps can all agree, at least, that the world is changing and it is healthy to re-examine how we should manage in this changed world.

There are clearly many responses that can be made to the challenges, opportunities, and problems you will face in the years to come. However, many experts argue that a revitalization of the management process is necessary to successfully respond to these sweeping changes (Deming 1986; Naisbitt and Aburdene 1985; Peters 1987; Waterman 1987). Our research and experience indicates that the more impressive organizations do tend to look to the management process as a "root cause" of good or bad performance. Therefore, a best place to start with an attempt to become an Organization of the Future and to successfully compete is with the performance management process.

Could you define and describe in detail the process by which your organization manages performance? Is that process systematic? Is the process effective and efficient? Is the process consistently understood and applied? Are strategies effectively linked to tactics and techniques? Is there effective implementation? Are the people that must implement plans a part of the development of those plans? We suspect that most of you answered these questions with some degree of hesitation and reservation. Over ten years' experience with organizational attempts to become Organizations of the Future led us to capture the process we will define and describe here. This process does not reflect exactly any of the organizations we have worked with over this period of time. Each organization's approach to improving productivity, quality, and performance is unique, and that is appropriate. However, when you stand back from the specific efforts and look for common threads, strategies, approaches, and techniques, you do find a rather generalizable process.

If you were to try to copy exactly the process as we have documented it in this chapter and later ones, you would surely fail. Our goal is to help you become "chefs," not just "cooks." You will have to tailor this process to your own specific circumstances and conditions. We provide you with a model, or prototype. You will have to design an application of the prototype that will work in your organization or specific organizational system.

So, our suggested response to the challenges, opportunities, and problems posed by your New Competition and competitive environment is a redesign and revitalization of your performance management process. We will now outline a prescribed performance management process that is based upon our work with excellent organizations attempting to become Organizations of the Future through the design, development and implementation of productivity and quality management efforts. (For a listing of organizations that form our data base, please refer to Appendix A.)

THE PERFORMANCE MANAGEMENT PROCESS

Managing performance means, by definition:

1. Creating visions of what the desired future state is;
2. Planning—assessing present organizational status relative to the vision, creating strategies for how the desired future state can be attained, and building on strengths so as to move toward your visions;
3. Designing, developing, and effectively implementing specific improvement intervention that have a high probability of moving us toward the desired future state, particularly in terms of levels of performance;
4. Designing, redesigning, developing, and implementing measurement and evaluation systems that will tell us whether we are going where we said we wanted to go and how well we are doing along the way; and
5. Ensuring that cultural support systems are in place so that we are rewarding and reinforcing progress, so that we can maintain the excellence we are achieving, and so we can control levels of performance necessary to compete with our New Competition.

Therefore, a performance management process is a process by which these things will take place in a systematic, consistent, persistent, patient, and comprehensive fashion throughout the organization. An organization's management process must both manage what gets done, as well as how those things get done. Examples will clarify that the management process must ensure plans are developed, ensure that the process by which plans are developed is constantly improving, ensure services and products are delivered on time, and ensure that the processes by which those goods and services are developed is constantly improving. The process by which an organization's management team accomplishes constant performance improvement in all aspects of the business must be given at least equal emphasis to the process by which the organization gets products and services out the door on time. These two aspects of management need to be well integrated in order for an organization to improve and meet the challenge of world-class, New Competition. As we said at the outset, in the Organization of the Future everyone will have at least two primary responsibilities:

1. Get the job done on time, within quality specifications, with the right amount of resources; and
2. Continuously improve individual, group, organizational, and systems performance.

Most managers today see their primary (perhaps even sole) responsibility to be getting the jobs done. They do not envision improving performance as a major responsibility; they are not measured against this objective; they are not rewarded for doing so. Therefore, they spend very little, if any, time on this objective. This must change if your organization is to become an Organization of the Future and successfully compete with The New Competition.

Figure 2-1 depicts a process flow diagram of the performance management process as it will be defined and described here. It represents the conceptual framework for this book.

The process begins at the top with a stimulus causing the organization or specific organizational system to attempt to improve performance. This stimulus may be:

1. The challenge posed by New Competition as we have suggested;
2. The executive order signed by President Reagan calling for a twenty percent improvement in productivity in all federal government organizations;

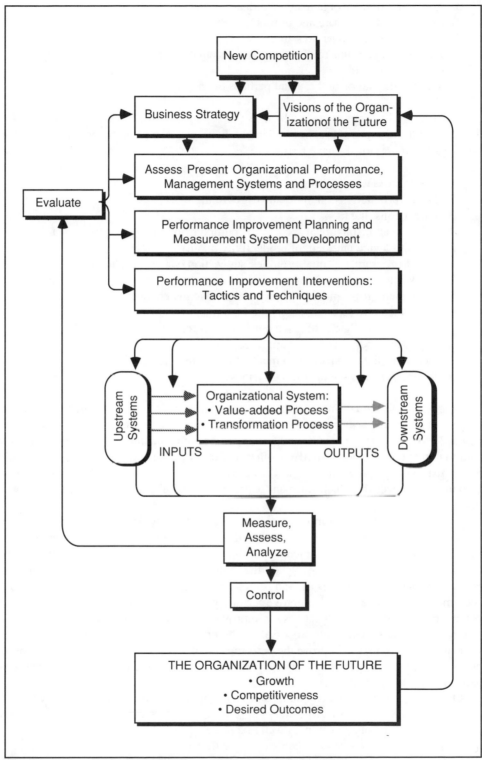

Figure 2-1.   The Performance Management Process

3. A champion in the organization with a vision;
4. Declining market share and profits;
5. Board and stockholder pressures;
6. The logic of wanting to get better in a systematic way;
7. Fear of failure; or
8. Some combination of these and perhaps other stimuli.

These stimuli evoke responses which, as you have seen in the literature, at conferences, on television, and in newspapers, vary considerably. Examples of typical responses to stimuli, such as the ones listed previously, have been:

1. Start a productivity center;
2. Start a productivity and/or quality program;
3. Hire a consultant;
4. Bring in an inspirational speaker to "pump up" our top management team;
5. Appoint a vice president of productivity/quality;
6. Start a program, e.g., quality circles, suggestion system, gainsharing, or cost reduction;
7. Automate the office, factory, warehouse;
8. Implement just-in-time inventory and production control;
9. Send a team to Japan and copy the Japanese;
10. Hire a famous "guru" to solve our problems for us;
11. Lay off ten percent of the work force;
12. Get rid of the union, or implement concessionary bargaining; or
13. Restructure and sell off losing businesses.

Of course, individually none of these responses can solve all your problems or achieve all the potential performance improvement that exists in your organization. Some of these interventions may even be strategically unsound, incompatible with other interventions, or ineffective at accomplishing your ultimate desired outcomes. For instance, we don't condone getting rid of the union or just starting a program. The most effective, longer-term response, as we have suggested, is to change the process by which you manage performance. This must start with a revamp of your planning process.

The planning process in most organizations is extremely deficient. We plan for capital investments, acquisitions, budgets, facilities, and staffing, but not for performance improvement. Most importantly, the process by which we plan is not effective. It does not involve, in an effective and efficient fashion, enough people or the right people. The output of the performance improvement planning process is a grand strategy by which we will, in a step function as well as an incremental fashion, constantly improve performance in strategic areas in the organization. We develop strategies, goals and objectives for improving performance. We focus on improving the performance of the systems and processes in the organization. This is not unlike the use of statistical process control to improve the performance of specific processes. The same concepts apply. The first basic step to improving the performance management process is to redesign and enhance the planning process.

Out of the planning process should come an integrated plan for improvement interventions. This plan would include the specification of improvement tactics and techniques to be employed in various areas of the organization, as well as a project plan. The project plan, milestone chart, and Gantt chart would sequence when each specific technique would be introduced into the various organizational systems. This project planning is extremely critical and difficult. It requires in-depth knowledge of the techniques themselves, as well as good wisdom relative to implementation strategy. The art of developing a grand strategy for improvement interventions is not widely practiced in American business and industry. Perhaps our disciplinary educational system and lack of holistic thinking causes this. Nevertheless, an understanding of what performance improvement techniques are available and what their specific operating character-istics are is critical to this step of the process. In Chapter 4, we will attempt to provide you with a reasonably comprehensive view of the range of techniques for performance improvement that exist today.

As we implement specific improvement interventions (note, the performance management process is, in itself, an improvement intervention) a need for measurement arises. We will want to monitor the performance of the organization or specific organizational system to confirm that our specific improvement interventions have had an impact. In this respect, we are developing what we call impact verification measures. Did the improvement interventions we implemented improve performance? We may need to do this as a part of an evaluation or justification follow-up study. Measurement of performance and feedback to people in the organizational system is, in itself, a powerful improvement intervention. Psychologists call this *knowledge of results* (KOR). Measurement as a routine part of the management process, apart from that associated with specific improvement interventions, is the most important aspect of measurement in the Organi-zation of the Future. We will elaborate significantly on the reasons for and the uses of measurement in the Organization of the Future in Chapter 5.

You will note in the performance management process (Figure 2-1) that measurement is separate from evaluation. This is appropriate and significant. The process of measurement is a non-value laden process. It is the process of deciding what to measure, collecting data, tracking over time, and analyzing the data. It can and should be separate from the evaluation process. Evaluation is the process by which we impose standards, specifications, requirements, values, and judgments to determine the degree to which performance meets the needs and/or expectations of our customers or our processes. We believe this separation in the two highly interrelated measurement activities is consistent with Deming's point on use of or inappropriate use of standards and with the literature from psychology on how to improve performance appraisal (Deming 1986; Kanter and Brinkerhoff 1980; Meyer, Kay, and French 1965).

In Chapters 5 and 7, we will discuss measurement and evaluation in considerable detail. At this point, let it suffice to say that measurement and evaluation are critical components of the performance management process. The figure identifies the feedback component from evaluation to:

1. Our perceptions of the challenge posed by The New Competition;
2. The appropriateness of our responses to the challenges;
3. Our perception as to potential new responses required;
4. Our strategies, goals, and objectives; and
5. The effectiveness, efficiency, and quality of specific interventions we have made to improve performance.

The performance management process reflects an open system (your organization is in constant contact with its environments) with a closed-loop feedback system (the evaluation component of your measurement process).

The process is designed to drive towards control and accomplishment of longer-term goals, such as becoming the Organization of the Future, survival, growth, competitiveness, and improving levels of performance. We argue that control is an outcome; a result of managing the process. We also propose that the bottom line for any organization is not profitability or managing to budget. In our opinion, bottom line is whether or not the organization is achieving its visions of what it wants to or feels it must become. Bottom line, long term, is survival, growth, constantly improving performance, competitiveness, and behaving in accordance to your values and principles. If you do these things, profits follow.

The Beginning: Visions of the Organization of the Future or Responses to Competitive Challenges

The performance management process, as depicted in Figure 2-1, seems to be driven in organizations today in at least two ways. It appears that some organizations are simply managing performance by responding to competitive challenges. Some organizations are clearly more successful at this than others. This process is not altogether reactive, and there are certainly many forms that this adaptive response can take. As we indicate in the process flow diagram, the response mechanism can drive planning or it can directly drive attempts to improve some aspect of performance without interfacing with any overall planning process. Planning might take place for a single intervention, such as a flexible manufacturing cell installation or an office automation project; however, overall organizational strategy implications may not be addressed. Ideally, it would be preferable to have the challenge-response approach begin with a strategic and comprehensive planning effort, then move to selection of specific improvement intervention tactics and techniques. This would minimize suboptimization of your improvement efforts.

It seems to us that planning has at least two important components: business unit strategy and performance improvement strategy. To address The New Competition, an organization's management team must define and reach some level of agreement regarding its sources of sustainable competitive advantage. What are our strategic variables, factors, and thrusts? What are our strengths and competitive advantages? The focus is on what we will do and on the business plan that centers on marketing, structures employed, markets to be served, technologies to be utilized, facilities, staffing, and products and services. We are talking about the portion of strategic planning that focuses on business strategy (Porter 1980, 1985).

In our opinion, the business plan is a background document. It might contain: long range objectives, i.e., 20-year horizon corporate objectives; strategic analyses, internal and external; and general strategy discussion. The business strategy is given life and meaning by a performance improvement plan/strategy that facilitates attainment of its business strategy. It links strategy to action. Moving directly to a micro plan, such as implementing computer-integrated manufacturing or automating the office in the absence of a larger, well thought out business strategy has limited value. We will tell you how to improve the quality of your performance improvement planning process in Chapter 4.

The other approach that appears to be taken is to drive the process toward a vision of the Organization of the Future. This might be termed a pull strategy as opposed to push strategy for the challenge-response approach. In one case, we are pulling the systems and process toward a vision of what the organization will have to look like in terms of problem solving, planning, decision making, structures, levels of performance, measurement and evaluation systems, and reward systems. In the other case, we are driving the systems and process in response to perceived challenges, threats, and competitive pressures. We're not necessarily suggesting that one is better than the other or that these two approaches exist in pure form in any given organization. Clearly, an organization could do and perhaps should do both. We believe it is important for American organizations to create a little better balance, in favor of the pull strategy. How important it is to create shared visions of the Organization of the Future, communicate guiding principles, and develop a grand strategy by which continual performance improvement can be attained cannot be over-emphasized.

So, the answer as to what is the beginning of the performance management process may be. It depends. Or that you can begin at either the top or bottom of the process, such as with responses to challenges or with the development of a vision of the Organization of the Future, or that you should begin at both the top and the bottom. For that matter, you could argue that the process of managing performance begins with measurement and evaluation of current levels of performance so that one can assess where to begin. Specific situations will probably dictate where you begin with the process. A suitable starting point or entry point to the process will then determine the sequence of steps to be taken from that point forward. Maybe the answer of where to start is answered best by Deming: "Start anywhere and anytime as long as you do it now!"

The assumed sequence of steps to the performance management process is revealed in Figure 2-1. A competitive challenge is perceived, and an awareness that performance needs to improve is created (Chapter 1). Appropriate responses are contemplated (Chapter 2). A vision of the Organization of the Future is developed and communicated (Chapter 3). A planning process is developed and implemented that creates strategies, goals, objectives, and action plans that will move the organization toward its vision of what it must become to compete and succeed (Chapter 4). Improvement actions are taken on an ongoing basis as a normal part of doing business (Chapter 6). Measurement and evaluation of the progress of the performance management effort takes place at all levels and across all functions on an ongoing basis (Chapters 5 and 7).

Planning: The Development of Integrated Strategies, Goals, Objectives, Action Items, Action Teams, and Action Plans to Improve Performance

A stimulus for change is developed either by creating a vision that pulls us toward it or by creating a crystallization of a competitive challenge, problem, or opportunity. You react to a situation or you proactively develop actions intended to improve the situation in anticipation of problems or opportunities. You have a sense of urgency: You must do something to improve performance. What next? The answer "to plan" is shallow and meaningless unless we tell you how to plan. In our opinion, the process by which you plan for performance improvement is of equal importance to the plan itself. The process by which you plan for performance improvement determines the level of quality and acceptance for the plan and actions necessary to implement the plan.

Knowledge of a competitive challenge or threat or even a vision of the Organization of the Future is insufficient alone to improve performance. A well thought out plan that is developed by all levels of management is essential to meet successfully the challenges posed by The New Competition and become your vision of the Organization of the Future. The planning process gives substance and meaning to what we perceive has to be done.

Figure 2-2 depicts a planning process we have used sucessfully to develop performance improvement plans for numerous organizations. We will describe this process in detail in Chapter 4. The basic planning process entails eight steps.

It begins with Organizational Systems Analysis (OSA), which has at least eight areas. In a planning process implementation for an autonomous organizational system, all eight areas of OSA would likely be appropriate. If the planning process were being completed for a quasi-autonomous department down inside the organization, the OSA areas might have to be tailored to fit the circumstance. The eight areas are listed in Table 2-1 and will be discussed in detail with examples in Chapter 4.

Organizational systems analysis is the interface step between business planning and performance improvement planning. We tell management teams that the purpose of Step 1 (OSA) is to prepare them to plan for performance improvement. In an organizational system that has done business planning and done it well, this step is largely redundant. The team may only need to review the business plan and discuss its relationship to their effort to plan for performance

39

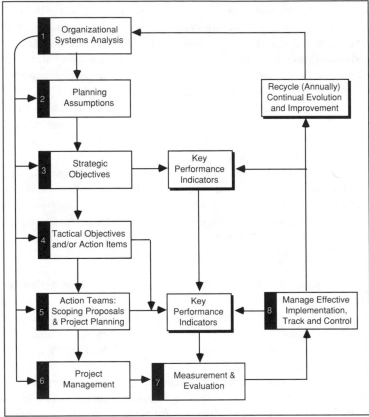

Figure 2-2. Performance Improvement Planning Process

improvement. The relationship between business planning and performance improvement planning you will face is hard to predict; however, there are common situations:

1. There is no plan of any type; therefore, the performance improvement planning process will develop *the plan*. In this case, Step 1 (OSA) will need to be done in detail and focus on business strategy issues.
2. You are in a semi-autonomous organization, i.e., a profit center/cost center within a strategic business unit (SBU). In this case, your performance improvement plan must support the SBU business plan. You will need the management team to carefully review the "upline" plans.
3. For a reasonably autonomous organization or organizational system, review of upline plans is always recommended if they exist; however, the performance improvement planning process can serve to develop both the business/organization plan and the performance improvement plan.
4. A department or sub-organizational system within a semi-autonomous or autonomous unit *should* clearly link its plans to the plans of the parent unit. The assumption is that the parent unit has a plan. We find this often is not the case in the real world.

Step 2 of the planning process entails developing planning assumptions upon which the performance improvement plan will be based. Assumptions are developed and analyzed in terms of their importance to the plan and their validity or certainty. These assumptions allow us to consider necessary areas for which contingency plans need to be developed and to assess our plan at later periods in time based upon critical assumptions that were made. Assumptions allow for a mechanism by which to account for uncertainty and risk.

Step 3 of the performance improvement planning process focuses on developing strategic objectives for performance improvement. This step is accomplished in a structured participative fashion. The output from this step is a prioritized list of strategic objectives for performance improvement for the organizational system for which the plan is being developed.

In Step 4, tactical objectives and/or action items are developed, again using a structured participative process. The output of Step 4 represents specific improvement interventions that need to be taken or initiated during the next year in order to begin to move toward the objectives established in Step 3.

Step 5 concentrates on forming action teams to develop scoping proposals for the priority improvement action items developed in Step 4. A scoping proposal outlines what has to be done, who has to do it, sequencing, measures of success (key performance indicators), and costs and benefits. Groups of three to five people comprise an action team. These persons normally volunteer to serve on an action team. Action team duties and effort are expected contributions to the organization beyond just getting the individual's job done.

Steps 5-8 of the performance improvement planning process essentially serve to link strategy to action. In this sense, Step 5 of the planning process makes a transition to the box in Figure 2-1 called Performance Improvement Interventions. We believe that this is where strategic planning has traditionally broken down, and as such, this is a critical step in the performance improvement planning process. It is important for the reader to see the fit between Figure 2-1, the performance management process, and Figure 2-2, the performance improvement planning process.

Step 6 is managing the implementation of the action item. Scoping proposals are reviewed and assigned to an implementation team. Implementation proposals are developed and the project management phase begins. A visibility system is developed to create "line of sight" for progress against the plan. Step 7 requires that each action team develop measures that will answer at least two questions: Have we successfully implemented the improvement project? What is the impact of the implementation on organizational system performance? Action teams must evaluate the results of their improvement project before moving on to another improvement project. Measures for improvement project success are integrated into the visiblity systems. Step 7 transitions into Step 8 by requiring that the action teams manage effective implementation and monitor progress of their improvement project for a sufficient period of time to ensure that steady state for the solution and design has been achieved. Continuous support and involvement from management and a visible tracking system will help to ensure effective implementation.

This performance improvement process is repeated in advance of the budget planning process. The planning process can be implemented in a top-down fashion to ensure congruity in goals, objectives, action items, and measurement from level to level. More will be detailed on actual implementation strategies for this process in Chapter 4. The recycle process occurs approximately once each year. For a given organization, this process may need to occur more or less often than once a year. The planning process itself is examined based upon lessons learned from the previous year, and any appropriate modifications are made at this point. It is reasonable to expect that the process itself will evolve, and it is here that this redesign and development process occurs.

1.1	Vision (Corporate Long-Range Objectives)
1.2	Guiding Principles (Values and Beliefs)
1.3	Mission (Purpose)
1.4	Input/Output Analysis
	1.4.1 Desired Outcomes
	1.4.2 Customers, Markets (Downstream Systems)
	1.4.3 Outputs
	1.4.4 Inputs
	1.4.5 Value Adding Transformation Processes
	1.4.6 Customers, Suppliers, Vendors, (Upstream Systems)
	1.4.7 Attributes (Quality, Quantity, Timeliness, Cost) at all checkpoints
1.5	Internal Strategic Analysis
	1.5.1 Structures Employed
	1.5.2 Staffing
	1.5.3 Facilities
	1.5.4 Technologies Employed
	1.5.5 Strengths and Weaknesses
1.6	Current Performance Levels
1.7.	Roadblocks to Performance Improvement
1.8	External Strategic Analysis
	1.8.1 Threats and Opportunities
	1.8.2 Review of Upline Plans

Author's Note: This list is not sequential nor comprehensive. It is meant to be a "shopping list" from which to choose areas that are appropriate for the system being studied.

Table 2-1. Areas of Organizational Systems Analysis

In Chapter 4, we will expand the level of detail provided for the process itself. However, at this early stage, it may be helpful to have several managers from various organizations who have experienced this process comment on their perceptions as to the value of the performance improvement process to their organizations.

> A college of engineering has been described as a collection of departments joined together by a common heating plant. The autonomy of academic departments and of faculty within those departments is without counterpart in business, industry, or government. At the same time, even an academic organization must look forward; it must establish priorities and it must move toward those common objectives. Our need for strategic planning coupled with the relative independence of faculty was a good reason for our decision to use Dr. Sink's Performance

Improvement Planning Process. We required a structured format to bring together and to achieve a measure of consensus among 300 opinionated professionals. We wished to develop and implement for the first time a strategic plan. The process was successful. A measure of consensus and support was obtained for a plan for the future.

Paul E. Torgerson, Ph.D.
Professor and Dean, College of Engineering
Virginia Tech

The Performance Improvement Planning process, as championed by VPC, is an extension of the planning process (the "other half of planning") that enables a company to proactively manage its way to the future it wants to achieve. UI was attracted to the VPC approach because of their linkage of performance improvement to planning which fits very nicely with the Company's functional, rather than departmental, planning process. We also found that VPC's manner of implementing a performance improvement process emphasizing participative management and reliance on every employee to be the best "authority" on his or her own job offers the most effective way of imbedding the concept into the very culture of our organization.

Dennis E. Hrabchak, Director
Strategic and Financial Planning
United Illuminating

The planning process from the Virginia Productivity Center provided a clear, concise focus for development of the Productivity Action Plan for the Department of the Navy (DON). This process was used to get top DON management consensus to:

- emphasize total performance improvements.
- identify key obstacles to improve performance.
- define true mission parameters.
- establish "guiding principles for productivity improvement."
- establish goals and action plans to achieve goals.

Many people believed that the strong traditions in the Department of the Navy would make change very difficult. Yet, in the nine months since the beginning of the Navy planning experience, the action plan was released and has already been updated; commitment has been obtained from the Secretary of the Navy and below; significant improvement has been made in most of the initial 12 goals; and we are just beginning. The opportunities that can result in tremendous improvements in total performance are there and must be nurtured and developed.

The planning process has been unifying, informative, challenging and uplifting to those involved. Expectations have been raised for positive change and substantive improvements through further planning, rewards, hard work and continued management emphasis.

G.C. Hoffmann
Specification Control, Advocate General of the Navy

(Author's note: The Performance Improvement Planning Process functions as the "backbone" of the Performance Action Team (PAT) Process described below.)

The first question should be, why PAT?

We—Burlington—looked at many different approaches to getting our employees more involved in day-to-day decision making. We evaluated gainsharing, bonus systems, and quality circles and decided that PAT had the most to offer to both the employees and the plant.

PAT is a process where decision making is taken to the lowest practical level. Our people who have participated (83%) do feel more involved in the day-to-day operation. It encompasses many areas of stimulating activity for our people and our performance. We feel the following are extensions of PAT rather than separate approaches: JIT, multi-skilled employees, machine set-up times, single sourcing, quality surveys with customers, employee vendor exchange and Process Control. All of the aforementioned are successful only if you have true employee involvement.

To fully understand our commitment to employee involvement we must go back and look at what we were doing prior to PAT. We had Profit Sharing and Retirement System, systematic depth interviews, annual appraisals, seniority, job opportunity rosters and elective vacation. We feel the benefits were all very good but did not totally give us the involvement and commitment that we felt our employees needed and wanted.

PAT is an excellent addition to involving our people and is directly related to our business's overall performance.

Taking decision making to the lowest practical level involves our employees in a way that allows for daily input and decisions that are both short and long range. It is a real approach that gets the activity of decision making back to the people who are actually doing the job.

Larry Maust
Vice President of Greige
Sales Division
Burlington Industries

The Navy and Marine Intermediate Maintenance Activities supporting aviation units have embarked on a major productivity improvement program. The initial focus was to improve the repair rate of items processed. This provides two beneficial outcomes: more ready for issue parts are available at the operating bases, and the more expensive and slower depot level logistics "pipeline" of transportation and repair is avoided. We quickly found that simply setting an improvement goal was not enough. We needed strategic planning of interventions, mission definition, process analysis, and the introduction of Statistical Process Control. In short, a broadbased planning strategy was employed to accomplish the required change. In this way we formed a coherent, integrated road map of actions to effect process changes at all levels of a rather bureaucratic system. An unexpected fallout of the formal process is that we established firm credibility with higher echelon organizations within the Navy and with personnel in the Department of Defense.

Capt. P. A. Monroe
Staff COMNAVAIRLANT
Naval Air Station Norfolk

When I first became a manager, I struggled for a long time with the question of what *long-range outcomes* my department should be striving to achieve. Once we had a good grasp of our long-range goals, I discovered that there was still something missing in our management process. We had no yardstick for measuring our progress toward achieving the goals that we had established for ourselves. It was only after we had determined explicit performance measures, and had established a systematic, periodic review process, that we began to feel that we were operating on a sound management basis. In my consulting work with many different companies and many different types of organizations, I always insist that we implement a process of establishing our long-range directions, and then systematically measure our performance on the key output variables. This approach has proven to be extremely successful in pushing organizations to better and better performance.

Joe H. Mize, Ph.D.
Professor (and Former Head)
School of Industrial Engineering & Management
Oklahoma State University

From now on there will be two eras at Rhodia: "Before-Sink Era" and "After-Sink Era". (Stated at the end of Rhodia's first Strategic Planning Session for Excellence in Performance.)

Edson V. Musa
President
Rhodia, S.A.
Sao Paulo, Brazil

Improvement Interventions: Integrating Action Items and Improvement Projects Developed in the Performance Improvement Planning Process with an Overall Strategy of Tactics and Techniques for Performance Improvement

As you can see, specific improvement projects are an integral part of the performance improvement planning process outlined in the last section. You can also perhaps appreciate that the improvement projects identified in Step 4 and implemented in Step 5 may not be comprehensive or well integrated. This component of the performance management process focuses specifically on integrating broader and more pervasive strategies for performance improvement with the detailed improvement projects that can be expected to come out of the performance improvement planning process. This component may involve nothing more than an audit of all the action items and improvement projects to ensure that all bases are covered. It may involve filling gaps where improvement projects do not address a needed improvement thrust. Or, it might involve evaluation to ensure that no new improvement techniques have been developed that have not been considered in the mix of improvement interventions being employed.

This component of the performance management process also involves analysis to ensure that no incompatible techniques are being employed. It focuses on coordination of what is being done throughout the organization to ensure that sufficient networking is being done to avoid reinventing the wheel or repeating mistakes, and to assure that implementation of techniques is as effective and efficient as possible. Chapter 6 will review performance improvement techniques available to your organization and attempt to categorize them for you. We are not advocating that you view our efforts in Chapter 4 as a "take-a-pill-to-get-well" approach. We advocate that you be good "chefs and cooks," not just cooks. However, we do feel that the book would be incomplete without a review of what's out there. We won't teach you the "how to's" for the techniques, but we will provide you with perspective and references as to where to go for more detail.

In the Organization of the Future, performance improvement planning is going to be pervasive, and tremendous amounts of proactive improvement will be taking place. This activity will supplement traditional improvement mechanisms that already exist in your organization, not replace them. The performance improvement planning process briefly discussed in the last section is a mechanism by which your organization can begin to move from being manager-led, control-oriented to being self-managed, commitment-oriented. This proactive performance improvement process cannot be overlaid on top of your existing improvement processes without considerable planning and coordination. This is what we mean by integration of improvement activity from the performance improvement planning process with the more global strategy for improvement in your organization or organizational systems.

Developing Improved Measurement and Evaluation Systems: The Art of Building Scoreboards

As you can see from Figure 2-1, the performance management process flow diagram, we now turn our attention to measurement, assessment, analysis, and evaluation of performance. By this point in the process, your organization would have: a clearly communicated awareness of the challenges posed by New Competition; a vision of what your Organization of the Future must look like in order to respond successfully to these challenges; developed comprehensive and integrated plans for responding to these challenges; implemented a performance improvement planning process to supplement and expand ongoing and perhaps traditional performance improvement efforts; and been coordinating the grand strategy or master plan for this performance management effort.

Involvement in the performance improvement effort would be pervasive throughout your organization. A tremendous amount of communication, training, development, patience, consistence, top management support, design, conviction, leadership, skill, ability, vision, coordination, planning, and belief would have been exhibited at this point if you are succeeding. You will be succeeding if you begin to sense that the culture is changing. If you begin to sense that people in the organization are beginning to see their jobs and their role in the organization in a new light, you are probably succeeding. You will feel a difference as you walk through the organization and observe behaviors and as you talk to people. You will see people excited about their work and performing at higher levels than in the past. You will see team building take place, and you will see improved focus on group performance as opposed to individual performance as a result of the performance improvement planning process.

And you will at times feel like the process is out of control. You will have heard the phrase "shove responsibility and accountability for planning, problem solving, and decision making to the lowest appropriate level," and you will wonder if you haven't perhaps shoved it too low, too fast. You will question the value of the experiment. You will be pressured by management for quicker results. You will be asked to tell the "bean-counters" how much money you have saved in relation to the costs of the program. You will face skeptics, cynics, devil's advocates, "snipers," resistors to change, challengers, and downright enemies. The percentage of people with you will represent the enlightened few, the early adopters, the inquisitive, the risk prone, and the frightened who don't know what else to do. This group very likely will amount in the first two to three years to no more than twenty-five percent of your organization. The percentage of people who are openly against you, or even worst, informally and via the grapevine system, will probably total twenty-five to fifty percent. The remaining twenty-five to fifty percent of your organization represent those who are indifferent, undecided, risk-averse, late adopters, and who will join the process as it begins to succeed. These percentages are in your favor! The twenty-five percent who are with you are a critical mass of followers and leaders. Make your strengths decisive. If led, the early adopters will ensure the success of the process as a result of their support and leadership throughout the organization.

The next step in the performance management process is to focus on improving performance measurement and evaluation systems. As you will recall, some measurement effort has already begun in Steps 6 and 7 of the planning process. However, this measurement focused on specific measures of performance for individual improvement projects and assessing the impact of these projects on organizational system performance. What needs to occur now is a more global analysis of the measurement systems in the entire organization. A good first step is to audit your existing measurement systems. We will present an auditing system in Chapter 5. The major developmental thrust of this step in the performance management process is to improve the quality of measurement systems. This means that we will have to design/redesign measurement systems for the following, often-neglected criteria: effectiveness, quality, productivity, quality of work life, and innovation. The assumption is that efficiency and profitability are the two best-measured criteria in most organizations. The objective is to build "scoreboards" that will provide everyone in the organization with appropriate information relative to how they and the organizational systems they are managing and working in are performing. They need to know whether they are progressing toward longer-range goals, as well as how they are doing on tactical and operational issues. They need to see good news, as well as the bad news. They need to see information that they can personally relate to and understand. They need to understand the relationship between their activity and performance and the larger organization's performance. This task is not an easy one and requires significant skill and knowledge.

In addition to building specific measurement systems, we must build mechanisms by which the measurement and assessment gets fed back to our perceptions of the challenges posed by The New Competition, our planned responses, our strategies for improvement, and our specific tactics and techniques to be employed to improve performance in order that "real time" adjustments can be made to the performance management process. Figure 2-1 depicts these feedback loops. By now it is clear that the performance management process, as depicted in our flow process chart and in our discussions to this point, is extremely complex and dynamic. Consider trying to translate this process in terms of a corporation the size of General Motors. The process might make sense on paper, yet when we try to think through how to apply it or how it corresponds to what is already being done in even a 500-person, autonomous plant, the process becomes just another abstraction of reality. We trust that as we move through the book and become more specific that the job you have to translate and transfer ideas to will become easier and more obvious.

At this stage of understanding, let it suffice to say that we have presented a process by which an organization:

1. Assesses competitive challenges and creates a vision of how to effectively respond to those challenges;
2. Enhances the strategic planning process in the organization to incorporate a pervasive performance improvement planning process;
3. Develops a grand strategy for performance improvement that integrates ongoing improvement thrusts with the improvement projects that flow from the performance improvement planning process;
4. Improves the quality of and pervasiveness of measurement and evaluation systems in the organization.

This process is not that complex to understand, nor is it really novel or unique. Again, it reflects an abstraction or generalization of what we see excellent organizations attempting to do as they strive to become Organizations of the Future. Their efforts are not as systematically thought through nor as systematically explained. We see our job as one of studying, translating in general terms, and helping to transfer the concepts to other organizations.

So, at this stage we have the four major components of the performance management process: awareness of the challenges and visions of responses; performance improvement planning processes that are coordinated throughout the organization; grand strategy development for improvement interventions that is integrated and coordinated with improvement projects that come out of the performance improvement planning process; and improvement in the quality of measurement and evaluation systems at all levels of the organization and in all organizational systems. The last major element of the performance management process is really focused on management of the process. It concentrates on infrastructure development, cultural support systems management, and continuing evolution of the process so as to maintain and build on excellence achieved.

Infrastructure for the Performance Management Process; Cultural Support Systems; Continuing Evolution; and Maintaining and Building on Excellence

The major components of a performance management process have been assembled. How do the components come together? How are they managed as an integrated whole? These are the issues that are addressed in the last component of the process. There are several perspectives from which you and your organization's management team could be reacting to our description of this process to this point:

1. We do this already, not exactly in this form, or in that sequence, but we do all these things. We may not do them consistently in all parts of the organization, but we do try to encourage our managers to do these things.
2. We go about productivity and quality improvement in a lot simpler way. You have made this too complex and academic. The process isn't this cerebral, it's much more intuitive and natural. We tell our managers we need them to cut costs by four percent and they do it. This process, as you've described it, won't work in our organization because it's too complex.
3. This is an oversimplification of the process. It is far more complex than displayed in the figure and discussed. There are critical elements left off, you can't capture our process on paper, it's just too complex. Furthermore, the process is different from level to level and function to function in our organization. Improvement means something different and how one goes about it in different parts of the organization is entirely different. It is an interesting attempt to capture our process, but it is too simple and too general to be of much use.
4. It is logical and it makes sense. We do not do a good enough job at improving performance as an integral part of what we all do and this explanation can help us to better communicate what we want our managers and management teams to be trying to do. It is an oversimplification in some respects, but that is necessary to communicate the basic, underlying process. It is too complex, in some respects, in that many of our managers are not used to thinking this systematically about their jobs and about performance improvement. We can't copy this process, but we sure can use it as a model, a prototype, from which to redesign and improve our existing approach. We can use this as a guide.

Our experience leads us to believe that the most honest and most common reaction, for American organizations, is the last one. We don't say this because we believe the other three reactions are necessarily wrong. We say this because our years of experience working with even the best of U.S. firms leads us to believe that the last reaction is the most valid and common at this point in the evolution of management process in this country.

Those of you who have reacted in a similar fashion to the manager's comments listed in Item 4 above, must address several issues at this point. Do we want to do something about how we presently manage performance in relation to how we ought to be managing performance? Do we want to tackle the whole organization or just start with some portion, a pilot project of sorts? How do we begin? Where do we start? How long will it take? How much will it cost? What are the tangible and intangible benefits we can expect? How do we get board, top management, employee, union, middle management, staff support? If I'm the top manager, how do I get this started without forcing it on the organization? If I'm not the top manager, how do I get top management's support? How do we manage and coordinate the program? How do we do this and still get all the other things done? How do we stop fighting fires long enough to work on this effort?

If you are from a successful organization, your problem may be one of complacency and a feeling that we don't need this, we're doing OK without it. If you are in a failing organization, your problem may be one of a sense of urgency, but a sense that this will take too long—you may need a "quick fix". The point is, that the decision to do something is not an easy one, regardless of the situation you may find yourself in. There will not be strong consensus, one way or the other, to do anything different than what you are already doing. There in fact will likely be stronger sentiments for maintaining the *status quo*. As we said earlier, the predominant, underlying belief is that maintaining the *status quo* will be sufficient for survival and success in the future. This means that most, if not all of you, regardless of your position in your organization face the challenge of how to sell a more systematic and proactive process for managing and improving performance. We believe, and hope you do too, that something different must be done in American organizations. We believe that the successful organization in the 1990s and beyond will look and behave significantly different than it does today. We agree with Deming that "everyone doing their very best is not sufficient" for the revitalization of American business and industry. If you believe your organization must change, you better have something to sell your management team. You cannot just go to them and say that we must change and that everyone is going to have to do a better job. As Deming has said, "we must know what to do". We would add that we must know what to do and be willing to pay the price to do it. We believe that the process we have outlined for you is a good example of what to do. It is not our process, it is a description of how excellent American organizations, like the ones Peters and Waterman talked about in *In Search of Excellence*, and others, are meeting the challenge of The New Competition.

In order to pull off an effective implementation of this process, or any other for that matter, an infrastructure has to be developed. The infrastructure is a management of the process design, if you will. We are so used to management structures that manage functions, plants, divisions, disciplines, that it is hard for us to think about management structures that are designed to manage processes. And, yet, the Organization of the Future will require that we do more managing horizontally, across functions and disciplines. In some respects the concept is not unlike that of the matrix organization. The performance management process is an umbrella program that cuts across the traditional vertical management structures we find in most organizations. The challenge is how to set up an infrastructure for the performance management process without establishing a vice president for performance improvement or a productivity and quality center. The reason this is the challenge and important is that performance improvement must be seen as an integral part of everyone's job. If you implement the process with a center or with a single champion you run the risk of not establishing shared ownership.

You will recall from Chapter 1, that Musashi Semiconductor Works spent over five years laying the foundation for their small group activity process. They trained, communicated, designed, developed and sold the process top to bottom in the organization. It is this kind of planning and preparation that is essential to the long-term success of a process like the one we are presenting. Programs can be pulled off in a shorter period of time. But you don't need another program if you truly want to become the organization of the future. You need a process that is an integral part of your culture, the way you do business. Will a few champions initially take the lead developing and selling these concepts? You betcha! Will that champion or small group of champions have to build a broader base of support and build a critical mass of champions? Absolutely! The design of the "grand strategy" for the effective implementation of the performance management process application in your organization will likely have to be developed by a small group of champions, with perhaps the assistance of select outsiders. Very quickly thereafter, that group will have to begin to build this thing called an infrastructure. Many American organizations do this by having a core staff group that coordinates the process with a council that is comprised of key decision makers in the organization. The council acts as a policy-making, planning, problem-solving, and decision-making body. It represents a critical mass of top and middle management who will share ownership for the management of the process. They will share the burden of deciding how to guide the design, development, and evolution of the process from its conception out into the future. The infrastructure is then the organization and management of the process itself. It is an organization within the organization that is designed to ensure that the performance management process is successfully implemented. The formality of the infrastructure will likely dissipate as the process evolves and becomes more firmly embedded in the way you do business.

CLOSURE

Chapter 2 was designed and written to provide you with an overview to the performance management process, which is the superstructure, if you will, for this book. The main theme of the book, the role of measurement in the Organization of the Future, is a linchpin in the performance management process. Taking the mystery out of measurement comes, in part, from better understanding the integral role that measurement plays in the management/improvement of performance (effectiveness, efficiency, quality, productivity, quality of work life, innovation, and profitability/budgetability). In the absence of that understanding and in the absence of an understanding of operational definitions for the seven performance criteria, one cannot use measurement effectively.

Our intent in this chapter was not to make the process of managing performance appear too simple or too complex. It was to present a clear, systematic model of the process we see excellent organizations using to better manage performance. It is useful to most people to be able to stand back from the trees and look at the forest. Many managers don't do that often enough. Looking at the performance management process in this structured fashion provides the opportunity to improve the clarity with which you can communicate what has to be done in your organization to move it towards your vision of the future. In the next part, Chapter 3, we will examine visions of the Organization of the Future in a little more detail. We will discuss the need for developing management processes that increase flexibility and adaptability. We will look more closely at specific characteristics of the Organization of the Future. And, we will discuss how to develop a compelling vision about the Organization of the Future.

REFERENCES AND SUGGESTED READINGS

Davidson, W. H. 1982. Small group activity at Musashi Semiconductor Works. *Sloan Management Review*. Spring, 3-14.

Deming, W. E. 1986. *Out of the Crisis*. MIT Press. Cambridge, Massachusetts.

Hackman, J. R. 1986. The psychology of self-management in organizations. Pallack, M. S., and R. O. Perloff, (Eds.), *Psychology and Work: Productivity, Change and Employment*. American Psychological Association. Washington, D. C.

Kanter, R. M. and D. W. Brinkerhoff. 1980. Appraising the performance of performance appraisal. *Sloan Management Review*. 21(3): 3-16.

Meyer, H. H., E. Kay, and J. R. P. French. 1965. Split roles in performance appraisal. *Harvard Business Review*. January-February.

Morris, W. T. 1979. *Implementation Strategies for Industrial Engineers*. Grid. Columbus, Ohio.

Naisbitt, J., and P. Aburdene. 1985. *Reinventing the Corporation*. Warner Books. New York.

Peters, T. 1987. *Thriving On Chaos*. Alfred A. Knopf. New York.

Peters, T. and N. Austin. 1985. *A Passion for Excellence*. Random House. New York.

Porter, M. 1980. *Competitive Strategy: Techniques for Analyzing Industries and Competitors*. The Free Press. New York.

_____. 1985. *Competitive Advantage Creating and Sustaining Superior Performance*. The Free Press. New York.

Sink, D. S. (1980, 1983, 1984, 1986, 1987). *The Essentials of Performance, Productivity, and Quality Management*. Short Course Notebook. LINPRIM, Inc. Blacksburg, Virginia.

_____. 1987. Guiding principles: The foundation of successful efforts to better manage productivity and quality. *IIE Integrated Systems Conference Proceedings*. Institute of Industrial Engineers.

Norcross, Georgia.
Waterman, R. H., Jr. 1987. *The Renewal Factor*. Bantam Books. New York.

3. VISIONS OF THE ORGANIZATION OF THE FUTURE

THE NEED FOR VISIONS

I n Chapter 2, we spoke of two basic strategies for energizing performance improvement. One strategy was a "push" strategy propelled through measurement. A second strategy was called a "pull" strategy that involved developing a shared vision of a desired future organization. In this strategy, once the vision is articulated, it serves to pull the organization in that direction. This is not a mysterious process despite the fact that the word "vision" is not the most frequently used word by most managers. This chapter will discuss some changes that will be necessary for organizations to become the Organizations of the Future. It will also discuss the role played by visions and values in helping make the transition.

There is scientific support for the notion of visions acting to help improve performance. Behavioral researchers call the phenomenon "mental practice." Positive effects of mental practice have been demonstrated for basketball players. Three groups of players of equal free-throw shooting ability participated in an experiment to test the effects of mental practice. Group One engaged in physical practice; that is they actually shot free throws. Group Two didn't engage in physical practice, but spent time in mental practice situations, thinking about the free-throw shooting process. Group Three engaged in no practice at all. The three groups were then tested for free-throw accuracy. The greatest improvement occurred in Group One. However, Group Two, the mental practice group, improved significantly more than Group Three. This phenomenon has been demonstrated in many other settings, such as, downhill ski racing, etc. The technique of visioning is often used by therapists to help clients create "futures" that are improvements over the past.

In organizations, the shared vision is a very powerful energizing force. William O'Brien, president of Hanover Insurance Companies of Worcester, Massachusetts, says: "We are each influenced by our own mental picture of what we are building with our efforts. I call these mental pictures visions and they play an important role in determining what our company becomes" (Naisbitt and Aburdene 1985). Naisbitt and Aburdene go on to write:

> Belief in vision is a radically new precept in business philosophy. It comes out of intuitive knowing; it says that logic is not everything, that it is not all in the numbers. The idea is simply that by envisioning the future you want, you can more easily achieve your goal. Vision is the link between dream and action... Ultimately, vision gets translated into sales and profit growth and return on investment, but the numbers are the vision.

The issues raised in this quote are central to our conception of the role of visions in the Organization of the Future. In the Organization of the Future, the numbers come after the vision. The vision serves to pull the organization in the desired direction, and the numbers provide a guidance system to help management steer the process.

In discussing the key role played by visions in organizations, Naisbitt and Aburdene point out that visions help produce alignment. What does that mean? Imagine for a moment two football teams. On one team, filled with outstanding talent, there are twenty-two players each attempting to beat last year's individual statistics in yards gained, passes completed, and tackles made. On the second team, equally talented, the players are all totally committed to one thing: winning the Super Bowl. On the first team, anything that interferes with individual performance will be resisted even if it may be better for the team as a whole. On the second team, if the players are truly committed to the vision, benching the first-string quarterback to help win a game is acceptable, even though it may cost the quarterback the chance to improve on last year's statistics and cost him in salary negotiations next year. Winning the Super Bowl becomes a compelling vision that brings all the members of the team into alignment with respect to goals and values. Individuals subordinate their personal welfare to the "common good." This is the power of visions.

What is a vision? Perhaps the simplest answer is that the vision statement is what the members of the organization will say in answer to the question "What is this organization trying to accomplish?" In the example shown here, winning the Super Bowl is the vision. A story is told of the differences between the views of two workers—both employed in auto manufacturing plants and both performing the same repetitive operation. The first worker responded to the question "What are you doing?" from a visitor. He said, "I'm welding door hinges on the door frame." When the second worker in a different plant was asked the same question, he responded, "I'm helping build transportation systems for the benefit of mankind." Two workers, two visions. Which would inspire the highest-quality performance? What would the people in your organization say?

The creation of a vision is normally the role of the leader. In fact, the creation of a compelling vision is what separates the leader from the manager. Of course, what separates the successful leader from the dreamer is that the leader has the practicality to convert the vision to reality. This conversion process involves establishing organizational systems that will operationalize the vision. Later we will discuss two of these systems in considerable detail: one is the planning system, the other is the performance measurement system. We believe that you can apply the ideas presented here, and they will help your organization move in directions that will allow you to meet and beat The New Competition.

IMPLEMENTING VISIONS REQUIRES NEW PARADIGMS

The example presented of the old- vs. the new-style organizations provides an illustration of an important concept as we attempt to understand and create Organizations of the Future. That concept is the notion of a paradigm. A paradigm is a set of rules that define boundaries (Kuhn 1970). In the example, the old paradigm is that an organization defines its vision in terms of numbers, e.g. sales, return on equity, and earnings per share. This "rule" establishes boundaries for what is in and outside of the vision. In this old paradigm, "winning the Super Bowl" as a vision would not fit. It would have to be defined in terms of won-lost records and post-season earnings per player. On the other hand, the new-style organization would define its vision qualitatively as "winning the Super Bowl." At first glance this distinction may seem trivial; however, when it becomes the basis for energizing and focusing the efforts of members of a team toward a goal, which vision will have the most impact? Can you imagine the coach in the locker room saying to his players, "Let's go out and win this one so we can have the highest post-season earnings per player?" It would never happen. Successful coaches are saying, "We have to win this one to make it to the Super Bowl." Successful coaches are leaders first and managers second. They inspire people through articulation and communication of visions that align the goals of individuals with the goals of the group. They also drill and drill the team to develop and consistently apply a set of skills and install systems that will convert this vision to reality.

There are many examples of paradigms in society and organizations: driving on the right side of the street; saying "hello" when you answer the phone; having meetings always start and end on time; constructing buildings and spaces that are rectangular; hierarchical organizational structures; and having the boss make decisions about pay raises, instead of having those decisions made by a work group. All of these are paradigms. Let us now examine some key ideas about paradigms and their role in organizations.

Key Points About Paradigms

In a videotape *Discovering the Future—The Business of Paradigms,* Joel A. Barker (1986) discusses six points about paradigms and the role they play for people in dealing with change. We will consider these points:

Paradigms are common. As the examples cited imply, there are many paradigms. In essence, our cultural norms can be considered to be paradigms. We find them in our homes (e.g., the way we load the dishwasher), in our offices (e.g., the way we construct files, or the way we handle employees birthdays), and in church and community organizations (e.g., religious sacraments). Virtually every structured activity involves the use of paradigms. These are the rules that guide our behavior. They are most often guiding us unconsciously. We are not aware of their influence.

Paradigms are useful. Because we do not have to stop and think about every action or activity, the paradigms save us considerable time. Paradigms serve as filters that enable us to focus on relevant information and filter out "noise." Without the influence of paradigms, we would undergo sensory overload and would have difficulty making sense out of our experience.

Paradigm paralysis can be dangerous. Paradigm paralysis is a "terminal disease of certainty" (Barker 1986). It occurs when your paradigm becomes "the paradigm" — the only way to do something. The engineering manager who insists that every person write the report his way may be suffering from paradigm paralysis. The instructor who insists on teaching via the lecture mode may be suffering from paradigm paralysis. In a changing world, paradigm paralysis makes us blind to new and potentially better ways to do things. Our paradigm filters keep us from seeing those things that do not fit our paradigms.

People who create new paradigms tend to be outsiders. New ideas tend to come from people who are not heavily invested in the old methods. A consultant who develops and standardizes a productivity audit process may spend his time attempting to improve the process; however, he is unlikely to become the advocate for a completely new way to perform the audit. Someone who has not been involved in the audit process development, perhaps someone from an entirely different discipline, is more likely to be the source of a new way to conduct the audit. The new ideas are most likely to come from the mavericks, those on the fringe of the existing paradigm. Innovative organizations need to find ways to "care and feed" these mavericks, because it is the new paradigms that lead to new products and services and breakthroughs in the production process.

Early adopters of new paradigms require great courage and vision. Practitioners of the old paradigm who switch to the new paradigm at an early stage do so at great risk. Think of some pioneers in new industries—Henry Ford, Thomas Watson, Ted Turner. They all took considerable risks because the new paradigms—automobiles, computers, cable TV news—were not fully proven. They had to jump to the new paradigms based on faith. There were insufficient data to prove that they were making the right moves.

You can choose to change your paradigm. Perhaps the most important point is that paradigms are not genetically "wired in." Paradigms are learned; they are acquired through experience. People can choose to change their paradigms; organizations can change their paradigms. The expanding movement for organizational culture change is concerned with changing paradigms.

Not only can an individual or organization choose to change paradigms, such changes may be essential if one is to be successful against The New Competition. Who would have dreamed ten years ago that organizations would have established day care centers in their office buildings? Who would have dreamed that a total organization would declare itself "smoke free" and ban smoking from its premises? Who would have imagined that an $800-million company would be able to operate with a corporate staff of twelve, as Nucor has done? Who would have believed that a country which produced "junk" in the 1950s would have the world's largest trade surplus and an outstanding reputation for quality in the 1980s? All these are examples of paradigm shifts.

As we consider the characteristics of the Organization of the Future, we must look more deeply at the types of paradigm shifts required for an organization to move from the old-style to the new-style organization. These are discussed in the next section.

Paradigms About Measurement

Organizations have many paradigms; without them they could not function. However, some of these paradigms get in the way of the organization's ability to continuously improve performance. We might call these dysfunctional paradigms "roadblocks" or "obstacles" to performance improvement. In Chapter 2, we have considered already some of these with relation to planning systems. Let's examine some of the paradigms that create problems for organizations with respect to the effective use of performance measurement systems.

Measurement is threatening. One paradigm that prevents creative implementation of measurement processes is the view that measurement systems are threatening. This paradigm is often grounded in objective reality. Almost every member of the organization can think of an instance in which a measure of performance was used to "beat up" on someone. Of course, the way people are harmed by measurement data is not physically, but through the loss of resources, the loss of autonomy, the imposition of additional reporting burdens, disciplinary actions, and, in some cases, dismissal. These stories are legendary and are part of the organizational mythology and culture. But they are very real; they exist and they serve to thwart the introduction of new or revised measurement procedures.

Of course, it is not the measurement system that is at fault here. Usually, it is simply that the measurement system is being used as a tool to implement a management style of fear and intimidation. While in most organizations fear and intimidation are not the predominant management style, remnants still exist. Thus, reasons the wise employee, "Why should I submit to a measurement system that might collect data that can be used to harm me?"

However, the other side of this issue is that people like to be measured. They like to get feedback regarding how well they are performing. So people don't fear measurement *per se*. What they fear is how measurement data may be misused by someone else.

The paradigm question buried in this fear is the assumption that measurement is for someone else. What has to be stressed is the fact that the primary audience for performance improvement measurement is the manager and group that are being measured. The key issue to removing this threat is to build a common vision that is accepted throughout the organization regarding what performance needs to be improved and why. A strategic measurement focus at all levels can help overcome the old paradigm.

Precision is essential to useful measurement. To many organization members, the term *measurement* is synonymous with *precision*. This is particularly true in white-collar, technical organizations. For engineers, scientists, and even accountants, there is in their discipline a culture of precision in measurement — or at least the appearance of precision. Thus, when we begin to talk about performance measurement in white-collar areas, these same people become very nervous. They realize that performance issues do not lend themselves to the level of precision they usually associate with measurement. Since measurement to them implies precision, the two concepts do not go together. This is understandable.

The paradigm issue is that performance measurement does not have to be as precise as the measurement in a laboratory to be useful. The basic purpose of performance measurement is to tell the organization whether it is headed in the right direction. In fact, if the organization insists on developing precise measures, it will probably never get started on the performance measurement trail.

Single indicator focus. Organizations are complex. Performance in organizations is complex. Therefore, performance cannot be adequately explained or measured by a single indicator. Regardless of whether it is IBM, McDonald's, or the local Little League baseball team, we must have multiple indicators of performance. However, a common paradigm is to search for the bottom-line single indicator. This always leads to trouble. When college basketball programs focus on won-lost records exclusively, they ignore academic performance of players. When General Motors focuses too much on profitability, it loses out on market share. When deregulated airlines attempt to focus too much on revenue or market share, the Department of Transportation mandates the release of information on on-time takeoffs.

The increasing focus on statistical process control is adding a different dimension to this issue. Not only is there a tendency for organizations to overemphasize single measures, there is a tendency to overreact to single data points on the indicators. Lacking a statistical understanding which points out that variability is expected, managers and employees often attempt to compensate for variation in measures that are normal for a system under control. By compensating, variability is increased and performance of the system is increasingly erratic. Therefore, both single-indicator and single data-point management are the tickets to trouble.

Overemphasis on labor productivity. When we focus on productivity as one of the most important dimensions of performance, there is a tendency to overemphasize labor productivity. Historically, the focus in manufacturing organizations is on decreasing labor costs. This tendency is driven by both competitive considerations and artifacts of measurement processes. For example, the arbitrary allocation of overhead to organizational units as a function of labor hours has made the reduction of labor hours a prime target of cost reduction efforts. We have reached the point where direct labor costs are a relatively insignificant component of many products, yet they continue to draw a disproportionate share of attention in the measurement systems. This is beginning to change as firms focus increasingly on indirect labor. While this change is appropriate, it simply shifts the problem, unless there is an accompanying increase of attention to the other input factors of production, such as capital, materials, and information. The paradigm shift called for is a shift from single-factor productivity measurement to multifactor and total-factor measurement. Only when such an approach is taken can the tradeoffs associated with management decisions be assessed truly.

Subjective measures are sloppy. As the measurement focus shifts to knowledge work and service organizations, there is an increasing need to measure "softer" dimensions of performance. These have to do specifically with employee morale and customer perceptions. As organizations attempt to focus reward systems on performance, these softer measures take on more importance in bonus and gainsharing systems. This shift is being resisted especially by the "bean-counter" community. There are two issues at stake here. Both relate to paradigms.

The first paradigm question is the ability to measure soft performance dimensions. There is a tendency to equate soft with sloppy. There is a great deal of sloppy measurement of these soft dimensions; however, the measurement technology associated with the measurement of attitudes and perceptions is well developed and can lead to reliable and valid measures. This has been the domain of industrial psychology for decades.

Secondly, the issue of a willingness to distribute rewards—including money—where the tangible savings are difficult to define is a very entrenched paradigm. It is also not without considerable logic on its side. However, sticking to this position effectively prevents the development of gainsharing systems based on a comprehensive definition of performance in many knowledge work and service organizations.

Standards operate as ceilings on performance. Performance measurement is relative measurement. In order to interpret performance measurement data, one must have something with which to compare the measures. Commonly used alternatives are standards, goals, or baselines. There is a subtle distinction between these alternatives. The notion of a standard is often used as if it were absolute. Even though its users often deny it, the standard carries the connotation of desired level. If the standard is met, performance is OK. In the organization of the past, prior to The New Competition, perhaps that was acceptable. However, in the organization that will successfully compete today and tomorrow, what was good enough for yesterday is not good enough for tomorrow. Standards which act as ceilings on performance, because they imply absolute desired levels, are an old paradigm that must change. When Deming argues against productivity measurement systems, this is what he opposes.

On the other hand, the concepts of baseline and goal are much more amenable to the philosophy of continuous improvement. Psychologically, it is easier for people to accept higher performance goals than higher performance standards. This is especially true when the goals originate from organizational objectives that are understood and accepted. Unless they are strategically linked, goals too can operate as ceilings on performance.

The dysfunctional paradigm is any term—standard or goal—which suggests that anything less than continual performance improvement is acceptable.

CRITICAL DIMENSIONS OF THE ORGANIZATION OF THE FUTURE[1]

"The paradox is that when introducing advanced technology calling for less labor per unit produced, people become more important and their competence more desirable" (Jonsson 1984).

This quote from the head of organization development for Volvo AB, one of the world's leading-edge organizations, provides an appropriate framework for this discussion. What is the Organization of the Future? Of course, no one is really sure. Obviously, there will be many Organizations of the Future, perhaps very different from one another. Nevertheless, we can speculate on some of the common threads that will characterize these organizations. Our discussion will address paradigm shifts in the Organization of the Future in four major areas: strategy, structure, technology, and management systems.

Strategy

The competitive strategy of a firm is a combination of the ends it seeks (goals) and the means selected to achieve those ends (policies) (Porter 1980). Competitive strategies are shaped by factors internal to the organization and factors external to the organization. Hage (1988) discusses some of the major external forces which will shape the strategies of the Organization of the Future. Hage addresses issues such as globalization of markets and organizations, shorter product life cycles, increased market segmentation and product differentiation, increasing concern about the educational ability of U.S. workers, and demographic shifts which will produce labor shortages.

---

1. This section is adapted from Tuttle, T.C. (1988).Technology, organization of the future and non-management roles. In *Futures of Organizations.* J. Hage (Ed.) Lexington Books Division of D.C. Heath & Co. Lexington, Massachusetts.

Survival in this era of New Competition will require development and implementation of strategies that lead to a sustainable competitive advantage.

What will be the key elements of these strategies? The essence of strategy development is an attempt to differentiate one organization from another. Despite this, similarities in the environments faced by organizations will lead to some general commonalities among successful strategies. From this writer's perspective these will be increased organizational flexibility, product and process innovation, cost reduction, and improved quality.

As Richard Foxen stated in the report from the NASA Symposium on Quality and Productivity:

> . . . . Surprisingly to many, in the last decade even our share of world exports of high technology products has declined from 25 to 20 percent. And the U.S. share of world trade in such services as insurance, finance, aviation, shipping and engineering also has declined from 25 to 20 percent. . . In order to seize the competitive edge, we must maximize the flexibility and adaptability of American workers and managers (NASA, 1984).

Increasing organizational flexibility. Increased competition, technological development, and shorter product life cycles all suggest that organizations must be able to respond more quickly to changes in the future than they have in the past. These conditions will require organizations to operate differently. These differences will be seen in structure, the integration of information systems across functional boundaries, decentralized decision making, fewer job classifications and multiskilled work forces, more effective communication between functional groups, strategic thinking at all organizational levels, and team problem-solving activities.

Product and process innovation. Responding to the new rules of competition requires an organization to creatively adapt through innovation to customer needs. Product innovation is the most visible evidence of the innovative organization. However, process innovation is equally important in sustaining competitive advantage. Creating a climate that encourages innovation requires dedicated management attention. It also places demands and expectations on non-management employees. "Business as usual" is no longer acceptable. Nonmanagement employees are expected to be a source of new ideas that will fuel the innovation process.

Cost. A key element of competitive strategy is the organization's position regarding its cost and pricing structure in the marketplace. In some product lines, cost is the major determinant of competitive success. However, more educated consumers increasingly view factors in addition to initial cost in product selection (e.g., quality, delivery time, and design). Nevertheless, global competition will continue to drive a strong concern for cost reduction in virtually every industrial and service sector.

Quality. Another product of the forces shaping the environment for the Organization of the Future is an obsession with quality. The essence of this quality revolution is a greater focus on products and services which meet the needs of the customer. Definitions of quality are changing from conformance to the designer's specifications to a concern with making sure the product specifications meet the customer's specifications.

Within the production process a concern with "process quality" has become a major focus. Process quality is concerned with building quality into the product as opposed to inspection and rework of poor product. Hayes and Wheelwright (1987) point out that before you can build quality in, you must first "think it in." These authors list five practices necessary to think in quality. These are:

1. Careful preplanning during the product design stage and involving engineering, production, quality assurance, and marketing;
2. Training workers so that they are capable of delivering high quality, and developing expectations of high quality in them;
3. Developing a working environment where people are encouraged to surface, discuss, and resolve quality issues, not hide them;
4. Work with suppliers to assure defect-free parts, and accept only perfect parts; and
5. Purge your thinking of the concept of acceptable quality level (AQL) and instead accept the concept of continuous improvement—no defect is acceptable.

Organizations that fully institutionalize these concepts find that quality increases and cost decreases. Hayes and Wheelwright quote a Japanese manager as saying:

> If you eliminate the production of defective items, things become much simpler and less costly to manage. You don't need as many inspectors as before. You don't need to have production workers doing rework through the process. Waste goes down. Inventory goes down. But morale goes up. Everybody feels proud when you produce only perfect products (Hayes and Wheelwright 1987).

When organizations adopt quality as a competitive strategy, they are committing to a major organizational culture shift. Nothing less will be sufficient to meet The New Competition.

Structure

A second major organizational trend is a shift in organizational structures. Figure 3-1 depicts the shift that is taking place in many organizations.

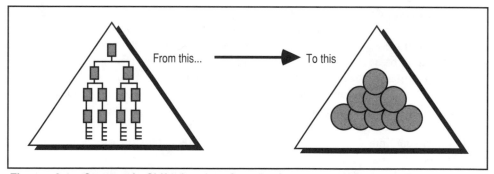

Figure 3-1. Structural Shift in the Organization of the Future

Naisbitt refers to this trend: computers and the whittling away of middle management are toppling hierarchies, flattening the pyramid. At Apple Computer, for example, fifteen people report to CEO John Sculley (Naisbitt and Aburdene 1985).

Replacing the pyramid are decentralized, product-oriented divisions, or profit centers. Within these divisions team structures are common. Names given to such new organization types vary from W. L. Gore's "lattice" to 3M's "biological" organization to Magna International's "organic" organizational structure. However, in many cases the objectives are similar. These objectives are manageable organization size, flexibility, and low management cost reflected in few layers and few managers relative to the number of "production" employees.

One of America's most successful firms at continuous innovation is 3M. As cited by Naisbitt and Aburdene, their commitment to decentralization is legendary. A firm with approximately 87,000 employees has a "biological" structure characterized by:

- A median plant size of 115 people;
- Five of ninety plants have more than 1,000 people; and
- Plants are located in small-town America.

While there are many variations of this theme with respect to organizational structure, the direction of movement seems inescapable. The rash of corporate restructurings occurring in the 1980s carried with it downsizing and a reduction of layers of management.

The moves toward restructuring are driven by strategic considerations. Foremost among them appears to be cost/profitability considerations. Either as a result of corporate takeover or as a defense against takeover, moves are made to increase profitability or stock value by cutting costs. A second motivation is to increase organizational flexibility and the capacity to react more quickly to environmental demands, including changing customer needs. From this author's experience, both of these strategies can lead to leaner and flatter organizational structures. Most restructurings are probably driven somewhat by both goals; however, in terms of its effect on the organization, there is a difference in terms of which of these motives are primary.

When cost reduction is primary, and it is implemented in a top-down autocratic fashion, this is likely to have negative consequences on flexibility, innovation, quality, and employee commitment. When flexibility and customer responsiveness are primary, innovation, quality, and employee commitment are likely to be enhanced; however, cost reductions will likely occur at a slower rate. Therefore, the competitive environment and the organizational culture will likely determine the approach taken to restructuring. Too often these decisions are made in a crisis mode, which leads to cost reduction strategies being primary. Organizations are then forced to attempt to recreate a culture that is more conducive to performance improvement.

By necessity and design, flatter organizational structures will push decision making to lower levels. However, as Lawler (1986) argues, this in itself is insufficient to create high-performing organizations. In addition to moving decision-making authority to lower levels, successful "high involvement management" (Lawler 1986) also requires that rewards, knowledge, and information be moved down concurrently.

Such an organizational design based on decentralized and more autonomous work groups places a greater demand on communication and information flow. Information must flow to the levels at which decisions are made. In addition, decision making must become more collaborative. Information technology, if properly designed, can facilitate these communication and decision requirements. However, person-to-person communication linkages will always remain vital.

Technology

Hage (1988) presents an innovative conception of "technology." He views technology as a subset of the broader category of knowledge. The more typical notions of technology Hage refers to are "machine" and "method." However, he accurately points out that these cannot be totally divorced from the other categories of knowledge, i.e., the theories or models and the skills of people.

The importance of this broad conception of knowledge vs. the typical narrow conception of technology is illustrated by the example depicted in Figure 3-2.

In the first column of this diagram, we can trace the steps required to produce a letter using the old electric typewriter technology. Column Two (without culture change) uses a potentially improved technology but the same method and same model, i.e., hand-written manuscript and mail delivery. As a result, the new technology leads to little improvement, only the elimination of the retype step. Column Three begins to reap the benefits of the new technology, and Column Four shows even greater benefits. In Column Three, we see a new model—the originator keys in the document. This also requires new skills—the skills of keyboarding. Column Four moves further toward a new model in that the document is transmitted electronically. This new model involves new machines (e.g., modem), new methods (e.g., direct data communication), and new skills (e.g., use of communication software and hardware). However, the process depicted in Column Four is the most efficient by far. In order to achieve these increased performance gains, more than new technology was required. Also necessary was a new way of thinking about document creation (a new model) and new skills. In essence, to reap the benefits of new machines, a new culture is required.

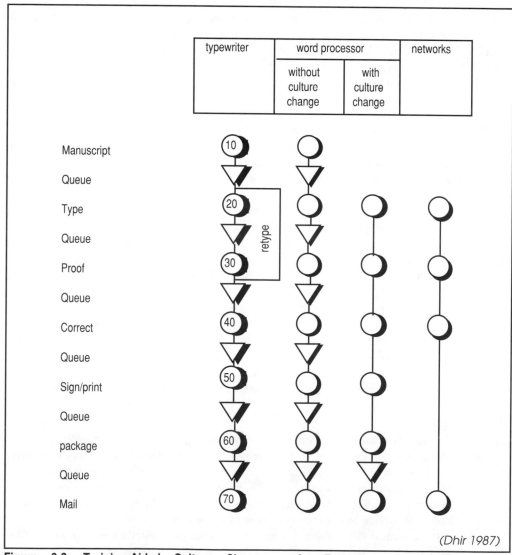

(Dhir 1987)

Figure 3-2. Training-Aided Culture Change - An Example

This rather simple example illustrates very clearly the difficulties associated with efforts to reap the promise of new technology. It also helps explain where the failure of new technology to live up to the promises made by vendors can occur.

This section makes no attempt to forecast specific types of technological gains in the Organizations of the Future. Rather, it attempts to describe this author's view of some major directions or purposes of this new technology. The discussion will focus separately on product and process technology.

Product Technology

Product technology refers to the characteristics of the final product that is delivered to the customer. With respect to product technology, three trends are readily apparent:

1. Product technology is becoming more sophisticated;
2. Product life cycles are being reduced; and
3. Increased differentiation of products is required in order to appeal to an increasingly diverse market.

From automobiles to toys to office equipment to weapon systems to food processors, our products are becoming technologically more complex. To some degree this increased sophistication is driven by the technologies themselves. That is, the technology exists, therefore it should be put to use. In other cases, it is driven by consumer or customer demand. For example, the combination of shifting tastes to gourmet food and a concern in a two-wage-earner family with time utilization leads to acceptance of an automatic coffee maker that can be programmed the night before to grind beans and then brew the morning coffee. Clearly the "high-tech" society expects products to grow in sophistication.

In the global economy, there are many more players in the marketplace than was the case in the past. Where Americans for most of the Twentieth century had a choice among three major automakers, today there are many more. A shrinking U.S. market is being subdivided into increasingly competitive spheres by new imports from Yugoslavia, Brazil, and Korea as well as the well-known Japanese and European models. Undoubtedly Soviet and Chinese autos are not far behind. Each of these new entrants seeks a competitive advantage. Initially, it is price; however, gradually the battleground shifts to other turf, such as quality or features. As each competitor strives for market share, new product innovations are introduced. With more competitors, this process occurs more and more rapidly. The result is shortened product life cycles.

This scenario is being played out in market after market. It does fuel innovation. Only organizations that are innovative and flexible will survive.

The third trend with respect to product technology is the need for increasingly differentiated products to appeal to identified market segments. After World War II, U.S. organizations virtually had an unlimited demand for products. Whatever companies could make they sold. Organizations were concerned with increasing output to keep up with demand. Today, and into the foreseeable future, this situation does not exist. The Japanese are moving into a similar period of stability following rapid economic growth. In a period of stable markets, competition is greater. Organizations cannot sell all that they make unless it has consumer appeal. As a result, we hear of organizations today describing themselves as "market driven."

The market-driven organization must be much more sensitive to the signals it receives from the environment. Instead of a few marketing people with their "ear to the ground," every employee

65

must become a marketing person. It must decentralize functions, be able to integrate information from diverse functions, and act quickly on that information to produce new products and services.

Process Technology

The most far-reaching impacts of new technology will result from changes in process technology. The forces driving product technology changes have considerable implications for the technology required to produce these products.

One view of how these processes will change is provided by a National Science Foundation Report (Solberg, et. al. 1985). These authors concluded that production technology in manufacturing organizations will be characterized by:

- Dramatically reduced cycle times from order to delivery;
- Flexibility—the range of capabilities of hardware will be expanded and set-up times will become negligible in order to make small batches economical;
- Transition to more machine intelligence—however, this must move beyond simply capturing human expertise in expert systems built on rational process models in physical laws; and
- Integration of technologies—advances in narrow fields of technology are wasted if bottlenecks occur at the interfaces.

These authors argue that these changes are being driven by manufacturers' requirements for increased quality, lower costs,and reduced flow times. These strategic variables, combined with product technology and image in the marketplace, are the basic ingredients of competitive advantage. Thus, what is happening in process technology is that organizations are attempting to use production processes as a strategic tool.

Significant changes are being made in production technology in manufacturing. However, the so-called indirect, or overhead functions, are also being affected by new technology. Since, for many organizations, the areas of greatest labor costs are the so-called white-collar areas, these increasingly have become targets for automation. Examples of one firm's efforts to modernize production technology in these areas can be found in the list of proposed projects in Figure 3-3.

Management Systems

The final aspect of the Organization of the Future to be discussed will be management systems. This is a broad category that encompasses human resource management systems, management control systems like performance measurement, budgeting, accounting, and planning systems. It is through management systems that organizational strategy, vision, and core values become institutionalized.

In the past, these management systems have often been viewed as separate systems, designed by professionals or technical specialists to help the organization control various facets of the operation. In the Organization of the Future these management systems will be viewed as strategic tools to help the organization develop and sustain a competitive advantage. This approach to the design of management systems requires that business strategy, core values, and operating principles have been defined. Next, this approach requires that organizations define the types of behaviors (e.g., risk taking, decisiveness, or collaborative decision making) required to achieve the strategy. Finally, the management systems must be developed to support and sustain these behaviors as well as provide sufficient organizational control. This discussion will center on changes that can be expected in human resource management systems.

SUPPORT	MODERNIZATION	AFFECTED SALARY WORKFORCE (%)	AFFECTED SALARY WORKFORCE (%)	MODERNIZATION	SUPPORT
Materials	Automated materials requirement and procurement	4	2	Computer-integrated manufacturing	IMOD
Human Resources	Computer graphics automation	2	1	Computer-aided facilities design	Facilities
Logistics	Technical publication automation	1	6	CAD/CAM	IMOD / Mfg. Engrg
Mfg. Control / Finance	Computer-aided estimation and pricing	3	2	Consolidated human resources data base	Human Resources
Logistics / Human Resources	Computer-based training	1	3	Computer-integrated engineering	Engineering
IMOD	Computer-aided configuration management	2	1	Plant work orders and spares inventory control	Facilities
IMOD	Artificial Intelligence-based gids and jproposals	1	2	Generalized budgets and control system	Finance
Facilities / IMOD	Capital resource allocation and control	1	3	Employee badge based automation	IMOD / Finance / Human Res.
Mfg. Control / Mfg. Engrg	Manufacturing information systems	6	3	Computer-aided quality assurance	IMOD / Quality
Human Resource	Computer-aided security administration	1	10	Other systems (to be indentified)	TBD
			55		

Information Systems Support

Figure 3-3. List of Projects for Office Administration (Adapted from Dhir 1987)

Employee selection. Driven by the paradox described in Jonsson (1984), organizations will begin to place greater and greater emphasis on employee selection processes. As job security selection and employment security become part of the organizational policy, this makes the selection decision a more critical decision. Therefore, applicants for full-time permanent employment can expect to undergo a more rigorous screening process.

Employment security. The strategic objectives of quality, flexibility, and reduced cycle times require a committed work force. Commitment is a two-way street. Organizations cannot expect employees to be committed to the organization unless those organizations exhibit a commitment to the employees. Therefore, employment security increasingly will be an issue in the Organization of the Future. The auto industry bargaining of 1987 was a harbinger of things to come.

The way this issue is likely to be resolved is that a very lean core of employees will receive employment security guarantees. In addition, it is likely that public policy changes will be enacted to ease the transition for displaced employees. At least for the core employees, employment security protection will enable them to make suggestions for improvements—even suggestions that could eliminate their own jobs. This is because they know they will be retrained and moved to another position.

Compensation system. Future reward systems will be consistent with the move to employment security. They will be implemented through various forms of variable compensation. A significant portion of the pay for core employees will be in the form of a bonus tied to the productivity or financial results of the organization.

In his prescription for restoring the U.S. competitive power, Lester Thurow addresses the need to modify reward systems.

> . . . .The place to start is by altering the present structure of salaries and wages. Instead of receiving straight wages or salaries with all of the residual profits allocated to the capitalists, part of each worker's or manager's income should come in the form of a bonus based upon increases in value added per hour of work. . .(bonuses should) account for, let's say, one third of total labor income. These bonuses become an important part of everyone's—blue collar workers, management—annual income and thus everyone shares a common interest in higher productivity and success (Thurow 1985).

Not only will reward systems provide for variable compensation, they will become more performance based. Advances in information systems will permit better accountability for individuals and groups. Pressure for performance will be strong, and this will be driven in part by the fact that there is a closer link between pay and performance for individuals, groups, and the total organization.

Employee development. Driven by the need for flexibility, organizations will require individuals who are multiskilled and who can be retrained. The ability to learn will be a selection criterion. Once employed, individuals will spend a considerable amount of work time in training.

To summarize, we envision the Organization of the Future to be a means of responding to The New Competition. It will operate in a global marketplace characterized by increasing competition. Markets will be increasingly differentiated, and consumers will be more demanding of product innovation and quality, as well as service quality. Product life cycles will become shorter and shorter. To operate successfully in this environment, organizations will have to evolve new paradigms with respect to strategy, structure, technology, and management systems—especially human resource management systems. While organizations will have fewer people, the ones who are there will be more critical than ever before.

Dynamic Stability in a Changing World: The Role of Values, Principles, and Beliefs

While organizations must change in order to become the Organizations of the Future, there is a concurrent need for stability. How can we reconcile the need for stability with the need for change? The answer to this apparent dilemma comes through the focus on organizational values, principles, or beliefs. Just as the principle of dynamic stability exists in physics, it can be found in organizations.

At IBM, Thomas Watson was quoted as saying that we are willing to change everything about ourselves except those core values. The values provide stability to an organization, just as the keel provides stability to a sailboat. While things change, some things remain constant. The core values provide that constancy.

Prescriptive Versus Descriptive Role of Values

In analyzing an organization, it is possible to examine the way the organization behaves and then deductively define the values that would produce these behaviors. In this manner, the operative values of an organization can be defined. An example of this process is presented in Chapter 4 under the organization systems analysis discussion. Once the operating values are articulated in this manner, they can be analyzed to determine whether they are the values the organization professes, or desires.

In many organizations that have not made a consistent, concerted effort to start and institutionalize their values, as has occurred in organizations such as IBM and Hewlett- Packard, it is likely that individuals are guided by their personal values. To the extent that these values differ from individual to individual, it is very difficult for an organization to achieve consistency in performance. Worse still, value conflicts that are wasteful of organizational time and resources are likely to occur.

Value-driven organizations actively teach their values to employees beginning with the first pre-employment contacts. They actively live these values through the recruiting process. The values permeate the management systems by which the organization selects, plans, allocates resources, rewards, promotes, and terminates. The values are explicit. Behavior exhibited that is contrary to the core values is treated harshly.

The need for shared values is similar to the need for a common vision. The vision and values are closely linked. Consistent performance in a dynamic environment requires a constancy of purpose. Shared values are a prerequisite to this consistency.

Organizations must shoulder the responsibility for instilling a set of values, because the values of the larger society have become fragmented, decentralized, and diverse. There are relatively few areas of the country where an organization can employ a working population with a set of values that will be homogeneous and conducive to high performance. Therefore, the organization must assume the responsibility to "grow its own" in an effort to establish a common organizational culture.

Organizational Value Statements

For the organizational values to play a guiding role, there are two essential ingredients. First, the values must be explicit. Second, they must be consistently lived. The first condition is relatively easy to meet; the second is exceedingly difficult. Therefore, simply reading statements of organizational values obscures their power. Also, the statements themselves often seem sterile.

The second author experienced this when addressing a group of managers. One of the points being made was that some firms operationalize their stated value that people are their most important asset by dropping the word "employee" from their organizational vocabulary. Instead, they substitute the word "associate," or some other term that connotes status equality. The point was made that you can do things to "employees" that you can't do to "associates." At that moment, someone in the back of the room stated that his organization tried that approach. They changed the term from employee to associate and nothing happened.

What this manager failed to understand is that it's really not the word that's important. What's important are the actions that are carried out to operationalize the values implied by the change in vocabulary. Just changing the term will not make an organization that does not value its people all of a sudden start changing its behavior. However, in an organization where there is a high value on people and where there is a concerted effort to behave in ways that promote this value, then using the term "associate" will be a powerful symbol of that commitment. However, the symbol not backed up with action will have little, if any, impact. In fact, it may have a negative impact since the failure of the organization to "walk the talk" will be highlighted.

The IBMs or Nordstroms or Hewlett-Packards are not effective because they have the most eloquent statement of organizational values. To the extent that they are effective, it is because they convert these values into actions that are tangible expressions of the values. With this caveat, we will present some examples of organizational statements of values, principles, and beliefs.

An organization recently selected as one of the ten best places to work in America is a trucking firm headquartered on Maryland's eastern shore. Preston Trucking Company has developed an extensive statement of corporate philosophy and values. This is presented in Figure 3-4.

Developing Organizational Value Statements

There is no one-two-three cookbook approach to developing a set of organizational values or guiding principles. In this author's experience, the process is an iterative one beginning with a draft authored by a single individual. Typically, the first cut will be by a senior individual in the organization. Often, the person will refer to statements from other organizations as a guide. However, it is not possible to transport a values statement from one organization to another. The words must attempt to capture the values around which the organization was founded and around which it attempts to operate. If the vision statement can be said to describe what the organization is trying to do, the values statement can be said to describe those principles by which it will operate and the standards by which it will manage.

Once the first-cut draft is written, it is circulated to members of the management team for comment and revision. The document is discussed and revised until it is accepted unanimously. At that point, it may be circulated to a wider group for comment and discussion. The point is to develop a statement that has the support of the senior management team. Once accepted, this document must be widely disseminated and consistently used to guide key decisions, to audit human resource management practices and policies, and to ensure that the values are put into practice.

CLOSURE

To respond to The New Competition, organizations must move from a control orientation to a commitment orientation (Walton 1985). However, this cannot be done simply with words. Managers are judged by their actions, not their words. You can write all the philosophy statements, vision statements, and core value statements you want. You can place them in your ads and in your public relations hype. But the bottom line is that if the actions don't live up to the words, they will do no good. However, if managers are truly willing to make the commitment, if they are willing

"**S**uccess is people working together." Preston's most important asset is people, not tractors, trailers, terminals, or management systems. The following quotation from the German philosopher, Goethe, summarizes our regard for people, 'Treat people as though they were what they ought to be and you help them become what they are capable of being.' This means that Preston People must be regarded as partners rather than as adversaries.

The person doing the job knows more about it than anyone else. It is the responsibility of managers to ask for suggestions, to listen to possible solutions to specific problems, and to help implement productive change. Each employee has unlimited possibilities. Good managers have the ability to recognize and unleash the potential for better performance. Managers have no more important responsibility than to develop our people and continually create a better, more productive environment. At Preston improvement is always possible and is continually sought.

Every Preston employee deserves to be treated with respect. Each group of employees must understand what is important for its success and how it contributes to the progress of the Company. Coordinators are expected to hold regular meetings which will accomplish this objective. Employees are encouraged to ask any questions which will give them better information about their jobs, benefits, the Company, or the performance of their group. The better informed each employee is about his job and how it relates to other jobs, the greater will be the opportunities for making the organization more effective.

It is the responsibility of those in management to regard each employee as an effective performer until specific results indicate where there are areas for improvement. To achieve this refinement, managers first pinpoint the performance areas, develop a baseline, and work with the employee to establish and reach a goal for improvement. As soon as progression is recorded, appropriate reinforcement is given.

Managers are to be fair, firm and positive in correcting substandard performance and inappropriate behavior. Discipline such as firing or time off without pay is employed only as a last resort for flagrant violations of ethical standards or work rules which have been clearly communicated. In all areas where correction is needed, managers must first councel the subordinate about his actions and obtain a commitment for constructive change. The manager must ask what he can do to help the employee bring about the needed change. If the worker perceives an obstacle to improvement, this hindrance should be addressed. Warning letters are used only after the individual has been clearly informed of the problem, and then has been given sufficient time and assistance to correct it.

Although managers observe and rectify errors, it is just as important that they give credit when a job is being done properly. No healthy work environment should have more negative comments than positive ones. The obligation of managers and supervisors is to create an atmosphere wherein employees constantly gain more knowledge and are able to participate in setting challenging goals to achieve outstanding results.

Customers. Our survival and success depend on how well we consistently serve our customers. Each job has an impact on the timeliness, quality, and cost effectiveness of what is expected to respect and have concern for customer needs. Once a commitment is made to a customer or another employee, it must be fulfilled on time.

Our dealings with our customers and each other are to be conducted in a professional and respectful manner at all times. This means that each person must strive to be a better listener than a talker. A professional is one who never stops learning from others, so he is always able to perform his job better for the benefit of Preston and our customers.

Figure 3-4. Corporate Philosophy Statement: Preston Trucking Company

No matter how excited a customer is about his problem, it is our obligation to remain calm at all times. Another person's problem is always important to him, so we must always treat it as such. Once the issue has been identified we must pinpoint the steps that are to be taken to correct it in a timely manner. If we are unable to accomplish our objectives in the time frame that has been established, we must call the customer and set a new timetable so he knows what progress is being made. After the problem has been solved, those responsible for its occurrence should understand what took place and what can be done in the future to prevent the problem from recurring. Acknowledgements of superior service from customers should be communicated immediately to those employees who are able to achieve outstanding results. Each person should never forget that when he talks to a customer, he is a vital part of our sales effort during each conversation. It always should be our objective to make the best impression on our customers whenever we have the opportunity. The respect that Preston earns from its customer is determined by the actions of each employee.

Satisfied customers are the best advertising that Preston can have. Although errors will occur, our goal is to achieve 100 percent customer satisfaction. It is our objective to constantly minimize the frequency of customer complaints. At the same time there can be no excuse for the same problem recurring when it is in our control to prevent this from happening. Dissatisfaction with Preston only benefits the competition. Dedicated customer awareness will enable Preston to enjoy sound growth in partnership with satisfied customers. At Preston customer satisfaction is the number one priority.

Figure 3-4 (continued).

to "walk the talk" and back them up, a statement of vision and organization values will provide the dynamic stability required to navigate a course that will enable the organization to meet and exceed The New Competition.

REFERENCES AND SUGGESTED READINGS

Barker, J. A. 1986. *Discovering The Future: The Business of Paradigms.* Film. Filmedia, Inc. Minneapolis, Minnesota.

Dhir, A. K. 1987. Office technology modernization — an approach. *IIE Integrated Systems Conference Proceedings.* Institute of Industrial Engineers. Norcross, Georgia.

Hage, J. Editor. In press. *Futures of Organizations.* D. C. Heath & Company. New York.

Hayes, R., and S. C. Wheelwright. 1988. *Restoring Our Competitive Edge: Competing Through Manufacturing.* John Wiley & Sons. New York.

Jonsson, B., L. Rehnstrom, et. al. Editors. 1984. *Ergo: Workshop on Productive Technology and Quality of Working Life. Volvo AB.* Gothenburg, Sweden.

Kuhn, T. S. 1970. *The Structure of Scientific Revolutions.* University of Chicago Press. Chicago, Illinois.

Lawler, E. E., III. 1986. *High Involvement Management.* Jossey-Bass, Inc. San Francisco, California.

Naisbitt, J., and P. Aburdene. 1985. *Reinventing the Corporation.* Warner Books. New York.

NASA. 1984. *A Framework for Action: Improving Quality and Productivity in Government and Industry.* Report from NASA Symposium on Quality and Productivity.

Porter, M. 1980. *Competitive Strategy: Techniques for Analyzing Industries and Competitors.* The Free Press. New York.

Solberg, J., D. Anderson, M. Barash, and R. Paul. 1985. *Factories of the Future: Defining the Target.* Report of research under National Science Foundation Grant MEA8212074. Purdue University, Computer Integrated Design Manufacturing and Automation. West Lafayette, Indiana.

Thurow, L. C. 1985. *The Zero-Sum Solution: Building a World-Class American Economy.* Simon & Schuster. New York.

Walton, R. 1985. From control to commitment in the work place. *Harvard Business Review*. March-April, 77-84.

4. PLANNING TO BECOME THE ORGANIZATION OF THE FUTURE

CURRENT PLANNING PARADIGMS AND PRESCRIPTIONS FOR PLANNING IN THE FUTURE

A ll organizations plan, and all managers within all organizations plan. Do you plan? Of course you plan. Could you and your organization plan better? Of course. Will you and your organization improve the quality of your planning in the near future? Probably not, unless you take a fresh look (break down old paradigms) at the process by which you plan. Planning to become the Organization of the Future, to improve quality and productivity, to ward off hostile takeovers, to anticipate contingencies, to develop businesses, to maintain the *status quo*, to develop budgets and anticipate financial needs and opportunities, and to implement solutions to problems are all valid applications of planning. What is planning? Thinking about the future; inventing desired future states; anticipating the future; forecasting future problems, opportunities, and needs; attention to detail; responsibilities and accountabilities—planning is all these things, and obviously, much more. We get locked into ways of thinking about planning that prevent us from becoming the Organization of the Future. For example:

- Only top management plans;
- There are planners, and there are doers;
- Planning should be done in a nonparticipative fashion;
- Planning is an art only;
- Since planning is so painful and difficult, it must be done at an expensive resort;
- The plan is more important than the process;
- There is one best way to plan;
- There isn't a structured way to plan;
- You can't plan with more than three to five people in the room—involving all managers and employees in the planning process would be inefficient and ineffective;
- People at the top think best—that's why they're there;
- We do too much planning already, our planning process isn't perfect but it works, you only need to do planning for capital, facilities, staffing, and marketing—anything else is redundant; and
- Planning is something you do when you don't have anything else to do.

These and other paradigms are holding back progress in the area of planning for performance improvement.

The word "planning" and particularly the term "strategic planning" create interesting and, in our opinion, negative and dysfunctional reactions on the part of most managers. Perhaps the consultants and business schools have created these reactions by shrouding strategic planning in a mysterious veil and creating the view that it is only done by "strategic planners". Planning is one of those management topics that is viewed with considerable suspicion by most real-world managers. They see planning as: unnecessary; something forced on us at budget time; non-pragmatic; inefficient; imprecise; painful; a waste of time; something that the planners should do; something to delegate; a necessary evil; mysterious; complex; difficult; warm and fuzzy; unstructured; crystal ballish; top management's responsibility; something that you do once every five or ten years whether you need it or not; something you hire consultants to do for you; or a natural and informal process that we already obviously do or we wouldn't be here. When we speak to top managers about planning, we are always intrigued by the variety of paradigms that exist. Most of these conceptions about planning are antiquated and dysfunctional relative to the task at hand— becoming or continuing to be competitive in the future.

Planning is almost always recognized as a primary function of the executive. It is generally agreed that planning should be an extremely pervasive management process and function. However, planning has traditionally been an activity or function engaging only top management and their consultants, once a year, in either Boca Raton, Palm Desert, or some other appropriate resort. The type of planning going on beneath the top management level in most American organizations is actually reactionary planning to either the environment or the plans passed down from above. The typical planning process and cycle tend to be very lock-step and bureaucratic in character. We often simply go through the motions, fill in the necessary forms and blanks, answer the bosses' questions, provide the requested data, turn them in on time, and then forget about them for another year. Planning is most frequently a very individualistic process and does not effectively tap "group or organizational wisdom and experience." It is rarely a group-oriented process, and if it is, the group process is usually very poor. Long, medium, and short-term concerns and perceptions for the organization and its subsystems are very rarely identified from an even smaller sample of managers and employees. Planning has become what top management and their consultants tell middle management to get the people at the bottom to do. "Don't think, stupid, just do what you're told," has become the culture of the day with respect to planning.

Of course, there is a far worse scenario than the one described here. That is the case where the organization has literally ceased to do any forward-looking, proactive planning at all. It is quite easy to fall into the trap of focusing only on "getting the job done" at all levels of the organization. It can become the perception that "maintaining the *status quo*" requires only that you fight fires well and perhaps do a little contingency planning. There are many organizations that only do budget planning and perhaps some facilities and capital investment planning. This narrow a domain for the planning process in an organization today almost ensures extinction. Planning must become more pervasive, comprehensive, and better integrated to move toward the vision of the Organization of the Future. There are many organizations that quite simply do not plan. There are organizations that do not plan well. There are organizations that plan for some things and not for others. There are organizations that have formal and informal planning processes, and those that have only informal planning processes. There are very few, if any we suspect, that effectively plan in a pervasive and comprehensive fashion. Table 4-1 compares and contrasts the characteristics of traditional planning efforts with the general characteristics of what we view effective planning must look like in the Organization of the Future.

The basic differences, as we see them, have to do with the pervasiveness of the process in the organization. We believe that the planning process, particularly the component that focuses on performance improvement, must involve a significantly greater percentage of the employees in your organization. Substantive, meaningful involvement in planning by more than a very small percentage of even your management team is rare. This must change in order for you to become the Organization of the Future. However, as we point out in Table 4-1, if the planning process involves more people, it must become more structured or else it will become inefficient. Hence, we need a structured but less formal and bureaucratic process. We also need a process that is more detached from the budget planning process and cycle. Too often, the budget drives the plan. To become the Organization of the Future there must be better balance, there must be a longer-term planning horizon, and the only way to do this is to allow the plan to drive the budget. This is

Table 4-1. Comparison of Typical and Forward-Looking Strategic Planning Processes

Characteristic Strategic Planning In "Type A" Organizations	Characteristic Effective Strategic Planning Processes For the 1980s and 1990s
• Formal	• Structured but less formal
• Focus on plan	• Focus on plan and process
• Budget driven	• Plan drives budget, not vice versa
• Top management and their consultants	• Involvement at all levels of management coordinated over time
• Marketing and financial imbalance	• Balance between marketing (product portfolio), financial, and operations issues
• Myopic	• Broadened perspective, more data tapped/ considered
• Limited involvement and participation	• Longer-term planning horizon
• Detached from many pragmatic operational realities	• Pervasive discourse on plans
	• Driven/managed top-down; data fed forward and backwards

obviously easier to say than do. There are tremendous pressures to succumb to short-term, budget-driven issues. It is critical to allow the planning process, particularly in early stages, to be free of the "can we afford it" type of reactions and judgments. When you are planning for long-term survival and competitiveness-type issues, you need to ask if you can afford not to do it. This mentality may be prevalent for big expenditures and decisions made by top management; however, down inside the organization, the "bean counter" mentality controls the culture. As a result, we are being surpassed by more adaptive organizations all over the world.

Paradigms about planning in America and in other countries are antiquated, myopic, and shortsighted. We need to broaden our views of planning and improve our understanding of what it is, how it should be done, what it entails, who should be involved, and how we can begin to redesign and evolve our current planning systems. Our thesis is that in order for organizations to compete with The New Competition in increasingly complex, dynamic, and competitive technological, sociological, and marketing environments they will have to sponsor, promote, develop, and create proactivity, innovation, and change at all levels of the organization. Capital investment in new technologies is critical to success. However, we are rapidly learning that we cannot just throw capital at a problem or opportunity and expect it to be remedied or capitalized upon. It takes the full commitment, ownership, and involvement of a lot of human resources in your organization to harness the full potential of new technologies.

We are managing complex socio-technical systems. Technological innovation must be driven by the people in the system. The people in your organizational systems tell you where the technology is needed most and how you can implement it most effectively and efficiently. Proactive participative planning for performance improvement drives technological innovation at a much more rapid pace than traditional methods. The Japanese, apparently, intuitively understand this. Perhaps it is their cognitive style and older culture that allows them to balance the requirements of social and technical subsystems. American managers listen, nod, but do not hear. We know but do not do. Our actions (Theory X behaviors) speak so loudly that our subordinates (managers, supervisors, employees) can't hear what we're saying (Theory Y philosophies). Employees today are better informed, have a greater level of knowledge, have greater visibility, are more technical and professional, and have stronger expectations for participation and involvement. For example, it is inconceivable for faculty members not to be a part of the strategic planning process at a university or college. It is clear that faculty have valuable input in the strategic direction of a university. And yet, it is extremely rare for a significant number of faculty to be involved in the strategic planning for a university. It is, unfortunately, true that very few universities have strategic plans. The point of this example is that in many respects your organizations are becoming more technical and professional in the makeup of employees. The same logic calling for a different form of governance and management process holds true for your organizations. The problems and opportunities your organizations are confronted with are more complex and dynamic, and the data necessary to solve the problems and take advantage of the opportunities are more dispersed. You must change the process by which you plan.

The need for acceptance of solutions, plans, and decisions is more critical in terms of achieving effective implementation today than it was yesterday. All these lead to the need to tap more data in more effective ways as we develop strategic plans. Those who must play a part in implementing the plans must play a role in developing the plans (Peters and Waterman 1982). If you want to become the Organization of the Future you must:

1. Break existing paradigms relative to planning;
2. Develop an understanding of the planning process described in this part;
3. Redesign your existing planning process incorporating techniques discussed in this part;
4. Continually evolve and improve the planning process.

Captain Phil Monroe of the U.S. Navy taught us an expression: "The difference between wanting and having is doing." If you want to become an Organization of the Future, you must be willing to pay the price to change how you think about planning, who does planning, and how you do planning.

To this point we have identified dysfunctional aspects of how planning is done today. We have discussed planning in a very general sense. In the next section, we will detail the concept of planning so that you may begin to more specifically identify how to integrate our prescriptions into your current planning systems.

PLANNING DEFINED AND DESCRIBED

Planning is a very broad term. There are so many types of plans, ways to plan, and terms associated with planning that it has created confusion in the field. What one finds in the conventional and even more current literature on planning is advanced discussions on specific issues associated with planning. One finds very little literature focusing specifically on the process by which planning is accomplished. We make no attempt to create a definitive or comprehensive treatment on the topic of planning. We simply want to clarify terms and conceptual frameworks for planning. And, we want to focus on how to develop performance improvement plans — the process by which planning is accomplished. First, let's examine terms associated with planning and their relationships to one another.

Figure 4-1 depicts a list of types of plans, planning horizons, the focus of planning, and various planning approaches or techniques. These four elements make up a basic taxonomy of planning.

As you can see, there is a variety of types of plans. It is likely that most of the types of plans

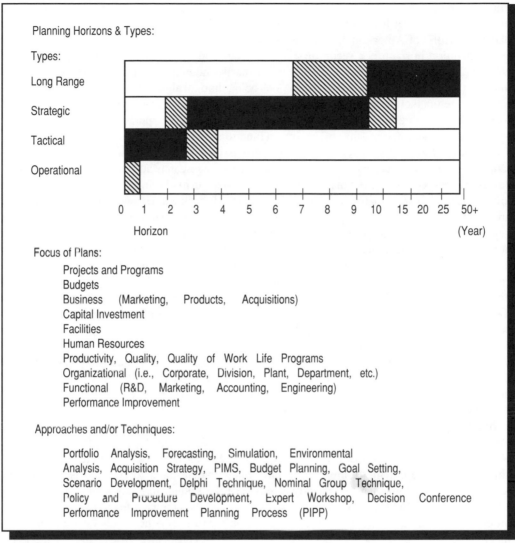

Figure 4-1. Planning Taxonomies

identified in Figure 4-1 exist, in one form or another, in your organizations. The questions we are raising for you to consider are: How good are the plans? How good is the process by which those plans are developed? Is there a performance improvement plan at all levels of your organization? Are these plans well integrated? Our suspicion and our experience suggest that your answers to these questions imply significant room for improvement. We are not proposing that the performance improvement planning process that we will describe in the next section will solve all of your planning problems. However, we do believe that the process can serve to improve the quality of your planning efforts in performance improvement planning, as well as in the other areas of planning identified in Figure 4-1. There are many focuses for planning efforts. Most organizations have formal planning efforts for projects, programs, budgets, capital investments, facilities, and marketing. It is not common for American organizations to have well-defined, effective planning efforts for their productivity and/or quality programs or for performance improvement. It is uncommon for planning efforts to substantively involve subunits of the organization or lower levels of management and staff. We believe these are serious flaws in the planning efforts of American organizations.

Planning horizon is a second important dimension of planning. The terms *long-range*, *strategic*, *tactical*, and *operational* are often primarily thought of relative to horizon. We view planning horizon as relating to the time periods being thought about as you plan. The terms long-range, strategic, tactical, and operational correlate to horizon but also address direction, desired future states, desired outcomes and outputs, paths, and more. The operational definition of what is meant by these four horizons will vary from function to function, organization to organization, level to level, type of plan to type of plan, and perhaps even person to person. For instance, long-range and strategic may mean twenty to fifty years in research and development or from a corporate perspective, while it may mean two to five years in marketing or at the divisional or unit level. There is no universal operational definition for what these horizons imply. However, there are some normative, industry-specific statistics on what these horizons imply (Szilagyi 1981). In general, when we speak of performance improvement planning, we use a ten- to twenty-year horizon for long-range, a three- to seven-year horizon for strategic, zero- to three-year horizon for tactical, and a zero- to one-year horizon for operational. Keep in mind that the words long-range, strategic, tactical, and operational imply horizon, path, and goal issues. The specification of horizon with respect to the planning process to be described is client/system-specific. It is a decision that the management team must specify as it begins the planning process. We find it common for managers to have difficulty thinking beyond three to five years. Most don't think beyond one to two years as a general practice, so asking them to think three to five years is often a challenge in and of itself. Our strategy has been to work at a corporate vision that is thought through for the longer term (i.e., five to twenty years). Most often this has to be done by the corporate visionaries, which typically will be a very small group of people or even one person. We then attempt to get the top management team to develop plans that are thought through for a two- to five-year horizon. This typically forces the management team to expand its horizon by two to three years. The assumption that strategic thinking can only be done by a few is invalid. Strategic thinking is a skill that can be developed with practice. Vision may be an art that few have, but the ability to think about the future and develop plans that respond to a vision is a necessary requirement for all managers in the Organization of the Future. In today's world, it is hard to clearly envision what the next two years will hold, much less the next ten to twenty years. The process doesn't assume that risk and uncertainty aren't realities; on the contrary, it recognizes the facts of life. The process does not lock you in; rather, it is a mechanism used to create "living" plans that allow you to be more flexible and adaptive in the face of risk and uncertainty and a more complex environment.

Planning approaches/techniques are hard to uncover in the business and planning literature *Group Techniques for Program Planning* (Delbecq, Van de Ven, and Gustafson 1986). The sort of traditional planning/budget cycle that is practiced in most organizations can be found described in much of the conventional literature on strategic planning (Szilagyi 1981, chap. 6; Steiner 1979; Byars 1984; Hammermesh 1986; Leontiades 1983; Marrus 1984; Naylor 1980; Miller 1971; Aaker 1984; Glueck 1980; Prasad 1983; McCarthy, Minichiello, and Curran 1987). We also find subcomponents of the general planning process discussed in the literature. For example, portfolio analysis, forecasting, opportunistic surveillance, problem solving, environmental analysis, policy and strategy formulation, acquisition strategy, budget planning, goal setting, scenario development, Nominal Group Technique, and simulation models are well represented in both texts and recent articles (McLaughlin 1985; Leontiades 1983; Hoffer, Murray, Charan, and Pitts 1984; Byars 1984; Aaker 1984; Miller 1971; Naylor 1980; Marrus 1984; Porter 1980, 1985; Prasad

1983; Glueck 1980). What we find lacking in the literature and in practice is a focus on general methodology or process by which plans themselves are developed. How does one plan so that:

1. The process involves a significantly greater percentage of the management team;
2. The plan drives the budget;
3. The focus is on the plan and process by which we are planning;
4. There is a better balance between the marketing, financial, and business aspects of the plan and the operational and performance improvement aspects;
5. There is a longer-term planning horizon;
6. The quality, effectiveness, and efficiency of implementation of the plans improve significantly;
7. The planning process supports a continuous improvement culture and orientation; and
8. There is better integration of all the various types of plans that exist in our organization.

We think that these are the really critical issues surrounding planning for the Organization of the Future. Unfortunately, they are not being substantively addressed in the literature. We see people discussing the problems and the symptoms but not the solutions.

Terms employed in the area of planning are a major source of confusion. There is no consistency with which many of the terms identified in Table 4-2 are employed in either the literature or practice. Table 4-2 depicts our understanding of the relationship between many of the terms used in the planning arena.

Table 4-2. Terms Employed/Associated With Planning

PurposeVision			
Policies	Mission	Goals	Superordinate Goals
Key Result Areas	Tactics	Projects	Programs
Strategies	Action Teams	Action Plans	Milestones
Action Items	Long-Range Planning	Self Studies	
Strategic Planning	Contingency Plans	Standards	
Business Planning	Implementation Plans		
Critical Success Factors	Specifications		
Scoping Proposals	Accountability		
Requirements	Key Performance Indicators		
Responsibility			
Opportunistic Surveillance			
Internal And External Audits			
Horizon			
Plans, Objectives, Activities, Milestones (POAMs)			

Several organizations we have worked with recently interchange the terms *goals* and *objectives*. Neither the literature nor practicing convention is consistent relative to the hierarchy associated with these two terms. We suggest you pick a convention that makes sense to you and be consistent. Clearly, we are discussing a logical hierarchy associated with planning terminology. Additionally, we are presenting a cause-and-effect relationship between these terms. Some would argue that this is unnecessary semantics. However, we contend that without a clear consensus of operational definitions and understanding of what these terms mean, you cannot make progress with improvement of your planning efforts. As Deming points out, and we will emphasize this again when we discuss performance criteria, "Meaning starts with the concept, which is in somebody's mind, and only there....and operational definition puts communicable meaning into a concept....An operational definition is one that people can do business with. Practice is more exacting than pure science, more exacting than teaching....The dictionary provides a concept, not a definition for use in industry" (Deming 1986). It is critical for you to arrive at an operational and reasonably agreed-upon understanding of what these terms mean and how they relate to one another in practice. Don't belabor this; don't argue about it. Have one person draft a straw-man position paper on the topic, discuss it for a while (how long a "while" is depends on the importance of having commitment—if it's a mission statement you obviously might expect to take longer than if it's the color of paper for a newsletter), then settle in on what your organization will use and communicate the results effectively and widely. As one observer of the strategic management process stated, "Management is still a kindergarten subject because of lack of agreement on terms. I like my clients, they're nice people. I don't have much respect for their tool kits" (Mascarenhas 1980).

The hierarchy for these terms that many feel comfortable with is as follows:

- Vision;
- Mission (purpose);
- Guiding principles (values and beliefs);
- Superordinate goals;
- Goals;
- Objectives; and
- Activities, action items.

Strategies, tactics, and techniques, in that order, are the mechanisms that we use to effectively implement goals, objectives, and action items. Goals, objectives, and action items can have various horizons. For instance, it is possible to have strategic goals, objectives, and/or action items. Some action items (projects, programs, and improvement projects) may take one to five years to implement. So, we see that horizon—the terms strategic, tactical, and operational—are independent of the terms goals, objectives, and activities. This is not well understood and is a common source of confusion.

Such terms as policies, procedures, strategies, tactics, action items, action plans, implementation plans, requirements, performance objectives, responsibility, accountability, milestones, standards, and contingency plans all relate to effective implementation of plans. You have four basic problems with respect to planning:

1. What should we be doing;

2. How do we get it done;
3. When do we want/need things done; and
4. How well do we need them done?

A process is needed by which to systematically define and describe the goals, objectives, and activities linkage for all functions and levels in the organization. There will be a corporate or organizational vision(s), mission(s), guiding principle(s), and superordinate goal(s) that will need to be defined and communicated. There will be vision(s), mission(s), guiding principle(s), and superordinate goal(s) for each subsystem in the organization. Without a structured process by which these elements of a plan can be developed, defined, agreed upon, and coordinated, the full potential of the effort cannot be achieved.

The most difficult aspect of planning is translating and transferring this simple model into a large, complex organization. You can grasp how the conceptual model presented in Figure 4-2 equates to your organization's planning process or how it would be implemented in your organization.

However, when one begins to consider moving the model application down in the organization, it often becomes very fuzzy. The first problem that has to be dealt with is that of understanding the unit of analysis. As you attempt to move the planning process down to subunits of the organization, the unit of analysis or focal system of the planning effort shifts. This is not unlike what happens in the budget cycle as a call for budgets goes out and functions, divisions, plants, and departments have to begin to put together their budgets. At some point in this process someone has to integrate all the budgets in aggregated pieces that make the total organizational budget. Planning is much more complex, because you are dealing with concepts, ideas, concerns, and perceived opportunities, not just with numbers. This makes the process of integrating plans more difficult, and this is why planning often breaks down at this point. As a result of this complexity, we have tended to involve subunits in our organizations in planning only through their budget process. The budget process is inherently short-term in nature, and, therefore, our plans are shortsighted and often myopic. Top management develops the strategic plans, middle management translates and interprets, the staff and operations people receive the translation, then a miracle occurs and our long-range goals are achieved.

To this point we have identified current planning philosophies and practices, and we have focused on discussing dysfunctional aspects and identifying prescriptive areas for improvement. We have attempted to pragmatically define terms and their relationships. We now want to turn our attention to an innovative planning process we call the Performance Improvement Planning Process (PIPP). It is a systematic, highly structured, participative and pragmatic methodology that has many potential planning applications in your organization. It is well-tested, and we will describe it using several case examples. We did not invent it, *per se*. We did design and develop it using knowledge gained from a variety of sources. It is innovative; it does work. It is an improved way to go about planning, and it does represent a good example of new management practices that will have to become a part of your Organization of the Future.

PERFORMANCE IMPROVEMENT PLANNING PROCESS

We started out this book by suggesting that for your organization to become the Organization of the Future all employees will have to accept as their job the responsibility to:

1. Get the job done; and
2. Constantly strive to improve their own performance, themselves, the work systems and processes, and the products and services of their organization.

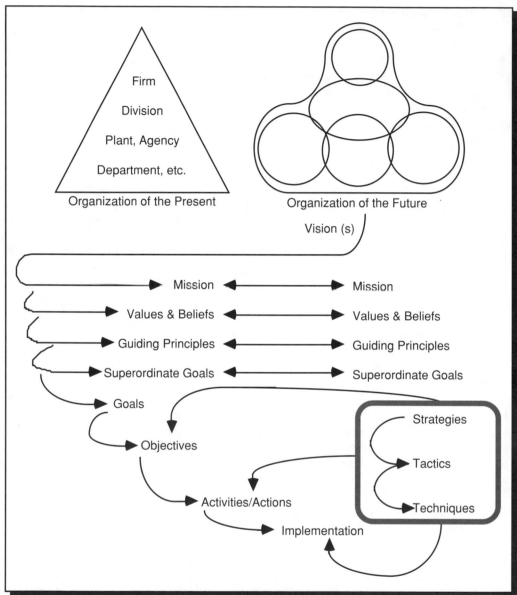

Figure 4-2. Basic Relationship Between Major PlanningTerms and Concepts

We suggested that the second aspect of job responsibility is probably going to be new for most of your employees. You could attempt to change your employees so that each, individually, constantly strives to improve his/her performance. However, we suspect that without some coordination between individuals, effort would prove less than effective. What if you tried to implant the constant improvement orientation by systematically exposing successively lower levels of management to a planning process that focused on performance improvement? At each level, you would get that layer of management to focus on goals, objectives, and action programs that would improve the performance of the system for which they are responsible. In this fashion, we would be turning their attention to constant performance improvement, not just individually, but also as a group. If we implemented this process throughout all layers of management, then we would eventually have the whole organization covered, and a systematic process for driving constant improvement of performance would be in place. Our focus in this section is on a pragmatic way to plan what will allow you to:

1. Effectively drive constant performance improvement;
2. Link planning to action;
3. Integrate much of what has recently been written about how to do strategic planning in one process;
4. Make your existing planning process more effective; and
5. Move towards becoming the Organization of the Future.

Background—Evolution of the Process

The planning process we will describe in this section has been developed over a period of about ten years. It integrates lessons learned and current research that is described in the references listed at the end of this chapter. We didn't really invent this process. We designed, developed, and tested it over the past ten years with a variety of sizes and types of organizations. Some of our applications have been with a large organization and with a large unit of analysis or application. For example, we used this process to develop the Department of the Navy's Productivity Plan. Other applications have been with small subunits within a larger organization. The process was also used for the Industrial Engineering and Management School of the College of Engineering at Oklahoma State University and a plant of 500 people within Burlington Industries.

Typically, an application of the process is tailored. For example, at the Naval Ordnance Station at Indian Head, Maryland, they are using the process to develop programmatic and departmental business plans. There are eighteen programs and thirteen departments. These thirty-one plans will be developed and then integrated into a corporate Station strategic business plan. Management at the Station does not use the term goals. They employ the term objectives. So in all of the documentation of the planning process, the words had to be changed to fit the specific language and application of this organization. This type of tailoring is essential to ensure that the generic process will be understood and accepted in your organization.

The generic planning process we will describe can be utilized to develop critical portions of: business plans, performance improvement plans, plans for productivity and quality programs, plans for developing measurement and evaluation systems, and more. The planning process was originally developed to fill a gap in the type of planning we saw being done in most organizations. We saw plans being developed that were not being implemented. We saw plans being developed in a vacuum, by top management and their consultants. We saw planning being viewed as an annual exercise that had no linkage to our operational, day-to-day decisions, behaviors, or performance. And, we saw no planning because people thought it was a waste of time.

We developed this planning process because planning is the most important of the executive functions and, unfortunately, it is one of the worst executed. We developed this planning process because those who must implement the plans must play a substantive role in developing the plans, and in too many organizations, planning does not substantially involve enough of the management team.

Eight-Step Planning Process: Step 1— Organizational Systems Analysis

Figure 4-3 depicts the basic flow of the planning process. We will first explain the steps in the absence of any implied specific application. Then we will discuss the process in relation to several

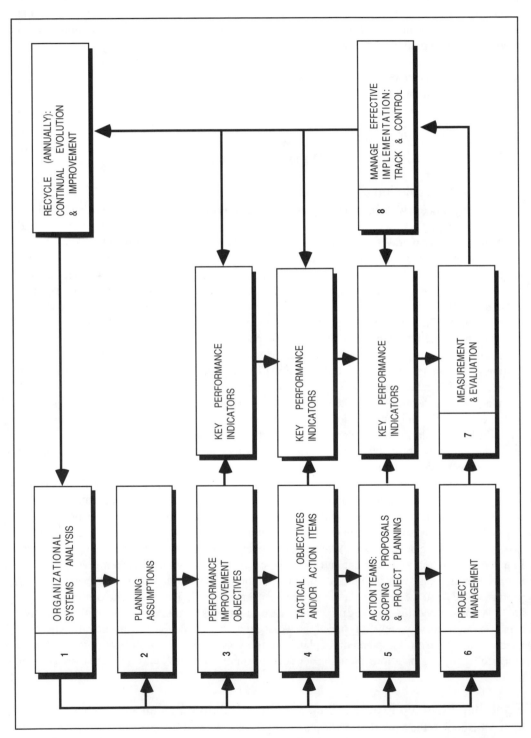

Figure 4-3. Performance Improvement Planning Process
The Eight-Step Planning Process

specific applications.

Step 1 of the planning process is called Organizational Systems Analysis (OSA). It is intended to provide and encourage a detailed analysis of the organizational system (firm, organization, plant, function, activity, department, college, unit, section, branch, division) for which the plan is being developed. It involves data collection, discussion, analysis, evaluation, and introspection into fundamental aspects of the organization. The purpose of OSA is to prepare a management team to plan. There are a variety of ways that OSA can be implemented. Group sessions, modified structured group processes, questionnaires and surveys, analyst data collection, and structured problem solving are all examples of techniques that may be employed. We identify eight basic areas that often are examined in OSA; however, you may choose to look at more or less areas depending upon your specific application. In our experience, no two applications have been done in exactly the same way.

The eight areas we suggest be observed are derived from the literature on strategic planning listed at the end of this chapter, from analysis of the results of two NASA quality and productivity symposia (1984), and from application experience with the process in the "real world." The underlying purpose of OSA is to provide a solid foundation for the heart of the planning process, which are Steps 2-4. The literature and our experience suggest strongly that the persons involved in the planning spend quality time examining some or all of the areas identified. The resultant quality of the plan itself, the goals, objectives, action items and plans, and final implementation and outcomes is highly dependent upon the quality of the effort and time spent in OSA.

The specific process by which each of these areas are examined can vary widely. The process will need to be structured and facilitated. However, the specific structure provided can vary. We will give you a few examples of how an area might be attacked and let you create your own approach based upon the range of alternatives we provide. Table 4-3 lists the eight basic areas we view OSA comprises. We will briefly discuss each area and recommend a process by which you might address the issues entailed in each area and develop the data to be utilized in future steps.

Table 4-3. Eight-Step Planning Process

Step1: Organizational Systems Analysis

OSA Area 1.1 Vision (Corporate Long-Range Objectives).
OSA Area 1.2 Guiding Principles (Values and Beliefs).
OSA Area 1.3 Mission (Purpose)
OSA Area 1.4 Input/Output Analysis.
    1.4.1. Customers and Markets We Want/Must Serve - Downstream Systems
    1.4.2. Suppliers, Vendors, Customers, Procurement - Upstream Sytems
    1.4.3. Business We Want To Be/Need To Be/Should Be/Are In, Products and Services Provided - Outputs
    1.4.4 Transformation Processes
    1.4.5. Materials, Supplies, Labor, Energy, Capital - Inputs
OSA Area 1.5 Internal Strategic Analysis
    1.5.1. Structures Employed
    1.5.2. Staffing
    1.5.3. Facilities
    1.5.4. Technologies Employed
    1.5.5. Strengths and Weaknesses
OSA Area 1.6 Current Performance Levels
OSA Area 1.7 Roadblocks to Performance Improvement
OSA Area 1.8 External Strategic Analysis
    1.8.1. Threats and Opportunities

OSA Area 1.1 Vision (Corporate Long-Range Objectives). What is your vision of your Organization of the Future? How would you like your organization to be in ten to twenty years? What are your corporate long-range objectives? We know these are difficult questions, and not many managers can provide the answers. But the best organizations did not reach the status they have achieved over just a few years. They were led by people who had visions. We're convinced that not everyone can develop visions. Our experience shows that visions need to be developed by leaders of organizations with, at best, consultation from followers. At the Naval Ordnance Station in Indian Head, Maryland, the technical director drafted the vision for his organization with the assistance of technical staff—seven long-range objectives. He then asked his subordinate managers to review and modify his list. They eventually ended up buying in to all the original

Table 4-4: Corporate Long-Range Objectives, NOSIH

1. To be internationally recognized as a center of engineering and manufacturing excellence in the areas of guns, rockets, and missile propulsion; energetic chemicals; missile weapon simulators and training shapes; ordnance devices (CAD/PAD); explosives; warheads; and special weapons
2. To achieve and maintain the best record of employee safety and envronmental protection throughout the ordnance industry.
3. To continually assess and adjust resource allocations and technica core capabilities so as to maximize effectiveness, competence, and productivity of the work force.
4.To constantly improve productivity and quality in our products and services.
5. To maintain a mobilization readiness posture and modernize our facilties and equipment through an aggressive investment strategy.
6. To maintain a quality of work life program that includes support for the Navy's Affirmative Action initiative.
7. To be the role model for excellence in the area of business practices.
8. To provide timely and quality response for products and services to the Fleet and all other customers.

seven, plus they added one more (see Table 4-4).

OSA Step 1.2 Guiding Principles (Values and Beliefs). We talked earlier about the importance of cultural support systems in an overall strategy to constantly improve performance. We provided a definition of culture that included terms like values, beliefs, and principles. What are the principles (implicit or explicit) that guide our strategies, tactics, behaviors, and practices? Are these principles consistently understood by all in the organization? Are the principles explicit, are they written down and communicated effectively? Behavior is a function of its consequences. It is guided and directed by perceptions of what will be rewarded or what will be punished. Behavior is guided by shared beliefs about what the organization wants and expects. It is generally true that we are much more likely to act our way into a new way of thinking than to think our way into a new way of acting. However, what things cause us to act—consequences, rewards, expectations, values, beliefs, guiding principles, or avoidance of punishment?

Research, literature, and experience lead us to believe that all of these things shape, direct, modify, and perhaps control behavior. Recently, it was suggested that principles shape our behaviors. Perhaps Deming began this movement by developing his fourteen principles upon which an organization should base its revitalization (Deming 1986). Many management teams have begun to examine the implicit principles that appear to be guiding the behaviors in their organizations. We find increasing numbers of organizations writing their principles down on paper and making them very visible within the organization as well as to their customers, suppliers and vendors. The implicit assumption is that writing the principles down will clarify and hopefully force people to behave in accordance with those principles. We believe this is important and will have a sustained effect if the measurement and reward systems are congruent with the principles. If this is not the case, we suspect that a temporary Hawthorne effect is all that can be expected from the exercise of explicating principles.

Our experience suggests that a good way to address this particular area of OSA is to go through a sort of role-play exercise with a sampling of persons in your organization. Ask the selected people to play the role of outsider looking in on their organization. This is often called the "man from Mars" view. Ask them to introspectively and perhaps critically, but most certainly honestly, examine behaviors in the organization and to write down principles upon which those behaviors appear to be based. The question is, "What principles appear to be guiding our behavior?"

The persons participating respond to this question after instruction—individually, anonymously, and in writing—and then turn in their responses for compilation. You may be surprised at what you will find.

In one organization where we tried this exercise, we obtained responses such as:

1. Don't make any decisions while the boss is gone.
2. Don't share power or you'll lose it.
3. Don't volunteer for anything.
4. Don't take any risks; don't innovate.
5. Don't share problems you're having or you'll reveal your inadequacies.
6. Top management shares in productivity gains while the rest of us pay the price for them.
7. The way to get ahead is to be visible and politically astute, not necessarily competent.

Clearly, this organization's management team was surprised by these perceived guiding principles. The list we have shown you is abbreviated; there were principles stated that were positive and congruent with what management hoped would be clear. However, critical to the art of culture management is the ability to bring out in the open and address the dysfunctional perceptions relative to principles. They represent counterforces resisting the progress of your organization. The first step in the change process for individuals, groups, or organizations is awareness. The purpose of this step in OSA is to create an awareness as to dysfunctional and unintentional perceived guiding principles. What we want to accomplish in this step of the planning process is simply to get this data out, not to make corrections at this point.

OSA Area 1.3 Mission(s). What is our mission? Is it explicit, clearly communicated to all in the organization? Are the various missions within the organization congruent with the overall mission of the organization? Are our behaviors and practices consistent with our mission(s)? Many organizations place great emphasis on mission. They view mission statements as being broader and more global than goals and objectives. They believe that the mission statement(s) must be written down and well communicated within the organization. They begin planning with a look at the mission statement(s). They believe that there is an overall mission statement for the whole organization and then sub-mission statements, if you will, for units within the organization. It would be during this step of OSA that mission statements are re-evaluated, modified, better communicated, or perhaps even written.

When we were involved in the development of the Department of the Navy Productivity Plan, a mission statement for the productivity effort was written. As a part of our investigation into how to write mission statements, we uncovered some tips (Table 4-5) on the process.

Table 4-5. Criteria for Writing and Evaluating Mission Statements

1. Clear and understandable, especially by rank-and-file employees
2. Brief enough for most people to keep in mind
3. Clearly specifies what business the organization is in:
   a. "What" customer or client needs the organization is attempting to fill, not what products or services are offered.
   b. "Who" are the organization's primary customers or clients?
   c. "How" does the organization plan to go about its business, i.e., what are its primary technologies?
4. Focus primarily on a single strategic thrust
5. Reflect and/or determine the distinctive competence of the organization
6. Broad enough to allow flexibility in implementation but not so broad that it permits a lack of focus
7. Serve as a template that managers and others in the organization can use in making decisions
8. Reflect the values, beliefs, and guiding principles of operations of the organization
9. Reflect and/or guide the formulation of attainable goals
10. Worded to serve as an energy source and rallying point for the organization

(Pfeiffer, Goodstein, and Nolan 1986)

Table 4-5 gives guidelines about writing and evaluating mission statements but not the process for formulating one. The common approach has been to assign staff persons to continuously work on drafts until the chief executive approves it. C. C. Lundberg (1984) recommends a structured group process for formulating a mission statement. Our experience suggests that mission statements cannot be written in a committee meeting. We found that the most effective and efficient strategy was to have one person (someone who is able and willing) draft a straw-man mission statement. In the case of the Navy Productivity Plan, Captain Phil Monroe from AIRLANT headquarters in Norfolk, Virginia, took on the task of drafting the first cut. We then took the draft to the Navy Productivity Steering Group and had them critique it. In a group session they first reacted orally to the draft. Then they individually had the opportunity to modify the draft. Captain Monroe and several others from the group took the input and came up with a second draft. At this point, there were few additional comments and we were very close to the final version, which is shown in Figure 4-4. Note that since the military has a previous definition of a "mission" they chose to call it "guiding principles," which is a combination of OSA areas 1.2 and 1.3.

OSA Area 1.4 Input/Output Analysis. Input/output (I/O) analysis is a technique developed

PRODUCTIVITY IMPROVEMENT GUIDING PRINCIPLES

In these serious and changing times, we must all improve the Department of the Navy's productivity and reach the two basic Department of Defense productivity goals. They are:

To contribute directly and indirectly in creating and keeping Armed Forces of such quality and excellence as will guarantee the fulfillment of basic national security objectives of the United States.

To ensure that the Department of Defense always attains the highest possible level of defense capability, and readiness, through the most efficient use of the funds provided by the American taxpayer.

We will maintain a level of readiness which ensures viable deterrence and supports the nation's defense.

We will emphasize the customer approach to working with others both internal and external to our organization.

We will work efficiently, effectively, and with maximum productivity within constrained resources.

We will improve the quality of what we do because better quality improves mission performance, increases productivity, and reduces cost.

Since people are our greatest asset, we will maintain an atmosphere of trust which fosters innovation, motivates superior accomplishments, and assures individual dignity and self-respect.

We will commit to excellence, to a relentless pursuit of continuous improvement, and to removing barriers to increased performance, productivity, and timeliness in all that we do.

We will use these principles daily to build on the excellence that has earned the Department of the Navy the public's trust and pride.

Figure 4-4. The Department of the Navy Improvement Guiding Principles

to create an improved understanding of the system being analyzed. In this case, we need to thoroughly define and understand the organizational system for which we are planning. There are five sub-areas in I/O analysis. The first two sub-areas seek to define the system for which a plan is being developed.

Sub-area 1.4.1. **Downstream systems** (i.e., customers—internal or external, or any other system or person that receives outputs from the organization) **are identified**. Customers are discussed in specific terms. Who are they? What do they want, expect, need, desire, and demand from us? What are their requirements? How can we serve them better? Where are our obvious problems at this particular interface? Do we really have a customer orientation? What do our customers think about us? Do we proactively work with them to ensure that we keep them satisfied? Do we manage our relations with internal customers as well as we manage our relations with external customers? Is there a customer orientation at all levels and in all functions in the organization? What markets do we, should we, and must we serve? These are the types of questions that could be raised in this sub-area of I/O analysis. The focus, customers, and markets should be examined descriptively as well as prescriptively.

This could be accomplished by sending a list of questions out to the management team for initial responses. The team could then assemble and discuss their responses. A comparison of descriptive statements (what is) with what should be would begin to develop a consensus as to what needs to be done in the area of customers and markets. On the other hand, it might be necessary to develop a strong analytical base of information relative to customer and competitor analysis. This sub-area serves to get the management team to introspectively and critically examine how well their organization serves the downstream systems it serves or supports.

Sub-area 1.4.2. **Upstream systems** (i.e., customers, suppliers, vendors, personnel, procurement, providers — any organizational system that you receive inputs of any sort from, again either internal or external to your larger organization) **are identified and discussed**. Who are they? What do we want, need, expect, demand, and get from them? How can they better serve us? How can we better communicate our needs to them? Do we cross that boundary frequently and effectively enough? Do we manage interactions with upstream systems? Do we strive to develop quality, long-term relationships with these systems? This part of Step 1 of I/O analysis serves to get the management team to introspectively and critically examine how well their organization is served and supported by upstream systems. Figure 4-5 shows an example of how input/output analysis should be done.

Sub-area 1.4.3. **Outputs**. This forces the management team to identify and agree upon what the outputs of their system are and should be. It is important in this sub-area to distinguish between outcomes (desired, undesired, dysfunctional, functional) and outputs. An outcome is something that occurs as a result of an output being received by a customer. For example, in a maintenance come, while "fixed machines or components" are output. Revenues and profits are outcomes, while delivered products or services are outputs. Customer satisfaction is an outcome, while the delivered product or service is the output. This is an important distinction if we are to measure productivity and effectiveness. The focus in this sub-area is on outputs.

What businesses are we in, do we need to be, should we be, and can we be in? What products and services do we, do we need to, should we, and can we provide to our customers and markets? Do we analyze our products, services, and businesses frequently enough and effectively enough? Do we constantly perform opportunistic surveillance? Are we in businesses we should not be in? These are the types of issues and questions that need to be raised in this sub-area of OSA.

Boundary clarification is important at this stage. What is an output for one system may be an outcome for another. Lack of discipline in defining the unit of analysis will cause problems relative to output definition. The key is to constantly strive to separate outcomes and activities

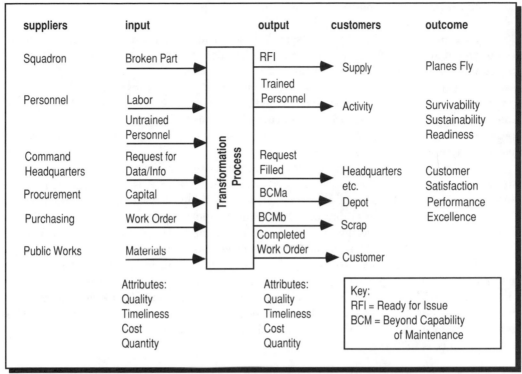

Figure 4-5. Example of Input/Output Analysis for an Aircraft Intermediate Maintenance Depot

from outputs. Do not assume that this sub-area is intuitively obvious or necessarily simple. Many organizational systems do not understand what their outputs are or who their customers really are.

Sub-area 1.4.4 **Transformation Processes**. This focuses the management team's attention on major activities or transformations that are made within their system to convert inputs into outputs. The secret at this stage is not to get too micro or too macro. We want the management team to develop a process flow diagram for the organizational system: the basic steps that take place to convert inputs received into outputs desired. We are not trying to do methods engineering at this point, so detail and perfection is not important. You want the team to develop a consistent, overall understanding of the transformation process for the organizational system for which the plan is being developed.

Sub-area 1.4.5. **Inputs**. This requires the team to identify major inputs to their system. We don't want a paper clip, staples, and pads of paper list of inputs; however, we also don't want a labor, energy, materials, and capital list. Again, the goal is too avoid being too micro or too macro. The primary focus in this sub-area should be linked to Sub-Area 1.4.2 where we looked at upstream systems. What are our inputs and how well do we specify what we need? You can begin to get the management team to evaluate the quality of the specifications for our inputs. In general, for inputs and outputs there are four basic attributes against which they can and are evaluated:

1. Quantity—how much do we/they need?
2. Quality—what reqiurements must we/they meet?
3. Timeliness—when do we need them, when does the customer need them?

4. Price/cost—how much can/should/will we/they pay?

We can evaluate the quality of our specifications for major inputs and outputs and the clarity of our communication of these requirements/specifications relative to each of these attributes in Sub-areas 1.4.3 and 1.4.5 of I/O analysis.

The purpose of input/output analysis is to improve clarity and consensus as to what the organizational system is really doing. In l.1, l.2, and 1.3 of OSA, the team will have looked at vision, mission, and principles. Now, OSA 1.4 gets them to examine the system in terms of customers, providers, outputs, inputs, and transformation processes. Most organizations have found this area useful as a preparatory exercise to planning.

This area of OSA has most frequently been done in a small group meeting using a facilitator to guide the group through the sub-areas and discussion. Forms are used to direct the process. Individuals first silently complete all five sub-areas, then discuss them as a group. The goal would be to develop one output that represents the combined inputs from the individuals in the group. Honeywell A&D uses this technique and has developed standard forms to assist groups with the process (*Honeywell A&D Performance Management Guide* l986).

OSA Area l.5 Internal Strategic Analysis. What are our strengths and weaknesses? What internal factors, issues, problems, and opportunities should we consider as we proceed with the development of our strategic plan? This area represents an internal look around. What is happening inside the organization that must be considered as we develop our strategic plan? This is an important area in the OSA and in the overall planning process. Our recommended approach for this step is as follows:

1. Convene the management team that will be participating in the planning session in a group session for approximately two to four hours. They will be completing area 1.5 during this period.
2. Provide each individual with a written task statement that says, "Please identify specific factors (issues, problems, trends, opportunities, programs, strengths, weaknesses, constraints, controllables, etc.) internal to our organization that we should consider as we proceed with the development of our strategic plan." They are to silently respond, in writing, to this task statement.
3. At the end of a ten- to twenty-minute period, a facilitator will go around the room, one person and one factor/item per round, soliciting and writing the items on a flip chart. This continues until all responses to the task statement are posted and numbered on the flip charts. It is quite possible to generate sixty to 100 ideas with a group of twelve to twenty people.
4. Once all the data are up on the flip charts, a controlled discussion can ensue for a short period of time.
5. At this point, an internal strategic, introspective, critical look at the organization has taken place and a general discussion of the results can occur.
6. The final step is to clean up the data and get it typed into a presentable format.

The following sub-areas may help in generating factors to consider in doing internal strategic analysis:

Sub-area 1.5.1. **Structures.** Is our structure one that supports and enhances our strategies? Does our structure facilitate the kind and levels of performance we are striving for? Is our first reaction to a problem to reorganize, or do we reorganize to support the management process as it attempts to respond to changing environments and technologies? Do we have old paradigms regarding organizational design? Does the organizational chart reflect reality or simply what we hope reality is? Does the organizational structure accommodate the informal organization? These are the types of questions that can be addressed in this step of OSA. Many organizations tend to turn first to changing the organizational chart when performance problems arise. It may be more realistic to view structure as one of a number of variables that has to be adjusted as others are manipulated to improve performance. The goal is to ensure that structure supports and enhances management processes, technologies employed, business environment, and management processes.

Obviously, you would begin an analysis of structure with a look at the organizational chart and a discussion with the persons who are "in charge" of organizational design. A group session that focuses on the extent to which the current structure "fits" other aspects of the organization is advisable. The desired output would be a summary analysis of structural problems. This data would then be utilized in the next several steps of the planning process (Mackenzie 1986; Robey and Altman 1982).

Sub-area 1.5.2. **Staffing.** Do we believe and practice that we win with people? Do we effectively concentrate on and ensure that we select and place the right people for the right positions? Do we constantly strive to develop management skills and employee skills? Do we invest in our human resources the same attention to detail and same level of commitment as we do our technology? Does our cultural support system support and reinforce the development and growth of our people? Do we view the human resource as the most important resource and behave accordingly? These critical questions must be answered in this area of OSA. In this, and perhaps other areas of OSA, an organizational survey might be utilized to gather a valid and representative sample of perceptions as to these issues. Numerous surveys that measure many dimensions being addressed in this sub-area are commercially available.

Sub-area 1.5.3. **Facilities.** For many organizations, facilities are a strategic variable. For rapidly growing organizations, they can be a limiting or constraining factor. For declining organizations, they can be a problem in terms of costs and investments. This sub-area focuses the management team's attention on strategic facilities issues. Obvious interaction between markets served, technologies employed, organizational design, and staffing must be considered. In this sub-area and in several others, it may be wise to bring in the specialists, if they exist, to discuss their forecasts and plans in this area. The desired output from this sub-area is a brief document that describes strategic facilities forecasts that can be utilized during Steps 3 and 4 of the planning process.

Sub-area 1.5.4. **Technologies.** What technologies do we employ to convert inputs into outputs? Do we constantly evaluate the appropriateness of each technology? Do we constantly strive to find more appropriate technologies? (Note: we use the word technology here in a very broad sense to mean "a way of getting something done." In this sense, technology can be hardware, software, methods, methodology, technique, policy, or procedure.) Do we constantly ask ourselves if there isn't a better way to do what we are doing? Do we have appropriate amounts of capital to support technological innovation? Do we encourage technological innovation? These are the critical issues and questions that need to be addressed in this sub-area of OSA.

Considerable data may need to be collected in order to effectively complete this area. Competitor analysis relative to technological employment and capital investment will be required, along with critical and realistic assessment of the culture to find out if technological innovation is really encouraged or whether the "bean counter" mentality stifles grassroots technological innovation. Are the people in the organization striving to constantly do their jobs in a better way, or do we get trapped in old paradigms about the best way to get something done? We suggest assigning to specific small teams of three to five people the task of investigating specific questions. After all the teams have finished their investigations, assemble them with the management team and discuss the results. A facilitator can assist in forming necessary closure so that this data can be utilized during Steps 3 and 4 of the planning process.

Sub-area 1.5.5. **Strengths and Weaknesses**. What are the strengths and weaknesses of the organization? What factors help or hinder the attainment of organizational goals?

OSA Area 1.6 Current Performance Levels. The purpose of this area is to provide as complete and comprehensive a picture of current performance levels for the management team as possible. This area will often require considerable time to develop the information, particularly the first time through the exercise. Analysts will probably be required to develop the information and work with the managers to present it in a format that is conducive to their evaluation. We recommend that this area include a look at key performance indicators, measures of performance against all seven of the criteria (effectiveness, efficiency, quality, productivity, quality of work life, innovation, and budgetability/profitability), as well as traditional and readily available measures of performance. This is a critical area of preparation for the remaining steps in the planning process. The Virginia Productivity Center (VPC) has developed an instrument called ASSESS. This instrument goes beyond just assessing current performance levels to also assessing performance improvement efforts. Several companies have used it to see how they are doing in their improvement efforts against other companies in VPC's data base and plan ways they can continuously improve.

OSA Area 1.7. Roadblocks to Performance Improvement. Some organizations have found it useful to do a roadblock to performance identification exercise. They utilize the Nominal Group Technique to gather this data. The output is a prioritized list of perceived roadblocks that the managers feel are preventing the organization from being as productive as it could or should be. We will discuss the Roadblock Identification Analysis and Removal Technique in detail in a later part of the book.

OSA Area 1.8. External Strategic Analysis. This area may be analyzed in the same manner as Area 1.5 focusing on the following sub-areas:

Sub-area 1.8.1. **Threats and Opportunities**. Many references listed at the end of this chapter show how "environmental scanning" could be done to know the threats and opportunities facing the organization. Data gathering could be done before the planning session.

Sub-area 1.8.2. **Corporate Goals/Objectives/Superordinate Goals**. **Review of Upline Plans**. If the system for which the plan is being developed is a subunit of a larger organization, then a review of the larger organization's corporate mission statement, objectives/goals, and more is necessary. In a recent planning process for a college of engineering at a major university, we asked the university and other major administrative support functions and selected state support activities to provide their strategic plans so that we might ensure that the college plan is congruent and compatible. We wrote to approximately ten other organizational units, including the university top management. We only received one semblance of a plan. The other units, including the university top management, either did not respond or informed us that a strategic plan did not exist.

The point of this case study is that although it would be nice to have other relevant organizational systems' objective/goals, you may not always be able to get that information. This will put you in the situation of having to develop plans for a subsystem in the organization without really knowing where the larger system is headed or wants to head. This shouldn't happen but often does, and, therefore, is something with which you must be prepared to deal. The absence of corporate objectives/goals will place greater importance and emphasis on Step 2 of the planning process-planning assumptions.

The purpose of Areas 1.5 and 1.8 is to give the individual managers who will be participating in the planning process a chance to "dump" what they know about internal and external factors that should be considered in the development process for the strategic plan. The objective is to get the data out; not to form any closure or to do any intensive analysis. Organizations that want to do an abbreviated OSA might just do Areas 1.5 and 1.8 prior to Step 2 of the overall planning process. This is only recommended if there are time constraints on the planning process that cannot be avoided.

We provide an example of the type of output that can be expected from an internal and external strategic analysis in Table 4-6.

The application of this planning process in a larger organization requires a number of design decisions. The following list represents the types of design decisions that we have been confronted with in the past eight years.

1. How much of the organization do we involve in planning, particularly relative to this particular process?
2. Do we implement the process top-down or bottom-up?
3. How do we integrate the plans we develop across the organization and from top to bottom in the organization?
4. Is the corporate plan simply a compilation of all of the divisional plans, or is there a separate corporate plan that is somewhat independent of the divisional plans? (Note: The same question is raised with respect to divisional plans. Note also that we use the term division to generically represent a second level of organization beneath the firm. The term for this level of the organization may not be division.)
5. How do we sequence and schedule all of the planning activities so that everything comes together and fits nicely with our budget cycle?
6. How do we coordinate and integrate all the different kinds of plans that we are required to provide?
7. How do we know that this much participation in planning is appropriate and will really pay off?
8. Shouldn't the corporate objectives dictate what the plans look like below?
9. What happens if the plans down inside the organization are incompatible with strategy developed by top management? What happens if the plans developed by top management are incompatible with the plans developed down inside the organization?
10. How do we find/train people to facilitate this planning process? How hard is it to pull this planning process off?

These are typical design-related questions that come up as applications of the planning process are being developed. As you can see, many of the questions focus on specific implementation questions that relate to how to begin, how to sequence applications, how to integrate results, and how to blend this process into an existing planning system. We can't answer all of your questions, or even all of these in this book, as many are too situation-specific. However, we will use a case example to address some of the more common and recurring questions.

The most common design question is, "How do we begin and proceed in a fairly large and complex organization?" Figure 4-6 depicts an organizational structure for a recent client of ours. We start with a general picture of the structure so that you can see layers of management, size of the organization, and the general hierarchical formal relationships built into their structure. When we design an application of this planning process for an organization, we always start by obtaining data on size, layers of management, formal relationships (organizational chart), matrix relationships (if they exist), numbers of people in each layer of management, key decision makers or key

Table 4-6. Example of a Strategic Analysis Output

Internal and External Strategic Factors

1. (Weakness) Number of available MSE's to recruit
2. (W) Lack of experienced people w.r.t. external world
3. (Strength &W) Deadline habit
4. (Competition) Arthur Anderson, Westinghouse, and A. Young
5. (Threat) 1988 Presidential Election
6. (T) Scott leaves
7. (Opportunity) Data base of customers who want to be served
8. (W) Competition has better marketing and visuals
9. (W) Continuing and increasing budgeting dilemma of D.F. and SP
10. (O) Client has bought services on faith
11. (S) The underlying philosophy of performance management
12. (S) Team spirit
13. (T/O) IE Dept. will rely on us to pay our own way
14. (TO) Competition with other VT centers and CIT
15. (W) Perceived lack of consistent set of products.
16. (O) Expanding our customer base
17. (T,O,S) Incorporate AI-based approaches
18. (T,O) New president at VPI
19. (W) Accounting system, MSS, Project Management System, and data base
20. (W) Assessment of our current performance levels
21. (W) Budgeting time
22. (W) Integration of business, tactical, and operating. plans
23. (S,O) Pervasive and consistent commitment of VPC staff to continually improving quality of products and services.
24. (S) Visionary leadership
25. (W) Complex products and service descriptions.
26. (T,W) Perceived ambiguity of MSE options
27. (W) Overload of activities between/with program manager, project manager and staff
28. (W) Target market segments not well defined
29. (W) Product and services not matched to market segments
30. (W) Low percentage of product sales
31. (O)Improved communications with MSL
32. (O) Ken Kiser on sabbatical and hiring a full-time professional
33. (O) Software development
34. (O) Basic research in productivity management
35. (W) Communications with other people in IEOR
36. (W) Don't have acceptable customer mix between public and private sector
37. (S,W) Often over spec our deliverables to clients
38. (O) Perfect timing for products and services in US economy
39. (T) Policing by IEOR Dept. & University
40. (W,T) Perception that participatory management at the VPC is a myth
41. (T) Disillusionment of GRA's
42. (W) Too hard on ourselves and sell our talents and abilities short
43. (T) No additional space ever
44. (T) Imbalance between management work and client contract work
45. (S) Senate Productivity Award

positions of power, sources of resistance, strategic areas in the organization, existing planning systems, existing measurement systems, planning cycle, desired outcomes of the client, and the specific design specifications as perceived at this point by the client. Once this data is collected, along with a general understanding of their business, we can begin to sketch out a strategy for implementing the planning process.

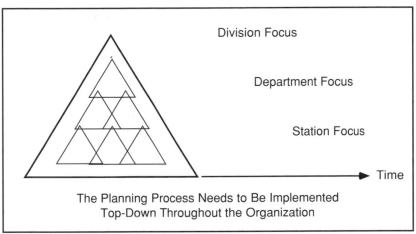

Figure 4-6. Example of an Organizational Structure

We generally recommend a top-down implementation of the planning process with information flow downward and upward in a lagged fashion. The question immediately gets raised as to what is top and what is bottom. The answer depends on who is initiating the intervention and what the intended unit of analysis or scope for the planning intervention is to be. If a plant manager three layers down in the management structure of a large corporation wants to do the planning process for his plant, top may mean starting at the top of the corporation—which might require a tremendous selling job—or with division management, or with his top management group of the plant. Planning down inside the organization with this process in the absence of higher level support and understanding can be difficult and will require a vision of what the process can do in the long run. Trying from down inside a large organization to pull off a change in the planning process at higher levels can be extremely difficult and time consuming. It is generally not wise to go on crusades that aren't blessed by the Pope.

Getting back to Figure 4-6 and our discussion of the issue of corporate goals and objectives integration with this process, as we said, it is possible for this process to be used to develop the corporate goals and objectives if the process is truly top-down. However, if the process is beginning somewhere down inside the organization or being applied at a lower unit of analysis, then Sub-area 1.8.2 calls for the consideration of corporate objectives as upfront data preceding the actual planning Steps of 3 and 4. The case example depicted in Figure 4-6 shows an organization that does top-down planning within the installation itself. The organization is a naval ordnance station (NOS) with the NAVSEA command of the Department of Navy. As you can see in the simplified organizational chart, there is a matrix type of operation with departments and programs. Figure 4-7 depicts the "grand strategy" planning process for the NOS. What you see in that figure is the planning cycle and the elements in the planning process, and we have highlighted the specific aspects of the overall planning process that NOS management has decided to use in the planning process described in this chapter. Management at the NOS has attempted to improve the quality of the existing planning process by bringing department and program managers more actively into the process. The long-range corporate planning guidance document, Row 1, is drafted by top management and the planning group at the NOS. The top management team, CO, XO, TD, and all department managers then got together and revised the corporate objectives during a one-day planning session.

The corporate objectives, guidance document, and program and department planning process guidelines were then reviewed at planning conference retreats with both program managers and department managers. The planning process being described to you in this chapter was presented to these managers, and they were walked through Steps 1, 2, and 3 of the process so that they could actually experience the process itself. The department and program managers were then asked to develop their program and departmental plans using this process, (i.e., Rows 3 and 5 in Figure 4-7). These resulting data/plans are then integrated into the Corporate NOS Plan. The horizon for corporate objectives at the NOS is twenty years. The horizon for program and department strategic plans is five to seven years. (Five- to seven-year objectives for the program and department are developed in Step 3 of the process being described.) The horizon for program and department tactical plans is one to three years. (One- to three-year objectives for the programs and departments are developed in Step 4 of the process being described.)

This short case example should give you some insights into how:

1. The process can be integrated into an existing and rather complex planning process and used to improve the quality of specific steps in that planning cycle;
2. Corporate objectives can be developed without the process being described, in a less participative fashion, and then fed downward into the planning process as it is developed at lower levels; and
3. A grand strategy looks for a large complex organization.

This completes our discussion of Step 1 of the eight-step planning process. This step provides data that will be the foundation for the next steps in the process. The step forces the management team to think through the questions and issues raised in these eight areas. Again, you may choose to address all eight areas, additional areas, or some subset of the eight areas. As we have indicated, there are a variety of ways that organizational systems analysis can be implemented. Group sessions, modified structured group processes, questionnaires and surveys, analyst data collection and analysis are just some of the specific ways to create the data necessary to proceed to Step 2 and to create the underlying awareness among the management team as to these strategic issues. Let's now turn our attention to Step 2 of the process—the creation of and analysis of planning assumptions.

Eight-Step Planning Process: Step 2— Creation of Planning Assumptions

Step 2 of the planning process is completed in a structured group session and focuses on developing assumptions upon which the plan will be developed. The appropriate group of managers is assembled and data from Step 1, OSA, are reviewed with the group. The group is asked to identify specific assumptions upon which the plan will or should be based. Each participant will silently generate responses to that task statement. After a ten- to twenty-minute period, a "round-robin" solicitation process is employed to obtain assumptions from each participant. One assumption per participant, per round is solicited and written on a flip chart. Each assumption is given a sequential number for later use. Typically, three to four assumptions can be written on

#	Activity	FY-87 / CY-87	FY-88 / CY-88	FY-89 / CY-89
1	Long-range corporate planning guidance document	FY 2006 (Aug)	FY 2009 (Mar)	FY 2009 (Feb)
2	program strategic plan specification	FY 88-94 (Aug)	FY 89-95 (Apr-May)	FY 90-96 (Apr)
3	Program strategic plan (14)	FY 88-94 (Sep-Oct)	FY 89-95 (Jun)	FY 90-96 (Jun)
4	Department strategic plan specification	FY 88-94 (Sep-Oct)	FY 89-95 (Jul-Aug)	FY 90-96 (Jul)
5	Department strategic plan (10)	Modernization FY 88-94 (Dec)	FY 89-95 (Sep-Oct)	FY 90-96 (Aug)
6	Direct workyears allocation methodology	FY 90 (Nov)	FY 91 (Oct-Nov)	
7	Indirect workyears allocation methodology	FY 90 (Nov)	FY 91 (Oct-Nov)	
8	Large project and MILCON reviews	FY 90-95 (large proj.), FY 93-95 (MILCON)	FY 90-95 (large proj.), FY 93-95 (MILCON)	
9	Large project and MILCON allocation methodology	FY 90-95 (large proj.), FY 93-95 (MILCON)	FY 90-95 (large proj.), FY 93-95 (MILCON)	
10	Facilities and ACP equipment allocation methodology	FY 90 (Nov-Dec)	FY 91 (Nov-Dec)	
11	Station strategic plan	FY 88-94 (Jan)	FY 89-95 (Jan-Feb)	
12	ORD-MIF workload plan	FY 88-94 (Jan-Feb)	FY 89-95 (Dec)	
13	MILCON plan	FY 91-95 (Jan)	FY 92-96 (Dec)	
14	ACP plan	FY 89-94 (Jan)	FY 90-95 (Dec-Jan)	
15	ORD-MOD plan	FY 89-95 (Jan)	FY 90-96 (Jan-Feb)	
16	Automated information systems plan	FY 89-94 (Jan)	FY 90-95 (Nov-Jan)	FY 90-95 (Apr)
17	Annual training plan	FY 88 (Aug)	FY 90 (Feb-Mar)	FY 90 (Jul-Aug)
18	Annual financial management budget (AFMB)			FY 91 (Feb-Mar)
19	NIIP quarterly status report to NAVSEA	(quarterly)	(quarterly)	(quarterly)

Figure 4-7. NOSIH Planning, Programming, and Budgeting Calendar

each flip chart sheet. This round-robin process is continued until all assumptions have been posted. At this stage, a short discussion on the general list of assumptions or on specific assumptions may take place. Often, people will dispute the validity of an assumption or will question how it is worded. This discussion can occur, but the next portion of this step usually clarifies concern about validity and wording. For example, somebody might suggest that revenues/budgets will increase at a rate of five percent per year for the next two to five years. Another might believe that they will increase at a rate of two percent per year for that period. As you can imagine, a lot of time could be spent arguing over wording and specific numbers. The process handles this by having each participant perform an importance-certainty analysis for each of the assumptions.

After all assumptions have been posted, every participant is asked to perform an analysis of each assumption on an importance-certainty grid (Figure 4-8). Each assumption, by the sequential number it was given on the charts, is placed in a cell in the grid representing the perceived importance and certainty. The importance axis, the y-axis or vertical axis, represents the degree to which the participant feels the assumption is important to the plan. The certainty axis, the x-axis or horizontal axis, represents the degree to which the participant feels the assumption is valid as it is written. This scale ranges from certain it isn't valid as written, to not sure or uncertain it's valid, to certain it is valid as written. So, for example, if a person felt that revenues/budgets would go up at a rate of two percent per year and not the stated five percent, he would indicate so by placing the assumption number further to the left on the validity scale. In this fashion disagreements on specific wording on assumptions can be analyzed and incorporated in a more efficient fashion.

The ultimate goal of this step is to create an awareness among the planning group as to assumptions upon which the plan should and will be based. The importance-certainty analysis allows for the incorporation of uncertainty and differences in perceptions about the future. There are many ways to process the data collected during this step. We haven't found a best way, and analysis and presentation of data collected from the importance-certainty grid are still not perfect. We are developing a computer program that will facilitate analysis and presentation of the grid. We suggest you experiment with different approaches to this analysis and overall step. This step normally takes about two to four hours depending upon how much time is taken to discuss the output from Step 1, OSA. At this stage you will be ready to proceed to Step 3 of the process— the development of strategic goals and objectives. Before proceeding to the discussion of the next step, we will insert sample output from Step 2 (Tables 4-7 and 4-8). The case example we provide

Eight-Step Planning Process: Step 3— Development of Strategic Goals and/or Objectives

Step 3 of the planning process builds on and should incorporate the data developed from Steps 1 and 2. The objective of Step 3 is to develop strategic goals (you must define the horizon; however, typically the horizon in this step is two to five years) and/or objectives. We have experimented with a number of techniques or approaches by which to develop goals and objectives, and it is our feeling that the Nominal Group Technique is the most effective and efficient technique for doing this if a participative strategy is desired. A tutorial on the Nominal Group Technique is provided in Appendix B for those who are not familiar with the structured group process. This step can and should be completed within two to three hours. You begin by ensuring that data from Steps 1 and 2 are reviewed by the participants either prior to the session or just prior to the session. This is par- ticularly critical if Steps 1 and 2 are completed much in advance of the Step 3 session. We might note at this point that it is possible to complete the first five steps of this process in a two- to three- day planning session. The level of detail and rigor desired for Step 1 may not be possible in that

ASSUMPTION #3

Shipyard workload, both level and type of work, will occur pretty much as expected.

	Certain isn't Valid	Uncertain	Certain is Valid
Critical to Plan	1	12	1
Uncertain	1	6	
Not Critical to Plan		1	

ASSUMPTION #7

Will continue to need highly trained and highly qualified personnel

	Certain isn't Valid	Uncertain	Certain is Valid
Critical to Plan	1		17
Uncertain			3
Not Critical to Plan			

ASSUMPTION #21

Competing shipyards will make a major change and continue to improve at a rate believed impossible.

	Certain isn't Valid	Uncertain	Certain is Valid
Critical to Plan	1	3	5
Uncertain	1	5	2
Not Critical to Plan	2		

ASSUMPTION #25

Our customers will become more consumer activists.

	Certain isn't Valid	Uncertain	Certain is Valid
Critical to Plan		4	5
Uncertain	2	6	5
Not Critical to Plan		1	

Figure 4-8: Example Output from Planning Process - Step 2 (Importance/Certainty Grid)

amount of time; however, an overview of the factors and issues addressed in that step is possible. Many organizations have chosen to break up the steps into chunks. For example, Tennessee Valley Authority has decided to combine Steps 1-3 into one planning module and Steps 4-6 into a second module. You might want to treat Step 1 as a module, Steps 2 and 3 as a module, Steps 4 and 5 as a module, and then Steps 6 and 7 as independent modules. Breaking the process down into modules may serve to minimize the disruption of having to find a two- to three-day period in which a group of managers can get away from their everyday responsibilities. On the other hand, if you stretch the steps out too long, you may have problems maintaining continuity.

Table 4-9 depicts an example of output from a Step 3 session with a worldwide agri-chemical firm. The organization is based in Brazil and employs approximately 14,000 people. The planning session was held offsite and took two days. We completed Steps 1-5 during that planning

Table 4-7. Sample List of Strategic Planning Assumptions
VPI&SU College of Engineering

1. Stature of college will continue at high level.
2. Electrical Engineering and Computer Engineering will become crowded.
3. Demographics will shift to urban areas.
4. There will be immediate space relief with the next building; however, little relief in the next decade.
5. Within the university, we will continue to fare better than other colleges in resource distribution.
6. Computers will become more integrated in our administrative tasks.
7. College administrative staff will increase, requiring further division of duties.
8. We will meet and plan on a more regular basis.
9. College of Engineering's favorable resource allocation will cause jealousy among colleges which will place more stress on Provost.
10. Methods of delivering educational programs will continue to change rapidly.

Table 4-8. Sample List of Strategic Planning Assumptions
VPI&SU IEOR Department

1. We will have to understand and adapt to, educationally and research-wise, the revolution taking place in American business and industry.
2. No major change in upper administration of the university.
3. Industry and business trend will be towards litigation and liability issues.
4. There will continue to be much emphasis on undergraduate education.
5. Undergraduate student enrollment will rise at an increasing rate.
6. We will balance curriculum quality with quantity; specialization with generalization; and socio-economic with technical considerations.
7. Resources will be available to achieve final goal of planning process.
8. University will continue to place strong emphasis on research.
9. Faculty shortage will rise.
10. Continued shifting of emphasis within sections of the national economy will make it difficult to predict future.

retreat. At the completion of the retreat, the president of the firm suggested that they repeat Step 3 again in a month to ensure that the goals were valid. This case example provides you with a feel of how the results are presented and the type of goals that result. This particular organization is now planning to move the process downward in the organization.

The nature of the goals that result from this step will depend on how you word the task statement. If you are building a business plan, one type of goal will emerge. If you are developing a productivity and quality management effort, another type of goal will be generated. A performance improvement plan may create yet another type of goal. The specified unit of analysis will influence the type of goal statements developed, as will the participants in the session. If you have fifteen supervisors from across the plant, the only unit of analysis they have in common will be the plant. So, in a session like this, you would have to ask the supervisors for goals for the plant. When you assemble a heterogeneous group of participants, your task statement will have to be written to accommodate the lowest unit of analysis that the participants have in common. So, again at this stage of the process you can see that there are a number of design decisions that need to be considered before holding a Step 3 planning session.

Table 4-9. Output from Step 3
2-5 Year Goals and Objectives

Date	:19 March 1987
Facilitator	:Tom Tuttle
Number of Participants	:14
Number of Goals Asked to Vote for	:7

Task: *Please identify 2-5 year goals and/or objectives that you feel our Performance Management Process should accomplish.*

Goal	Votes	No. of Votes/ Total Vote Score
To maintain ethical level of behavior at least at current levels	Superordinate	
1. Successfully implement a new organizational structure	7-7-7-7-6-6-5-2-2-2-1	11/52
2. To create and implement process for performance improvement • Create a critical mass of persons who understand process within next 6 months.	7-7-7-7-5-5-4	7/42
3. To promote/spread the values of the company to all people	7-7-6-6-6-6-4	7/42
4. Increase profits by 20% over 5 years	7-7-5-4-2	5/25
5. Reduce non-quality costs by 10% year	7-6-5-4-3	5/25
6. To increase the level of participation of all employees at all levels in decision making	6-5-5-5-3	5/24
7. To be a leader in agricultural & pharmaceutical business and be as profitable (% sales) as we are in other markets	6-5-5-4-1-1	6/22
8. Management & training staff should increase education/training of all personnel (coaching)	6-4-4-3-1-1	6/19
9. Attain international quality levels in all products	6-3-3-1-1	5/14
10. To implement a performance measurement system for innovation and set a goal of 20%/ year gain from baseline. • To develop or increase conditions that will stimulate innovation	4-3-3-2-2	5/14

Audit check. At the end of Steps 3, 4, 5, 6, and 7 a check back to the output from previous steps is important. For example, once goals, objectives have been developed in Step 3, those goals and their priorities should be "audited" against the results from Steps 1 and 2. The planning process was designed to build on previous steps for there to be internal, sequential consistency, unless for some reason the management team decides otherwise. Goals would be checked against planning

105

assumptions to see that no assumptions were violated and that assumptions were built into the plan at this stage of its development. This step will be even more critical if you decide to stretch the steps in the planning process out over time.

You may also need to begin, at this stage, to integrate this plan with other planning efforts or planning documents in your organization. There may be capital investment plans, facilities plans, or acquisition plans with which this emerging plan will need to be compared and contrasted. This effort may be something that is better done by a small group of analysts than during the actual planning session for Step 3.

Development of key performance indicators. The issue of the relationship between measurement and strategy, goals, effective implementation, and improvement is critical and is the theme of this book. At the recent World Productivity Conference in Washington, D.C., a speaker on the opening panel asked if measurement preceded improvement or vice versa. At first glance it is a rather simple question, but after some thought it becomes clear that it is a very difficult and important question to address. There is considerable discussion as to whether measurement precedes strategy formulation or follows it. The same issue arises at each of Steps 3, 4, and 5 in this planning process. Recently, the technical director from a Naval Ordnance Station raised a similar interesting question in this vein: "Shouldn't the measurement be implicit in the goal/objective statement?" It is traditionally thought that objectives should include in their written statement standards to guide measurement. However, written goal statements have traditionally been developed in broad, global, non-specific terms.

In our opinion, measurement should be an integral part of each step of the planning process. The question as to "what an integral part means" will be subject to some interpretation and some variation in terms of how it is implemented. However, our suggestion is that there be:

1. Key performance indicators (linked to the mission/strategy) at every level in the organization, including the corporation, firm, agency, etc. Measures and a measure ment system should exist for the highest down to the lowest organizational subunit.
2. Key performance indicators/measures that exist for the corporate objectives (i.e., the overall corporate strategy). Whether these precede or follow the goal/objective development is subject to your assessment of what makes sense. The measurements can be included in the goal statements themselves or attached separately. We suggest that the goals/objectives be written in one column and that indicators/measures for each goal/objective be identified in a separate column.
3. Key performance indicators/measures developed after Steps 3, 4, and 5 in the planning process. Therefore, the measures will become more and more specific as you move from strategic goals/objectives (Step 3) to tactical objectives or action items (Step 4) to plans of action/implementation (Step 5).

We provide an example of measure development for corporate objectives from our naval ordnance station case example (Table 4-10).

We will provide specific advice in terms of how to develop key performance measures/indicators in Chapter 6. We do recommend that it be an activity that the group of managers contribute to; however, our experience suggests that they will struggle with the task. The Maryland Center for Quality and Productivity has developed, tested, and implemented in many organizations a process (MGEEM) that makes this struggle less painful. Many of the ideas for this process are included in the methodology described in Chapter 6. One strategy would be to have a small group of analysts develop straw-man measures for the goals/objectives and then have the management planning group add to, modify, and delete from the list. The development of measures and measurement systems is definitely difficult, and the approach of having... "experts" (i.e., someone who has done it before and has done a lot of thinking about the process and perhaps a lot of reading on the subject) guide the process appears to be most effective and efficient.

Eight-Step Planning Process: Step 4— Development of Tactical Objectives or Action Items

Now that strategic goals have been developed along with key performance indicators for each major goal, the planning process focuses on getting the management team to think more tactically. What must we do in this organization in the next one to three years to begin to move towards our five- to seven-year goals and objectives? (Again, the horizon would be selected by you; we simply picked one to three years as an example.) In some organizations, there are budget cycles that span one to three years. In such cases, tactical objectives are often tied to the next budget cycle. The basic purpose of Step 4 is to have the management team translate strategic goals into more tactical views of how we will accomplish those longer-term goals. We are trying to get closer to "rubber meets the road" type of issues.

The Nominal Group Technique (NGT) is again utilized in this step as the technique for developing the tactical objectives or action plans. The same group that developed the strategic goals will develop the tactical objectives. The session will take about two to three hours depending upon how much backtracking and stage-setting is done. The actual NGT session will only take about one and one-half to two hours. Table 4-11 depicts sample output from a Step 4 session. This output comes from a college of engineering planning process implementation. The data itself is less important than the format and general type of things that come up at this stage in the process. At this point, the group will now have participated in at least one NGT session, and they should begin to feel much more comfortable with the overall process itself. We normally see management teams going through this process for the first time really start to open up at this stage. The session usually seems to go more smoothly, discussion is very substantive, and the group is generally more productive. The quality of the output from this step should improve due to previous exposure to the group process.

At this point, let us make a comment about our last sentence. Many managers are disappointed with the "quality" of the output from some of these sessions, particularly the first time through the process. In particular, top managers feel that subordinate managers lack vision, perception, and strategic awareness. This is due partly to the fact that most organizations share very little information, knowledge, and power; therefore, most subordinate managers don't have a good feel for what's going on across the organization from a strategic perspective. This process is designed as an attempt to resolve that problem through involvement of the total management team in the planning process. It forces sharing of information and power; it is designed to do that. The overall quality of the output from this process will improve exponentially over time as the management team becomes comfortable with the process and their new-found roles and responsibilities. For too long the organization has said, "Just do, don't think," and when all of a sudden they are expected to think, too, it is an adjustment. Patience, persistence, and consistency are the key words to follow.

Audit check. Again, the output from Step 4, Tactical Objectives/Action Plans, must be audited back to Step 3. We are looking to ensure that all strategic goals/objectives are covered by tactical objectives. (Note: Not all strategic goals might be addressed by one or more tactical objectives, and not all tactical objectives have to be cause and effect linked to a strategic goal.) If a strategic goal does not appear to be represented by a tactical objective, then the group must

**Table 4-10. Corporate Objectives with
Measures Development**

Top-Ranked Strategic Objectives	Key Performance Indicators
1. Implement transition plans for NAVAIR products.	Transition plans signed and in place Obtain MK36 TDP form NWC Received vs. Submitted Number of programs
2. Develop/implement business plans for commodities.	Plans published and in place Increased programs brought into Department
3. Increase Department personnel retention rate (technical and administrative.	Comparison to baseline (track) - Attrition rate - Average length of employment Increase average experience by 0.5 years
4. Implement Dept. work prioritization system.	People work 8-10 hrs. instead of 12-14 % of managers using system In place and working in 6 mos. Deadlines met
5. Develop staff to properly manage the programs.	(Individual Development Plans?) IDPs developed % of planned division staff filled Have a training program
6. Develop the Department Facilities and Equipment Plan.	Identify requirements and prepare POA&M within 4 months Facility/equipment upgrade/procure
7. Department will implement reward program(s).	Implement the system $s of awards per program year Increase rewards by 10% "Employee of the Month" system in place
8. Develop control systems/ techniques for programs.	Cost tracking in place Product schedule/cost planned/actual Spending plans in place for all programs PM has decision-making/internal control system in place New financial system in place by end of FY 88
9. Pursue product transition from design to production.	Compelete transition Revised MOA with NWC Major program retained at NOS from design phase into new product line

10. Establish a Junior Manager training program.	Establish course outline
	Candidates from within department available for
	  supervisory positions
	Training program established for
	  GS11/12-potential managers
	(Rotation, intense management training, OJT)
	One trainee per division by EOY

ask themselves why. This may require the insertion of another action item or the translation of the strategic goal into tactical objective format. Often, certain strategic goals are written such that they can, as written, become a tactical objective. Figure 4-9 depicts an example of how one organization has performed this audit check. Note that we are simply trying to establish cause and effect linkages between action items and strategic goals.

Table 4-11. College of Engineering Step 4 Sample Output

1. Develop Mission Statements and Plans.

2. Identify Sponsored Research Problems

3. Produce Space Action Plan

4. Plan to Increase U.S. Ph.D.s

5. Assign College Development Officer.

6. Justify Additional Support Personnel.

7. Develop Universal Teaching Evaluation.

8. Identify University Service Problems.

9. Evaluate Academic Standards.

10. Re-Define Faculty Career Paths.

11. Increase Physical Plant Responsiveness.

12. Require Educational Methods.

Key performance indicators. Measures that will help the management team know whether or not the action items are accomplishing the objectives intended and their impact or relationship to overall performance need to be developed at this step also. As we mentioned earlier, it is common to see objectives written with standards of impact, targets for completion, and more. Our suggestion is that the objective be written and then standards of impact and targets for completion and other quantitative enhancements be added as addendums. These are the key questions to be answered in this part of Step 4:

1. Are we accomplishing or have we accomplished the objective/action item?
2. Does the objective have the intended impact on our strategic goals?
3. What impact does the action item have on performance?
4. Is the process of implementing the action item in control?

At this stage you will now be ready to focus on implementation of action items. The next step, Step 5, forms action teams that are responsible for the development of implementation plans

Action

A. Create a Navy P/P Plan for FY 87.

B. Establish immediate action item that focuses on success, pilot studies/ demonstration - "initial success".

C. Come up with a well-written mission statement consistent with DoD's - SYSCOM commitment.

D. Develop "PR blitzkrieg" aimed at CNO, CME, SECNAV, SYSCOM, Shore activity, Nonsupervisory people and Fleet command.

E. Document problems & concerns of C&L study.

F. Develop a Navy performance improvement awareness course/ training.

G. Establish early and strong top management commitment.

H. Have each activity (HQ and Shore) develop by end of 1987, a 2-5 year productivity plan with broad policy guidance from DoN.

I. By 1/1/87, establish accountability mechanisms and initiatives for revising personnel, financial, and procurement policies.

J. Measurement - develop and implement by FY 87 (end) P/P measurement systems to:

    a. Define base line (where are we starting from?)
    b. Define and implement Macro Navy indicators
    c. Positive local scoreboards developed by local users
    d. Shift IG focus and emphasis to performance/productivity measurement

K.   By 1/1/87, publish directive that local gain savers will retain and redirect 50% of all cost and personnel savings and profit.

Goals

9. Establish mechanism for sharing local efforts.

12. Create mission statement for effort.

6. Establish P/P awareness program for military/civilian personnel.

1. Establish and demonstrate top management support, commitment, and involvement.

4. By end of FY 87, each Navy HQ's and shore command will have a yearly 3-5 year productivity improvement plan which is measurable and increases employee participation.

5. By October 89, DoN will revise personnel and financial policies to promote productivity improvement.

8. By October 1987, DoN will institute system for procuring based on factors other than lowest initial cost.

2. Create and establish management philosophy that emphasizes customer satisfaction and motivation of people to improve quality/performance continuously.

3. Ensure effort meets Executive Order, DoN and OMB specifications/ requirements

7. By January 88, DoN will publish policy outlining how to spark and promote innovation; create climate that encourages change.

10. Require that all top management get P/P management training.

11. Eliminate unnecessary regulations in DoN; Cancel 50% of regulations by 88.

Figure 4-9. Audit Check on Action Items and Goals

for top priority objectives/action items.

Eight-Step Planning Process: Step 5— Formation of Action Teams and Development of Plans of Action

The most commonly experienced and most frequently written about problem in planning is the linkage of action to plans. How do we ensure that plans developed will be implemented effectively? How do we translate plans into action? "The plan is nothing. Planning is everything," said Dwight D. Eisenhower. Planning is a continuous and systematic process of thought about the future; assessing the environment, imagining the future, recognizing opportunities, and defining relative strengths and weaknesses. The result, a plan, is a specific course of action that is essential to communicate, coordinate, and control the activities necessary to accomplish the objectives established in planning. Most organizations don't know how well they have performed, because they don't have explicit statements of what they are trying to achieve. Many organizations have plans that are never effectively implemented due to how they were developed, how they were written, lack of accountability, lack of measurement, and lack of commitment and ownership. A vision and a sense of direction without a mechanism by which to motivate follow-through is a futile effort of improvement. To this stage in the planning process you will have developed direction; however, you are not assured that follow-through will take place.

At the level in the organization for which the planning process is being implemented, we force implementation accountability to reside with the management team at that level. Once the management team has developed prioritized action items in Step 4, the top priority action items are assigned to groups of two to five members of the management and planning team. For example, if we ended up with twenty top priority action items and had fifteen members in the planning team, each member might end up in three to four action teams. The purpose of these action teams is to develop "scoping proposals" for the assigned action items. A scoping proposal consists of the following information:

1. What has to be done to accomplish this objective?
2. What is the sequence of activities that must take place?
3. Who must be involved at each stage of implementation?
4. Who should provide overall management for this action item?
5. What are the anticipated costs and benefits?
6. What must be done to ensure effective implementation?
7. How will we know if the objective is successfully implemented?
8. How will we know if the objective is successful?
9. What are the major milestones in the implementation?
10. What other objectives and projects must this be integrated with?

We depict an example of a completed scoping proposal in Table 4-12. This example is abbreviated.

We mentioned that specific action items are "assigned" to members of the management team. Typically, the assignment process is a voluntary one. That is, members of the management team select the action items they want to further develop. The first time through this process we typically limit action team involvement to one or two per member of the planning team. The implication is that not all action items/objectives will be covered the first time through the process. The reason for doing this is to ensure that the management team learns the process before loading them up with too much work. "Establish the process, control the variance, then shift the

111

Table 4-12. A Sample Scoping Proposal

Action Plan 12

Goal 12: By October 1987, all shore activities will establish measures of performance/productivity and develop a yearly 5-year productivity plan.

Functional Lead: Each echelon 2 Command

Milestones:

1. Feb. 87 - Each command will distribute this DoN Productivity Action Plan to each subordinate activity with guidance on development of the yearly 5-year productivity plan.
2. Aug. 87 - Each activity is to establish measures with baselines and a draft of their plan to their command level.
3. Oct. 87 - Each activity will submit their first plan.

Measures of Success:

1. An organized approach to productivity improvement.
2. Activity level buy-in to improvement.
3. Improved support to the Fleet and Marine Corps.

mean." The process by which the management team determines what action items will be covered and what will be deferred is something that you will have to work out on a case-by-case basis.

The product from this step is a set of plans of action and milestones (POAMs), or project plans, for the top priority action items. The scoping proposals represent implementation plans. The developers of scoping proposals may not necessarily be members of the implementation team. Once an implementation team is identified, a more detailed implementation plan may need to be developed. On large, complex action items/objectives, subplans may be necessary for specific tasks in the overall implementation project. The purpose of this step is to transition the organization from strategic and tactical planning to effective implementation. It will require that management stay with the process longer than they are accustomed to devoting to a process. They will have to become the linking pins from strategy to effective implementation. The secret to success is attention to detail with respect to responsibilities and accountabilities in the action plans. This step is the most critical one in the process. If you allow the process to break down here, all will be lost. The nature of the process—highly participative—will make your job easier at this stage. However, participation may be necessary for high quality plans, but it is clearly not sufficient alone.

Audit check. At this step in the process the audit check involves monitoring how many of the objectives are being further developed. The Nominal Group Technique will provide you with a prioritized list of goals, objectives and action items. The reason this prioritization is important goes beyond the obvious search for consensus. Your organization, as is the case for all organizations, has limited resources. The two most valuable resources—time and money—are often the most highly constrained. You can't possibly implement all the goals/objectives and action items arising from Steps 3 and 4 of this process. It's not a question of whether all deserve to be implemented; it's a question of whether all can realistically be implemented with the resources you have at hand. The critical question is whether you implement the right ones—the ones that will best move you towards your strategic objectives, the ones that will best facilitate your becoming the Organization of the Future.

Key performance indicators. Measurement is an integral part of this step, as you can see by the requirements for the scoping proposals. The focus for measurement in this step is on successful implementation of action items/tactical objectives. Are we successfully implementing the top priority action items identified in Step 4? Does the implementation of these action items have a positive impact on the performance of the organizational system for which they were developed? Are we successfully driving toward our strategic goals and objectives developed in Step 3? Are we effectively and efficiently tracking our costs and benefits associated with each action item? These are the types of questions that need to be answered by the measures developed during this step.

At this point in the process members of the management and planning team should be actively involved in the implementation management for major action items developed during Step 4. People often ask, "Where does the time to do this work come from?" It is estimated that in the professional, managerial, and technical positions of most organizations in excess of thirty percent of available time for productive effort is what might be termed "discretionary." By discretionary time, we mean time for which the individual has some or total control over how it is spent. The person can choose what project to work on, can choose not to work, can daydream, can think, can write, can plan, or can solve a problem. But, the point is what the person does is at his or her discretion. A NASA manager once told us that winning organizations use their discretionary time wisely. Losing organizations do not manage how they use their discretionary time. This planning process is an attempt to redirect some of the discretionary time and effort in your organization towards team performance improvement objectives. Our more than ten years of experience with this process suggests that there is plenty of time available to drive this process. We have not seen one organization yet that could not implement this planning process with its existing staff. It's simply a matter of redirecting resources.

The next step in the process focuses entirely on integrating and adding to the key performance indicators developed to this point in the process.

Eight-Step Planning Process: Step 6— Project Management

Steps 1-5 have provided us with a rough plan; now we must begin implementation. The scoping proposals are reviewed for approval by the planning group as a whole or by a planning committee created for this purpose. Upon approval, an implementation team is assigned to the objective. The implementation team may or may not be the members of the action team. The nature of the work involved may require that it be delegated. Either way, the action team is still responsible for managing implementation and tracking the progress of the tactical objective/action item. If necessary, the teams may have to develop and present more detailed implementation proposals prior to approval for the more complex objectives.

Quarterly and midyear reviews are held by the planning group to monitor progress. A grand strategy for the process is developed. The grand strategy may simply be a calendar or Gantt chart with all significant activities and milestones on it. The grand strategy might be a document capturing all the output from Steps 1-5 or an executive summary of these.

A plan now exists, at least in "skeleton" form. The pieces or components of a plan have been developed. There is a vision, corporate objectives, strategic goals/objectives, tactical objectives/action items, and implementation plans and action teams. What is lacking at this point is a document that brings all of these elements together in a coherent, systematic, and integrated fashion. This is one of the purposes of Step 6 of the planning process, grand strategy development. A grand strategy is actually a master plan and master schedule for the plan components. It brings all of the elements of the plan together and presents them in a concise, understandable fashion. The grand strategy can exist in many forms. It could simply be a document that presents and discusses all the output from Steps 1-5. This would be what one might consider to be the long form of a grand strategy. The appropriate audience for the long form might be the people who developed and must implement the plan. The long form would not be appropriate for other audiences (i.e., the board, stockholders, upper management, and union) as it would present too much detail and reduce the probability that these audiences would read and understand the plan. A shorter form for the grand strategy might include a summary sheet of top priority goals, action items, and action plans, along with key performance indicators that reveal measures of perceived success. Figures 4-10 and 4-11 depict several examples of pieces of a grand strategy from a number of case examples.

In this step, you want to develop a document or perhaps several documents (different ones for different audiences) that will clearly communicate the results of the planning process (Steps 1-5) without necessarily providing all the data that will have been accumulated to this point. This is clearly a design task, and there is no one best form or format for this document. Step 6 puts all the data developed to this stage together in one coherent package. This step actually creates the plan.

Eight-Step Planning Process: Step 7— Continued Development and Enhancement of Measurement and Evaluation Systems

Key Performance Indicators for the entire organization, organization strategy, strategic goals/objectives, tactical objectives/action items, and Implementation Proposals/Action Plans (POAMs) have been developed. There has been no attempt to integrate these measurement activities into a coherent, single system. This is the purpose of Step 7 of the planning process. A plan now exists. The questions to be addressed in this step are: How will we know if we are headed in the right direction? How will we know if we are making progress? How will we know if our plan is succeeding? Are we getting better? Are our plans of action working? Are our action items/tactical objectives accomplishing the strategic goals/objectives we identified? Are we accomplishing our superordinate goals, mission, and key performance indicators? Are we living up to our guiding principles? Are we effective? Are we efficient? Are we productive? Are we managing total quality at all five checkpoints? Are we managing quality of work life successfully? Are we innovative? Are we profitable? Are we managing our budgets? What needs to be changed in the planning process next year to make it more effective? These are the types of basic questions that should be addressed in Step 7 of the planning process. Key performance indicators and other measures will be available from earlier steps and other sources, and these will have to be compiled and integrated into one system that can address the types of questions listed here.

The purposes of Chapters 5 and 7 are to provide you with some specific tools, techniques, and approaches that can be taken to accomplish Step 7 in a systematic fashion. At this point, we will not elaborate on how to do this step.

Eight-Step Planning Process: Step 8— Manage Effective Implementation Continuously

The final step in the process focuses on effective implementation. Peter Drucker has been quoted as saying, "What we [Americans] need to learn from the Japanese is not what to do, but to do it." Other countries seem to be innovative, while we seem to be content to be inventive. We appear to fall down when it comes to follow-through, execution, patience, persistence, and consistence. We seem to have lost the capacity for attention to detail. We are enamored by Japanese techniques

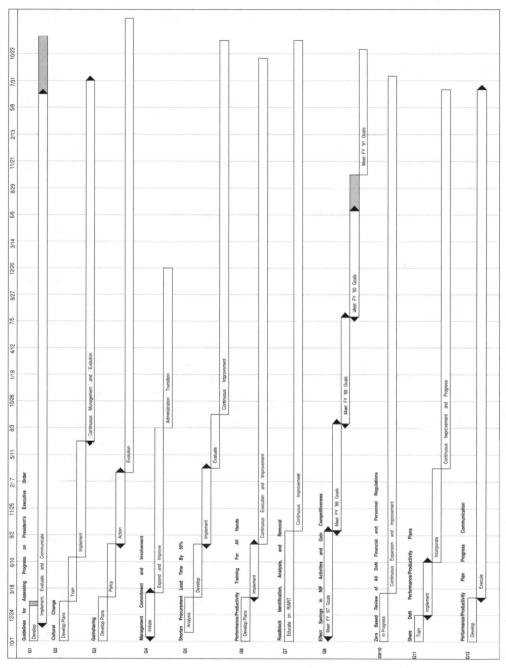

Figure 4-10.   Department   of   Navy   Grand   Strategy

taught to them by our industrial engineers, quality control specialists, and management experts. Somehow, when the Japanese put their cute little words on a technique, it becomes vogue to use it. I am always a little amazed when I hear an American manager give me a lecture on some new-found Japanese technique that we have been teaching in industrial engineering as methods engineering for over fifty years. I guess maybe they have just found a way to better communicate the concept.

The point is that at some period in this planning process, as well as with other improvement efforts, some basic attention to detail, hard work, accountability, follow-through, patience, persistence, and stick-to-itiveness will be required to achieve the results desired. We may live in a society and in an era where things have and do come so easy; as a result we have lost the drive and ability to accomplish things that take time. We don't have any new techniques for you, any quick fixes, or even any tips on how to accomplish Step 8. Basic project management techniques and skills will be required to pull off this final and most important step. However, we will discuss in the next chapter how linking measurement to improvement techniques such as employee involvement and gainsharing may be the answer.

Eight-Step Planning Process: Recycle, Evolve, Improve

Planning is a continuous and continuously improving and evolving process. Planning is more like sailing than speed boating; it requires constant mutual adjustment to a dynamic and sometimes turbulent environment (internal and external). To be successful, planning must achieve commitment built through involvement at all levels of the organization and in all functions. Planning requires awareness, willingness and ability, and a willingness to pay the price for effective implementation. If this planning process is to succeed in your organization, it must become more than just a new program; it must become a process, a way of doing business. Like other systems and processes in your organization, the planning process must continually improve. As you move through the planning process and the implementation of action items, needed modifications and enhancements will become obvious. These must be captured and integrated into the process for next year. This obviously will require a planning coordinator/manager who is as concerned with the process by which your organization plans as he/she is concerned with whether the forms are being filled out on time, the i's dotted and the t's crossed.

Earlier, we depicted a grand strategy for our naval ordnance station case example that showed three planning cycles (see Figure 4-7). It depicted how the various plans lead into one another and how the overall corporate plan was developed. This particular organization is already thinking through how their planning process will evolve and improve in the years to come while they are in the development and implementation stages of the first year. In the second year of this process, you will find that certain steps can be abbreviated or perhaps even deleted. You will discover new ways to complete a given step or substep. You'll learn what to concentrate attention on and what you can simply add to or modify from previous years' plans. This learning, developing, and growing process will not occur if you don't have a competent champion for this process. In many organizations, this may logically fit in a planning department. In others, you may need to develop a position or add this responsibility to an existing position.

Treat the planning process like any other process. Apply statistical process control concepts to it as developed and espoused by Deming, Juran, Ishikawa, and others. Enhance your existing planning efforts by integrating this planning process into them, and you will be well on your way to becoming the Organization of the Future you must become.

Process Applications/Case Examples

The participative planning process just described can be applied to many planning situations and needs in your organization. We believe its strength lies in applications directed towards performance improvement planning. It appears to be tailorable to any unit of analysis within the organization. It has been successfully used in a specific department within a larger organization that was not involved in the process. Conversely, it has also been applied in a top-down fashion creating consistency from level to level in terms of how plans are being developed. You have to view the process as we have described it to this point as a technique that can be tailored to most planning situations. This will require development of a strategy for how the process will be employed within a given organization. Prior to holding a planning session with any of our (VPC's) clients, we hold a one-day initial design session with key personnel responsible for the implementation of the process. This often involves the "change masters," who will be managing the process, and key decision makers from the top management team. (Let me reinforce that the term top management implies the appropriate level of top management relative to the unit of analysis for which the intervention is being made. It does not imply that the highest-level manager in your organization should be involved in the initial design session. It does imply that the highest-level manager for the unit of analysis for which the planning session is being held should be involved.) During this session, desired outcomes and expected products are discussed. A specific agenda for the planning session is worked through. Decisions as to what parts of OSA should be done as "homework" prior to the session are made. The specific focus of the planning effort is agreed upon.

This planning process has been successfully used to develop productivity, quality, performance improvement program plans, and operations/business plans that focus on productivity and quality improvement, performance improvement plans, measurement system development plans, and the annual business plan. The process can be, and has been, tailored to meet a number of planning needs in organizations. It has been designed to help you develop the performance improvement portion of a strategic business plan. We do not see it as a substitute or replacement for conventional strategic planning. We view this planning process' strength as being in the area of linking strategy to action, focusing on what we should do and how we should do it to constantly improve performance in the organization. We believe that the strategic business plan should interface with this planning process during Step 1, OSA. There are many issues involving strategy, long-range visions, and business and market plans that may not be sufficiently addressed in this process without sufficient time and effort spent on preparation to plan for performance improvement. This is the purpose of OSA, to prepare the group to plan for performance improvement. This is the intended interface to other types of planning ongoing in the organization.

The fact that the process has been specifically designed to focus on performance improvement planning and linking strategy to action has not prevented organizations from adopting this process as their strategic business/operations planning process. What we have seen is that with certain modifications the process can be used for a number of planning applications. However, we would like to end this chapter with a variety of performance improvement planning process applications. We present those case studies that are the most developed, for which we have the most data to share, and that represent a reasonable cross section of business, industry, and government. The three case studies we will detail are the Department of The Navy's Performance Improvement Plan, Burlington Industries Greige Sales Division's Performance Action Team Process application, and the University College of Engineering Strategic Planning efforts.

Performance Improvement Planning for the Department of the Navy

How does the Department of the Navy (DoN) of the 1980s become an Organization of the Future? How does the DoN respond to President Reagan's executive order calling for a twenty percent gain in productivity by 1992? How does the DoN ensure that constant improvement in perform-ance is a goal embraced by all DoN employees? These are tough questions that deserve top management's attention and involvement. Without well thought-through strategies, the questions cannot be answered successfully. Without plans to implement answers that are developed by key management and staff in the DoN, the issues won't be addressed successfully. These tough questions require pragmatic answers and solutions implemented by committed people and supported through involvement of visionary and supportive leaders and managers. Those who must implement answers to these questions must play a role in developing the strategies for success. On September 15-17, 1986, thirty-two senior level captains and Navy (or equivalent) personnel from the major communities and activities in the Navy and Marines assembled in Blacksburg, Virginia, to create a productivity plan for the Department of the Navy. The three-day workshop produced data that represented a solid foundation for a follow-on planning workshop with the Navy's Productivity Steering Group in Washington, D.C. on October 16-17, 1986. The Department of the Navy's Productivity Steering Group added to, modified, enhanced, endorsed, and reviewed the straw-man plan developed by middle management in Blacksburg in September. Out of the October session came a refined plan that was "cleaned up" and eventually published as the *Department of the Navy's Performance/Productivity Improvement Plan*. (Copies of this plan are available from either the VPC or the Navy Productivity Principal's office.) The two workshops held in September and October of 1986 employed the planning process described in this chapter as the mechanism for developing a high-quality and "bought into" plan for perform-ance improvement.

The DoN's performance improvement planning effort specifically focused on: ensuring as much top management support and legitimization through involvement as possible; development and/or recognition of a critical mass of champions and masters to drive the process once the external "change masters" have completed their tasks; ensuring effective staff-to-operations linkages for the plans (ensuring that the plan had its origin from a pragmatic, operations-oriented perspective); an appropriate amount of educational interventions to ensure that the plans are of high quality; getting the "right" people to plan with the "right" process; facilitating the planning process with "masters"; effective communication up and down the line with respect to the results of the process (effective public relations to ensure that the product is made as visible as possible); and performance improvement rather than business planning. The DoN began this effort committed to meet these design specifications in order to ensure that strategy was linked to action. Gerry Hoffmann, the productivity principal for the Navy, wanted to ensure that a high-quality plan emerged that satisfied upline and downline requirements. He was committed to completing the planning process in such a way as to ensure that action followed. In doing so, compromises were made and costs were incurred that sometimes made it difficult to defend the approach to upper management. Inherent in the decision to utilize this planning process are considerations of the need for quality, need for acceptance, availability of time, desired outcomes for the plan, and, in this case, political factors and motives surrounding the decision to develop a plan.

The DoN has partially addressed each of these issues. By developing the DoN Productivity Plan the way it has, some "top management" involvement has been achieved. However, there is still skepticism that the level of management reached is high enough to successfully support an effort of this scope. The process used to develop the plan was designed to create a critical mass of champions with which to work. It is essential that this core group of senior-level managers and the Productivity Steering Committee stay "on board" and are active. This requires communica-tion, coordination, and attention to detail. You can't buy champions and you can't coerce them; they usually enlist voluntarily, and you must nurture their roles.

The staff-to-operations linkages are critical to the eventual success of the DoN Productivity

Plan. The relationship between DoN headquarters offices and the field operations relative to this plan, their plans, and the execution of those plans will "make or break" the effort. The field operations obviously have to feel an ownership of the plan and commit to necessary actions at their level that will support the overall plan. The Secretary of the Navy needs to define and manage roles, responsibilities, and accountabilities in such a way as to create cooperation and coordination.

An audit for evaluating the quality of a performance/productivity plan/effort was developed by the VPC. One element of that audit focuses on the extent to which the performance/productivity plan "covers all the bases." Successful performance/productivity plans incorporate consideration for the following components:

- Awareness and culture change;
- Performance management;
- Basics understanding and execution;
- Planning for performance improvement;
- Measurement and evaluation systems;
- Control and improvement systems;
- Action planning and effective implementation;
- Cultural support systems; and
- Maintaining excellence.

The approach taken to develop the Navy Productivity Plan has ensured that many of the design specifications mentioned have been initially considered. A quick check of the goals and action items developed for the plan will reveal attention directed to the eight components for a comprehensive performance/productivity plan effort. The DoN's initial performance/productivity plan represents an excellent example of how to begin such an effort in a large, complex organization.

The Eight-Step Performance/Productivity Improvement Planning Process

The eight-step planning process developed by Dr. Sink guided the design of the two DoN workshops. The following describes how each of the steps were implemented and gives examples of the outputs.

Step 1. **Organizational Systems Analysis** —Both workshops generated a prioritized list of roadblocks to productivity using the Nominal Group Technique. Examples of the roadblocks generated were:

1. System and tradition encourage *status quo*;
2. Bureaucratic barriers to effective management;
3. Need for top level "champions";
4. No clear, cohesive, compelling long-range vision and plan;
5. Diffused focus on what's important and how to measure success; and
6. Lack of incentives to improve productivity.

Both external and internal strategic analyses were also done. Outputs from these analyses were used for the next step.

Step 2. **Developing Planning Assumptions**—Using the importance/certainty grid, each participant in Workshop 1 evaluated the thirty-eight assumptions generated. The following resulting assumptions were presented and validated in Workshop 2:

Critical but not certain:
1. There will be top management commitment and leadership.
2. Navy will seek lowest cost/high quality goods/services regardless of source.
3. There will be an avenue to allow change in law, policy, instruction, etc.
4. There will be a method for measurement and analysis of utilization and productivity.
5. The current lack of awareness within the DoN will be corrected.
6. There will be participative management to gain productivity gains.
7. The capital investment program will be converted into a productive one.

Critical and certain:
1. Incentive program will be the key to developing productivity effort.
2. The productivity effort will be killed by excessive management.
3. Need for training will continue to exist.
4. Technology and information systems will be exploited.
5. There will continue to be a shortsighted focus on peace-time efficiency, not mobilization readiness.
6. President's executive order will remain in effect.

Step 3. **Developing Strategic Performance Improvement Goals**—After participants of Workshop 2 generated a prioritized list of goals using NGT, these were compared and consolidated with goals generated in Workshop 1 to come up with the following list:

1. Establish guidelines for achieving and measuring progress towards the President's Executive Order (Goal 3 from Workshop 1).
2. By October 1988, DoN will implement a plan for organizational cultural change within DoN, which emphasizes continuous improvement, customer satisfaction, and cultivation of people (Goals 2 and 7 from Workshop 1).
3. Establish a policy to reward increased productivity through gainsharing.
4. Establish and demonstrate, from the highest level of command to the activity level, management commitment, support, and involvement (Goal 1 from Workshop 1).
5. By September 1988, modify processes/policies to shorten procurement leadtime by fifty percent (Goals 8 and 11 from Workshop 1).
6. By March 1987, implement performance/productivity training and awareness programs, top-down in all DoN activities (Goals 6 and 10 from Workshop 1).
7. Identify and remove productivity roadblocks (rapid handling as in Model Installation Program ([Goals 5, 7, and 11 from Workshop 1]).
8. By FY 89 effect savings in NIF activities that meet SECNAV targets and ensure ability to compete with private industry (Goal 4 from Workshop 1).
9. By March 1987, develop and initiate implementation of a master plan for aggressive use of capital investment programs.
10. By 1988, conduct zero-based review of all DoN financial and personnel regulations, and cancel/revise at least fifty percent (Goals 5 and 11 from Workshop 1).
11. By October 1987, all shore DoN will establish measures of performance/productivity and implement a yearly five-year productivity plan (Goal 4 from Workshop 1).

The following two Navy examples are outcomes of this last goal.

Step 4. **Developing One-Year Action Items and Improvement Projects**—Due to time limitations in Workshop 2, the goals were used as action items. Examples of action items generated in Workshop 1 are:

- Establish clear, concise, accepted, and understood measures of performance at all levels and in all functions of the DoN.
- Develop and communicate a Navy Performance/Productivity (P/P) Plan during FY 87 using the data provided from this workshop. This should be completed no later than December 31, 1986. Communication of plan would occur January 1, 1987-October 1, 1987. Theplan should institutionalize the P/P management principles and philosophies by defining principles, vision, philosophy, core values, beliefs, and developing a mission statement, establishing broad policy guidelines that are consistent with the DoD-SYSCOM's commitment.

Step 5. **Implementing Improvement Projects**—Participants in both workshops were asked to volunteer for action items to develop scoping proposals. An example of an action plan/ scoping proposal is:

Action Plan 11

Goal 11: By October 1987, all shore activities will establish measures of performance/productivity and develop a yearly five-year productivity plan.
Functional Lead: Each echelon 2 Command
Milestones:

1. Feb. 87—Each command will distribute this DoN Productivity Action Plan to each subordinate activity with guidance on development of the yearly five-year productivity plan.
2. Aug. 87—Each activity is to establish measures with baselines and a draft of its plan to its command level.
3. Oct. 87—Each activity will submit its first plan.

Measures of Success:

1. An organized approach to productivity improvement.
2. Activity level buy-in to improvement.
3. Improved support to the Fleet and Marine Corps.

Steps 6 and 7. **Project Management and Measurement and Evaluation of the Impact of Performance Improvement**—The scoping proposals include measures of success. These measures are used by the implementors of the action plans to evaluate progress. At this point, significant improvements have been reported on the DoN-wide level. The productivity principal's office has been monitoring what is actually happening in the different commands and installations within the DoN. The steering committee will meet again after a year to assess implementation of plans.

Recycle and Continuously Improve the Process—The following recommendation was made by the VPC in our final report:

"Continued planning for the effort using processes such as the ones demonstrated in the two workshops is essential. We recommend that a modified planning workshop be developed and executed in FY87 in the April-July time frame. The performance/productivity planning process should precede the budget process, such that budget implications can be absorbed. Similar planning must take place within each community and activity. Again, we re-emphasize that 'the process by which you plan is as important as the plan itself'."

This case study has shown a pragmatic technique for a participative performance improvement planning process applied to a large organization such as the Department of the Navy. The process has been used in smaller organizations and has yielded noteworthy results, particularly in some Navy installations such as NOSIH and NNSY. These small successes have partially influenced the response of the DoN to President Reagan's call for a twenty percent improvement in productivity, i.e., to come up with a comprehensive and integrated performance/productivity improvement plan for the DoN. This could have been done by a staff group and signed by the Secretary of the Navy. However, DoN has realized that for an effort such as this to be implemented by committed people, participation must be solicited even at the planning stage. And while there was skepticism about whether a participative process would work in a traditionally autocratic environment, the process itself has surfaced a critical mass of champions committed to implementing high-quality plans which they developed with an effective and efficient process facilitated by highly qualified people. It may be too soon to judge the overall success of the process within DoN, but based on the response of different activities and levels within the DoN, the process is definitely spreading and gaining acceptance. The following are examples of two organizations within the DoN that are using the process.

Naval ordnance station. Figure 4-7 depicts the recently redesigned planning cycle and process for the Naval ordnance station. As you can see from the figure, the cycle and process is complex—about thirteen to fifteen months long and contains numerous planning documents and steps. The actual strategic plan at the NOS is really a collection of documents and plans. However, you will note that there does exist one document called the Corporate Strategic Plan. As mentioned, the NOS is comprised of thirteen departments and eighteen programs and is structured in a matrix organization design format. The overall strategy guiding the redesign of the planning process at the NOS appears to be to move the responsibility and accountability for planning, problem solving, and decision making to the program and department management team level.

Corporate long-range objectives (horizon twenty years) were drafted and consultatively reviewed by the department managers. The participative planning process was presented and reviewed with program managers. The intent is to expose and integrate the planning process at the program and department management level over the next three years. Changing the organization's management team habits relative to planning will obviously not happen overnight. The first year of the grand strategy calls for exposure, awareness creation, early stages of skill development, overall planning process design and development, debugging, educational interventions, and the execution of the overall planning process on schedule in whatever fashion is feasible. Several pilot applications of the eight-step participative planning process are scheduled for selected departments. The majority of the departments and programs are left on their own to decide how to develop their departmental and programmatic plans. The intent over the next three-year period will be to lock in on a process that will be consistently utilized by all departments and programs.

We have highlighted the elements of the planning cycle for the NOS where the eight-step participative planning process is intended to be employed in Figure 4-7. The participative planning process is intended to be used to improve the consistency with which the plans are developed and to improve the quality and acceptance of the resulting plans. Note that the participative planning process described in this chapter is only utilized to develop selected parts of the overall plan. It is a technique that can be employed to improve the overall quality of the strategic plan and to improve the assurance that strategic plans will be effectively linked to tactical plans and implementation. In addition, the integration of the participative planning process into the planning cycle at the department and program level is used to place emphasis on the must do, business plan aspects, as well as the continuous performance improvement objectives. The simultaneous focus on what must be done to satisfy demand, customers, and requirements along with what must be done to continuously get better must be successfully accomplished in the organization in order to become the Organization of the Future. It is in vogue to read and listen to the current popular gurus on productivity, quality, "one-minute management," "passion for excellence," or "quality without tears." They inspire us, entertain us, provide us with simple explanations of our problems, offer us training and education to improve awareness, provide implementation assistance if we do it their way, and often imply there is a quick fix. In the world of "rubber meets the road," it is important to translate philosophy and concepts into pragmatic techniques and processes. We think that the participative planning process, when facilitated correctly, can make a lot of what the leading authors and public speakers of the day say should happen in your organization actually happen.

When you attempt to redesign and improve the planning system and process in a large complex organization, as the NOS has, it is imperative that you adopt at least a five-year horizon for the change effort. Anyone who has tried to change a major management subprocess, such as planning, will identify with this requirement. It has taken many years for the NOS and your organization to develop their culture and their habits associated with management process. If it takes as long to change these things as it did to create them in the first place, the NOS and your organization are very likely to be going out of business. However, these changes cannot occur overnight. This is precisely why the technical director of the NOS has mapped out a five-year grand strategy for changing the planning process. He has made a five-year commitment to his management team and a long-term commitment to the facilitators who are helping him design and pull off the transformation. This is a necessary, but not a sufficient, condition for success.

The NOS is now, as you can see from Table 4-13, in the beginning of cycle two of their three-cycle plan to incorporate the designed changes in the planning process (i.e., 1988). Department and program manager training and development are occurring, productivity coordinator training is taking place, and facilitators to assist each department and program, if they so choose, with the application of the planning process are being trained and developed. The second year/cycle of the intervention is the first full year during which the redesigned planning process is actually implemented in full form. A great deal of infrastructure development, continuing training, open discussion, and continued acceptance and buy-in development will take place in year two. By year three, the planning process should be a way of doing business for most of the management team and they can focus on actually improving the process. Just like statistical process control, we establish the process, learn the process, control the variance, and then shift the mean (i.e., improve the process and its performance).

Naval shipyard. We don't have as much to share with you on this case application because the application of the participative planning process in the development of the operations plan for the shipyard is just underway at this writing. However, we can describe how the decision to apply the process was made and the context within which the application is being made.

One of the top twelve goals identified in the Navy Productivity Plan focused on ensuring that all field activities develop productivity measurement systems and five-year productivity

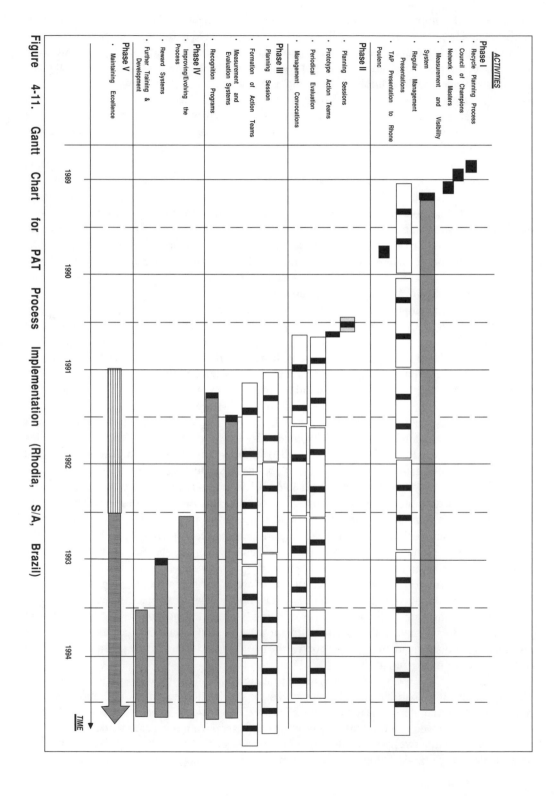

Figure 4-11. Gantt Chart for PAT Process Implementation (Rhodia, S/A, Brazil)

plans by October of 1987. The Navy Productivity Plan was sent out to all major commands in early 1987. Since that time, we have been aware of responses to that plan from the NAVAIR and NAVSEA Commands. In particular, in the NAVSEA Command a strategic operations/business plan was forwarded to the subsystems in the Naval Sea Command. Reference to the Navy Productivity Plan was made, and a call for strategic plans at the major field activity level is consistent with the goal established in the overall Navy plan. A shipyard operations plan has been developed and sent down to each of the eight major shipyards, along with a request for a strategic operations plan. In all of these business/operations plans for NAVSEA and the shipyards, strong reference is made to productivity improvement, continuous improvement, and quality. The plans are fairly traditional narratives focusing on mission, background data (environment, growth, facilities, technology, budgets, staffing, world politics, current and upcoming initiatives, strengths and weaknesses, and trends), and goals. The plans appear to have been written by staff groups for signature by command leadership. They provide excellent background for planning; however, in my opinion, they fall short of being a plan that will be operationalized. How these planning documents are utilized by the field activities is critical to the ultimate success of the process.

The naval shipyard we are using as a case example received the call to develop a plan by October of 1987 from Shipyard Command leadership. The overall shipyard planning document was forwarded with the request; however, no other background information was forwarded, such as the Navy Plan or the NAVSEA plan. The naval shipyard commanding officer (CO) had been involved in the Navy Productivity Plan development process and had developed a feel for what the participative planning process could do. As such, when the call came from Shipyard Command leadership for specific shipyard plans, the CO sought approval upline to utilize the participative planning process as the mechanism for responding to the upline request. Initial indications from upline command were favorable.

The request for a plan called for a focus on an operations plan. There were no planning specifications provided other than those perhaps implied by the overall Navy shipyard plan provided with the request. Essentially each shipyard was left to its own devices as to how it would respond to the plan. We spent one day with the design team of the case shipyard outlining the planning retreat session. We reviewed the Navy plan, the NAVSEA plan, the overall shipyard strategic business plan, and discussed the fact that a current strategic plan for the case shipyard did not exist. It was decided by the CO that the focus of the planning session would be on developing a strategic operations plan; however, strong emphasis would be placed on integrating plans for the productivity and quality improvement efforts into the overall operations plan. We concurred with the case shipyard planning process design team that one integrated plan, though more difficult to develop, was preferred to numerous plans (i.e., a business plan, a productivity plan, and a quality plan). We also decided that the top management team at the shipyard would receive background information prior to the actual planning session in the form of the Navy Productivity Plan, the NAVSEA plan, and the overall shipyard plan. We also decided to provide the top management planning team with a number of current, provocative articles focusing on Organization of the Future type issues. The final agenda for the two-day planning session appears in Table 4-13.

You will note that the session calls for completion of Steps 1-5 of the participative planning process detailed in this chapter. As mentioned in our description of Step 1, OSA, some of the work for that step is done prior to the session itself. In particular, the background preparation relative to upline plans is "homework," if you will, done prior to the session itself. Note also that the planning session design team selected relevant portions of the OSA to be completed during the planning session itself. In this case, they selected OSA Areas 1.2 and 1.3 Mission Statement and Principles, respectively—and Areas 1.5 and 1.8—Internal and External Strategic Analysis, respectively. The focus of the planning session was to develop an operations plan that effectively integrated quality and productivity improvement initiatives. Therefore, during Step 3—Objectives Development—and Step 4—Tactical Objectives Development—the participants were asked to focus on business and operations-related objectives as well as quality- and productivity improvement-oriented objectives. This places importance on identifying and distinguishing between must-do objectives and should/would like-to-do objectives. As mentioned earlier, the Nominal Group Technique can handle this by forcing the planning team to separate objectives into must and want objectives. The want objectives are subjected to the fourth step, voting and ranking, in the NGT process. In this fashion, you then can effectively wind up with a business plan as well as an improvement plan.

Table 4-13. Sample Planning Agenda

Time	Event	Mode
MONDAY 9/7		
1500	Arrival of VPC Staff (Sink, Kiser, Rossler, Das)	
1600	Tour of Norfolk Naval Shipyard	
1930-2130	Reception at Capt. McGinley's residence	Social
TUESDAY 9/8	PLANNING SESSION DETAIL AGENDA	
0730-0800	Coffee and Donuts	
0800-0815	Kick-off by Capt. McGinley	
0815-0900	Organization of the Future	Educational
0900-0945	"Discovering the Future"	Film
0945-1000	BREAK	
1000-1015	Business Planning & Performance Improvement Planning	Educational
1015-1200	Step 1 - Strategic Planning	Group
1200-1300	LUNCH at the Holiday Inn	
1300-1345	Step 1 (continued)	Group
1345-1500	Step 2 - Strategic Planning	Group
1500-1515	BREAK	
1515-1715	Step 3 - Strategic Planning	Group
1715-1730	BREAK	
1730-1830	Executive Session with Capt. McGinley	
1830-1930	Hospitality Suite at Holiday Inn - Hosted by VPC	Social
WEDNESDAY 9/9		
0730-0800	Coffee and Donuts	
0800-0830	Review of Day 1	
0830-0900	Overview of Navy, NAVSEA and Shipyard Plans	
0900-1000	Performance Definitions	Educational
1000-1015	BREAK	
1015-1200	Step 4 - Strategic Planning	Group
1200-1300	LUNCH at the Holiday Inn	
1300-1430	Step 5a - Strategic Planning	Group
1430-1630	Step 5b - Strategic Planning (Need breakout rooms)	Group
1500-1515	Working BREAK	
1630-1700	Closure by Capt. McGinley	

Developing plans, communicating plans, coordinating plans, and integrating plans are all uncommon activities in most American organizations. The focus has tended to be more on the plan than on the process by which we plan. Planning has tended to be an exercise, like a homework assignment, that once completed signifies the end to the process. The linkage between the strategic plan and the tactical and operational activities and behaviors is weak, to say the least. Many, if not most managers I have talked to and worked with, condemn planning not so much because they think it is unimportant, but more so because they have never seen a process or technique for planning with which they felt comfortable. We condemn the goal because we don't have a path. Planning is a process that can be designed and engineered to work in any situation or setting. We tailored a planning process to work for a naval shipyard, and engineered it to create a quality product and to ensure that the process was meaningful—increasing the probability that the plan would be implemented. The only really important reason to plan is to improve. You can't improve if the strategic plan is detached from reality or if it does not link successfully to operational actions. The planning process, just like the measurement process, must be completed in a fashion that ensures action is taken.

Department of the Navy performance improvement plan closure. These two case examples, although not particularly detailed, do provide some insight into how the participative planning process presented in this chapter can be utilized to develop performance improvement plans in a large, complex federal government setting. The process we have presented need not replace existing planning procedures. It will be easier for you to simply attempt to integrate this process into existing planning systems. You saw an example of how this can be done with the NOS example. If the desire is to develop a business plan that places more emphasis on quality and productivity improvement, then the naval shipyard example provides some insight into how this can be achieved. The process presented in this chapter is simply a technique or process by which critical aspects of your plan can be more effectively developed. Let's now look at how this process has been utilized in the private sector—the manufacturing sector.

The Use of Performance Improvement Planning in a Performance Action Team Process Implementation for Burlington Industries Greige Sales Division

A detailed case study of a performance action team (PAT) process implementation at the New River Textiles Plant within the Burlington Greige Sales Division can be found in the Summer 1986 issue of *National Productivity Review* (Sink, Shetzer, Marion). I won't replicate the information in that case study, but will attempt to focus briefly on how the participative planning process fits into a broader effort to involve all employees in an organization—from the vice president down to the lowest level in the organization—in a process designed to continuously improve performance (effectiveness, efficiency, quality, productivity, quality of work life, innovation, and profitability/budgetability).

In the late 1960s and early 1970s, quality circles were transplanted to this country from Japan. The legacy they have left is one of participative management (management of participation) out of the textbooks of the previous ten to twenty years and onto the factory — and later the office floor. By 1970, many Japanese firms had close to twenty years of experience with employee involvement. Firms like Musashi Semiconductor (Chapter 1) were achieving outstanding results with their efforts. In this country, managers searched for the answer as to why the Japanese were beginning to dominate certain industries and markets. The search revealed an answer, albeit a simplistic one, that pointed to quality circles and robotics. Continued analysis has revealed that there are other reasons, and they too have caused other "single data point managers" to rush off implementing techniques such as JIT in hopes that they have found the quick fix.

Quality circles in this country were sold to top management and done to the workers. As such, a whole group of critical employees in the American organization—called middle management, technical, and professional employees—were left out of the employee involvement process. As a result, quality circles as implemented in this country have tended to exhibit a life-cycle that lasts three to five years (Lawler 1986). We have tended to view quality circles as a program, not a process, and they generally have not been tied to a larger strategy to improve overall performance. Quality circle efforts have been typically designed and developed by people in non-pivotal positions with little power.

In contrast, my observation of the remarks from high-level Japanese managers at conferences on quality and productivity (i.e., the IIE-sponsored Pacific Basin Productivity Conference in 1986 and the Tenant/JMA Quality Conference in 1987) is that employee involvement is viewed as a strategic thrust imbedded in a larger, overall, and integrated strategic effort to constantly get better. The Japanese, it seems to me, appear to view quality circles, small group activity process, semiautonomous work groups and autonomous work groups as stages of evolution, where American managers see them as alternatives. The result is that their efforts at management of participation are more mature, sophisticated, and hence, more productive. They generate more ideas, proposals, and innovation; involve a higher percentage of the employees in the organization; and implement more of the proposals for performance improvement than we do. Their employee involvement efforts also appear to be better integrated with overall corporate strategy as a result of better information and power sharing. Participative management works in Japan largely from a fear and rigid status hierarchy basis. Participative management in this country can work just as well but for different reasons.

We tackled the problem of ineffective participative management in this country as compared to Japan by redesigning the process. We looked at critical design issues that appear to be required to make employee involvement work and built them into the PAT process. In doing this, we needed to have a mechanism that would get all levels of management more actively involved in the process. The answer we came up with was to integrate a participative planning process as an integral part of the overall performance improvement effort. Line employees and supervisors focus on participative problem solving, such as in quality circles, and the management team focuses on participative planning. The result is a comprehensive process focusing on performance improvement that involves everyone in the organization. Plans for performance improvement and implementation of those plans is added to the job expectations of the management team, and proactive problem solving to eliminate roadblocks to performance improvement is added to the job expectations of the employees and supervisors. The structured and systematic process and inherent infrastructure ensure that, over a period of time (say two to three years), the more proactive performance improvement process becomes a way of doing business.

The case study for the New River Plant describes how the PAT process works and how it was implemented in the plan. It also describes how the participative planning process fits into the overall participative management effort, how it works and how it was implemented in the plant. The process is developed in a top-down fashion so that upper management is exposed and involved in the participative planning process prior to any involvement of line employees and supervisors. The process has to reach a point of acceptance and success with management before you can expect it to succeed at lower levels. My experience is that employee involvement almost never fails because line employees can't or won't do it. Employee involvement almost always fails due to lack of management support, understanding, and commitment.

This case example, then, depicts how the participative planning process can be used to specifically focus on performance improvement planning. The process was not used at the Burlington plant to develop a strategic business plan. It primarily focused on performance improvement. At the time of this writing, the Burlington plant has achieved approximately 100 percent involvement in the process at all levels of the plant. The initial PAT process coordinator and facilitator has been promoted and moved to another plant within Burlington. A first-line supervisor has been assigned the responsibility of becoming the new PAT process coordinator and facilitator based upon interest and ability. The primary focus in the third year of the process development was on how to stabilize the process and ensure 100 percent recycling each year. The thrust to accomplish this was on improvement of the understanding of the process on the part of first-line supervisors. Several supervisors who were able and willing to run the participative problem solving process in their own work groups, without external facilitator assistance, were identified. Hostile takeover attempts, understandably and unfortunately, sapped the energy and attention of most of upper management in the division and company. Nevertheless, it appears that the process is well established and maturing. Long-term survival, success, and continued evolution will depend upon the continuing development of a critical mass of champions for the process. The case does exemplify many of the issues discussed to this point in the book and provides an example of how to integrate the participative planning process into an overall attempt to build a continuous performance improvement process.

Strategic Planning in a University Setting: Planning for Academic Departments And a College of Engineering

Choosing the strategic planning process. Virginia Tech's College of Engineering experienced significant growth between 1970 and 1985. By 1985, the faculty had grown to 275 and research expenditures had increased by a factor of five. The higher level of performance of research faculty increased their vocal opinions regarding college and university-level priorities and decisions. The dean was long tenured—fifteen years—and wanted faculty input into future plans. By 1985, the time had come to include these talented faculty in strategic planning. In the spring of 1985, the dean appointed a faculty committee to complete a strategic plan. As one of the committee members, I was a proponent of participative planning. The committee chose me as chairperson and recommended a full faculty effort using VPC's strategic planning process.

Initiating the process. The first step was to collect background material from university administration and other colleges within the university. Then each of the twelve departments organized planning meetings during December and January 1985-86. Most departments set aside six hours for the session. A few set aside three to four hours. The length of time chosen was unusually an indication of the department's feelings about the usefulness or seriousness of participative planning.

Using VPC's planning process and the original committee members as facilitators, each department agreed upon a list of recommendations for action items. The recommendations were often redundant across departments. To bring together these twelve departmental lists, a planning session was held with the head and an elected faculty from each department. These people completed the same process, weaving in the recommendations from the departments during the round-robin phase of the NGT. Synthesized, as well as new ideas, surfaced. At the end of the twelve-hour session (held over two days), a list of twelve prioritized action items was ready to be presented to the faculty.

At this stage, the planning committee was nine months into the process, and many of the department heads and faculty had devoted a great deal of time to it. There was a sense that more than the twenty-six faculty and department heads should be involved in the implementation of the final twelve action items. In fact, many of the action items were philosophical in nature and did not have specific recommendations for implementation or measures of success. However, this group of twenty-six wanted to turn much of the work over to other faculty for finalization. This turning over would cause discontinuity in the process in that the people voting on the priorities of the twelve action items would not be the same people carrying out the implementation. People who participated in the definition of the action items and understood the nuances of the statement of the action items would not carry forward their understanding. To reduce misinterpretations of the twelve original action items, this group of twenty-six prepared scoping proposals for each of the action items. These scoping proposals would pass on to other faculty the rationale behind the action item and suggestions for measures.

Implementation of the action items. A faculty forum was held in May 1986 where all twelve action items were presented. Faculty volunteered to serve on action implementation teams. The dean appointed chairpersons of each team. Each team met several times during the next academic year, 1986-87. In the winter of 1987, the dean called all twelve chairpersons together for a progress report. Final reports from each team were submitted to the dean by September 15, 1987. Under the action teams, the reports presented additional action items. In spite of the scoping proposals, understanding and nuances of priorities and action item statements were misinterpreted.

A summary of the report recommendations was sent to all faculty. At the end of two years, there were still no implementation plans—only recommendations.

A few action item recommendations were resolved during the years of meetings of the college. This may have been the result of the visibility of the college's progress in the planning process. Some recommendations needed continued follow-through for implementation, which was handled by individual champions—not necessarily the action team members.

In January 1988, another summary report was made to the dean and department heads on the implementation of action items. Two major items are presently being discussed in the engineering faculty organization and will be brought to the entire faculty through a mail ballot. Other issues are pending decisions and discussions by department heads and university administrators.

Problems. An important issue throughout the process was the definition of "by consensus." Many issues became high priorities that did not have a majority vote. Some new items were presented in summary reports that were not consensus items but rather the pet idea of the author of that portion of the report.

Lack of experience in such a planning process caused quality control problems in the number of new action items presented by the action teams. Twelve action items from the planning sessions of twenty-six faculty and department heads resulted in nearly 200 action items from the action implementation teams. The scope and quality of the action items varied. Some items were philosophical and difficult to effect or measure. Others were so narrowly focused that they had limited appeal to the general faculty.

The nature of many action items was the definition of mission and identification of operations resource problems rather than proposed strategic action. Many faculty members did not want to participate in the broader planning effort. They were narrowly focused on their pet subjects.

Over a three-year period, the cast of characters and champions changed. Continuity and understanding of the intent of action items was lost. Occasionally, there was little relationship between the original twelve scoping proposals for the action items and the recommendations of the action teams.

There was political upheaval in the university during the last year of the process. Many action items could not be followed through immediately because of the number of changes in top university officials.

Promises. The faculty was consulted and they debated endlessly. No one could feel left out, even if they didn't agree with the outcome. The huge investment of time pushed the process toward completion. During the three-year period, enough changes occurred that were related to the recommendations that optimism increased about implementing other recommendations. The reports from the action teams were perceived as faculty consensus and proved more impressive to university officials than would a report from a small committee.

CLOSURE

Other recent case applications of the participative planning process for the purpose of developing performance improvement plans specifically are: the Departments of Chemical Engineering, Industrial Engineering and Operations Research, and Agricultural Engineering at Virginia Tech; United Illuminating of New Haven, Connecticut; the NAVSEA CENLANT; NADEP-NI; and others.

We have introduced a structured, systematic, and participative planning process that has been developed over the past ten years in a variety of settings and for a wide range of applications. Most of the planning literature—and we provide you with a fairly complete bibliography at the end of the chapter— fails to provide the reader with technique. The literature is filled with what not to do, issues that plague planning applications, theory on what will work, strategy and policy guidance, timely decision rules, current strategies for success, and plenty of rhetoric about what planning should be and is not. Planning, in our view, like measurement, has one basic purpose or desired outcome—to improve performance. In order to accomplish this, planning must: be pragmatic; involve those who must implement the plans; be simple (but not too simple); and ensure that long-range, strategic, and tactical thinking are effectively linked to action. Planning, to be effective at improvement, must create a commitment to—an ownership for—the plans the process develops. Planning is a continual process. It is not something that is done once a year, once every three years or once every ten years whether you need it or not. Planning is an integral part of the management process and must be a responsibility and accountability of every manager and management team. Complete planning in a complex organization requires that different managers and management teams play different roles in the overall planning process. It is a concerted team effort, one that is coordinated, communicated, and that inspires cooperation. It is more like the sport of sailing than motor boating in that it requires constant adjustment and attention. Managing the culture and the planning process may be the two most important functions of a manager and management team.

We believe that this planning process has been designed to accommodate much of what planning must be in the future. We feel strongly that this process can help your organization chart a path towards the Organization of the Future. We believe that without a process like this you will have a very difficult time competing with your New Competition. We know that it will be difficult to translate and transfer what we have presented in this chapter to your organization. We also know that once someone decides not to do something, almost any excuse will do. What will be your excuse for not experimenting with this important innovation?

REFERENCES AND SUGGESTED READINGS

A & D's Future and You: A Performance Improvement Guide. 1986. Honeywell, Aerospace and Defense Management Development Center.

Aaker, D. A. 1984. *Developing Business Strategies.* John Wiley & Sons. New York.

Barret, M.E. 1981. OST at Texas Instruments. *HBS case study* (9-182-609). Harvard Business School.

Bennis, W. G., K. D. Benne, and R. Chin. 1985. *The Planning of Change.* 4th ed. Holt, Rinehart, and Winston. New York.

Byars, L. L. 1984. *Strategic Management: Planning and Implementation Concepts and Cases.* Harper & Row. New York.

Camillus, J. C. and J. H. Grant. 1980. Operational planning: The integration of programming and budgeting. *Academy of Management Review.* 5(3): 369-379.

Chakravarthy, B. 1982. Adaptation: A promising metaphor for strategic management. *Academy of Management Review.* 7(1). 35-44.

Delbecq, A. L., A. H. Van de Ven, and D. H. Gustafson. 1986. *Group Techniques for Program Planning.* Green Briar Press. Middleton, Wisconsin.

Deming, W. E. 1987. *Out of the Crisis.* MIT Center for Advanced Engineering Studies. Cambridge, Massachusetts. 276-279.

Emshoff, J. R. and A. Finnel. Spring 1979. Defining corporate strategy: A case study using strategic assumptions analysis. *Sloan Management Review.* 41-52.

Gardner, J. R., R. Rachlin and H. W. Sweeny. 1986. A *Handbook of Strategic Planning.* John Wiley & Sons. New York.

Glueck, W. F. 1980. *Business Policy and Strategic Management.* McGraw-Hill. New York.

Gupta, J. and G. Hirsh. 1986. Managing the planning process: Recent trends and challenges. *European Management Journal.* 4(2).

Hamermesh, R. G. 1986. *Making Strategy Work.* John Wiley & Sons. New York.

Hofer, C. W., E. A. Murray, R. Charan, and R. A. Pitts. 1984. *Strategic Management.* 2nd ed. West Publishing Co. St. Paul, Minnesota.

James, B.G. Summer 1984. SMR forum: Strategic planning under fire. *Sloan Management Review.*

Kast, F. Fall 1980. Scanning the future environment: Social indicators. *California Management Review,* 23(1): 22-32.

Kelley, C.A. Jan-Feb. 1984. Auditing the planning process. *Managerial Planning.* 32(4): 12-15.

Lawler, E. E. 1986. *High-Involvement Management.* Jossey-Bass Publishers. San Francisco, California.

Leontiades, M. 1983. *Policy, Strategy and Implementation: Readings and Cases.* Random House. New York.

Lindsay, W.M. September 1980. Impact of the organization environment on the long range planning process: A contingency view. *Academy of Management Journal.*

Lundberg, C. C. Sept.-Oct. 1984. Zero-in: A technique for formulating better mission statements. *Business Horizons.*

Mackenzie, K. D. 1986. *Organizational Design.* Ablex Publishing Corp. Norwood, New Jersey.

Marrus, S. K. 1984. *Building the Strategic Plan.* John Wiley & Sons. New York.

Mascarenhas, M. 1980. *Strategic Management: The Strategic Planning Process.* Management Development Program Lecture at Oklahoma State University.

McCarthy, D. J., R. J. Minichiello, and J. R. Curran. 1987. *Business Policy and Strategy.* Richard D. Irwin. Homewood, Illinois.

McCaskey, M.B. June 1974. A contingency approach to planning: Planning with goals and planning without goals. *Academy of Management Journal.*

McLaughlin, H. J. 1985. *Building Your Business Plan.* John Wiley & Sons. New York.

Miller, E. C. 1971. *Advanced Techniques for Strategic Planning.* American Management Association.

Nadler, D.A. Summer 1982. Managing transitions to uncertain future states. *Organizational Dynamics.* 37-45.

Naylor, T. H. 1980. *Strategic Planning Management.* Planning Executives Institute. Oxford, Ohio.

NASA. 1984. *A Framework for Action: Improving Quality and Productivity in Government and Industry.* Report from Symposiums on Quality and Productivity.

O'Connor, R. 1978. *Planning Under Uncertainty.* Conference Board. New York.

Pearce, J.A. II. Fall 1981. An executive-level perspective on the strategic management process. *California Management Review.* 24(1): 39-48.

Peters, T. J., and R. H. Waterman. 1982. *In Search of Excellence.* Harper & Row. New York.

Pfeiffer, J. W., L. D. Goodstein, and T. M. Nolan. 1986. *Applied Strategic Planning: A How to Do It Guide.* University Associates, Inc. San Diego, California.

Pinnell, B. 1986. Keeping corporate planning relevant — A key task for the planning department. *Long Range Planning.* 19(1).

Porter, M. E. 1980. *Competitive Strategy: Techniques for Analyzing Industries and Competitors.* The Free Press. New York.

_____. 1985. *Competitive Advantage: Creating and Supporting Superior Performance.* The Free Press. New York.

Prasad, S. B. 1983. *Policy, Strategy, and Implementation.* Random House. New York.

Rhyne, L. C. Jan.-Feb. 1984. Strategic information: The key to effective planning. *Managerial Planning,* 32(4): 4-11.

Robey, D. and S. Altman. 1982. *Organization Development.* Macmillan Publishing Co., Inc. New York.

Sink, D. S. Spring 1983. Using the nominal group technique effectively. *National Productivity Review.* 173-184.

Sink, D. S., L. Shetzer, and D. Marion. Summer 1986. Performance action teams: A case study. *National Productivity Review.* 233-251.

Sloma, R. S. 1984. *No-Nonsense Planning.* The Free Press. New York.

Steiner, G. A. 1979. *Strategic Planning: What Every Manager Must Know.* The Free Press. New York.

Steiss, A. W. 1985. *Strategic Management and Organizational Decision Making.* D. C. Heath and Co. Lexington, Massachusetts.

Stonich, P .J. and S. G. Wernecke. May 1982. Strategy formulation: What to avoid; how to succeed. *Management Review.* 25-42.

Szilagyi, A. D. Jr. 1981. *Management and Performance.* Goodyear Publishing Co. Santa Monica, California.

Tichy, N. M. 1983. *Managing Strategic Change: Technical, Political, and Cultural Dynamics.* John Wiley & Sons. New York.

5. HOW WOULD YOU KNOW?

BASIC MEASUREMENT CONCEPTS, THEORY, PHILOSOPHY FOR THE ORGANIZATION OF THE FUTURE

The top manager of an organization recently requested that we train a management team in a given department in the area of productivity measurement. He wanted us to teach them how to develop high-quality measures and measurement systems for their department. He gave us one day to satisfactorily complete this task (i.e., six contact hours). The top manager's objective was to train one department—an important one—have them do it, then transfer the knowledge and skills across the organization. You can appreciate his challenge and ours.

In thinking through what we would teach that management team in six hours about measurement, we developed a strong sense of what represents the absolute essentials of measurement. We came up with an agenda and course content that we feel reflects the basic knowledge that any manager must have in order to systematically and effectively design, redesign, develop, and improve the quality of his/her measurement systems. This chapter, particularly the first half, is essentially what we taught that management team in six hours. By the way, the management team felt we had captured, in fact, the essence of what they needed to know in order to fulfill their top manager's request. We might also mention that this particular management team was typical—in that they were skeptical, confused, ambivalent to the task of measurement, in a compliance mode, somewhat resistant, brainwashed/indoctrinated by the system as to how to do measurement and how to use it, as well as bright but slow to change their views due to the years of exposure to poor-quality measurement systems. The point is that face-to-face we can deal with questions and concerns and skepticism. In written form, we must rely on your willingness to read and then think carefully about what is being said. You'll have to break your paradigms about measurement in order for these concepts and approaches to make sense. We're confident you can do this, and as a result, a whole new way of thinking about and approaching measurement awaits you.

What did we tell that management team in six hours that altered their thinking about measurement and pointed them in the direction of designing/redesigning, developing, and implementing improved measurement and evaluation systems?

First, we presented a management systems view of their organization. Figure 5-1 is exactly the picture we drew on the white board for them. We explained that their department is a management system, complete with upstream systems (suppliers and vendors—internal and/or external), inputs, transformation processes (value-added processes), outputs (goods and services, tangible and intangible), and downstream systems (customers—internal and/or external). We explained their role in the management system:

1. Ensure that the jobs get done, on time, within specifications, and within budget; and,
2. Constantly improve the performance of the system(s) they are managing as a team.

They liked this and agreed that the second role has not been an emphasis on the past. We showed them the box in the management systems model that represented them. We pointed to the improvement interventions, indicated by the arrows going from the management team box to the organizational system box, and discussed that these arrows represent their constant attempts to improve the performance of the system. We mentioned that, often, in order to justify and make certain improvement interventions, they needed information to support the interventions and that was what the arrows coming up off the right side of the organizational systems box through the tools box and then into the management team box represented. Those arrows represent the data collection, data processing, data presentation, and data evaluation parts of a management system. We pointed out that this, in graphic form, is a portion of the measurement process. We spent about an hour talking about this model and its implications for their task of measurement. They liked the model and felt it helped them crystallize their thoughts about their task at hand.

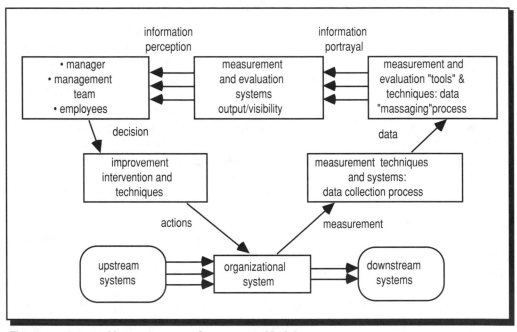

Figure   5-1.   Management   Systems   Model

Second, we taught them how to think about the performance of their organizational system. From the first hour's portion they came to agree that a critical part of their job as a management team is to constantly improve their department's performance. It seemed very logical and natural that they must measure their department's performance, either before improvement interventions or at least after them, in order to really be managing. The question "Are we getting better?" deserves an answer. You cannot measure performance or performance improvement if you cannot operationally define performance. We spent another hour operationally defining perform- ance and its subcriteria for this management team. We drew an enlarged picture of their department, as a management system (see Figure 5-2), on the white board and operationally defined each of the seven performance criteria (effectiveness, efficiency, quality, productivity, quality of work life, innovation, and budgetability since they were a cost center) in relationship to their department.

We started with generic, department-independent definitions for each of the seven criteria and then evolved toward developing department-specific definitions. We explained that the seven criteria are like the seven clusters of instruments on an airplane's instrument panel (i.e., navigation instruments, engine performance instruments, communication instruments, etc.) and that the attributes or subcriteria for each of the seven performance criteria are like the actual instruments themselves (i.e., the compass, the directional gyro, the oil temperature gauge, the gas gauges, the tachometer, the radio frequency indicator, etc.). You don't start to build an instrument panel at the second or third level of detail, you start at the first level. We explained that this is where a lot of measurement efforts go awry; they start at the detail level and have no conceptual level of understanding to guide them. We spent about an hour and a half on this, and they really enjoyed this second cut at improving their understanding of what to measure. They felt that the overview did give them perspective on a critical area that had troubled them in the past. They confirmed for us that you cannot measure what you cannot or will not operationally and conceptually define.

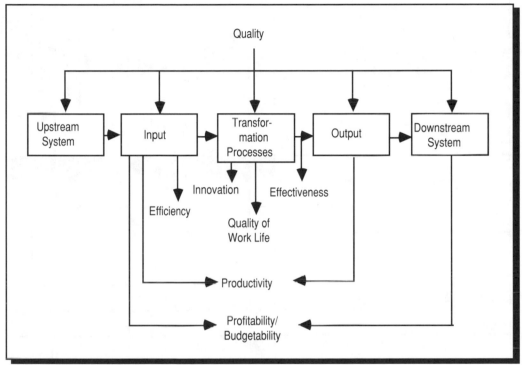

Figure 5-2. Organizational System and the Operational Definitions of Seven Performance Criteria

The third thing we did to help this management team understand how to go about improving the quality of their measurement and evaluation systems was to run them through a Nominal Group Technique session. (For more detail on this technique, see the Reference section at the end of this chapter.) The focus of the NGT session was to have the management team identify specific measures of performance for their department. In fact, the task statement read almost identically that way. We spent an hour and fifteen minutes on this exercise. At the end of that period, the management team had created a prioritized list of measures of performance for their department. They were pleased with the results, although they admitted to struggling through the thought process for the first time. We then handed out an instrument called AIM (audit to improve measures/measurement) and had them complete it. Figure 5-3 depicts an AIM example. They listed the measures identified from the NGT session across the top of the form and audited them against the elements list down the side of the form. The process forced them to think about what

Audit to Improve Measures X = Objectives or criteria whose performance is measured by the measure being audited	Top-Ranked Performance Measures	1. Average of station workload man-yrs. generated	2. Letters of appreciation/ commendation(complaints)	3. Personnel attrition rate	4. MATS items completion rate	5. CONS in deficit	6. People from other depts wanting to work in our dept	7. Risk taking at low levels	8. Exit interviews-data (reasons people leave)	9. Percent of major recommendations accepted	10. Branches in one div. that work with .those in another	11. Personnel attendance data
Performance Criteria												
Effectiveness		X	X		X					X	X	
Efficiency												
Quality (6 checkpoints)			Q5						Q3		Q3	
Productivity												
Quality of Work Life				X			X	X	X			X
Innovation								X				
Profitability/Budgetability		X				X						
Input/Output Analysis												
Input: Labor		X					X					X
Material		X										
Capital		X										
Energy		X										
Data/Information												
Processes				X		X	X	X	X		X	X
Outputs		X			X					X		
Outcomes			X	X			X			X		X

Figure 5-3. Audit to Improve Measurement (AIM) Naval Ordnance Station Case Example

they had, as a team, agreed ought to be measured. In this case, the results revealed that they were not going to measure innovation, quality of work life, or productivity. They felt this was a problem that should be corrected, and we made the point that AIM had done its job. At this point in the session they really began to sense progress and increased understanding, and as a result, began to sense the task their top manager had given them was doable and important. We were now-four- and-a- half hours into the workshop and were ready to provide the management team with measurement technique introduction.

The fourth and final portion of the six-hour workshop on measurement focused on technique and application issues. We went back to the management systems model (Figure 5-4) and highlighted the measurement tools and techniques box. We explained that many improvement interventions and management team decisions, problems, and opportunities would require information regarding how well the organizational system is performing. They clearly recognized the need for techniques with which to collect, process, and present that information. We pointed out that we had time to provide technique and application overview but not skill development. We reviewed the concepts of unit of analysis and scope with them and discussed that these two issues had to be addressed in order for measurement applications to be effective. Unit of analysis has to do with the boundaries of or definition of the system for which the measurement system is being developed. There are unique measures for different units of analysis. Lack of clarification of unit of analysis can cause frustration and failure with a measurement application. Scope refers to the length of the time period being analyzed by the measurement effort. Is the reporting period to be a week, a month, a quarter, or a year? The answer to this question will affect the type of technique chosen for the measurement application.

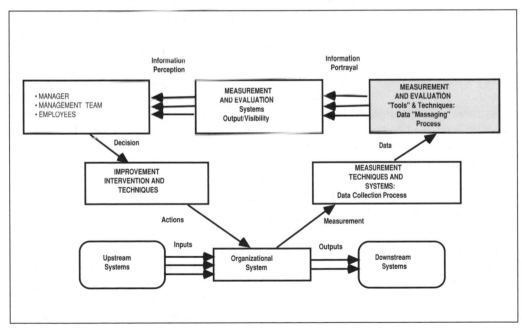

Figure 5-4. Measurement Tools and Techniques

We also discussed other critical issues associated with successful application of measurement efforts, such as audience and purpose clarification. The intended audience for the measures/ measurement system will have obvious impact on what is measured and how the results are portrayed. Purpose, for example improvement vs. control, will have similar critical impact on the measurement application.

We then reviewed two specific techniques for productivity and performance measurement that represent state-of-the-art and practical applications. We demonstrated how the total factor productivity measurement model works and how SCORBORD—a software support—facilitates the storage, retrieval, processing, and presentation of data and information. We also presented a measurement methodology called PRFORM and discussed how it could be used in white-collar settings. We demonstrated how PRFORM software also facilitates storage, retrieval, processing, and presentation of data and information relevant to these types of measurement applications.

The group of seven managers from this department went away happy with the day; comfortable that they had a solid foundation with which to respond to their assignment, but challenged by the prospects of having to put the knowledge gained in six hours to work in the real world. They left worried that, although they had a foundation of knowledge, they didn't have the experience and skill to pull off the assignment. We tended to agree with them, acknowledging that becoming a master at measurement doesn't happen in six hours.

This real-world scenario is intended to preview the types of pragmatic, measurement-related topics and issues that will be discussed in this chapter. We've spent the better part of ten years, and collectively, we've probably spent well over forty years, studying and doing measurement. Measurement is so important and so natural, and yet it has such a bad reputation and is given so little emphasis and attention by managers. We want to present measurement, in this chapter and throughout this book, in a very nonthreatening fashion and as a very natural and integral part of the management process. We realize that even if we accomplish this we may not succeed in getting upper-level management in your organization to read this and think about the implications. However, we do believe that the wisdom shared in this chapter, in particular, can help you and your organization to make progress in the critical area of improvment in the quality of your measurement and evaluation systems. There are some fundamentals that have to be learned, and they will be represented as an elaboration of the case example just discussed. As we have learned from Deming, Ishikawa, Juran, Crosby, and others, in the area of quality, much of what we must learn about management in the global economy is of a philosophical and conceptual nature. This is true for measurement also. Note that the concepts presented in the area of quality today, particularly by Deming, regarding measurement, are also directly applicable in the broader area of performance measurement, productivity measurement, and more. As we saw in the case example presented here, measurement is an integral part of the management systems process. Let's explore how to go about improving the quality of measurement systems in your organization in a systematic and structured fashion.

HOW WILL YOU KNOW IF YOU ARE CONSTANTLY GETTING BETTER? BECOMING THE ORGANIZATION OF THE FUTURE

"How would they know?" is another Deming challenge commonly leveled at audiences. It's an almost cynical question, intended to challenge American managers' awareness as to how little they know about management, in general, and quality and measurement, in specific. We're just doing our very best. How would they know? Everyone just doing their very best isn't enough. Everyone must know what to do, know how to do it (knowledge and skills), be willing to do it, and then pay the price to do it. The president, chief executive officer, chief operations officer, director, and top management team of every organization in America must hold themselves responsible and accountable for quality and productivity and, most importantly, for constant improvement. As the saying goes, they are ultimately held accountable for everything that goes on or doesn't in the organization. This truism has taken on added meaning when it was suggested that greater than eighty-five percent of the quality and productivity problems in the American organization are caused by management. The reason—the logic—is simply that top management defines and controls, directly or indirectly, knowingly or unknowingly, the management process, systems, and culture in the organization. By not managing the management process, by not constantly improving the management process, top management in America has created the crisis. Nothing less than a catharsis in the way top management thinks about the management process will take us out of the crisis.

The development of a management process which will constantly improve quality, productivity, and total performance must become a top priority. If the top management team in your organization isn't willing to plan for, become a part of the design process, or spend time thinking about the journey, I suggest you find work at another organization. If you've been asked by top management to lead the quality and productivity crusade and you then found out that top management wouldn't become intimately involved, I suggest you decline the crusade leadership opportunity. Life's too short to go on crusades that aren't blessed by the Pope. If you've found that top management's support and interest was high at first, but that there are now new thrusts, new bandwagons, and new quick fixes, I suggest that you resign the crusade to make a point. Life's too short to go on crusades that aren't supported for the duration. Of course, the point to productivity and quality improvement is that it must be continual. So, in this sense, it's not a crusade or program; it's a never-ending process of continual improvement. If you are top management and you've been guilty of starting up crusades and programs, I urge you to think carefully about the realities of The New Competition, the Organization of the Future, and the global economy of the 1980s, 1990s, and beyond.

How will you know if you are constantly getting better becoming the Organization of the Future? You won't if you don't engage in a systematic effort to design/redesign and develop the measurement and evaluation systems in your organization. You are the pilot, a part of the flight crew of a complex airplane, and the question is "Do you have all the right instruments necessary to fly the airplane successfully and safely?" What is the level of quality of the cockpits/instrument panels that the managers and management teams in your organization have at their disposal? Should they get better, can they get better; if so, how? These are the kind of fundamental questions that this chapter has been designed to answer.

Deciding to Measure

The decision to measure is not easy, obvious, or even often considered. It is often decided for us, at least in the control-oriented situation. It is often implied, frequently avoided, and almost always misunderstood. It is certainly influenced by management style and preference. It should be motivated by the need to support and enhance improvement; it is often motivated by unnecessary or unwarranted desires to control, or at least create the illusion of control.

Why measure?

The most important, and perhaps the only really valid, reason for measuring performance of an organizational system is to support and enhance improvement. We measure because the process tells what system capabilities are, and the levels of performance we can statistically expect from the processes and systems in our organization. We measure because an innate human need is for feedback—how did we do? We measure because we want to know how to get better—what to focus our attention on and where to put our resources.

What to measure?

Managers and management teams are responsible and accountable for the performance of organizational systems; measure the performance of organizational systems. The complete panel of instruments for an organizational system will include information about effectiveness, efficiency, quality, productivity, quality of work life, innovation, and profitability (profit center)/budgetability (cost center). Measure total performance. You get what you inspect, not what you expect. If your instrument panels are incomplete, your performance will be, too.

How to measure?

Managers and management teams measure constantly, whether they know it or not. Measurement is a very natural process. Human beings were provided with a number of senses so that they could measure, constantly, the environment around them. We were provided with a brain so that we could store, retrieve, and process data and information. We have invented and developed computers, software packages, and other tools and techniques to supplement the human mind. The human mind is fantastic at some tasks and not so good at others.

The best measurement system is an appropriate blend of the qualitative with the quantitative, the subjective with the objective, the intuitive with the explicit, the hard with the soft, the known with the unknown, the knowable with an appreciation for the unknowable, the human mind with tools for support. How do we measure? We measure with our senses, with our minds, with computers, and with techniques—guided by models, theories, and so forth.

Style and Preference Versus the Role of Measurement in the Organization of the Future

The cognitive style and personal preferences of a manager or management team have played a large role in whether formal measurement was done and how it was done. This isn't necessarily bad. However, in the Organization of the Future, the critical and necessary role of measurement won't allow for these factors to determine whether or not to measure. Measurement is a necessity and is becoming more critical as organizations, technology, and environments become more complex. Reflect on any of the futuristic movies—*Star Trek*, *Star Wars*, *2001*, *2010* — and think about the increasingly important role of measurement in those visions of the future. Note that artificial intelligence (i.e., *Hal* and *Sal*, the fifth- or higher-generation computers in *2001* and *2010*) requires tremendous amounts of measurement as an integral part of developing cause-and-effect understandings that can be built into the logic of a computer. Personal, often irrational, dislike or fear of measurement will have no place in the Organization of the Future.

Style and preference will play an increasingly important role in how we measure and how we portray the results of measurement. We are beginning to understand how different people collect and process information (Wonder and Donovan 1984; Hampton 1981; Morris 1979; Wright 1980; Myers and Myers 1986). This improved understanding will assist in tailoring measurement systems for specific managers and management teams. All pilots essentially have to adapt to the same instrument panels. There is very little flexibility built into most control panel design. The human being adapts to the system, not the reverse. In the Organization of the Future, the measurement systems will adapt to the human beings. We will be able to specify how we prefer to see information, what information we want to see, when we want it, and we will be able to tailor information for problem solving, decision making, and planning by accessing common data bases and designing our own individualized reports.

We will be able to adapt the measurement activities to individual and team styles and preferences in the Organization of the Future so as to improve the quality of the management support system. We will not be able to continue to allow personal style and preference to determine whether or not we measure.

THE ROLES OF MEASUREMENT

Measurement tends to be viewed and used in a very narrow fashion in most organizations. Our perceptions of the proper role for measurement and of the range of applications for measurement are undoubtedly shaped—biased by current usages. Finance, accounting, management by objective (MBO), work standards, and budgets dominate our thinking about the roles of measurement. In short, tradition has established a very control-oriented view of measurement applications in the organization. A control orientation for measurement should not necessarily imply a negative connotation. Although, like Theory X—a control-oriented view of human behavior— control and commitment are slowly becoming value-laden terms. As with leadership, the notion of situational measurement needs to be considered and developed. Autocratic, tight control orientation, leadership and management styles and behaviors tend to create positive effects if they are appropriate and negative effects if they are inappropriate. Of course, the question is how to define and determine appropriateness. In the same sense, the use of measurement for control versus measurement for improvement must be considered in light of the situation. Even in saying this, I reveal a narrow concept of measurement by implying there is a two-point continuum of control versus improvement. The use of the word versus implies control may always be at odds with improvement—that they are incompatible. However, I suppose it is possible to have a measurement system that could serve the purpose of control and improvement.

Just as we have begun to expand our thinking about leadership and management styles and behaviors to include a more refined continuum, we should begin to refine our thinking about measurement. We have gone beyond Theory X and Theory Y notions of style and behavior to include at least a four-point continuum containing autocratic, consultative, participative, and delegative dimensions. As a manager moves from autocratic to delegative behaviors, it is implied that less control, power, and influence is exerted, in a one-way fashion on planning, problem solving, decision making, and so forth. The better the match between the style and behaviors exhibited by the manager/leader and variables such as maturity (willingness and ability) of the subordinate, availability of time, need for quality, need for acceptance, and others, the higher the probability that the desired outcomes for the specific situation will be achieved. Similarly, a more sophisticated, contingency, or situational approach to measurement approaches will increasingly yield improved results in the Organization of the Present and Future. We're going to help you better understand the factors that have to be considered as you approach measurement and the alternative approaches at your disposal.

The job of being a manager and leader in the 1980s, 1990s, and beyond is definitely getting more complex. I believe the anybody-can-manage philosophy is an obsolete belief. Einstein once said that we should keep things as simple as possible, but not simpler. The demands of being a successful manager require that as the organizational systems we manage become more complex and dynamic our knowledge and skills for managing those systems develop and increase. I believe the task is an important and relatively straightforward one. Those that have chosen to learn about situational management, have applied it, and developed skills for it are better managers today and are succeeding. It took a vision, a willingness to learn and change, a commitment to improve, and the discipline to pay the price to develop knowledge and skill through application and practice. Most complex skills require the same sequence of activity. Learning how to better utilize measurement to constantly improve the quality and productivity—the total performance—of the organizational systems you are a part of and you manage will be challenging and rewarding.

We'll start to better understand the expanded views of measurement by considering the variety of roles that measurement can play in the management process. As we have said, the use of measurement for control is probably the most common and best-understood application. We also use measurement for forecasting, prediction, variance analysis, cost estimation, planning, bid preparation, personnel evaluation, testing, quality control, production control, scheduling, project management, gainsharing and incentive systems, budget analysis and control, capital investment decisions, cost/benefit analysis, and engineering economic analysis. In general, any activity in the organization that has a data requirement will necessarily involve measurement. When you closely examine the underlying intent and motive for many, if not most, of these applications, you find control, prediction, estimation, decision making, and problem solving (of a reactive type) as the major theme.

However, measurement can also be a very effective driver of performance improvement. Measurement can be used as a tool to ensure that strategy is implemented, as an integral part of high-quality management support systems, as an improvement and development device, as a motivator, as a natural and integral part of the management process, as continual and real-time feedback on how individuals and groups are performing, and as a mechanism for supporting continuous improvement behaviors in the organization. Measurement can be done and used in such a way as to minimize or eliminate fear. Measurement can be used without evaluation and judgment; only focusing on analysis of data for the purpose of understanding, as an example, how we are doing—getting better or worse. Measurement can be used in a very positive and effective fashion relative to the goal of constant improvement.

In this sense, I am very concerned about the implications of Deming's statements regarding measurement. His points about standards, quotas, merit systems, and MBO are being misinterpreted by those who don't understand the difference between measurement and evaluation. He is being misinterpreted by those who don't understand the difference between measurement for improvement versus measurement for control. Those who misinterpret have come away believing that Deming is saying "don't measure"—that measurement is bad. I'm convinced, after reading, re-reading, and listening carefully that Deming is attempting to distinguish between measurement for improvement versus measurement for control. I believe he is saying that standards, quantitative goals, and quotas are naturally a part of the evaluation process but are insidiously dysfunctional if used in the improvement aspect of the measurement system. As he says, when you set a standard, some have to reach up and some have to reach down. On the average, the standard will be met. The standard can and has become a limiting factor to performance in the American organization. The only standard with any merit in the Organization of the Future is that of "constantly get better." Having a standard of constant improvement does not imply, in any sense of the word, that measurement is bad. In fact, conversely, it makes measurement ever more critical. Deciding what constitutes performance and then tracking indicators against our concepts of performance is the measurement process. Statistically, all measures, all processes will exhibit inherent variation. Measuring that variation and defining it with statistical parameters is not a standard-setting process in a strict sense of the word. We are simply quantitatively defining what the system, process, and person is doing relative to a defined measure. We can learn what the process can be expected to do in the current state. The current state may be stable, steady or unstable, or unsteady. The mean level of performance, as measured against a defined criterion, and the measured variability are caused by things inherent in the process and by things independent of the process itself, such as management, leadership, and environment. Deming speaks of special causes and common causes of variation in the performance of processes. Some of the variation in levels of performance are in control of the manager, the management team, the employees, and the management process and systems. Change a variable in the management system and the mean and variance of a process can change due to changed behaviors of the people in the particular process. Assume that everything about the management system were perfect; management did a perfect job and adopted and effectively implemented all of Deming's principles. There would still be variance in the levels of performance achieved by the process. The only way to improve the mean level of performance and reduce the variability would be to redesign/change the process itself. The aim in the first half of this century was to apply the principles of mass production so that we could reduce costs and increase the availability and opportunity for more people to have more at a lower cost. The aim of the last half of this century is to reduce/minimize variance in every possible process so as to achieve the goal of constant improvement of quality (Deming 1987. Let's look at an example to clarify.

Measurement as the driver of performance improvement. In the summer of 1969, I worked in an appliance manufacturing plant as an assembly-line spray painter. The line I worked on is depicted in Figure 5-5.

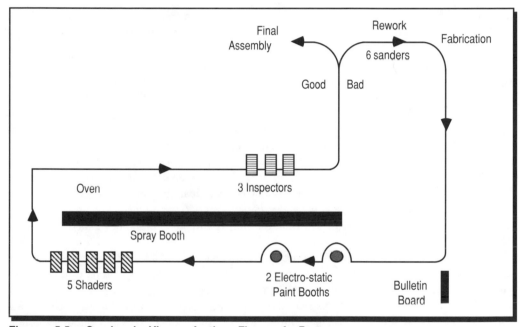

Figure 5-5. Overhead View of the Flow of Parts

The figure represents an overhead view of the flow of parts that make up the outside panels for refrigerators. The front doors, freezer compartments, and refrigerator compartment would come from fabrication and be hung on the overhead conveyor line shown in the figure. The parts would come through two electrostatic paint booths that automatically painted the base color— avocado, harvest gold, brown, or white—onto the door panels. The conveyor would then bring the panels through a shading booth where five shaders would hand spray a slightly darker shade of avocado, harvest gold, or brown on the edges of the door panels. This process was manual, because at the time, robots with the level of precision required for this process were not common in American manufacturing facilities. (They may still not be common.) The painted panels would then pass through an oven where the paint was baked and dried. Out of the oven, the panels would pass three inspectors whose job was inspecting quality into the product. I later learned that the inspectors were looking for runs in the paint and shading that was too wide, too narrow, or too inconsistent. The inspectors would mark panels not in compliance with their visually applied specifications with a red grease pen. The panels then proceeded down to the first floor of the factory, where they were removed and stacked to go to the final assembly line if they had no red mark, or thrown in bins to go to rework if they had a red mark.

When door panels were run that were painted white, the shaders—and I was one of the five shaders—basically did not have a job. So I would go over and stand by the spot where the overhead conveyor would bring the panels up from the first floor. I would watch for a ticket that would tell us which color to paint the next batch. As I waited for the tickets to come up, I noticed the inspectors and observed them using their red pens a lot. One day I went over and asked the inspectors what they were looking for when they decided whether to give a panel a red mark. They impatiently described the specifications they were instructed to apply. I asked them where most of the errors appeared to be coming from, and their reply was "the shaders." I then asked if they kept data on errors, and they shared the daily report sheets with me. I asked for these reports daily —while the white parts were run—and began to track good parts/total parts run (my measure of performance).

Figure 5-6 presents the basic findings. After about a week of tracking this data, I decided to post the results on a bulletin board (something in American organizations that could be used effectively as scoreboards if management only knew how) at the end of the paint booth work area (see location as marked on Figure 5-5). The data I presented was for the past four weeks, good parts to total parts painted, first shift and second shift, tracked day-by-day. Note that the paint line was apparently in steady state, performing at seventy percent, plus or minus a couple of percent. I explained to my team of shaders what the numbers meant and what the inspectors on the other side of the wall had told me they were looking for as they marked up parts. (Note: This was the first time, I learned, that the shaders had been told what the specifications were for the job. The training for the job had entailed placing a new shader in between two experienced shaders and saying, "Look to the left, look to the right—Do what they tell you to do." I think they called this "on the job training.")

After a week, a little competition between shifts had set in, a little Hawthorne effect had undoubtedly set in, and performance (as measured, partially at least, by good parts to total parts painted) had improved substantially (see Figure 5-7).

As you can see, performance increased from seventy percent to ninety-seven percent—plus or minus a couple of percent—and then settled down to about ninety-five percent after a couple of weeks. Performance stayed at ninety-five percent for almost three months. I kept the charts updated daily in my spare time as white parts ran on the line. One day, close to the end of my summer job period, our shift supervisor came up to me and asked me to explain the charts on the bulletin board. I proudly explained what I had done and explained the results. At the completion of my explanation, he shook his head and stated that he had severe reservations about my actions. First, he explained that I had created a major problem for him in that he now didn't have anything for his rework people to do! Second, he explained that it wasn't in my job description to analyze and post data. Third, and finally, he explained that the bulletin board was for official company business only and said that I should remove the charts from the board and cease spending time on the activity.

Several interesting and revealing points can be made from this case example:

1. Industrial psychologists tell us that the content of the job has significant motivational potential. They tell us that jobs have five basic core dimensions:

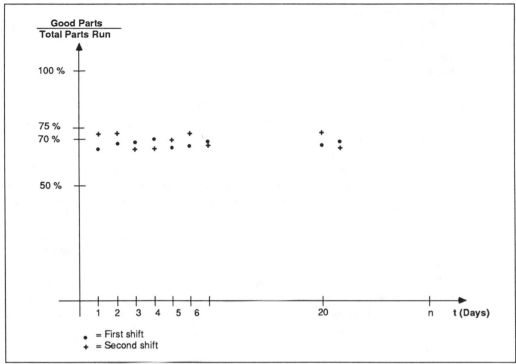

Figure 5-6. Run Chart (Before Intervention)

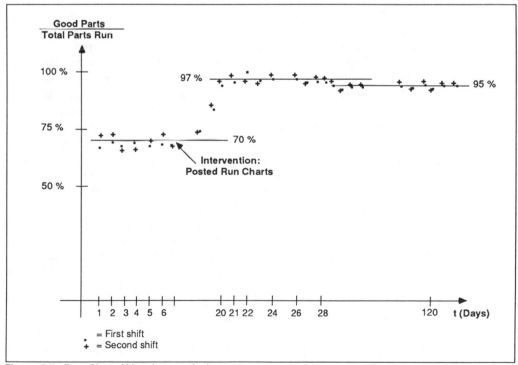

Figure 5-7. Run Chart (After Intervention)

- Task significance;
- Skill variety;
- Autonomy;
- Task identity; and
- Feedback (Hackman and Oldham 1975).

2. Many jobs do not automatically or inherently satisfy all of these dimensions. What I had done was to enrich the job by providing feedback. I did not speed up the line, change the technology, implement gainsharing, involve the employees in participative management, change the standard or the method, or train the shaders. I simply built a scoreboard and gave them some feedback. *Measurement can be used effectively to drive and motivate performance improvement. It costs you very little to achieve these gains. The amount of gains to be achieved will vary from system to system. I had eliminated a specific cause of error from the system.*

3. The supervisor in this story is not the villain—he was not stupid, he was not wrong, *per se*, in what he did. He was simply doing the very best he could in a system that measured and rewarded and sanctioned the kind of behavior described. I had created a problem for him in that the rules of the game he had survived by and succeeded under called for empire building, not empire slashing. In improving performance of the paint line, I had inadvertently created an opportunity for the plant to improve its performance, but the opportunity for the plant was a threat to the supervisor. His world—domain—of twenty-two persons (ten shaders and twelve rework people) now could shrink to twelve persons (ten shaders and two rework people). His measurement and reward system—his perception of what constitutes a good job—does not call for constant improvement, but maintenance of the *status quo* or building a bigger empire.

4. A young, inexperienced industrial engineer or statistical quality control specialist might have looked at the data in Figure 5-7 and inferred that the system was in control—in steady state. By the numbers, this would be an understandable interpretation. They might have established a standard based upon the data that called for the shaders to never go below seventy percent good parts to total parts run. This scenario, as you well know, is all too conceivable. As Deming has pointed out, and as the data clearly show, some people have to reach up to standards, some have to reach down. In this case, almost all shaders were clearly reaching down. Standards for forecasting, or estimating, control are fine. The only acceptable standard for improvement and setting expectations is that of constant improvement. Do the best you can with the resources and culture and operating environment within which you exist. If management does their job, doing the best you can will be competitive. Building a culture that expects and measures and rewards constant improvement will alleviate the type of situation described in this case example. This process was not really in control at seventy percent good parts to total parts run. There was a significant level of special causes of error in the system. By providing feedback to the shaders, we were able to remove some of the special cause of error and increase performance to ninety-five percent. To improve the performance of this particular system to ninety-nine percent or higher would probably have required dealing with common causes of error inherent in the technology associated with painting (handspray) operations. Improvement of the quality of your management processes can significantly impact special causes and increase performance. How will you know if you don't develop the knowledge and don't measure?

5. My final comment: This example is not the exception but the rule in American organizations. Given the opportunity, I could replicate this example in your organiza-

tion. Measurement, when done properly, (i.e., linked to a purpose or goal that managers/ employees have accepted) can drive and motivate performance improvement. Measurement is the only mechanism by which you will know if you are systematically removing special and common causes of error from your systems and processes at a rapid enough rate. (Note: We have used the term special and common causes of error and not defined the terms. Our understanding from Deming, Juran, Ishikawa and others is that common causes of error are problems and causes that are common from plant to plant, operation to operation, location to location, and that cause performance to be less than perfect. Technological constraints might be a good example. There is inherent variation in all processes. Special causes of error in a system or process would be site or situation specific and, as Deming says, are the responsibility of management. The example just provided is a potential example of a special cause of error. In other plants, and specifically on other paint lines like the one described here, we might expect to see different patterns of variation due to differences in management processes. In this respect, the error we saw in the example is due to special causes, perhaps unique to this plant and line.)

Measurement can tell us where we need improvement, it can help us to prioritize where to devote our energies and resources, it can motivate, it can tell us when we've gotten better, and it is a natural and inherent part of the management process. Good, high-quality measurement systems don't just happen; they must be designed and developed and maintained. Well-designed and developed measurement systems linked to a business strategy that is understood and accepted can drive constant performance improvement. *Without improved measurement systems your New Competition is going to drive you out of business!*

Improvement as the driver of measurement. At the World Productivity Forum sponsored by the Institute of Industrial Engineers in May 1987, one of the plenary panel speakers asked a provocative question: "Do we motivate to measure or measure to motivate?" Do we or should we measure to drive improvement or improve and use measurement to confirm? As with most philosophical questions, the answer is probably that it depends, or that we do both. However, a recent project with Goddard Space Flight Center (GSFC) of NASA brought home to us the importance of thinking about improvement as the driver of measurement.

In 1985-86, Tuttle and Sink were invited by a productivity director to develop a white-collar productivity measurement pilot study. What we found, after several visits, was that interest on the part of the pilot organization for measuring white-collar productivity was not high. In fact, even though the pilot project was paid for by headquarters, the pilot organization management were not interested in sponsoring the project. They conveyed a strong interest in improving performance and removing roadblocks to performance but low to no interest in beginning with a measurement focus. Out of these discussions came a small project that developed a technique we call the roadblock identification, analysis and removal technique (RIART). This project is discussed in a short paper by Sink, Tuttle, and Das (1986).

We won't discuss this case example in detail; however, we do want to emphasize the lessons learned. In the action-oriented, firefighting, hectic, short-interval scheduling, pressure-packed world that you live in and that most management lives in, measurement beyond what is required to comply with requirements is extremely hard to justify. Most managers believe that they already measure too much—they are drowning in a sea of measurement. It's a Catch-22, in that most managers know they need and they want better information with which to make decisions, solve problems, and plan, but they also know they don't have time to do something about it. So they hire people to improve their management information systems who have not been trained to be customer-driven and, therefore, who add to the sea of data in which the manager is drowning. Measurement is not a high priority of most managers. This is true not because measurement isn't important, but because measurement is not done properly to support decision making, problem solving, and planning. Most, if not all, managers would rather act on intuition, impulse, and experience rather than work to improve the quality of their information system (Mintzberg 1986).

We have no general theory of measurement and few, if any, masters of measurement in our organizations. We have master accountants and standard setters but few, if any, master measurement systems people. As a result, measurement is simultaneously desired and rejected. This is why a user, customer-oriented process like management systems analysis (to be discussed in detail later in this chapter) to design the measurement system to truly support the manager's needs is so critical. Without theory, techniques, and masters to guide us, no progress will be made (Deming's personal remarks in an August 1987 teleconference).

We have learned from this experience and others that most managers would prefer an improvement/action-oriented approach to a measurement-to-improve approach. We have learned that coming in the back door to get at measurement is often the best tact to take. We developed a structured process by which engineers and scientists could identify roadblocks that were impeding them or preventing them from performing as well as they could or should, and found that it was extremely well-received by the engineers and scientists, and eventually by management. We involved the scientists and engineers in the process of developing ways to remove roadblocks and found that they enjoyed it and did a good job at it. We forced the engineers, scientists, and management to identify specific measures that they could monitor to tell them if, in fact, they were removing roadblocks and if, in fact, the roadblock removal was actually improving performance. We had to provide knowledge of what performance is and how to measure it. However, we found that the process was easier following the improvement orientation than it was when we had attempted to begin with measurement. We believe (we don't have a lot of empirical evidence, so we can't say we know) that beginning with an improvement orientation in many situations will make the measurement process much easier. In our opinion, this is because there is a natural motivation for measurement when it follows improvement—the need to have feedback.

In summary, in many settings the process for improvement of the quality of measurement systems may best be begun with a structured approach to improvement. We personally suggest that the improvement approach be structured and participative; however, the participative specification is less important than the specification for structure and follow-through.

Measurement as a tool to ensure strategy is implemented. The performance management process detailed in Chapter 2 and the performance improvement planning process discussed in Chapter 2 and detailed in Chapter 4 both emphasize the importance of linking measurement to strategy. The process by which we plan and the measurement and reward systems play major roles in determining whether or not an organization will effectively carry out its plans. Measurement systems and measures need to be designed for various units of analysis or levels of the organization, for various purposes, with various users and audiences in mind, and to consider data requirements and data availabilities. At all levels and for all users of measurement systems and measures, there exists, in our view, a need to use measurement as a mechanism for ensuring that plans are effectively implemented.

In the performance management process (Figure 2-1), we depicted at least two steps in the process where measurement is a predominant focus. We suggested that at the same time the organizational system is developing its performance improvement plan, the management team ought to be designing and developing, redesigning, auditing, or at least reviewing its total measurement systems for the organization. This would entail looking at all measurement systems within the organizational system and evaluating the effectiveness and quality. These systems would range from work measurement and performance appraisal to budget systems to total organizational productivity measurement systems to corporate finance systems to gainsharing measurement systems to project and program measurement systems. At this stage in the performance management process, we inferred that a thorough audit of all measurement systems was in order and that new systems might be required, old systems might need to be revamped or even deleted, or a total redesign might be in order. Note from Figure 2-1 that management systems development is preceded by an assessment of present organizational system performance and a review of management systems and processes, business strategy development, and visions of the Organization of the Future. All of these efforts are influenced by an analysis and understanding of The New Competition, by ongoing evaluation of our efforts to constantly improve performance, and undoubtedly, a number of other factors that we have neglected to depict in our model of this complex process. The point to be made is that measurement system development for the organizational system must be influenced by and reflect strategy. An element or subsystem of the measurement system must focus on tracking the extent to which the management team is progressing toward the specific business strategies identified in the process. In simplistic terms, we speak of effectiveness measures and impact measures. The effectiveness measures focus on simply answering the question as to whether or not we are doing what we said we would do. The impact measures focus on answering whether or not doing what we said we were going to do is having the impact we thought it would have on organizational systems performance.

Every level in the organization should have a plan and a strategy that is influenced, at least, by upline plans and strategies. We would hope that each organizational system within the whole organization is implementing in its own inimitable way the performance management process. The challenge becomes one of integrating and coordinating all of these management processes. Measurement systems and measures that focus on strategy implementation and strategy implementation impact and help to accomplish this goal of integration and coordination. Measurement in the form of key performance indicators (or whatever term you choose to give the measures that result from the measurement activity) creates a visibility for what the organizational system has actually committed to in terms of behavior accountability. It's very common for strategies to emerge from the planning process that sold well on paper, but when we begin to implement them we realize they either can't be done or shouldn't be done. As we said, planning is a very dynamic process. Developing measurement systems and measures that specifically link to the goals, objectives, and strategies developed forces those who must implement to think through cause-and-effect linkages, costs and benefits, and strategy implications. These effects are good. Measurement can also force the management team to think about the realities of implementing the strategies developed. They face the reality of being held accountable, and this can cause certain management team members to re-examine the risks and costs of implementing selected strategies. This introspection may cause managers to shift strategies from what really ought to be done to what we can realistically, easily, or without too much risk of failure actually do. These effects are bad. So, the point is that measurement, specifically measures that relate to strategy implementation and strategy implementation impact, is important but can create some dysfunctional as well as functional outcomes. This has to be managed.

Simply stated, what we have been talking about is the input, activity, output, and desired and actual outcome linkage. Figure 5-8 graphically depicts these relationships.

Our plan, in a sense, clarifies what our desired outcomes are. How will we know if we have achieved our desired outcomes? Our plan also describes and hopefully achieves some measure of consensus as to what specific outputs the organizational system is going to produce. These outputs, as you know, will be both of the tangible and intangible type. How will we know if we have produced the outputs, at the level of quality, we said we would produce? Our plan, in particular the plan coming from the performance improvement planning process described in Chapters 2 and 4, forces us to develop strategies for implementation. These strategies for implementation necessarily include specific action plans and activities that are designed—based upon beliefs and knowledge of cause-and-effect relationships—to accomplish outputs and outcomes. Should we measure activities? If we measure activities (path), do we run the risk of falling into an activity trap? Who should measure activities? My bias is that we would focus our measurement energies starting at the right side of Figure 5-8 and move to the left slowly, and when we run out of measurement energies or resources, stop measuring. My experience suggests that this is a fairly effective measurement strategy that, unfortunately, isn't practiced in many of the management processes I've seen.

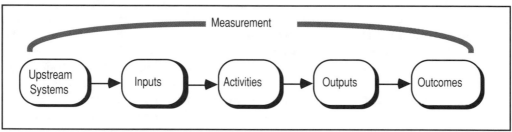

Figure   5-8.   Organizational   System   -   Measurement   Linkage

If done properly, measurement is an effective, perhaps necessary but probably not sufficient, tool to ensure strategy is implemented. Strategy at what level? Strategy at all levels! Starting with the largest unit of analysis the firm, corporation, center, or agency— the process of using measurement as a tool for forcing, in a natural way, accountability for strategy implementation is important to becoming the Organization of the Future. The process can work at the individual level and must work at the organizational level if the organization is to achieve its goal of constant improvement.

Measurement as a management support system. Electronic data processing systems, management information systems, decision support systems, management support systems: Are these buzz words? A management support system is a system that supports management. What does that mean? Kurstedt (1986) defines, or describes, and depicts a management system as three components and their interrelationships. Figure 5-9 presents Kurstedt's Management Systems Model.

KURSTEDT'S MSM

Who is managing, what is being managed, and what is managed with—these are the three components of a management system. Kurstedt defines the interrelationships and associated interfaces. He describes three interfaces:

1. The measure-to-data interface between what is being managed and tools (what it is being managed with);
2. The portrayal to perception interface between tools and who is managing; and
3. The decision-to-action interface between who is managing and what is being managed.

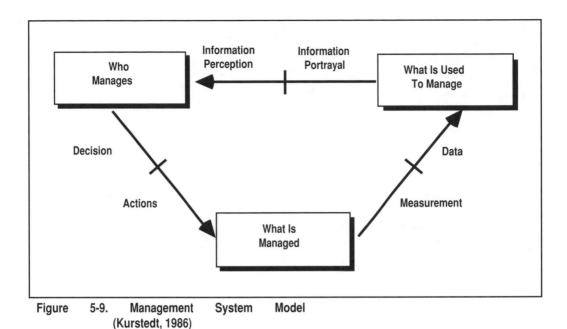

Figure   5-9.   Management   System   Model (Kurstedt, 1986)

The model clearly comes at the management process from an information flow perspective, and with minor modification we can focus on the measurement process perspective.

Modified MSM

Figure 5-10 depicts a slightly modified view of the management systems model. If, as we have suggested from the beginning of this book, we view the most important job that a management team has to perform as constantly improving the performance of the organizational system for which they are responsible, then we see that this process is represented by the improvement intervention process in the model. This is what Kurstedt calls the decision-to-action interface. We identify this with a number two in a circle. Can improvement interventions on an organizational system be made without support information (i.e., inference is that measurement of some sort will take place?) In the real world, the answer is that some can be made without any formal information and some can't. Many decisions and actions are made in your organization without formal support information. On the other side of the coin, however, there are many decisions and actions that require formal information and analysis. The management systems model developed by Kurstedt and expanded upon by Sink doesn't neglect the informal nature of decision making and improvement interventions. The "tools" box in the model includes the managers' and management teams' wisdom, judgment, intuition, and experience as a form of data-to-information transformation process. The model recognizes that measurement happens formally and informally and that both forms of measurement are the basis upon which decisions and actions to improve performance are made.

Then one important role of measurement is as a management support system. Measurement does support the process of management. What is the process or are the processes of management? Barnard (1939) suggests that there are three functions of the executive:

1. To provide a system of communication;
2. To maintain the willingness to cooperate; and
3. To ensure the continuing integrity of organization purpose.

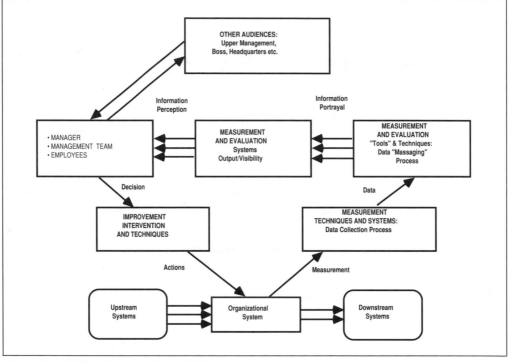

Figure 5-10.   Modified   Management   Systems   Model

Barnard ends his dissertation of the executive function with a discussion of leadership as the personal capacity for affirming decisions that lend quality and morality to the coordination of organized activity and to the formulation of purpose. Others, namely Szilagyi (1981), view the manager's job and management process as:

1. Deciding what to do;
2. Deciding how to do it;
3. Directing performance;
4. Evaluating performance; and
5. Deciding what should be changed.

He goes on to conceptualize the process of management as planning, organizing, leading, control, and change. Thompson (1967) sees the management process (he calls it the administrative process) as one of co-alignment of people, institutionalized action, technology, task environment, and organizational design and structure. When the process is working well, he suggests that the organization is "kept at the nexus of the several necessary streams of action." He views the management process as a continual and complex attempt to manage:

1. The certainty associated with and consensus for preferences regarding desired outcomes (goals, objectives, and strategies);
2. Beliefs and knowledge about cause-and-effect relationships (technology/path); and
3. The crystallization and clarity of standards of desirability or assessment criteria (measurement).

All the management-related books I've read in the past ten years have merely elaborated upon or embellished the views of these three authors. In my opinion, the management process is clearly depicted. The management process is clearly not as easily executed as it is written about. I borrow a quote from the end of Barnard's classic book entitled, *The Functions of the Executive*:

> Anyone who sees this, naturally rushes to the conclusion of which I was speaking, that no mortal legislates in anything, but that in human affairs chance is almost everything. And this may be said of the arts of the sailor, and the pilot, and the physician, and the general, (author insertion: and the management systems engineer?) and may seem to be well said; and yet there is another thing which may be said with equal truth of all of them. What is it? That God governs all things, and that chance and opportunity cooperate with Him in the government of human affairs. There is, however, a third and less extreme view, that art should be there also; for I should say that in a storm there must surely be great advantage in having the aid of the pilot's art. Would you agree? (Plato, *Laws*).

As the complexity of the system being managed increases and our knowledge of cause-and-effect relationships improves, the sophistication of and maturity of our measurement systems will or can or should increase/improve appropriately. Measurement is an integral part of the management process. Measurement is the foundation of the development of support systems for planning, problem solving, decision making, improvement, control, adaptation, motivation, and even leadership. Measurement plays a critical role in the development of improved management support systems.

Measurement as a control device. Do we measure: to improve? to control? to gain visibility? because we are required to? to satisfy someone else's needs? because it's what we've always done? or to comply? Does control precede improvement, or does improvement lead to control? If we measure to control, do we hinder our chances for improvement? If we measure for improvement, how do we know if we are in control? Does Deming mean don't measure when he says, "throw out all standards, numerical quotas, targets"? Is measurement for control a legitimate goal in the Organization of the Future? These are tough questions, some of which we have already attempted to answer.

Measurement as a control device is probably the most familiar and most frequent application of measurement. We measure or someone or something measures for us, we evaluate, and we exert influence or make an intervention on the thing we are measuring in an attempt to control. Control is an outcome resulting from an intervention. Control is not an output. The intervention we make to establish or re-establish control is one of improvement. It is a common misunderstanding that one controls to establish improvement. The self-control of a process is an improvement intervention. Imposed control is less improvement intervention than we would like to believe. The effective implementation of a control intervention is directly related to the quality of that intervention and the acceptance of that intervention. If we have a high-quality intervention that is not accepted by those who must ultimately implement and maintain implementation of the control intervention, follow-through and actual implementation will be of low quality.

One of Deming's fourteen principles suggests that we should throw out all standards, remove all quotas, and cease managing by the numbers. Many have interpreted, incorrectly we believe, this as saying we should not measure. We assert that Deming is making an important point about measurement as a control device. In particular, we believe that he is sharing wisdom regarding the important difference between measurement as a control device and measurement as an issue —the red bead experiment (Deming 1986); "some have to reach up, some down"

(Deming 1986); and define the process, control the process, then improve the process, as well as the need for and importance of operational definitions (Deming 1986).

Measurement is useful and necessary for gainsharing systems, incentive systems, forecasting, cost estimating, budgeting, decision making, problem solving, planning, and many other management activities. Measurement is also useful and necessary for motivation, improvement, feedback, knowledge of results, driving constant improvement, and many other management activities. Research in the area of performance appraisals has indicated that managers and performance appraisals have at least two major functions— that of development, improvement, assessment and appraisal and that of control, evaluation, distribution or rewards (Meyers, et. al. 1965; Kanter and Brinkerhoff 1980). The research called this the "split roles in performance appraisal." The conclusion of the research was that performance appraisal—a measurement-oriented activity—has two roles to fulfill, and that one system, one performance appraisal session cannot satisfy both of those roles since they conflict with one another. One role of performance appraisal is that of evaluation—grading performance and linking to reward systems; this is a control-oriented measurement system. Another role of performance appraisal is that of assessment, development, and improvement and requires another set of behaviors related to measurement from the manager and the employee. Anyone who has ever sat through a performance appraisal session has felt the incongruity between the two intended roles. You also know that the role that dominates and wins out in these sessions is the one of evaluation, judgment, control, and grading. The reason is simple—the manager has an immediate and pressing need to fill in blanks on a performance appraisal form that has to be turned in to personnel by Friday noon. Raises, budgets, promotions, and other important systems are dependent upon this information. As such, the upline need for this information and the unwillingness of most managers to separate the performance appraisal process into two separate sessions is one of the most critical roadblocks to the success of this process in American organizations. We try to make one measurement system satisfy two uniquely different requirements and that hasn't and won't work.

Let's try to extrapolate from lessons learned with performance appraisal — a measurement process— to measurement as a control device. "When you establish a standard, a target to meet, some people have to reach up to achieve it and some people have to reach down" (Deming 1987). He speaks to the different applications of measurement and standards. He speaks of the difference between measurement for control versus measurement for improvement. Measurement and standards are important for communicating specifications, forecasting, budgeting, and knowing whether the system is in or out of control. Standards used for the purpose of improvement, driving continuous improvement, are self-defeating. Measurement is necessary for the purpose of improvement, driving continuous improvement. Industrial engineering is alive and well, and the role of setting standards is still a valid role. However, the industrial engineer had better learn how to apply work measurement. We must learn to separate the process of measurement from the process of evaluation in our applications.

When we measure an attribute for a specific criterion, track it over time, and establish an understanding of statistical variation, perhaps even develop upper and lower control limits, all we have done is to define what the particular process we are studying can do relative to that specific attribute. Say we are measuring paint runs on parts coming off a paint line or number of misaligned pages on copy jobs. We track these errors over time, statistically analyze the variation and develop some parameters for the variation (i.e., means, measures of dispersion, and so forth). We can determine if the process, with respect to these attributes, is in or out of control. The upper and lower control limits and the mean don't really tell us whether performance is good, bad, or indifferent. The data simply tell us how well the process can perform relative to the particular attributes we are measuring. This is the measurement process. The evaluation process involves judgment and discretion, as well as actual knowledge of what the requirements and specifications are relative to how well the process is performing. The actual act of comparing actual performance to the standards (i.e., engineered standards, customer specifications, past performance—how well we did yesterday, heuristically developed standard, and organizational system requirements) is the process of evaluation.

Let's use the appliance manufacturing plant's refrigerator paint line example to clarify. You will recall from the recent section where we discussed measurement as a driver of performance improvement that I decided to post the number of good parts/total number of parts run as the measure of performance for the shaders on the paint line. I decided what to measure somewhat autocratically—decided how to operationalize the specific measure (which in this case wasn't that hard since the measure was countable and the data was available), plotted the data over time, shared the results, and, as you saw, performance improved significantly. I'll repeat, briefly, the points made in that section. I measured and shared results—created feedback/knowledge of results—and the shaders did the evaluation. There were no engineered standards; there wasn't even a statistical upper-control limit established. I just plotted the data over time and shared the results. Again, this does not imply that evaluation is not an important part of measurement. In order for measurement to be utilized, put to work, evaluation has to take place. Deming and others are simply asking us to examine our paradigms and consider the effectiveness and efficiency of having someone other than the people doing the work do the evaluation.

Does evaluation lead to control? I think the answer is yes. Unknowingly, I was after control of the shading process on the paint line. With knowledge of results, we almost simultaneously controlled variance and shifted the mean. The process came under control, and we could now move to other processes and do the same thing. What prevented us from spreading this success throughout that entire plant? The bottom-line answer was management. However, the direct aspects of the organizational system that prevented further success was the culture—the lack of a performance improvement management process, improper measurement systems, lack of measurement systems, a messed-up reward system, incorrect knowledge and perception of what the organization really needs and wants from its employees, no management of participation, and an operating principle that is guided by the fallacy of the "one great brain" strategy.

Is measurement a control device? The answer is yes. Measurement is inextricably linked to evaluation, which is intended to improve and control. The questions being raised regarding measurement today focus on how we are measuring, how we are evaluating, and how we are controlling and improving performance in all the processes within our organization. The concern is that we are not nearly proactive enough at improvement and control to respond to the challenges being posed by the new competition. The concern and belief by Deming and others is that we have assumed that someone besides the people doing the work should measure, evaluate, and control performance. As we move from control-oriented organizations toward commitment-oriented organizations, we will have to modify, sometimes significantly, how we use measurement as a control device. An important outcome of measurement is control of variance in performance—the question is who is doing the control. Your organization can continue to operate with the paradigm that promotes attempts to inspect performance into the products and services your organization is producing. Or, you can become an Organization of the Future and develop a new operating philosophy and culture that supports moving the responsibility and accountability for measurement, evaluation, and control to the lowest appropriate level.

Measurement as an improvement device. Measurement, evaluation, control, improvement; measurement, evaluation, improvement, control; improvement, measurement, evaluation, control: What is the proper sequence of these components of the measurement process? Ishikawa, Juran, Deming, and other quality management experts suggest that we must understand the process (define it), control the variance in the process, and then shift the mean in the performance of the process. They view everything that goes on in the organization as a process. I guess the fundamental question is, how does improvement in complex organizations come about? What role does measurement play in the improvement process? We've discussed this relationship at reasonable length in this section, and I don't want to be repetitive. I hope by now that you are convinced that measurement is an improvement device, in and of itself. I hope you now know that you can't have control—true control—without measurement. You cannot manage what you cannot control. I guess that would infer, logically, that you can't manage what you can't measure. It's really not that complex, but it sure is easy to lose sight of the forest for the trees when you try to do it in a real organization. We know that because we do it for a living to our own organizations and for other people's organizations. The struggles and challenges we have experienced and encountered over the past ten years or so have lead us to a fairly systematic thought process regarding how you go about the task of designing and developing measurement and evaluation systems for complex organizations. We each have slightly different preferred methodologies or approaches, however, we've tried to blend them into one integrated approach. We will share the lessons we've learned and wisdom we've gained in the remainder of this chapter. Let us repeat, for emphasis, at this point the belief/conviction we hold regarding measurement: "The most important role of measurement is that of an improvement device."

The Decision to Measure

We have said that performance measurement should be viewed as a tool for improvement. We have also pointed out that measurement should be viewed as an integral part of the management process that is required to enhance organizational system performance. In making the decision to implement a new measurement process or to redesign an existing measurement process, there are several considerations that the designer should bear in mind. These include the impact of measurement on performance, the need for acceptance of the measuring process, measurement to enhance observation, the limitations of measurement, and the applicability of measurement.

Measurement of an aspect of an organizational system's performance sends signals throughout the organization as to what the manager views as important. Because of this impact of measurement, it is important that we measure the right things. Since resources, time, and materials tend to flow from unmeasured to measured aspects of organization performance, we need to ensure that the measurement system covers the key facets of an organization's mission, purposes, and objectives.

A second consideration is that, in order for a measurement system to serve as a force for improvement, it must be understood and accepted by users of the system. If not, users will find ways to avoid, fake, or otherwise defeat the system. This is especially true when measurement is used to drive improvement. Many elegant measurement systems imposed by top management or staff experts have failed because they did not gain the acceptance of those being measured. One way to increase understanding and acceptance by users of a measurement system is to involve them in its development.

A third important consideration is that measurement is a substitute for, or can at least enhance, direct observation. When measurement for improvement is the goal, measurement can serve as a substitute for direct observation of performance. In this sense, measurement gives us visibility where it might otherwise be difficult. An axiom that has guided managers through the years is to ensure that critical aspects of performance are carried out through inspection. In most organizations of any size, it is impossible for the manager to inspect physically all aspects of performance on an ongoing basis. Therefore, measurement becomes a substitute for direct observation. In addition, in white-collar jobs, knowledge work, or service organizations, products or services are often intangible; therefore, measurement becomes a way that the efforts or organizational system members are made more concrete and visible. Thus, measurement serves as feedback to allow members to know how well they are doing. In this way measurement is a critical component of the motivation process.

The point is that users of measurement data must understand its limitations. At best, performance measurement is imperfect. It is subject to fluctuations or special causes that are sometimes out of the control of the measured organizational system. Usually, despite considerable efforts, not all aspects of performance are feasible to measure in a formal way. Thus, measurement data must be interpreted with judgment. For example, when the number of hours to design a new work process exceeds the estimate by thirty percent, this may be understood to be just a necessary price of on-the-job training for two new engineers who joined the design team. However, someone up the chain of command who notices this drop in efficiency might attribute it to other causes (e.g., poor engineering management) and take actions that are inappropriate.

The final point to consider is that despite protestations to the contrary, most organizational systems' performance can be measured. Given the time and resources, and a master to drive the process, almost anything can be measured. However, the utility of measurement may be a different issue. Not all aspects of performance that can be measured are worth the cost. Determination of measurement feasibility and utility is ultimately a judgment of the manager of the organizational system. However, it is often difficult to determine the value of a particular measurement indicator until it has been tracked for some time period. Therefore, managers are cautioned to reserve judgment on the feasibility and utility of indicators until there is some data on which to make a valid judgment.

Who decides to begin? The decision to develop and implement or modify a measurement system maybe the decision of the manager of the organizational system or an improvement team. While the manager must commit if the process is to work, there may be outside influences on the decision. A corporate mandate, a presidential executive order, an audit report, or increased competitive pressure could all be forces that would trigger a manager to decide to begin. The best motive, even when there is outside pressure, is for the manager to decide that the measurement system is to be developed primarily for his management team's own needs. If the manager feels coercion, then communicates to his subordinates that someone else is forcing us to develop the measurement system, the likelihood of successful implementation is very low.

President Reagan issued an executive order that required all federal agencies to identify selected functions that must increase productivity by twenty percent by 1992. As we observe agencies approaching this activity, there is a clear difference between those who are simply trying to comply with a requirement from the Office of Management and Budget and those who look at the executive order as an opportunity to make fundamental changes in the way the organization does business. Those taking the latter approach have a much greater chance of successfully implementing a performance measurement and improvement effort. Those taking the former approach are essentially saying to staff people, "Do what you have to to comply but don't rock the boat or bother me with the effort." The reports will show that the agency is in compliance, but nothing will have changed.

In the Organization of the Future, we suspect that the decision to continually improve measurement systems will be made by the management team, not just the manager. There will be a critical mass of masters of measurement in the organizational systems of the Organization of the Future, and these masters will be driving the continual development of improved measurement.

How is the decision made? As with any organizational decision, the process depends on the nature of the decision. A decision regarding the development of a productivity measurement process normally is not especially time critical. It does require acceptance for successful implementation. The information required to successfully develop and implement a system is generally dispersed, although the manager may be the primary person with access to information regarding the need to develop or improve the measures currently in use. These conditions argue for a consultative or participative decision process. However, the manager should be cautioned not to present the decision as a participative one if a decision has already been made or if the organization has no choice in the matter. In that case, the manager may present to the group the issue of what type of measurement process to implement, since a decision to implement a process has already been made.

As we have indicated before, four basic factors need to be considered when determining the approach to take in making the decision:

1. The need for acceptance on the part of users of the measurement system as it relates to driving improvement with the measurement system must be considered;
2. The need for quality in the resulting measurement system as it relates to who has the information necessary to develop a successful measurement system and drive improvement;
3. The availability of time for development of the measurement system; and
4. The maturity (ability and willingness) of users of the system as it relates to the task of developing and using the measurement system.

As we move from control-oriented, manager-led organizations toward commitment-oriented, self-managed organizations a greater and greater percentage of the decisions associated with measurement system development will be shared with the management team.

How should the process be implemented? There are a number of implementation issues facing the manager who decides to implement a measurement process. Once you have decided to begin, your first task is to clearly frame in your mind the reasons why you feel performance enhancement is essential to your organization. This step is necessary because you will have to write down this rationale and articulate this vision to members of the organization many times as the process unfolds. People don't get excited about having their performance measured for its own sake. While feedback regarding how well they are doing is interesting, and while setting up competition against themselves over time or against similar organizations can stimulate performance gains, people need reasons for their actions. As a manager, you must help your people understand why performance improvement can help your organization, and perhaps most importantly, "what's in it for them." The most important phase of a performance improvement effort is creating awareness at all levels in the organization regarding why it is important.

As you work through this phase of the process you should discuss your ideas with your boss, your subordinates, and the individuals you select to be the measurement masters for your organization. Your vision must become a shared vision if it is to energize and guide your efforts to improve performance. You cannot depend on measurement as the driver of performance improvement. If you do, and there is no shared vision or understanding of the business strategy, you will generate resistance and motivation to fake the measures, and performance improvements that do occur will be difficult to sustain. This highlights the importance of linking your measurement efforts to the planning process we have discussed.

A critical early decision is who to involve in the measurement development process. A simple guideline is to involve those who will be affected by or will use the measures; if not all those who will be affected, at least involve people who represent the viewpoints of all those who will be affected. While there are major benefits from involvement, there are also costs that must be weighed. The tangible costs are the time of people who will participate and the inevitable anxiety associated with change. If the organization has not had a history of participative management, there will be costs with respect to moving to a new management style (e.g., more time to make a decision, managers will need to learn new behaviors, and so forth). If there has not been a history of involving people and sharing business information, the quality of input from organization members may be low due to their lack of opportunity to understand the broader issues that may impact measurement system development. These issues are raised to point out that participative approaches are not a panacea. For most organizations, involving management and nonmanagement employees in the measurement development and implementation process will be the recommended approach. However, this should be a conscious decision, not one made because it is in vogue or because we recommend this approach.

If the decision is made to use a participative approach, then a measurement master with good facilitation skills will be needed. The measurement facilitator generally is someone external to your organization, who is skilled in group process activities (e.g., running meetings, facilitating group discussions, interviewing, and listening) and who understands the basics of organizational performance measurement. Experience suggests that the combination of skills is critical to the success of the process. If it is not possible to find someone with good group process skills and measurement knowledge, then go with someone who has group process skills. It is easier for that person to learn what they need to know about measurement than for an individual with measurement knowledge to learn group process skills. The worst mistake a facilitator can make is to try to steer an organization toward the facilitator's solution. In our experience, management analysts and industrial engineers who are in staff roles relative to the target organization often have a tendency to try to impose their solutions. In every case, this strategy backfires and the measures are rejected.

The implementation plan. The culmination of the decision to measure is the development of a measurement implementation plan. This may be a formal, detailed plan as is appropriate for a multiyear implementation in a very large multinational organization. For a small organization it may be a very informal list of things to do. However, regardless of the scope of the plan, the thought process is basically the same.

The first step is to consider the audiences for the measurement information. Who will the measurement data be reported to? Obviously there are many choices at this point. For an improvement-oriented measurement system, which we are discussing, you as the manager of the target organizational system are a principal audience. However, to engage the power of feedback, the measurement data should also be reported to your organization members. If you keep the numbers in your desk, you are failing to gain the power for improvement that is possible from a participatively developed measurement process. The appliance manufacturing example discussed earlier is an example of what can happen when the members of an organization receive feedback on a measure they accept and understand. So your people are another audience.

What about your boss? What do you tell your boss? Not so much that he can micro-manage you. On the other hand he probably needs enough information to feel comfortable that you have things under control and that performance is moving in the right direction. Also, he needs to avoid surprises. So he will probably need enough data to convince him that you will keep him out of trouble. Over time, as he understands that your system is under control, the amount of information he needs should decline.

There are other potential audiences, e.g., control agencies, internal staff groups, board of directors, the media, advertising department, and more. At this stage you need to identify the major ones; the others you can take care of later.

Once you have identified the audiences, you need to decide what they need and when they need it. While you haven't yet decided what you will be measuring, the easiest thing to do is to sketch out a blank report format for each of the target audiences. This will surface some important questions. First, it will make you more explicit about the exact purpose for the measurement data. Will it be for a monthly operations report to help you judge whether your organization is moving toward strategic targets along a family of measures representing your mission? Or will the data be used to develop a formula for sharing productivity gains with your people? Perhaps you will decide that the purpose is really twofold. One is to provide data to corporate in three strategically selected areas, but it is also to guide my resource allocation decisions to allow me to make sure that these three corporate screening indicators actually improve. Honeywell Aerospace had such a measurement system. Each Honeywell facility had to report to corporate on three areas of strategic focus—value added per employee, inventory reduction as a percentage of sales, and scrap/rework as a percentage of sales. Anything else the managers tracked was for their own information.

Once you are clear on the purpose for the improvement-oriented measurement effort, you need to think about the frequency of reporting and the form of the report. Frequency depends to a degree on the nature of the operation and the nature of the aspect of performance being measured. However, a rule of thumb for performance improvement is the more frequent the feedback, the better. For in-process quality measurement, hourly measures on most processes are desirable in short-cycle operations. The most common time periods are weekly or monthly. However, the measurement time period should fit the need, not the calendar or the demands of the bean-counters.

The format for the measurement report should respond to the needs of the users. You may have to ask them for those other than yourself. You may want your people to help design the feedback to employees. Using the analogy of the aircraft instrument panel, the issue here is not what the gauges are at this point, but what should the instrument panel look like and where should the gauges be located. The basic choice here is between graphic portrayal and tabular data. Generally, for feedback to employees— e.g., on a bulletin board or a visibility room—graphic is preferable.

Once the audience analysis has been conducted, it is important to analyze the driving and restraining forces associated with measurement system implementation. The technique suggested for this analysis is force-field analysis. Force-field analysis is a structured way for an individual or a group to analyze the "forces for" and "forces against" the successful implementation of a decision or change. When applied in this context, the goal is successful implementation of a performance measurement process.

Figure 5-11 presents a sample force-field analysis conducted for an organization considering measurement system implementation. This was done with the division managers of the organization. The force field technique allows for the scaling of the forces so that it is possible to quantify their relative strength. This is usually not necessary in the present applications.

Once the force-field analysis has been conducted, it leads directly to the implementation plan. The implementation process must essentially have two parts. It must focus on accomplishing the tasks—generating the data that is called for in the audience analysis. It must also deal with acceptance by the various audiences. The force-field analysis provides data that allows the management team to plan implementation actions that will serve to increase the "forces for" successful implementation and minimize the "forces against" successful implementation. Using the example presented here, a carefully developed communications program can help minimize many of the forces against successful implementation. It can address the fear of losing resources and the fear of exposing inadequate performance by pointing out how the data will be used and noting that identification of poor performance areas provides opportunities. Honesty is important in communications, so the manager should point out that if the performance continues to be

Figure 5-11. A Sample Force-Field Analysis

inadequate then action may have to be taken. However, this will be a last resort after ample opportunity has been given to correct the problem.

Of course, it is possible to impose the measurement process on the organization through an increase in management support: You can ram it down their throats. When implementation plans focus only on increasing the "forces for" without acknowledging and reducing the "forces against," they generally encounter resistance that may come back in other forms. People may not fight this implementation if enough force is applied, but this hostility will be redirected toward other targets to the detriment of organizational performance.

Deciding What to Measure

Once the decision has been made to measure and support measurement, a second fundamental question arises: What are we going to measure? Just as the decision to measure question seemed simplistic on the surface, so does this question. However, as we saw with the decision to measure, there is a lot that might not meet the eye at first glance. Easy answers to this question are: let the people in the system decide what to measure; let management decide what to measure, and let the people in the system do it; let the industrial engineer decide; let a consultant decide; go to the literature and find out what people like us measure, and copy what makes sense; and the government has already decided—we'll just measure what they tell us to measure. How do we know if any of those approaches are really getting at the right set of measures—the complete set or the best set? We would like to start this section off by giving you some background information that many have found very useful for developing a high-quality answer to this important question of what to measure.

Operational definition of performance and its major subcomponents

"Meaning starts with the concept, which is in somebody's mind, and only there: it is ineffable. An operational definition puts communicable meaning into a concept. An operational definition is one that people can do business with. Practice is more exacting than pure science; more exacting than teaching. The dictionary provides a concept, not a definition for use in industry" (Deming 1986). There is a deficiency in the operational definitions of the term performance and its components in present practice in American organizations. We find a field filled with academicians who are attempting to approach measurement and improvement of organizational systems with weak conceptual models and no operational definitions. We find the field filled with practitioners with no conceptual models and weak operational definitions. The result is confusion in the literature and in practice. What follows is another attempt to reduce some of the confusion. Our goal is to operationally define the performance of an organizational system. The purpose is to provide operational definitions such that the task of measurement can become less mysterious.

The analogy we prefer to use is one of an instrument panel for an airplane. The discussion to follow will define the major categories or clusters of instruments your organizational systems need to be looking at in order to measure, evaluate, control, and improve performance. In other words, we will be defining, operationally, clusters of instruments, not the specific instruments themselves. An airplane example would be: engine performance instruments, not cylinder head temperature; or airplane location instruments, not an altimeter or compass; or airplane perform- ance, not an airspeed indicator or rate of climb indicator. We will be operationally defining what we believe to be a comprehensive set of performance measurement criteria that every organiza- tional system must monitor. You will have to determine the specific measures that will operationalize each of the criterion. This approach has provided many mangers and management teams with a much more systematic and higher-quality approach to developing measurement systems over the past five years. We'll begin by examining your organization and sub- organizations from a general systems model perspective.

Systems view of your organization. Every organizational system (again, an organizational system is a firm, corporation, plant, function, group, branch, section, division, strategic business unit, department, or even small group activity) can be described and depicted in a general systems model fashion. Figure 5-12 depicts your organization in this fashion.

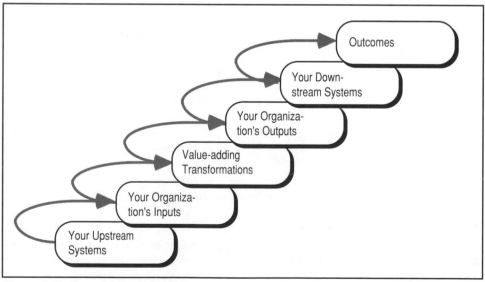

Figure 5-12. Organizational System

Note that this isn't a very complex or sophisticated view of your organization. However, it does contain some of the major components and the basic flow of resources. In particular, it provides a useful way of thinking about the performance of your organization. Note, also, that this figure is essentially the same as the middle portion of the performance management process flow diagram that has been presented and discussed throughout the book to this point. Important aspects of this view of your organization are the fact that we identify upstream and downstream systems and, of course, their respective interfaces. So, we see a picture that reinforces that every organization, every individual, and every organizational system has customers, suppliers and vendors, systems or people they receive inputs from and systems or people they provide outputs to. Every organizational system has inputs, value-adding transformation processes or activities, outputs, and outcomes. This all seems simple, and yet we find that when we work with management teams in specific organizations that there is not a good understanding of these elements. Our observation is that it's pretty hard to measure productivity, or any other aspect of performance, when you can't agree on issues such as what your outputs are.

Now, representing your department or work group or division or plant or company using this resource flow systems model isn't that unique. General systems analogies for organizations have been around for a long time. Ludwig von Bertalanffy is credited with the development of general systems theory in the 1950s. He published a book entitled *General Systems Theory* in 1973. Since that time, most management texts have relied on these concepts to develop improved understanding of complex organizations. Several classic management texts that have relied heavily on systems models for describing complex organizations are: *Organizations* (March and Simon 1958); *The Social Psychology of Organizations* (Katz and Kahn 1978); and *Organizations in Action* (Thompson 1967). It seems academicians have grown tired of the analogy, and practitioners have had difficulty seeing the pragmatic application. Is the systems view of an organization more than just an interesting way of conceptually depicting what an organization does? We think it is if, and only if, you develop practical applications from the model itself.

We want to do at least two practical things with the systems view of your organization. First, we want to use this view to operationally define performance. We believe this has not been done successfully in either the rigor or relevance literature in the business arena. Second, we will use the systems view of your organization to develop a technique called input/output (I/O) analysis. Input/output analysis is a technique that is useful for assisting management teams with developing a better understanding of what they are supposed to be doing; building an improved customer focus, an improved supplier, vendor, upstream system relationship, and a solid foundation from which to develop improved measurement systems. A sneak preview of the results of an input-output analysis may help you to better understand how we will actually apply the systems view of your organization. We insert Figure 5-13 at this point to accomplish this. Figure 5-13 is a completed input/output analysis for an aircraft Intermediate maintenance department aboard an aircraft carrier. A simplistic description of what AIMD does would be that they fix "Top Gun's" airplane when he comes back from missions. The input-output analysis output reveals, however, that a lot more happens in an AIMD than just fixing parts. We won't, at this point, go through a detailed description of this completed I/O analysis, but we encourage you to study it for a couple of minutes in order to get a feel for the types of things that are captured.

Let's now transition to using the systems view of your organization as a tool for better understanding performance. The systems view of organizations presented earlier provides a framework for analyzing performance in terms that are amenable to measurement. Therefore, the first step in the decision of what to measure is to gain a better understanding of the organizational system for which measures are to be developed. The basic system concepts defined earlier are the primary issues to be addressed. A useful way to define the system is to construct a system diagram as shown in Figure 5-14.

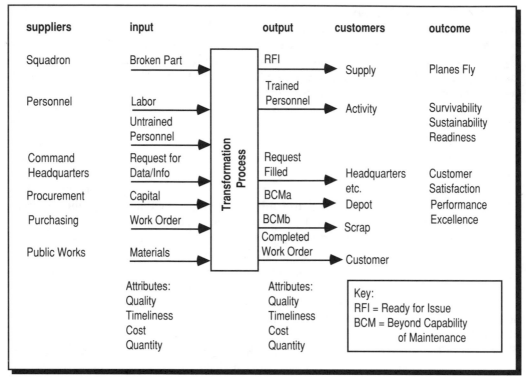

suppliers	input		output	customers	outcome
Squadron	Broken Part		RFI	Supply	Planes Fly
Personnel	Labor	Transformation Process	Trained Personnel	Activity	Survivability Sustainability Readiness
	Untrained Personnel				
Command Headquarters	Request for Data/Info		Request Filled	Headquarters etc.	Customer Satisfaction
Procurement	Capital		BCMa	Depot	Performance Excellence
Purchasing	Work Order		BCMb	Scrap	
			Completed Work Order		
Public Works	Materials			Customer	

Attributes:
Quality
Timeliness
Cost
Quantity

Attributes:
Quality
Timeliness
Cost
Quantity

Key:
RFI = Ready for Issue
BCM = Beyond Capability
       of Maintenance

Figure 5-13. Example of Input/Output Analysis for an Aircraft Intermediate Maintenance Depot

This diagram depicting a federal government agency, the Office of Device Evaluation in the Food and Drug Administration, illustrates a completed diagram. The measurement facilitator completes this diagram in conjunction with the representatives of the target organization. A completed diagram for a public power company is presented as Figure 5-15.

This framework can also be utilized to provide a way of considering the relative importance of the seven performance criteria defined here. While all seven criteria are relevant to all organizational systems, their relative importance varies as a function of the type of system.

Direct outcome, indirect outcome, and unknown outcome systems. For this discussion we can consider three types of systems: direct outcome, indirect outcome, and unknown outcome. A direct outcome system is depicted in Figure 5-16. In this example, the output of the system virtually assures the outcome. While there is some choice of the form, design, or means of presenting the output, the range of output variability is quite low. Examples of direct outcome systems include automated batch manufacturing, a copy center, an automated emissions testing facility, a supply room, an appliance repair facility, and bank tellers. In each of these systems, the outcomes follow the outputs with a high degree of certainty.

As a result, the major considerations on the part of the producing system are efficiency, productivity, and quality. The organization is concerned with efficiency because it must be concerned with using its resources skillfully in order to produce a sufficient quantity of outputs in the appropriate time period. It is concerned with quality because a principal outcome—customer satisfaction—is directly related to the extent to which the output corresponds to customer requirements. In this type of system, effectiveness—choice of the appropriate output—is less of

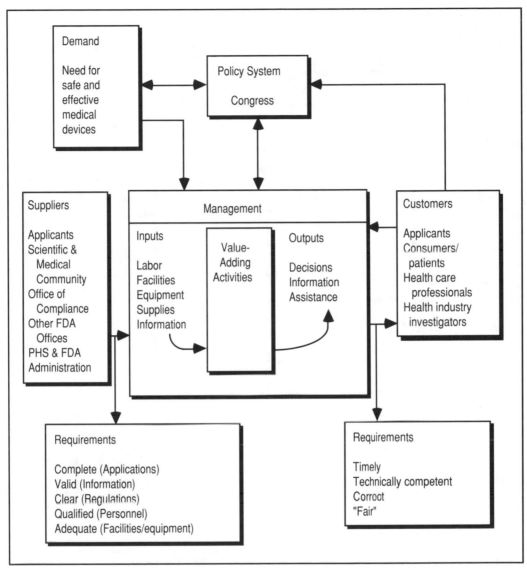

Figure 5-14. A System Diagram for the Office of Device Evaluation

a concern because there is little discretion on the part of people working in the system with respect to the outputs produced.

Figure 5-17 depicts an indirect outcome system. In this type of system, the range of variability of outputs is considerably greater. The system must choose among a range of possible outputs those which will produce the most favorable outcome. Only after the outputs are clearly specified should the system focus on improving the efficiency with which those outputs are produced. The first concern is whether the outputs are the right outputs. Examples of indirect outcome systems are weather forecasters, design engineering groups, software development organizations, consulting firms, and bank trust officers. In each of these organizations, the manager or organization member makes choices among a range of possible outputs those which are most appropriate in terms of helping the organization accomplish its mission. Effectiveness,

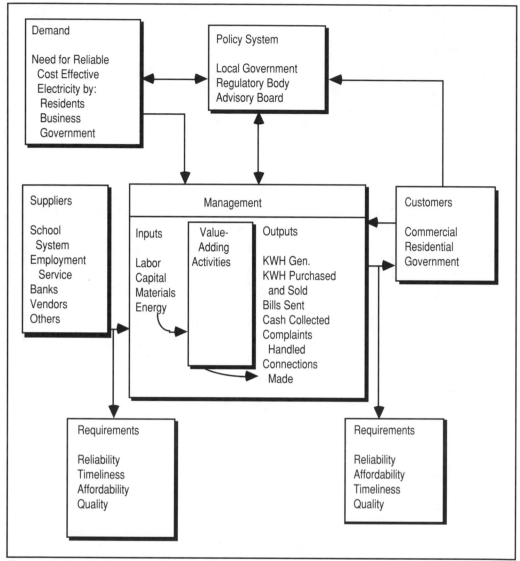

Figure 5-15. A System Diagram for a Public Power Company

the extent to which the outputs lead to desired outcome, is a major criterion of organizational performance. Efficiency and productivity are also very important but only after the organization has determined that it is producing the right outputs.

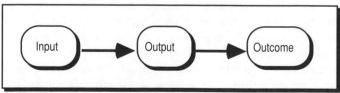

Figure 5-16. Direct Outcome System

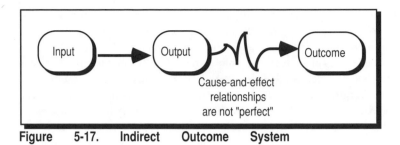

Figure   5-17.   Indirect   Outcome   System

Figure 5-18 presents a third type of system, the unknown outcome system. An unknown outcome system is one that prepares to perform its mission but may never actually have to perform in an operational environment.

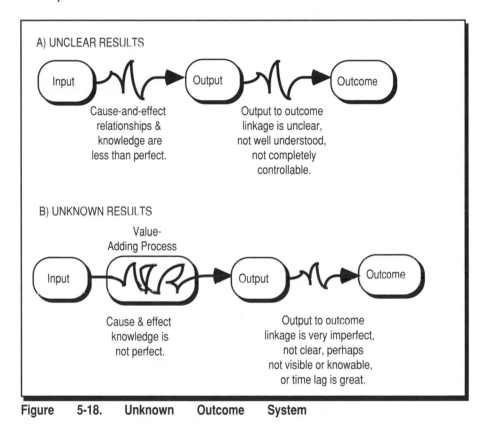

Figure   5-18.   Unknown   Outcome   System

Many fighting military organizations are unknown results systems. However, there are a number of civilian counterparts; disaster preparedness organizations, mine rescue teams, and police SWAT teams all fall into this category. In effect, many social service and educational institutions fall into this category. For example, the ultimate outcome of a child welfare organization may occur many years after the services are terminated; therefore, for all practical purposes they are unknowable. Educational institutions can track graduates, but the ultimate outcomes of the educational institution are frequently unknown. This is particularly true for general education as opposed to education for a particular career field. Unknown outcome systems assess performance through surrogate measures or intermediate criteria. In military and disaster preparedness, there are simulated battles or disasters. Education organizations use test scores as a surrogate. Child welfare organizations measure accomplishment of treatment plan milestones. For these organizations, the critical dimension is effectiveness, which is never really known. Effectiveness using surrogate measures is the best we can do. Such organizations fight constant battles with bean counters who seek to reduce resources to unknown outcome organizations because they have difficulty demonstrating their effectiveness. Such organizations often strongly resist measures of efficiency or productivity because they feel these criteria are not appropriate, since they are in business to respond to a contingency. The military commanders frequently complain that the bean-counter mentality is reducing their wartime effectiveness in an effort to achieve peacetime efficiency. In days of large federal budget deficits, these arguments are likely to become even more heated. The fact that the organizations are indirect results systems means that basically the arguments are fought on emotional, rather than rational, grounds.

The conclusion from this discussion is that the manager and measurement facilitator must understand which of the three types of systems the target organization most closely resembles. Then the facilitator should steer the organization toward the most appropriate blend of criteria for that type of system.

Dimensions of performance of organizational systems. We have studied the literature on performance of organizational systems over the past ten years. We have worked extensively with real-world managers in the development of performance measurement systems for all kinds of organizational systems.. Our pragmatic summary of our findings includes the following observations:

1. There is no consensus as to performance criteria for organizational systems.
2. There are no consensus operational definitions for the commonly cited performance criteria such as effectiveness, efficiency, quality, or productivity.
3. Much of the research that looks at the impact of various improvement strategies—such as reorganizing, quality circles, vertical integration, mergers, quality of work life programs, gainsharing, technological innovation (CIM, office automation, and ASRS), culture management interventions, MIS design/redesign, and so forth—is difficult, at best, to translate, evaluate, and interpret because there is no consistently applied concept of what constitutes organizational systems performance.
4. We repeat this conclusion from earlier—the field is filled with practitioners with no conceptual models and weak operational definitions; the field is filled with academicians with weak conceptual models and no operational definitions. The result has been confusion in the literature and in practice with respect to performance measurement and improvement.

We have worked with organizations that have given up trying to define productivity or that are spending inordinate amounts of time on the task. We have sat through numerous presentations where high-level managers and leaders of the productivity and quality movements in their organizations showed slides that said "Productivity = Quality." We have read too many articles in prestigious journals that talk about improving productivity and quality, but fail to operationally define what the terms mean and indicate the authors don't know what the terms really mean in an operational sense. We are reporting observations, not necessarily criticizing.

What are the dimensions of organizational systems (again, a department, a work group, a function, a division, a plant, a firm, a section, or a branch) performance? We have already revealed our answer in numerous places in the book to this point. We are convinced that the general categories, comprehensive set but not necessarily mutually exclusive set (i.e., it is the complete list of criteria but the criteria do overlap with one another), of performance criteria are effectiveness, efficiency, quality, productivity, quality of work life, innovation, and profitability (profit center) or budgetability (cost center). We have arrived at this list through extensive literature review of what a wide range of authors have said. A less rigorous explanation or defense can be made using Table 1-6.

The table provides a simple correlation analysis of the various views on performance for organizational systems. We contend that closer study reveals that the seven criteria can and should subsume all of the KPIs, KRAs, CSFs, attributes of excellent organizations, and more discussed by other authors. The seven criteria represent the generic set of performance criteria for organizational systems. The other items presented in the figure are, in fact, specific indicators of one or more of the seven basic criteria.

We are obviously dealing with a semantics and logic issue. We can endlessly argue for another criteria or that someone else's conceptual framework is more sound or complete. We are not necessarily trying to convince you or the rest of the world that we're right, and you or they are wrong. The really important thing is that we move toward more consistency with respect to how we define, operationally, performance for organizational systems. We encourage you to develop your own set of criteria, operationally define them, establish consistent understanding and use of them in your organization. If we can spark that process, then we will have succeeded. Let's now turn our attention to providing operational definitions and descriptions of each of the seven performance criteria.

Effectiveness. Figure 5-19 depicts the systems view of your organization with the criterion *effectiveness* shown in relation to what it operationally represents. Effectiveness is an output and outcome side issue. That is, it focuses on aspects of performance for your organizational system that are on the downstream side. The operational definition for effectiveness is "the accomplishment of the 'right' things." Right is in quotes because what is right is often subject to interpretation, discretion, judgment, and individual or group perception. Did we do the "right" things? Did we

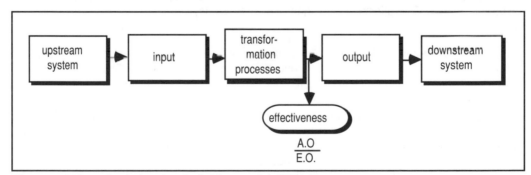

Figure   5-19.   Operational   Definition   of   Effectiveness

get them done? These are the operational issues associated with effectiveness. Most frequently, two attributes are used to further define effectiveness—timeliness and quality. So, the operational definition of effectiveness becomes "the actual accomplishment of the 'right' things, on time, within the quality requirements specified." The operational measure for effectiveness is actual output (AO) divided by expected output (EO). If the number is bigger than one, we were more effective than we thought we would be; less than one, less effective than we thought we would be. A number bigger than one isn't necessarily better; less than one necessarily worse. Again, we must be careful to separate the process of measurement from the process of evaluation.

Efficiency. Figure 5-20 depicts your organizational system and shows the efficiency criterion in the location that it relates to. Note that efficiency is an input side issue; it deals with resource consumption issues. The operational definition for efficiency is "resources expected or predicted or forecasted or estimated to be consumed (REC) divided by resources actually consumed (RAC)." If the number from this ratio is larger than one, then we are more efficient than we "expected" to be; less than one, less efficient than we "expected" to be. What is the relationship between efficiency and effectiveness? The number for resources expected to be consumed relates to or comes from our number representing what our expected output should be. In other words, REC is linked to EO. Numbers for resources expected to be consumed come from industrial engineers, forecasters, estimators, or managers when they develop budgets and so forth. The number or quantities of resources actually consumed relates to or comes from actual output; RAC is linked to AO. Numbers of or quantities of resources actually consumed come from cost accountants, cost accounting systems, or our cost tracking systems. Efficiency is an input/resource consumption issue. An organization can be effective and not efficient, efficient and not effective, neither effective nor efficient and still survive.

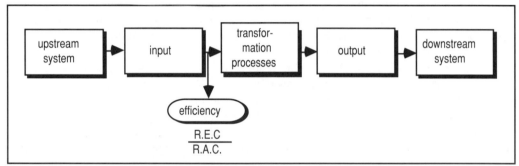

Figure 5-20. Operational Definition of Efficiency

Quality. Figure 5-21 depicts your organizational system and now represents the quality criterion at the positions in the systems model where it must be operationally defined, measured, and managed. You will notice that where effectiveness was an output side issue and efficiency an input or resource consumption issue, quality is more pervasive in that it is a critical criterion at all stages of the life cycle of an organizational systems resource and management process flow.

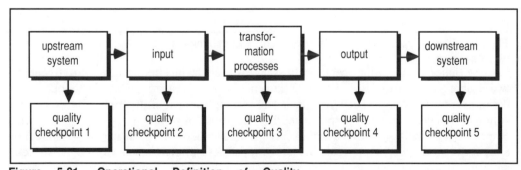

Figure 5-21. Operational Definition of Quality

The conventional, quasi-definitions we see for quality in the popular literature, such as "quality is free," "quality is giving the customer what he or she has a reasonable right to expect," "quality is conforming to specifications," "quality is zero defects," and "quality = productivity," are not really operational definitions with which we can do business. Most importantly, they do not convey the complete picture of total quality management. In order to understand quality, we must operationally define it by at least five checkpoints.

Quality Checkpoint 1 is operationally defined as being the selection and management of upstream systems. It includes such activities as: design and development of products and services; communication of specifications and requirements; selection of upstream systems such as vendors and suppliers; crossing boundaries and communicating with customers as to their expectations, specifications, needs, and requirements; working with and being willing to manage conflict with the people and organizational systems that provide your inputs or who support your organizational system's performance; and being concerned about the quality of the management process for your upstream system and working with critical upstream systems to ensure that they are giving you what you require to do a good job.

I have been told by a reliable source that McDonalds has a very limited number of vendors (i.e., one to three) for their french fries and that they ensure those vendors are managed as well as, if not better than, they are. This is an example of what we mean by Quality Checkpoint 1. There are an almost exponentially increasing number of examples of very positive actions that are being taken by American organizations and managers that reflect initiative at this particular checkpoint in the total quality management process. Write to us and let us know what you're doing in this area, and we'll consider incorporating your examples in future updates of this section.

Managing this checkpoint inside your organization (i.e., for internal upstream systems) is as important as it is to manage it between your organization and external upstream systems. Our experience is that it is very difficult and often painful to do this because the customer-supplier role clarity is often so poor in the American organization. Who works for whom? Who's the customer? Who manages specifications and requirements of the user/customer inside your organization? Who cares whether your internal customers are satisfied or unsatisfied with the support they are provided? How do you change the "I just work here" mentality? These are all critical, often white-collar (i.e., office, professional, and technical employee), issues that are not being addressed at all or are not being addressed proactively enough in most organizations.

We have developed and are developing audits that can be administered to test perceptions as to how good a job your organization's management processes are doing to manage this checkpoint and others. (ASSESS from the Virginia Productivity Center does this, as well as Organizational Productivity and Quality Self-Audit from the Maryland Center for Quality and Productivity).

Quality Checkpoint 2 focuses on the confirmation that your organizational system is receiving from the upstream systems as to what it needs, wants, expects, and deserves. A simple descriptor for this checkpoint is incoming quality control/assurance. We often find statistics prevalent at this checkpoint, as it is helpful in determining, quantitatively, whether or not upstream systems/processes are in control. The use of statistical methods simply assist or facilitate this predominantly verification-oriented process. The most important part of this checkpoint is the action that follows confirmation that the process might be out of control. Going back to the upstream system that provided a defective product or service is time consuming and sometimes painful and conflict creating. It is all too easy to simply say, "We'll just do it over ourselves" or "We'll live with it" rather than providing feedback to the upstream system. I find us doing this constantly in the VPC.

We're not going to get into the statistical procedures associated with this checkpoint; it is not our area of expertise, and it has been successfully done, in our opinion, in the literature (Deming 1986; Ishikawa 1985; Juran 1988; Feigenbaum 1961; Imai 1986; Walton 1986). We will make the observation that the most difficult and important aspect of this checkpoint is not associated with the statistical procedures but with the problem-solving processes that follow application of the statistical procedures. We include in Table 5-1 a list of the principles, points, and issues raised by Juran, Deming, and Ishikawa that relate to this particular checkpoint.

Table 5-1. Principles in Quality Checkpoint #2

Ishikawa (1985)	Juran (1988)	Deming (1986)
• Many factors influence the production of a product; one main factor is raw material. • You must check each purchase; (e.g., purchasing); to see if incoming material is in accordance with the standards set. • Quality for each individual item is important. • Reworked goods, especially accepted goods, and adjusted goods are all <u>defectives</u>.	• Checking for human errors should be planned on an 'active' basis. • Detection of errors should be made at the earliest opportunity. • Enforcement of quality policy. • Make use of statistical techniques for incoming materials. • Inputs are all the means employed by the process to produce the product. Inputs include information, materials, components, and human effort. • Inputs should be secured from everyone; non-clients as well as from clients.	• Eliminate the need for inspection on a mass basis by building quality into the product in the first place. • Defective material and workmanship not permissible anywhere on the line. • A defective, once produced, stayed until and unless it is discovered on a later test, to be corrected and replaced at what is usually great cost. • Defects beget defects. • It is for best economy to have theory for guidance in the use of incoming items. • Detective incoming part cause the assembly to fail. • One should take at all incoming material, possibly on a skip-lot basis. • Management needs training to learn about incoming material.

Quality Checkpoint 3 is the part of the total quality management process that focuses on building quality into the product or service. Statistical procedures are used/can be used here also, but more generally speaking, measurement and evaluation processes are critical at this checkpoint. In-process quality control is employed at this check-point. More importantly, this checkpoint requires supportive management support systems to ensure that quality being built into the product or service is measured, promoted, encouraged, and rewarded. This checkpoint is far more mental than statistical, in our opinion. Success at this checkpoint is far more dependent upon what the organizational systems' guiding principles reflect and what the measurement systems and reward systems communicate than whether our statistical procedures are in place and working perfectly. We are not suggesting that the use of measurement and statistical procedures isn't critical at this stage—it clearly is. We are suggesting that there are other far more subtle and insidious factors that have to be dealt with at this checkpoint.

Table 5-2. Ten Rules for Stifling Innovation

1. Regard any new idea from below with suspicion — because it's new and because it's from below.

2. Insist that people who need your approval to act first go through several other levels of management to get their signatures.

3. Ask departments or individuals to challenge and criticize each other's proposals. (That saves you the job of deciding; you just pick the survivor.)

4. Express your criticisms freely, and withhold your praise. (That keeps people on their toes.) Let them know they can be fired at any time.

5. Treat identification of problems as signs of failure to discourage people from letting you know when something in their area isn't working.

6. Control everything carefully. Make sure people count anything that can be counted and that they do so frequently.

7. Make decisions to reorganize or change policies in secret, and spring them on people unexpectedly. (That also keeps people on their toes.)

8. Make sure that requests for information are fully justified, and make sure that it is not given out to managers freely. (You don't want data to fall into the wrong hands.)

9. Assign to lower-level managers, in the name of delegation and participation, responsibility for figuring out how to cut back, lay off, move people around, or otherwise implement threatening decisions you have made. And, get them to do it quickly.

10. And above all, never forget that you, the higher-ups, already know everything important about this business.

Does your culture support constant improvement of all processes and all aspects of performance or do you have a "maintain the *status-quo*," "I just work here," or "don't fix it if it isn't broke" attitude prevalent? Are your management processes really effectively tapping the insights and creative potential of all employees relative to value-adding process improvements that need to be made, or do you still operate under the "one great brain" assumption? In Rosabeth Moss Kanter's outstanding book, *The Change Masters,* she identified ten rules for stifling innovation in an organization (Kanter 1983). They are insightful and relate directly to critical Checkpoint 3 issues. If your organization or organizational system adheres to any of these rules, then you probably have problems at this checkpoint (see Table 5-2).

We include in Table 5-3 the principles, issues, and points raised by Deming, Juran, and Ishikawa that we feel relate to this third checkpoint.

Quality Checkpoint 4 focuses on the assurance that what is coming out of the organizational system meets the specification , requirements, and expectations established. Some people have misinterpreted Deming's third point, "Cease dependence on inspection." It does not suggest

Table 5-3. Principles in Quality Checkpoint #2

Ishikawa (1985)	Juran (1988)	Deming (1986)

• All processes involved in developing, planning, and designing a new product must be placed under control.
 	
• Companies must strive to control design and process in such a way as to attain a go-straight percentage of 95 to 100 percent.
 	
• Quality cannot be created through inspection; it must be built into each design and process stage.
	• Eliminate error-proof operations.
	
	• Replace error-proof human workers with nonhuman operators.
	
	• Emphasize a capable manufacturing process, not on product inspections.
	
	• A processor is anyone who conducts a process.
	
	• Must ensure these factors in a process:
	  - adequacy of the system of self-control
	  - completeness of the list of control subjects
	  - assignment of responsibility for the various control actions and decisions
	  - adequacy of facilities maintenance procedures and schedules
	
	• Improve planned process controls - the activity of keeping the operating process in a state that continues to be able to meet process goals
		<u>All-or-none-rule</u>
		
		The rules for minimum average total cost for test of single incoming part turn out to be extremely simple under certain conditions, labeled Case 1 and Case 2 in what follows:
		
		Case 1: The worst lot to come in will have fraction defective less than k_1/k_2. In this case, suppose that the process is in statistical control delivering lots in which the defective items are binomially distributed around the mean p. Then the rules for average minimum total cost will be equally simple.
		
		Case 1: If $p < k_1/k_2$, no inspection
		Case 2: If $p > k_1/k_2$, 100 per cent inspection
		
		Even though the distribution of fraction defective in lots straddles the break-even point k_1/k_2.
		
		<u>Defective material and workmanship is not permissible anywhere on the line.</u>
		
		<u>Dispose of standard acceptance plans</u>
		
		• Quality comes not from inspection, but from improvement of the production process.
		
		• The four steps of manufacturing (design it, make it, try to sell it, test it) leads to a helix of continual improvement of quality.
		
		• Every activity, every job is a part of a process.
		
		• There are many stages in a process at every stage, there is 1) production, and 2) continual improvement of methods and procedures.

that Quality Checkpoint 4 goes away or that outgoing quality control/assurance should not be done. It suggests that outgoing quality control does not ensure that quality is built into the product or service; the quality is there before you ever inspect. Again, we will not even review the statistical procedures associated with Checkpoint 4, as they are well documented in the literature cited for Checkpoint 2. Those interested in more detail are directed to those references.

Recall the appliance manufacturing firm example. The experience in that situation and others is that the communication between the people building the product or service and the people inspecting the product or service (note that the people inspecting the product or service might be Checkpoint 4 inspectors or Checkpoint 5 customers) is not as good, if it exists at all, as it could or should be. There was no feedback loop from quality control in the appliance manufacturing firm's paint line example I discussed in this chapter. This is the rule, not the exception in many American organizations. It is particularly prevalent in white-collar settings. American organizations are typically well differentiated and poorly integrated. When we perform a roadblock identification exercise using the Nominal Group Technique with managers, common highly ranked roadblocks are turf protection, "stove-pipe" management, "rice bowl" protection, empire building, and "Balkanization." These terms are descriptive of organizational behavior that can be functional; however, they are most frequently—particularly in these times—dysfunctional. The communication between suppliers and vendors (more generically, upstream systems), customers (upstream and downstream systems), and providers is essential to being able to accomplish the goals and desired outcomes of total quality management. If Checkpoint 4 is a "Balkanized" activity, as it was in the appliance manufacturing example I provided, the whole quality management process is likely to fail. Ineffective execution at any of the five checkpoints endangers the entire process.

Quality Checkpoint 5 focuses on downstream systems. I describe it as being the proactive, detailed understanding of what your customers want, need, expect, and demand, as well as how they are reacting to the delivery of the goods and services you are providing. I tell the following story in my three-day short course to exemplify.

I recently went through the process of buying a car. I am and have been committed to buying American, which meant the process was, for me, a painful process. Dealers for automobile companies are, in fact, part of the Quality Checkpoint 5 process; they should be. I contend that this is true for Japanese auto companies and not true for American companies. Now, I would be the first to admit that this is probably more dealer-specific than auto-company specific. However, it appears to me that Japanese auto companies have reached out and influenced their dealers more effectively than have their American counterparts.

My data base is not large; however, as I have told this story, many in the audience have related to it, which might indicate that the small data base contains some valuable information. I visited numerous, four to be exact, General Motors dealerships looking for an Oldsmobile, Buick, or Cadillac. My experience in the first three dealerships was the same—lack of cooperativeness, general lack of skill and knowledge on the part of the salesman, lack of interest in me as a customer, unwillingness to share information, and no timely follow-up. I provided name, address, and phone number to all contacts. In one case, I never received a follow-up note or call. In two other cases, I received follow-up calls a year after my visit and purchase of a car from another dealer. The fourth dealer I visited, a GM dealer also, is the one I eventually bought a car from. It was an exceedingly well-run dealership, and I purchased my car from them for that reason alone. They toured me through their well-maintained service department and introduced me to their service manager. They worked with me to arrange a loan with a local bank, getting me the best rate, and using a well-organized computer system to print out a payment schedule. They did not offer the best deal on the car I purchased. They did send my wife a dozen roses the day after we bought the car and have followed up with letters several times in the past year. Ask yourself this question: Do you think GM caused this dealer to manage this well? Also, do you think GM caused the other three dealers to manage that poorly? This is a quality Checkpoint 5 issue.

I also visited several Japanese auto dealerships just to see what they had to offer and to see how they did business. In each case, I first received a note from the salesman—within a week—thanking me for stopping in and encouraging me to stop back and discuss details. Within three weeks, I received a note from the owner of the dealership thanking me for stopping by and informing me that they would do whatever it took to keep me happy, and that they would ensure that my car had the best service possible. The attention to detail, the follow-up and follow-through were very impressive. Ask yourself this question: How does a Japanese company positively influence dealer behaviors all the way from Japan?

As I have sat in and ridden in Japanese cars and as a result of my recent search for a new car, I have come away with the following impressions. A 4-foot-10-inch Japanese design engineer in Osaka, Japan knows more about and cares more about a 6-foot-2-inch American living in Blacksburg, Virginia than a 6-foot-2-inch American design engineer in Detroit, Michigan. Japanese automobile companies view dealers as an integral part and extension of their organization. They manage these upstream systems because they know that this is part of the total quality management process and will give them a competitive edge. The Japanese are managing Checkpoint 5 better than we are. American dealers have an arrogant attitude about American consumers; most don't really care about the little things.

Before I end this little treatise on Quality Checkpoint 5 and automobiles, let me reconfirm that I did end up buying a GM car and have been very happy with it. I still believe that we engineer better cars. I still don't like the smallness of the Japanese imports. I am more convinced now than ever before that there are huge gaps, deficiencies in the management process—particularly the quality management process—in American automobile companies. Some dramatic changes need to be made in what we are doing and how we are doing it if American automobile companies are to regain competitiveness and leadership. A good place to start would be with a massive campaign to better manage Quality Checkpoint 5. I think the money GM is spending on advertisements would be more wisely spent on a well thought-through Quality Checkpoint 5 process.

During my tenure at Eastman Kodak, the Customer Equipment Services Division adopted some interesting and effective Quality Checkpoint 5 innovations. The service engineering department was responsible for service cost estimates, technical service publications, spare parts estimates, assisting equipment service representatives on problems in the field, and, in general, the life-cycle management of a line of equipment from a serviceability, maintainability, reliability, and customer satisfaction perspective. In particular, the business systems equipment department (microfilmers, reader-printers, copiers, and computer-oriented micrographics) developed a position called service systems engineer. This position was responsible for working on management support systems that would provide improved feedback from the field as to where problems were occurring. We made field visits to find out, from the customers, their perceptions of problems with our equipment. We focused on the specific equipment, locations, and components where it appeared we had our biggest problems. Without measurement—improved measurement systems—we would not have known where to begin. So, we worked first upon improving the quality of the data being collected in the field by the equipment service representatives. Then we worked on how to store, retrieve, and portray the data in such a way that meaningful information could be gleaned by management. We used the information to provide feedback to market research and development, design engineering, manufacturing engineering, central parts services, and our equipment service representatives. We had difficulty getting all these parties to cooperate and to think Kodak as opposed to their own divisions, but we persisted and succeeded. Now this story isn't a new one, and some would argue that it isn't innovative. It's really quite basic. My question is: If it's so basic, then why don't more companies make it work? It boils down to a matter of execution and attention to details and leadership. The point to this second little case example is that there are many ways to go at managing Quality Checkpoint 5. They all involve getting closer to your customers.

Quality Checkpoint 6 is the quality management process. I know, you thought I said there were only five checkpoints; I was wrong. Figure 5-22 depicts the six quality checkpoints in a slightly different fashion than shown before.

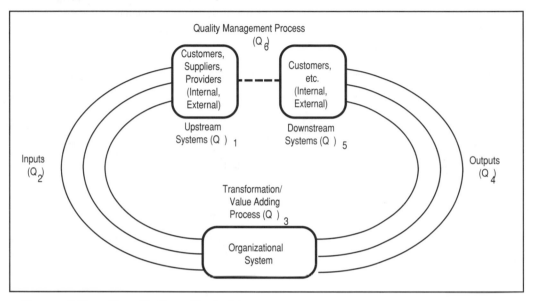

Figure 5-22. Six Quality Checkpoints

Note that Quality Checkpoints 1 and 5 wrap around and interface with one another. This signifies that customers are upstream and downstream systems. Customers play an important role on design and development, specification, input side of what you do (white-collar or blue-collar), and on the output side of what you do. Quality Checkpoint 6 is the quality management process; it's the coordination and overall management for the process. We don't have the space to completely define and describe the entire process, and it wouldn't be appropriate for this book as it has been done quite successfully in at least four other current books. The four outstanding books that are must reading for the manager and/or master desiring to better understand Quality Checkpoint 6 are: *Juran on Planning for Quality* (Juran 1988); *Out of the Crisis* (Deming 1986); *What is Total Quality Control?* (Ishikawa 1985); and *Managing Quality: The Strategic and Competitive Edge* (Garvin 1988). The serious student of quality management will gain all they need to know about this final checkpoint by starting with these four books and then "boot-strapping" to other more detailed references.

So quality, unlike effectiveness and efficiency, is not just an output side issue or an input side issue. Quality is a pervasive aspect of performance of an organizational system that must be measured and managed at all checkpoints. Therefore, it follows that the operational definition for quality is necessarily more complex than those for effectiveness and efficiency. Our understanding of quality must go beyond the popular concepts of "it's free," zero-defects, "it comes without tears," giving the customer what he/she has a reasonable right to expect, conformance to requirements/specifications, and others. Quality has to be operationally defined and measured for at least each of the five quality checkpoints. We have tried to provide at least an improved operational understanding of what each of these five checkpoints involves. Let's now turn our attention to the fourth of the seven criteria—productivity.

Productivity. Figure 5-23 depicts the by-now-familiar organizational systems model and includes a representation of what productivity operationally means for an organization. Productivity is operationally defined as being the relationship between what comes out of an organizational system divided by what comes into an organizational system. Productivity is output over input. This seems so simple that one wonders why people struggle so much with the measurement of productivity. The answer lies in examining several operational issues associated with actually measuring output over input.

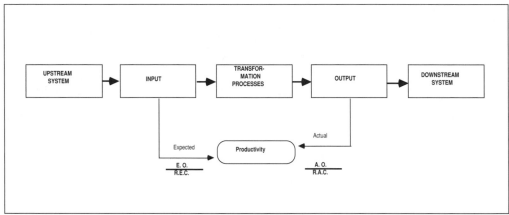

Figure 5-23. Operational Definitions of Productivity

1. The "tangibility" of outputs. In many organizational systems, much of the output is difficult to quantify. This creates problems in ensuring that the numerator of the productivity equation is complete. If, as is often the case, the numerator is incomplete, then users of the numbers question the validity of the ratios.

2. The fuzzy unit-of-analysis problem. Failure to lock in on an understanding of what the unit of analysis is for the measurement of productivity causes inconsistency in what we define as outputs and inputs. An input/output analysis can solve this problem, but few people take the time to do a thorough one prior to launching into measurement.

3. The undefined scope problem. Measurement scope has to do with the unit of time for which we are measuring performance. It's analogous to how long you leave the shutter of the camera open. Are we measuring for a period of a day, week, month, quarter, year, or more? Matching outputs and inputs for a given unit of time is a correlate problem associated with scope.

4. The define-productivity-in-our-heads-one-way-and-operationalize-it-another-way problem. People have a tendency to cognitively define productivity as output over input, and then when they go to measure it, they operationalize it as if it were in fact the broader issue of performance. This happens for a number of reasons. In my opinion, the most important is that people are subconsciously saying that performance tells the whole story—productivity just a part —and I want to make sure the whole story is told so that I don't get evaluated unfairly.

Productivity is an important criteria of performance because when you measure it well, you end up learning something about effectiveness, efficiency, and quality. It is a good diagnostic measure in that sense. It's a nice dial to have on your instrument panel because it can efficiently tell you what is happening to the organizational system. The actual measures for productivity you end up with may not be complete, comprehensive, tell the whole story, or be perfect, but they will give you insights as you track them over time. You will need to have other dials on your instrument panel to help you understand why productivity is going down or up.

It is important to keep in mind that productivity can improve in five basic ways (see Figure 5-24).

	Output	Input	Productivity Improvement
1	Increases	Decreases	Output ⬆ / Input ⬇
2	Increases	Remains Constant	Output ⬆ / Input —
3	Increases	Increases, but at a lower rate	Output ⬆ / Input ⬆
4	Remains Constant	Decreases	Output — / Input ⬇
5	Decreases	Decreases, but at a higher rate	Output ⬇ / Input ⬇

**Figure 5-24. Five Basic Ways
To Improve Productivity**

Note that these combinations of outputs and inputs can be caused by external factors (i.e., business conditions) or can be caused to occur due to things we do as managers and management teams. We can be proactive about making Scenario 5 happen, or we can wait around for our competitors to make Scenario 3 have to happen. The choice is up to you and your management team. Many argue that there are certain situations where Scenarios 4 or 5 are forced on an organization. Many federal, state and local government agencies and organizations see themselves being forced to increase the quality of and level of service while budgets are being cut. Of course, this scenario would be the most difficult to manage—particularly if you were reactive versus proactive. The do-more-with-less scenario is difficult, if not impossible, under traditional American management process and practices. In my opinion, the only way to respond to this type of challenge is to change how you manage. This is true for the private or public sector.

The point to examination of the five ways that productivity can improve is to attempt to break a paradigm that exists in this country that productivity means do more with less, cost reduction, loss of jobs, less inputs, less job security, loss of power, and pain. I'm not arguing that productivity doesn't conjure up these impressions today; I'm suggesting that it need not and should not. Productivity has become value laden, and the value implications are negative. We have allowed a term like productivity to take on negative connotations. We have confused measurement with evaluation. Productivity is simply the relationship between what comes out of an organizational system and what goes into that same system for some given period of time. We track the ratio over time to see whether the number goes up or down. We evaluate why the numbers are going up or down to control performance and maintain competitiveness. Productivity has become a negative term in America because we have allowed it to happen. This is most unfortunate because productivity is a concept that must be embraced by unions, employees, staff, management, the private and public sectors—everyone. To constantly improve the relationship between outputs and inputs is important and good. The consequences of doing this should be good. This is one specific area where globally competing Japanese firms have a distinct competitive advantage. They have made the consequences of productivity improvement positive for almost all involved, while their American counterparts have made the consequences of productivity improvement negative for almost all involved. It's very hard to have a successful productivity program in the United States without addressing—head on—the job security issue. It is politically and practically unastute to really be too proactive about productivity in an American organization.

Operationally, then, productivity is the relationship between what comes out of a system (an assumption is made that the outputs meet the attributes established for them i.e., quality, timeliness, and price) divided by what comes into the system (i.e., labor, capital, materials, energy, and data/information, and again, we assume that these inputs pass Checkpoint 2 and meet the specifications established for them) for some given period of time. There are a variety of specific types of productivity measures, such as partial-factor, multifactor, and total-factor ratios and indexes. These are described in detail in *Productivity Management: Planning, Measurement and Evaluation, Control and Improvement* (Sink 1985). We will discuss a specific technique/ model that can facilitate development and use of productivity measures later in this chapter.

Quality of Work Life (QWL). Figure 5-25 depicts the location on the organizational systems flow model that quality of work life addresses. As you can see, it is a performance criterion that focuses on an aspect of the value-adding process.

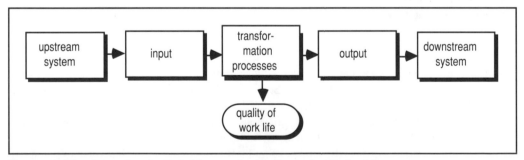

Figure 5-25. Operational Definitions of Quality of Work Life

QWL is operationally defined as "the affective response or reaction of the people in the organizational system to any number of factors, such as pay, working conditions, culture, leadership, coworker relations, feedback, autonomy, skill variety, task identity, task significance, the boss, amount of involvement in planning, problem solving, and decision making. "Affective" means "of affects, of feelings, emotional." So, we are talking about how people feel about various aspects of work life. This criterion is located beneath the transformation process box in Figure 5-25 because it has to do with the people in the organizational system. It is the people in the organizational system that specifically determine what factors they choose to affectively respond to and, as we know, there will be tremendous variation in which specific factors are focused on by individuals.

The implicit assumption regarding QWL made by most managers is that if people feel negatively about factors they feel are important it will negatively influence their performance and, hence, negatively influence organizational system performance. Conversely, if people feel positive about factors they feel are important it is assumed that this will positively influence their performance and, hence, positively influence organizational system performance. However, the research findings, for many years, have shown that the relationship between attitudes, feelings, and performance is low. The prevailing view is that feelings may be a measure of the extent to which the organizational systems reward employee efforts.

It is difficult to find, in the literature, good operational definitions for what QWL is. The definition we have provided is the most pragmatic, least value laden, and most directly operationalizable. As with the previous four criteria, we have provided an operational definition for the criterion only. We have simply provided a definition for a cluster of instruments you should have on your instrument panel. We have not provided you with the instruments themselves. You will have to determine which specific factors you will monitor and how you will do this.

How people feel about perceived important dimensions of their life in organizations is critical to overall organizational system performance. We're not suggesting that happy people are necessarily productive people. Nor are we suggesting that productive people are always necessarily happy. The research does not support these simplistic cause-and-effect linkages. We are suggesting that there is a complex and important link between quality of work life and performance of an organizational system. There are effective ways of measuring quality of work life, and there are certainly ways to develop management processes that improve system performance while simultaneously improving quality of work life.

Innovation. Figure 5-26 identifies innovation also as a criterion that relates to Quality Checkpoint 3, the transformation process. Innovation is operationally defined as " the creative process of changing; what we're doing, how we are doing things, structure, technology, products, services, methods, procedures, policies, etc. to successfully respond to internal and external pressures, opportunities, challenges, threats." There are several key words in this operational definition. First, creative—innovation involves creativity. Second, change—innovation necessarily involves change. Third, successful response—innovation is successful, if it isn't then maybe we're just talking about invention. It seems to me that the Japanese have proven themselves to be very innovative, while the Americans have, of recent, proven themselves to be, in cases,

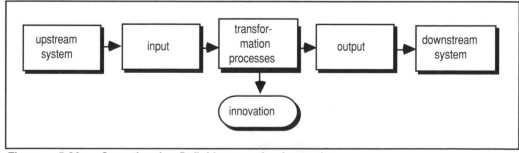

Figure   5-26.   Operational   Definitions   of   Innovation

just inventive. For example, we invented the technology for the VCR; however, we don't make any in this country. Finally, it seems to me that innovation is both a reactive and proactive process, hence the choice of the words opportunities and pressures, challenges and threats. Innovation is the creative process of successfully changing whatever it takes to survive, compete, grow, and attain whatever your desired outcomes are.

Richard Foster (1986), director of McKinsey and Company, wrote a book entitled *Innovation* in which he reintroduces the concept of S-shaped curves (see Figure 5-27). An S-shaped curve represents a technology, a way of getting something done, in a broad sense of the term. Our figure depicts two S-shaped curves because Foster suggests that S-shaped curves always come in pairs. This is analogous to saying that there is always a better way to do something. The x-axis— horizontal axis— represents cumulative and incremental effort put into learning and using the technology. The y-axis—vertical axis—represents the level of performance achieved with the technology. Notice that an S-shaped curve is another representation for learning curves. As we become more familiar with the technology—learn more about it—we begin to gain greater amounts of benefit and performance for smaller increments in effort, until we reach the top of the S-shaped curve where we reach a point of diminishing returns. We have reached the limits of the technology.

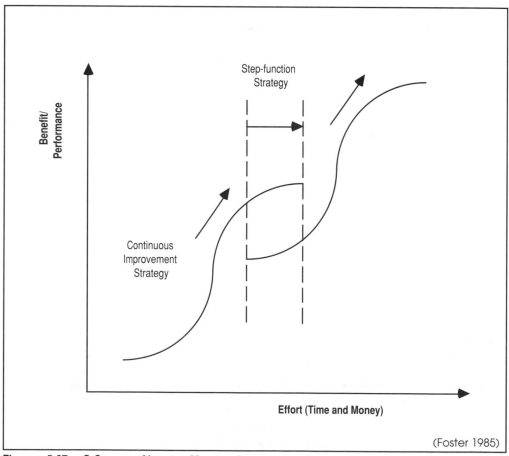

(Foster 1985)

Figure   5-27.   S-Curves   Almost   Always   Appear   in   Pairs

Foster points out that, at this point, we have two choices: continue to attempt to refine and improve upon the performance of the current technology or search for a new S-shaped curve. The measurement implications associated with this decision are fairly obvious. How will you know if you are at the top of an S-shaped curve? Foster's excellent book is filled with examples of organizations; that successfully transitioned to new S-shaped curves; that searched and failed; that switched to new curves and failed; or that failed to search for new S-shaped curves and failed. He talks a lot about what I call the big delta—big technology shifts. These are clearly important. However, as the Japanese have proven, the little delta—little technology shifts—are also important. Moreover, the small constant improvements in current technologies determine the rate at which we will move up a current S-shaped curve.

We have cultures, measurement, and reward systems that do not promote, encourage, or reward for doing the kinds of things Foster is talking about on a large or small scale. We have already discussed this at great length and won't repeat our observations and opinions. We like this book and the concept of S-shaped curves because they enhance our understanding of the operational definition for innovation. How we spark and promote and control innovation is an issue to be taken up later. How we operationally define innovation is our task at hand. Innovation is the creative process of changing whatever it takes to succeed. How will you know if you are doing this if you don't measure it?

Profitability/budgetability. Profitability and budgetability are depicted in Figure 5-28 as the relationship between an outcome and inputs. Profitability, for a profit center, is a "measure or set of measures that relates revenues to costs." Budgetability, for a cost center, is a "measure or set of measures of the relationship between budgets and agreed upon goals, deliverables, and timeliness with actual costs and actual accomplishments and timeliness." Budgetability isn't really a word, so don't start looking it up in the dictionary. I invented it; not to proliferate complex words but to solve a problem I had. When I presented these seven criteria to public-sector audiences, they would inevitably invalidate the seventh criteria because it didn't relate to them. Then, they would invalidate the whole concept of seven criteria because of a perceived private-sector bias. Then they would argue that I didn't understand their business. They would point out that life in the private sector is so much easier because there is a bottom line—the seventh criteria. They don't have a bottom line, which makes measurement difficult, if not impossible.

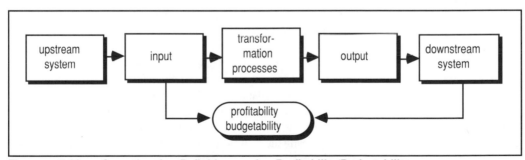

Figure   5-28.   Operational   Definition   of   Profitability/Budgetability

So, I thought long and hard about this issue. I concluded that every organizational system has a bottom line—they may or may not have crystallized what it is. The fact that they think they don't is an indication of a cause of some of our problems. I reasoned further that if people in the public sector feel that profitability is the bottom line for the private sector, then people in the private sector ought to feel that "budgetability" is the bottom line for the public sector. It seems to me, and has made sense to most, that budgetability is the relationship between budgets, stated deliverables, deadlines and actual costs, actual deliverables, and actual delivery dates. It seems that this is the seventh criteria for a "cost center." I have a philosophical "heartburn" over calling profitability the bottom line for the private sector. I feel that the bottom line is survival, growth, competitiveness, or whatever other long-term desired outcomes you have established in your strategic longer-term goals.

Performance criteria interrelationships. We have now discussed and defined, operationally, the seven dimensions of performance for organizational systems. By now it should be clear that this may be a comprehensive list, but it is not completely mutually exclusive. There is clear overlap among the seven criteria. Effectiveness incorporates quality attributes, productivity includes quality,k effectiveness, and efficiency, and quality is quite pervasive. Figure 5-29 depicts the relationship between these seven criteria.

The arrow pointing from left to right in this figure infers that the job of a management team is to drive the equation from left to right. Focus on effectiveness first: What are the right things for us to be doing? Once effectiveness has been defined for your organization, then turn attention to efficiency and quality. What resources will we need to consume to accomplish those "right" things and what are the quality specifications? If an organizational system manages these three criteria well, productivity will follow. White-collar productivity is a buzz word with few operational implications. The concern in the white-collar arena must be on effectiveness, efficiency, and quality. Productivity will follow if we better manage these three criteria.

We view quality of work life and innovation as moderating variables in the equation. They moderate the relationship between productivity and profitability/budgetability. They can enhance your performance or detract from it. In the longer-term, poor performance in the areas of quality of work life and innovation usually spell failure for an organization. A near-term outcome is profitability (profit center) or budgetability (cost center). Long-term desired outcomes such as survival, growth, improvement, and excellence are achieved by driving the equation from left to right.

There are strong, pervasive pressures in your organization that cause management teams to drive this equation from right to left. There is a propensity to allow the budget to drive the plan. The comptroller and the budget are very powerful in most organizations. Unless there is offsetting power in the planning process, an organization runs the risk of too much right-to-left drive in the management process. Perhaps Lee Iacocca said in better words what we are trying to describe in model form:

> By their very nature financial analysts tend to be defensive, conservative, and pessimistic. On the other side guys in sales and marketing are aggressive, speculative, and optimistic. They're saying let's do it, while the bean counters are cautioning why you shouldn't. If the bean counters are too weak, the company will spend itself into bankruptcy. But, if they are too strong the company would not meet the market or stay competitive. In a company you need both sides of the equation.
>
> *Lee Iacocca,*
> *Iacocca: An Autobiography*

I didn't read Iacocca's quote when I designed the model depicting the interrelationship between the seven criteria; conversely, Iacocca didn't see my model when he wrote his book. Both express the same basic concept.

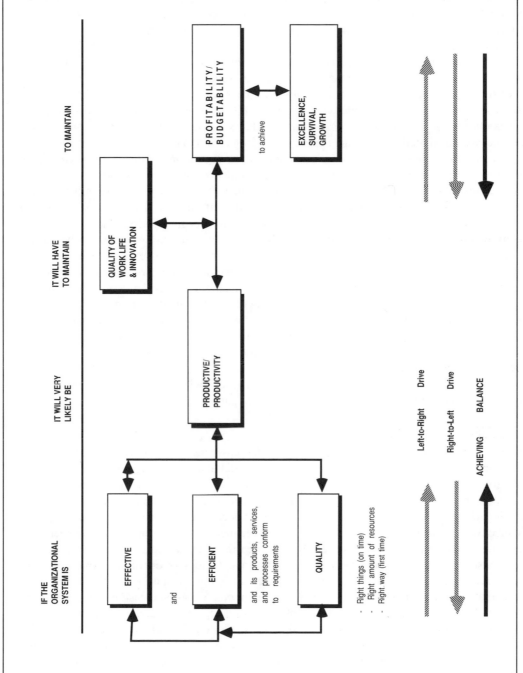

Figure 5-29. The Inter-relationship Between Organizatioal Performance Criteria

The secret, of course, is to achieve balance. What constitutes balance? Clearly there was more right-to-left drive the day Mr. Iacocca joined Chrysler than the day they obtained the government loan guarantees. Business conditions will affect what constitutes balance. A research and development laboratory will weight the seven criteria differently than will a production department. No two organizational systems or managers will equally weight the seven performance criteria, nor will they weight equally the seven criteria. Balance will, necessarily, be a very situational issue.

You cannot survive and succeed, long term, unless you achieve balance. You will not succeed and survive, long term, unless you manage all seven performance criteria. The interrelationships are complex and dynamic. Your job is analogous to an aeronautical engineer's and a pilot's if the laws of aerodynamics were constantly changing. Instrument panels would have to constantly change if this were the case. This is what's happening in your world, and without flexible, well-designed measurement systems your organization is going to crash.

Instrument panels, clusters of or types of instruments, specific dials and instruments. We have now defined for you the clusters or types of instruments you will need on your management teams' control panels. The instrument panel is analogous to the visibility room, the bulletin board, and the report packages that you use to present specific information. The clusters or types of instruments are analogous to navigation, communication, engine performance, and aircraft position information to which the pilot has access. The seven performance criteria are the clusters of instruments/information that is needed for your management teams to effectively manage. The seven performance criteria do not represent the specific dials and idnicators. Your job is to identify the altitude of the aircraft, an airspeed indicator to indicate speed, an oil pressure gauge, a glide slope indicator to indicate whether the plane is in control during an instrument approach, and more. What are the instruments that will tell you whether your organizational system is effective, efficient, managing quality at all five checkpoints, productive, innovative, managing quality of work life, and is profitable or managing budgetability? We're going to help you answer this question in the next chapter.

Are you comfortable managing with an instrument panel of the past or the present, or are you willing to pay the price to develop an instrument panel of the future?

CLOSURE

Our collective experience and wisdom suggests that basic measurement concepts, theory, and philosophy for measurement in the Organization of the Future is lacking. We don't find many masters of measurement in American organizations. We are both participants in the higher education process in this country, and we don't find that measurement masters are being developed by our universities. We have well-trained accountants, financial analysts, corporate finance types, industrial psychologists, work measurement specialists, industrial engineers, and personnel and human resource managers, but few measurement masters. Someone once said that we only see that which we are trained to see. Unfortunately, most of our disciplines train people only to see that aspect of measurement for which their discipline is responsible in the organization. This creates and has created often shortsighted and myopic views on measurement's role in the organization. We are in the midst of a revolution in management practices and processes not unlike the one we experienced during the industrial revolution at the turn of the last century. We are being forced to re-examine and change how we manage. As we have indicated, key management processes that must be redesigned include measurement systems, reward systems, and planning systems.

We have attempted to provide in Chapter 5 the foundation for designing, developing, and implementing measurement systems in the Organization of the Future. Many of the concepts

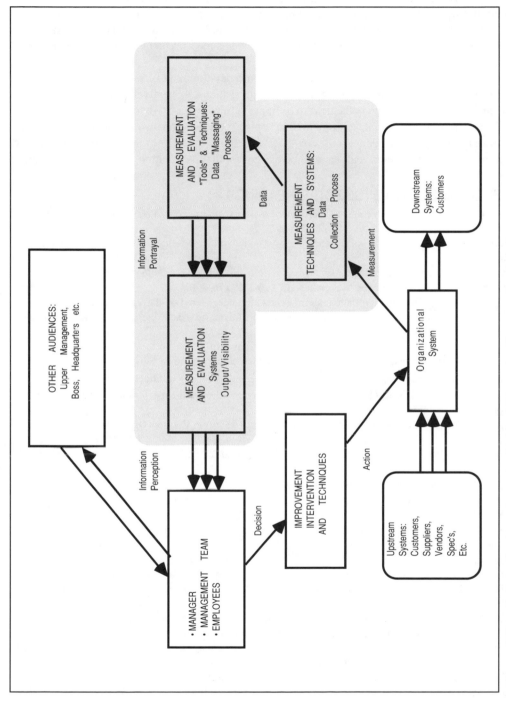

Figure 5-30. Design, Development, and Implementation of Measurement Systems

presented will be reinforcing for some of you and threatening for others. Some will argue that we have made it too complex; some too simple. Some will disagree with our seven criteria and how we have operationally defined them. If we cause you to think about these fundamental issues surrounding measurement, we will have succeeded. In particular, if we cause you to consider how to design measurement systems to support constant and continual improvement and to create better balance between measurement for control versus measurement for improvement, then we will have indeed succeeded.

The next two chapters focus on design and development of measurement systems and development and implementation of measurement systems, respectively. Figure 5-30 highlights the areas to concentrate on in the next two chapters. In Chapter 6, we focus on developing a plan for measurement systems development. In Chapter 7, we focus on developing and implementing a measurement system. We are at the how-to level in this chapter. The management systems model and management systems analysis will be our conceptual roadmap for these next two chapters.

REFERENCES AND SUGGESTED READINGS

Bernard, C.I. 1939. The Functions of the Executive. Harvard University Press. Cambridge, Massachusetts.

Bertalanffy, L. V. 1973. General Systems Theory: Foundations, Development, and Applications. Brazillier. New York.

Deming, W. E. 1986. Out of the Crisis. Massachusetts Institute of Technology, Center for Advanced Engineering Study. Cambridge, Massachusetts. 110-112, 276-296.

_____. 1987. Total Quality Management. Teleconference offered by the Virginia Productivity Center, Virginia Tech, and sponsored by George Washington University. Blacksburg, Richmond, Norfolk, and Lynchburg, Virginia.

Feigenbaum, A. V. 1961. Total Quality Control. McGraw-Hill. New York.

Foster, R. 1986. Innovation, The Attacker's Advantage. Summit Books. New York.

Garvin, D. A. 1988. Managing Quality: The Strategic and Competitive Edge. The Free Press. New York.

Hackman, J. R., and G. R. Oldham. 1975. Development of the job diagnostic survey. Journal of Applied Psychology. 60. 159-170.

Imai, M. 1986. *KAIZEN—The Key to Japan's Competitive Success*. Random House Business Division. New York.

Ishikawa, K. 1985. *What is Quality Control? The Japanese Way*. Prentice-Hall. Englewood Cliffs, New Jersey.

Juran, J. M. 1988. *Juran on Planning for Quality*. The Free Press. New York.

Katz, D., and R. L. Kahn. 1978. *The Social Psychology of Organizations* (2nd ed.). John Wiley & Sons. New York.

Kanter, R. M., and D. W. Brinkerhoff. 1980. Appraising the performance of performance appraisal. *Sloan Management Review*, 21 (3). 3-16.

Kanter, R. M. 1983. *The Change Masters*. Simon and Schuster. New York.

March, J. G., and H. A. Simon. 1958. *Organizations*. John Wiley & Sons. New York.

Meyers, H. N., E. Kay, and J. R. P. French. 1965. Split roles in performance appraisal. *Harvard Business Review*. January-February.

Mintzberg, H. 1986. The manager's job: Folklore and fact. *Management Classics*. Edited by M. T. Matteson and J. M. Ivancevich (3rd ed.). Business Publications, Inc. Plano, Texas.

Morris, W. T. 1979. *Implementation Strategies for Industrial Engineers*. Grid Publishing, Inc. Columbus, Ohio. (Currently out of print. Being rewritten under new title by D. S. Sink.)

Myers, I. B., and P. B. Myers. 1986. *Gifts Differing*.   (9th ed.). Consulting Psychologists Press, Inc.

Sink, D. S. Spring 1983. Using the nominal group technique effectively. *National Productivity Review*. 173-184.

_____, T. C. Tuttle, and S. K. Das. 1980. Measuring and improving white collar productivity: A NASA case study. *Productivity Management Frontiers-I*. Edited by David J. Sumanth. Elsevier. Amsterdam, Holland.

6. GETTING STARTED

W e have presented and discussed some basic measurement concepts in the last chapter. How does one use these basic concepts to actually develop working measurement systems? This chapter is designed to answer this question for you. We have attempted to present a pragmatic and straightforward methodology for the design and development of an effective measurement system. We have chosen not to give the methodology a name; we'll let you do that. It represents the combined wisdom of Tuttle and Sink. We— Tuttle and Sink—have been building and helping others build measurement systems, collectively, for over 25 years. We both have preferred jargon and specific approaches, and we have attempted to merge our knowledge and experience into one methodology that makes sense to both of us based upon what we see working.

We are in the midst of designing and developing measurement systems for our own organizations and are also involved in helping other organizations develop their own measurement systems. There is emerging a systematic approach that can be utilized to successfully develop measurement systems. Research and development on this approach is ongoing; however, we feel confident that the steps we present represent the foundation of what is required.

MEASUREMENT SYSTEMS DEVELOPMENT AND IMPLEMENTATION PLANNING

Good measurement systems, like good aircraft instrument panels, don't just happen. They are designed, human-factors engineered, developed, and constantly improved. If we haven't succeeded in convincing you of the importance of well-engineered measurement systems, then you probably don't need to read further. But if, as we suspect, you believe that improving measurement systems is vital to your organization's success, then we are about to show you how to engineer measurement systems. When we say engineer, we infer human factors engineering and inclusion of sociological, psychological, as well as industrial engineering issues in the design and development.

Management systems analysis will ensure that the entire management system is considered as we develop the measurement system. Revisiting the performance improvement planning process results will ensure that measurement is linked to strategy. In fact, the methodology we will present in this chapter is our recommendation for how to complete Step 7 of the performance improvement planning process. An early step in the methodology is that of defining the target system—clearly defining and delimiting the unit of analysis. A measurement systems audit can ensure that the team of people designing and developing the measurement system are aware of the variety of existing measurement tools and techniques that are currently in place. Audience analysis focuses on identifying the various audiences for the output of the measurement system. Who should and who will be receiving output from the measurement system and how will they use the results? Knowing what's available in the area of measurement tools and techniques is essential to the successful design of improved measurement systems. What principles will/should guide our development and use of these improved measurement systems? Who will be the masters that will design, develop, and implement the systems? Do masters exist? Will we have to hire some, develop some? Without masters, your efforts will fail. Which specific techniques and models will we use to help us convert data into information? The selection of tools for data collection, storage, retrieval, and processing is an important step in the methodology. Most critical perhaps is the question of how to overcome the predictable resistance to change and resistance to measurement in general. Finally, what are the components of a complete design for a measurement system development and implementation plan?

This is a quick rundown of the "getting started" portion of the methodology. These things represent the critical issues that the measurement systems development team will have to address. We will discuss each of these points in some detail and then move to the next chapter where we will present the heart of the methodology, the actual measurement system development.

Management Systems Analysis (MSA)

The management process has been described, depicted, and discussed in many ways in the past. All major business textbooks on the subject of management and organizational behavior adopt a conceptual framework to guide the development of the text and to help the student put the management process in perspective. We won't review the variety of ways used to explain what the management process is since we provide references at the end of this chapter for the interested reader to investigate. A representation of the management process that we are impressed with comes from Dr. Harold Kurstedt of VPI. Kurstedt is director of the Management Systems Laboratory at Virginia Tech and is the Prillaman Professor in the Department of Industrial Engineering and Operations Research. He has developed a management systems model (Kurstedt 1985a) and is involved in continuing research into aspects of that theory and model. Figure 6-1 depicts his basic model.

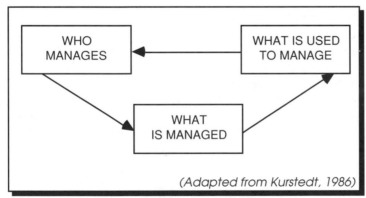

Figure 6-1. Management Systems Model

He considers the three boxes to represent a management system. Every manager who manages has a domain — a set of things for which he/she is responsible. Within that domain are people, tools, systems we manage, technology, relationships, information, and more. There are also three interfaces: decision-to-action interface, measurement-to-data interface, and information-portrayal to information-perception interface. He suggests another ABCs of management as presented in Figure 6-2.

Managers can administer the process, build the business, and/or cater to crises. Kurstedt suggests that unless we administer the process effectively and efficiently we cannot build the business and will constantly cater to crises. There are significantly more intricacies to this model and the current ongoing research. We reference Kurstedt's work for the interested reader.

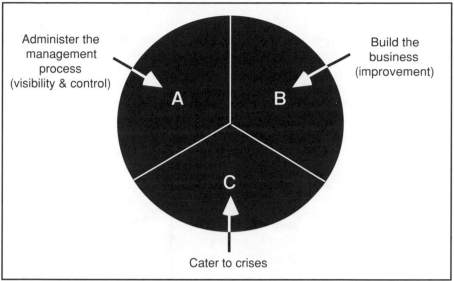

Figure 6-2. Managers Spend All Their Time Doing Three Things

We have modified the management systems model for the purpose of focusing specifically on performance measurement and improvement. Figure 6-3 presents our modified model.

Like Kurstedt's model this modification contains interfaces between the three major components of the model: the decision to action interface between who manages (the manager/management team) and what is managed (the organizational system); the portrayal-to-perception interface between tools (data storage, retrieval, processing models, techniques, and heuristics) and who manages; and the measurement-to-data interface between what is managed and the tools used to convert data into information. Note that we have added three boxes and highlighted what happens at these three interfaces. We have previously discussed in the presentation of the performance improvement planning process an example of the first interface. Chapters 5 through 8 focus on measurement and evaluation and therefore attend to Interfaces 2 and 3.

I have worked hard to operationalize the management systems model theory particularly as it relates to performance measurement and improvement. Kurstedt is deeply involved in doing this as it relates to management support systems and management systems—in general, design, development, and implementation. I have developed a technique called management systems analysis (MSA) that is a five-step process of systematically walking through this model and answering key questions focused at developing performance improvement and measurement systems. We have numbered the steps of MSA on Figure 6-4.

To review, Step 1 of the MSA is entitled "Gaining a better understanding of the organizational system." The reason for starting here goes back to an underlying principle of this book: you cannot define and measure what you do not understand. Gaining a better understanding of the organizational system or even the domain that a management team is responsible for is important. I won't even attempt to sell you on this statement. In my opinion, this either makes sense or it doesn't; it's an issue of guiding principles and goes beyond logical defenses. If you assume that management teams have a good understanding of the organizational systems for which they are responsible, I think you are in trouble. Ten years of experience suggests that most management teams don't share information and knowledge and, therefore, tend to have limited awareness about mission, goals, improvement interventions, customers, environments, and what the left hand or right hand is doing.

There are several ways for management teams to improve their understanding of the organizational systems they are managing. Table 6-1 lists examples of activities that will accomplish this goal.

Note that OSA from the performance improvement planning process is largely designed, in fact, to do what Step 1 of the MSA requires. If you have successfully completed Step 1 of the PIPP, then it is likely that you will not need to do step one of MSA. In this sense, Steps 1 of PIPP and MSA overlap.

Step 2 of MSA focuses on identification of ways to improve the performance of the organizational system being analyzed. As mentioned previously, management teams in the

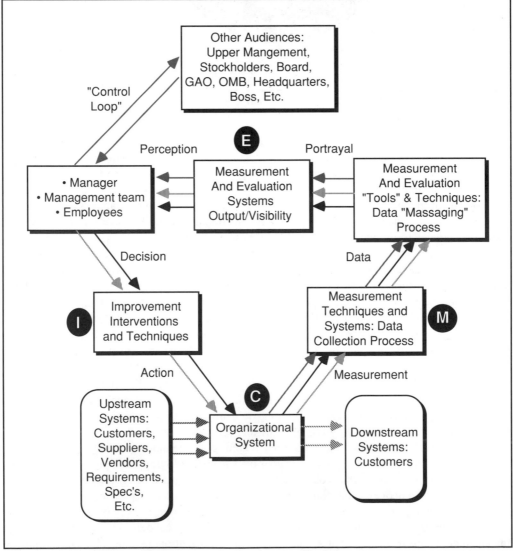

Figure 6-3. VPC's Management Systems Model

Organization of the Future will have at least two major responsibilities: ensure that the organizational system does what it is expected and needed to do—get the job(s) done on time within specifications; and constantly improve the performance of the organizational system. As we have said, in order to ensure that the second area of responsibility is successfully being accomplished throughout the organization, a major change in culture, planning, measurement, and reward systems is required. This is consistent with what Deming and Kurstedt are suggesting. Deming is calling for this in his fourteen points and Kurstedt expresses it in his ABC model. You can't build the business and stop catering to crises if you don't administer the process. The focus of Step 2 of MSA then is on how to improve administration of the management process and how to build the business. This is relevant and important for all organizations, not just the private sector, although the language might imply that.

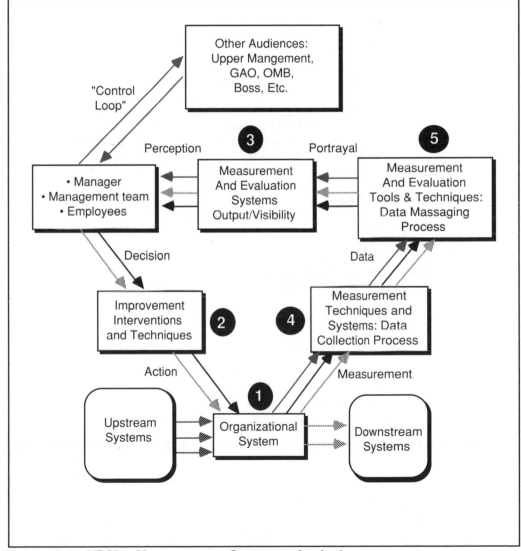

Figure 6-4. VPC's Management Systems Analysis

Note that the second step of MSA is equivalent to Steps 3 and 4 of the PIPP. The purpose of the performance improvement planning process is, in fact, to systematically identify ways to improve the quality of the management processes and to identify ways to build the business. So, we begin to see the interrelationship between the MSA and the PIPP. To this point in the MSA process, there is significant overlap. The purpose of Steps 5, 6, and 8 of the PIPP is to manage implementation of the ideas that come from the management team relative to improving the quality of the management processes and building the business.

Table 6-1. Areas of Assessment for Organizational Systems Analysis

Area 1.1 Vision (Corporate Long-Range Objectives)

Area 1.2 Guiding Principles (Values and Beliefs)

Area 1.3 Mission (Purpose)

Area 1.4 Input/Output Analysis

1.4.1.	Customers and Markets We Want/Must Serve - Downstream Systems
1.4.2.	Suppliers, Vendors, Customers, Procurement - Upstream Systems
1.4.3.	Business We Want To Be/Need To Be/Should Be/Are In, Products and Services Provided - Outputs
1.4.4.	Transformation Processes
1.4.5.	Materials, Supplies, Labor, Energy, Capital - Inputs

Area 1.5 Internal Strategic Analysis

1.5.1.	Structures Employed
1.5.2.	Staffing
1.5.3.	Facilities
1.5.4.	Technologies Employed
1.5.5.	Strengths and Weaknesses

Area 1.6 Current Performance Levels

Area 1.7 Roadblocks to Performance Improvement

Area 1.8 External Strategic Analysis

1.8.1.	Threats and Opportunities
1.8.2.	Review of Upline Plans

Step 3 of the MSA begins to get into the area of attention of Step 7 of the PIPP. A management team, it seems to us, has several measurement needs. First, it needs to know, on an ongoing and timely basis, how the organizational system is performing. Kurstedt suggests that there are three stages of maturity of management systems: gain visibility, gain control, and optimize. He goes on to suggest that there are different types of pursuits or organizational systems and areas of endeavor within organizational systems. He identifies the following:

1. A perplexity—we don't know where we're going (no knowledge of desired outcomes or outputs or ends);
2. A problem—we know where we want to go, but are not clear how to get there (knowledge of goals, lack of knowledge as to path);
3. A program—is a pursuit with a definite starting point but for which you have only a qualititive fix on the end;
4. A project—we know where we want to go and how to get there, but we have uncertainties to deal with and the project may be unique and nonrepetitive, hence we may be inefficient (still high on the learning curve); and
5. A process—we know what we want and how to get it and we can repeat it over and over again (Kurstedt 1985b).

A management team's information needs will be different depending upon what they are managing. There are different types of organizational systems, different types of improvement interventions, and different types of problem solving required for different types of situations. Our information needs will vary and our ability to satisfy those information needs for different situations will also vary accordingly.

Thompson (1967) addresses this in his classic book on *Organizations in Action*. In his chapter on the assessment of organizations, he presents a two-dimensional grid that looks at situations and types of assessment. Figure 6-5 presents that grid. The horizontal axis relates to "beliefs about cause/effect knowledge." Do we know what causes what? Are we managing a perplexity, a problem, a program, a project, or a process? Note that belief in cause/effect tends to improve/increase as we move from perplexities to processes. The vertical axis of the grid addresses "standards of desirability." Are our specifications clear, crystallized? Do we know or have we agreed upon what constitutes performance? Thompson then goes on to fill in the cells of the grid. He answers the question: What sorts of assessment techniques might we expect in each of these cells? I would suggest that he also was asking: Which of the seven performance criteria

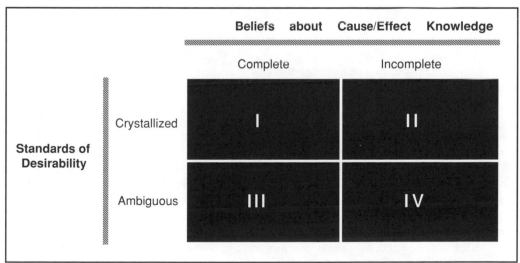

Figure 6-5. Situations and Types of Assessment

(Adapted from Thompson 1967)

are of most importance in each of these cells? He goes on to suggest, for example, that the efficiency test is used in Cell 1. He suggests that an effectiveness test, (he calls it an instrumental test) is appropriate in Cell 2: Was a desired state of affairs achieved? He provides some insight but not much specific guidance for Cells 3 and 4.

In Thompson's chapter on the control of complex organizations, he presents another grid (see Figure 6-6). The horizontal axis of this grid is the dimension called "preferences regarding possible outcomes." I interpret this to mean: Are we certain? Is there consensus regarding desired outcomes? Do we know where we are going? Is there a clearly communicated strategic plan? What are our preferences relative to the variety of outcomes that the organizational system could create? The purpose of Steps 3 and 4 of the PIPP is to create certainty for some of these things.

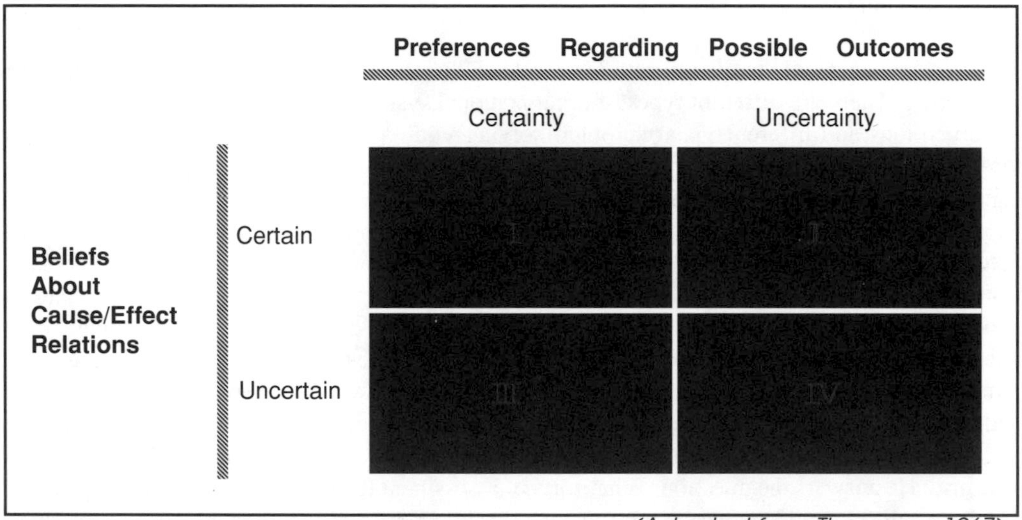

Figure 6-6. Process of Decision   *(Adapted from Thompson 1967)*

The vertical axis captures the dimension, beliefs about cause/effect relations. This is a path issue in my interpretation and, therefore, relates to the horizontal axis from the previous grid. The difference in the two axes appears to be beliefs about cause/effect knowledge versus beliefs about cause/effect relations. Do we think we know how to accomplish our goals versus do we think we understand cause/effect relationships? Again, we end up with a four-cell grid. He calls the axes basic variables of decision. The four cells represent four types of decision issues. Each decision issue calls for a different strategy. Cell 1 calls for a computational strategy, Cell 2 calls for a compromise strategy, Cell 3 a judgmental strategy, and Cell 4 an inspirational strategy.

If you were to merge these two grids, making the assumption that there are actually three unique dimensions, you would end up with a cube. The x-axis could represent the preference for possible outcomes (goals) dimension. The y-axis could represent the belief about cause/effect knowledge and relations (paths), and, the z-axis could represent the standards of desirability (assessment criteria). This conceptual integration appears in Figure 6-7.

Each of the eight cells of the cube represents a different situation. We can place Kurstedt's pursuits in specific cells, for example. We can place different stages of the problem solving process in specific cells. The stages of the problem-solving process are:

1. Issue identification;
2. Issue analysis;
3. Problem identification;
4. Problem analysis;
5. Decision analysis;
6. Design analysis;
7. Decision making;
8. Implementation analysis;
9. Implementation; and
10. Evaluation.

More specific to Step 3 of MSA, we can classify information needs/requirements in relation to the type of organizational system or specific problem that a management team is attempting to manage. We can identify the type of information that they should have and the type of information they can have depending on the specific situation. Management teams managing perplexities and issues need, and can obtain, different types of information than teams managing processes. Management teams managing perplexities, those in Cell 1,1,1 (don't know where they're going, don't know how to proceed, and don't know how to measure progress) or Cell 2,1,1 (know where they're going, don't know how to proceed, and don't know how to measure progress) are fortunate if they can create visibility with measurement systems. Management teams managing processes, those in Cell 2,2,2 (know where they're going, how they're going to get there, and know how to measure progress) need to measure to optimize. The intermediate requirement, as we mentioned, is to gain control.

So, there is a rich theoretical foundation upon which to develop answers to Step 3 of MSA. We haven't even reviewed the literature from the field of information systems. In the next chapter, we will show you how to help a management team decide what information it wants/needs to improve performance. The question we will answer is: "What does the management team need to know in order to tell them (a) how well the organizational system is performing, and (b) if the organizational system is getting better?"

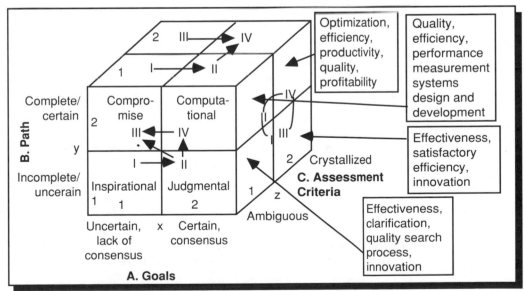

Figure 6-7. The Performance Management "Cube"

Step 4 of MSA focuses on the data requirements to provide the information identified in Step 3. Step 4 entails more than just an identification of data needs; it also requires addressing the following questions:

1. What data do we need?
2. Where will we get the data?
3. How will we access the data effectively and efficiently?
4. How will we store and retrieve the data effectively and efficiently?
5. How will we obtain the data that is not readily available?
6. Who will ensure that data needs are met on an ongoing basis?

Step 4 is the trench work of measurement. Supporting new information needs of management teams is hard work. We are so used to providing information that is easy to provide — that is so readily available from existing systems—that it is difficult to break out of the paradigm that says if it isn't a part of our current MIS it can't be important. Data-base design and implementation is a major impediment. Despite our talk of centralized data bases and integrated systems, the reality is that data support for measurement systems for organizations striving to improve is difficult to obtain.

Step 5 of the MSA focuses on what Kurstedt calls the "tools" box in the management systems model. It addresses the data to information transformation. Processing data, report generation, audience and purpose analysis, systems analysis, and model/technique selection and implementation are examples of activities encompassed by this step in the MSA. Spreadsheets, the total factor productivity measurement model, the objectives matrix, the multi-criteria performance measurement technique, statistical performance control, accounting packages, productivity map, the one page management system, intuition, judgment, experience, expert systems, data-base systems, report generators, and decision and management support systems are all examples of tools in this box and are the kinds of approaches that will be analyzed in Step 5 of MSA. Step 5 requires us to answer. How can we best convert our data into the information that has been required by the management team? The management team has indicated that if they had this information they could manage the organizational system better. How can we best provide that information?

This, in summary form, is management systems analysis. It is a logical sequence of steps that will guide you through the development of improved measurement systems. It is customer-focused (the customer is the management team) and it is improvement-oriented (the development is driven by our information requirements in support of our improvement strategies developed in Step 2 of MSA). In the next section, we will specifically speak to Steps 3 through 5 of the MSA.

Eight-Step Planning Process Revisited

In Chapters 2 and 4, we examined, in detail, the eight-step performance improvement planning process. We provide another look at the flow diagram for the process in Figure 6-8. Notice that the key performance indicators' (KPIs) boxes and Step 7 of the process specifically address the measurement issue. We mentioned that the KPIs focus on the effectiveness, efficiency, and quality with which we have implemented our objectives identified in Steps 3 and 4. Did we do what we said we would do to improve performance? Did we consume the right amount of resources? And, did we implement the objectives in a quality fashion? If we consider the action items identified in Step 4 to be projects, then the KPIs are project management measures of performance. Step 7 of the PIPP focuses on assessing the impact of our performance improvements on the performance of the organizational system. Is the organizational system actually getting better as a result of implementing our performance improvement plan? How will we know?

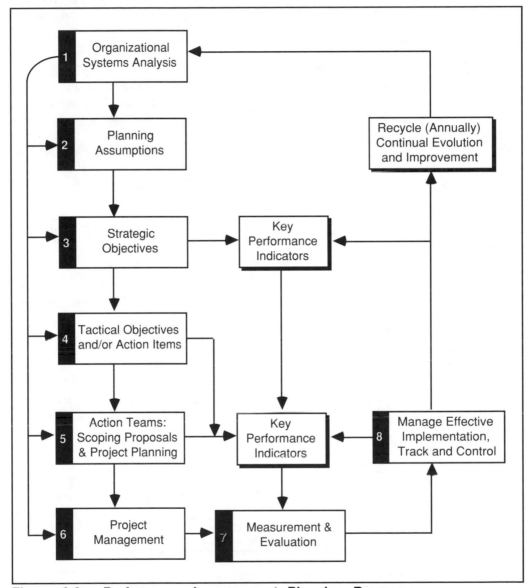

Figure 6-8. Performance Improvement Planning Process

Another critical relationship between our plan and measurement is the linkage between overall strategy, long-range goals, visions, guiding principles, missions, and our resulting measurement systems. Are there measures—information requirements—identified by the management team that will tell them whether or not they are progressing towards their long-range goals and visions? It is possible for the result of Step 3 of MSA to be myopic and shortsighted;

that is, the measures the management team identify focus only on tactical or operational issues. It is possible that the measures identified in Step 3 of MSA to be provided to the management team focus on near-term horizons and ignore longer-term considerations. If MSA were done in the absence of the planning process or a planning process, it is possible that the results from Step 3 would be deficient in this regard. When developing and implementing a measurement system you must consider this concern. In the next chapter, we will show you how to audit your measures to ensure that this does not happen.

Defining the Target System (Unit of Analysis)

When developing a measurement system, an early requirement is to identify and define the target system. This is a purpose of Step 1 of MSA and requires defining and delimiting the unit of analysis. What is the organizational system for which the measurement system is being developed? Boundaries must be established in order for measures to be developed. Not firmly establishing the unit of analysis is one of the major reasons for failure and frustration with the measurement process. It is impossible to differentiate between outputs, outcomes, intermediate outputs, activities, and various kinds of inputs unless this has been accomplished. We essentially are defining the boundaries of the system on the input and output side.

We reprint the input/output analysis for the aircraft intermediate maintenance department in Figure 6-9 to clarify our point. If we fail to clearly define the boundaries for the target system, we can end up classifying activities as outputs (if we allow ourselves to look inside the transformation process for outputs, we have allowed the unit of analysis to get smaller) and we create confusion, for example, with respect to what productivity really is. Conversely, we might

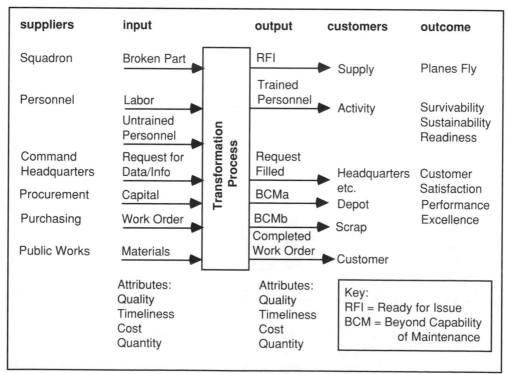

Figure 6-9. Example of Input/Output Analysis for an Aircraft Intermediate Maintenance Depot

allow the boundary to slip to the right and start to confuse outcomes with outputs. Many times we have less control over outcomes than outputs and, therefore, when a management team begins to identify productivity improvement ideas, they become frustrated because they perceive they have no control over the output side of the productivity equation. This happens frequently in white-collar settings. They confuse outcomes with outputs and then argue they can't measure or manage productivity.

The target system/unit of analysis must be defined, understood, and delimited in order for effective measurement to occur. How do you select a target system? Where do you start? One answer is to start at the top and work down. Start with the largest unit of analysis (i.e., the organization as a whole) and slowly begin to work down and decompose into smaller units of analysis. This would be a big, but not impossible, task in a large organization. If all management teams within the organization were trained in the techniques presented here, the task would happen quickly and easily. The management teams, in a sense, would be the measurement systems developers.

Another strategy would entail focusing on those organizational systems that have the greatest need for improvement, represent the areas with largest cost drivers, are the most responsive to making progress in the area of measurement systems development, have the weakest measurement systems, are the least accountable, have the poorest visibility and control, and are the most innovative and progressive. We personally have had the opportunity to work with organizations that are the most innovative and that recognize the importance of measurement. Of course, we also get the opportunity to work with a number of organizations that are failing and don't have time for measurement. We also have a lot of business from organizations that have been mandated by a president or other pivotal person in a position of power to measure. There are right and wrong reasons to measure.

Our bias is that all organizations ought to strive to improve the quality of their measurement and evaluation systems. All organizational systems within a larger organization ought to strive to do the same. Therefore, we recommend that a top-down strategy be employed. All organizational systems ought to be picked as target systems, and all target systems must be defined using a technique such as input/output analysis.

Process X function diagram

In addition to the issue of the type of organizational system, the decision regarding what to measure differs in terms of whether the target system is a function or a process. Consider the diagram in Figure 6-10.

Assume that processes are organizational activities that cut across functional lines, e.g., capital budget, power plant design, purchasing, job evaluation, and strategic planning, or programs or projects in project management organizations. Functions, on the other hand, are intact organizational entities usually referred to as departments, sections, or branches.

If you are attempting to develop measures of performance, it is possible to define the system as the vertical dimension in Figure 6-10 or the horizontal dimension. For example, in one organization we are working with, the system for measurement has been defined as lab tests. In effect, this is the horizontal dimension of the chart cutting across multiple functional organizational entities, e.g., individual laboratories. This would be fine except for the fact that the accounting system is set up on the vertical dimension of this chart. While measures could be defined for the horizontal dimension, it will be very difficult to obtain the data required to operationalize the measurement indicators.

This discussion is especially relevant for the following reason: most U.S. organizations

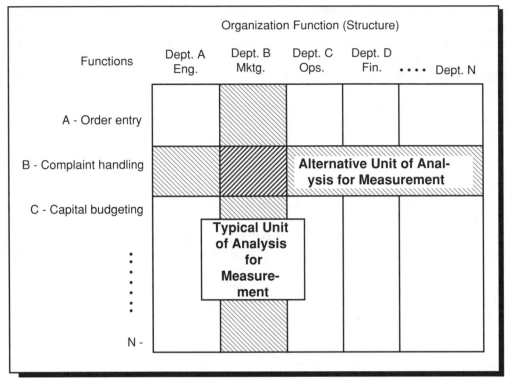

Figure 6-10. Process X Function Diagram

set up cost accounting systems and measure in the vertical dimension of this chart. However, organizations moving in to total quality management (TQM)t are increasingly slicing the organization horizontally in terms of processes to examine and improve. However, there is frequently a mismatch between the improvement orientation and the existing data systems. Some organizations are trying to cope with this situation by reorganizing more along process or product lines. Others are trying to cope by developing accounting systems that can track costs in either direction.

Measurement Systems Audit

The first step in the measurement system audit process involves clearly understanding the business strategy of the target system's parent system. In essence, this step involves identifying, for the manager of the target system: What aspect of performance is your boss (your upline system) trying to improve? For some organizations, this will be very obvious because the organization will have clearly articulated the key strategic performance dimensions to all organizational levels. In other organizations, there will be very little information relative to upline plans and strategies.

Examples of what we mean can be drawn from three very different organizations. A few years ago, the Honeywell Aerospace and Defense (A&D) Company defined three strategic performance dimensions for all Honeywell A&D organizations. These were value-added per man-hour, and scrap/rework and inventory reduction both expressed in relation to total sales (*Honeywell A&D Performance Improvement Guide* 1986). Another organization, the Anne Arundel Department of Utilities in Anne Arundel County, Maryland, a Senate Productivity Award recipient in 1987, had a different focus. This organization stated its key strategic performance dimensions as QCI (quality, cost, and image). A third example derives from work the Maryland Center for Productivity and QWL is doing for General Motors. In the course of developing a quality awareness training program for hourly employees, an analysis was made of the ways in which General Motors, in its manufacturing process, adds value for its customers. The sources of value identified were determined to be cost, availability, quality, features, and reputation.

In all three examples, the common element is that key dimensions of performance that are essential for competitive success have been defined. Ideally, these dimensions derive from the business strategy and the basis on which the organization seeks to sustain competitive advantage. Three generic strategies for competitive advantage rest on having lower costs than competitors, differentiating the organization or its product or service from competitors on attributes that are important to customers, or through focusing on a specific niche in which you can seek cost advantage or differentiation (Porter 1985).

The process of identifying these performance dimensions in an organization that has not made them clear may be difficult. However, as a manager you cannot develop a set of measures that will help the organization achieve its strategic objectives unless you are clear on what those objectives are. Therefore, you should require this information from your boss, your boss' boss, and so on until you have clarified these strategic dimensions for all upline systems. If you uncover the fact that there is no commonly agreed upon set of dimensions, you might tactfully suggest that the organization engage in a planning process session such as that described in Chapter 4. Use the NGT process to define key result areas as described in Appendix B. However, until this happens, you must do the best job you can to define the strategic performance areas for your organizational unit. The last section reviews the process of revisiting the eight-step planning process.

Once the strategic performance dimensions are identified the dimensions can be included in a section of the AIM form. See Figure 6-11 for an example of an AIM tableau.

Define linkage between the seven performance criteria and strategic dimensions

Chapter 5 operationally defined seven criteria of organizational systems performance. The chapter also defined different types of organizational systems and the relationship between organizational system type and types of performance criteria. Using these two pieces of information, it is possible to rank the seven performance criteria in terms of their relative importance for the target system. In general, this can be done by starting with the performance criteria that are most closely linked to the strategic performance dimensions. For example, if the organization is attempting to differentiate itself from competitors through quality, then we would expect to see the quality criteria weighted heavily among the seven performance criteria. There is substantial evidence to support the idea that quality of working life is also related to product and service quality, hence we would expect to also see this criterion ranked highly. In addition, if the organizational system is a direct result system, then efficiency and productivity are also very relevant criteria. The resulting prioritized list of seven criteria should also be included as a section of rows in the AIM tableau. So, we have identified strategic performance dimensions and target system performance criteria priorities.

Other sections of AIM can include the long-range goals (i.e., twenty years) of the target system, the objectives from Steps 3 and/or 4 of the eight-step planning process, and even goals and objectives from upline systems where appropriate.

Identify current performance measures for the target system

Performance Measures / Audit Factor	Current								Newly Developed								
Long Range Objectives																	
Upline																	
Target Systems																	
Strategic Performance Dimensions																	
Upline																	
Target System																	
Performance Improvement Objectives																	
Upline 0-3 year																	
5-7 year																	
Target System 0-3 year																	
5-7 year																	
Performance Criteria																	
Efficiency																	
Effectiveness																	
Quality Checkpoint 1																	
Quality Checkpoint 2																	
Quality Checkpoint 3																	
Quality Checkpoint 4																	
Quality Checkpoint 5																	
Productivity																	
Quality of Work Life																	
Innovation																	
Profitability/ Budgetability																	
Audience																	
Mgmt. Team																	
Upline																	
Purpose																	
Control																	
Improvement																	
Checkpoint																	
1. Upstream																	
2. Inputs																	
3. Trans. Process																	
4. Output																	
5. Downstream/ Outcome																	

Figure 6-11. Audit To Improve Measurement (AIM) Tableau

Performance Measures / Audit Factor	Current							Newly Developed							
	# New Programs	# Written Programs	Percent Time Spent on Priority Projects	New Products	# Task Loading Changes	Quality of Cost Estimates	"Time Sharing"	Turnover Rate	Capital Equipment Requests	Letters of Recognition					
Long Range Objectives															
Upline															
Target Systems															
Strategic Performance Dimensions															
Upline															
Target System															
Performance Improvement Objectives															
Upline 0-3 year															
5-7 year															
Target System 0-3 year															
5-7 year															
Performance Criteria															
Efficiency															
Effectiveness															
Quality Checkpoint 1															
Quality Checkpoint 2															
Quality Checkpoint 3															
Quality Checkpoint 4															
Quality Checkpoint 5															
Productivity															
Quality of Work Life															
Innovation															
Profitability/ Budgetability															
Audience															
Mgmt. Team															
Upline															
Purpose															
Control															
Improvement															
Checkpoint															
1. Upstream															
2. Inputs															
3. Trans. Process															
4. Output															
5. Downstream/ Outcome															

Figure 6-12. Audit To Improve Measurement (AIM) Tableau

Step 7 of the eight-step planning process called for developing performance measures for the target system. Current performance measures may be identified or new ones developed in this step. These measures will be attributes and indicators of the seven performance criteria. The complete set of current and newly developed measures of performance for the organizational system should be placed in the columns (across the top) of the AIM tableau (see Figure 6-12).

Complete the audit tableau

The next step in the audit process involves completing the audit by checking appropriate boxes. We are mapping the measures to the various rows within each section of AIM. We would identify which measures relate directly to each of the long-, medium-, and short-range objectives identified in Steps 1, 3, and 4 of the eight-step performance improvement planning process. We would also identify with a check those measures that directly correspond to the strategic performance dimensions identified, as well as the prioritized list of the seven performance criteria. We can also map measures to the five quality checkpoints—the upstream system, inputs, transformation process, outputs, and downstream systems/outcomes phases—of the organizational system resource flow model we have previously discussed.

There may be other sections and rows you want to add to audit your measures, attributes,

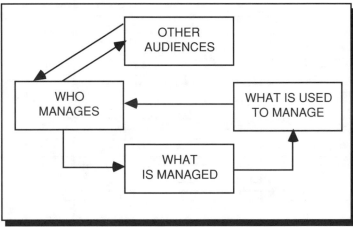

Figure 6-13. Management System Model

and indicators against. The intent is to ensure that your measures are comprehensive, valid, and thought through in an integrated fashion, and that they cover all the aspects of total performance for your target system. This step of completing the audit is not as easy as it might appear on the surface; however, upon completion others have found the process very rewarding.

Conduct the analysis

Gaps may appear in your audit tableau. They will become very visible with the use of this instrument. You may uncover areas where you have no quality measures and you will need to develop some. You may wish to revisit and rethink your upline plans data, your target system plans, or Step 7 of the planning process to develop a more comprehensive list of measures. Or the needed measures to fill in gaps may become obvious and you may want to employ a consultative strategy by developing straw-man measures for members of the target system to approve. In the next chapter, we will discuss the next steps in measurement system development once AIM has been completed. We want to turn our attention to the users of the measures you have just audited— the audiences for measurement.

Audience Analysis

There are multiple audiences for measurement information and data. Most simply, there are external audiences—those who are not a part of the organizational system being measured— and internal audiences—those who are a part of the system. Figure 6-13 graphically represents these two audiences.

Obviously, the external audience could be further segmented to include other parts of the organization, the public, regulatory bodies, financial analysts, and more. Even the internal audience can be segmented to include managers, nonmanagers, staff, union officials, and employees.

From a measurement system design standpoint, the important issue is the requirements of each audience with respect to the relevant performance measures, the frequency of reporting, and the format or portrayal of the measures. With respect to measurement as an improvement tool, the most relevant audience consists of the members of the organizational system itself—the management team of the target system. For this internal audience, the information required to support their tasks of continual performance improvement are identified in Step 3a of MSA. We will discuss exactly how to complete this step of MSA in the next chapter. The same process that is applied to developing information requirements/measures of performance for the internal audiences can be applied for external audiences also.

The point to performing an audience analysis is that different audiences have different information needs and requirements. Therefore, a single measurement system will rarely suffice, although a single well-designed data base of measurement data might be developed to supply a variety, if not all, of the information systems. A simple form for performing audience analysis is depicted in Figure 6-14.

Identifying or Developing Masters

Peters and Waterman discuss the role of champions in excellent organizations. I believe they elaborated on several types of champions. Recently, Deming has discussed the concept of masters. I recall a master being defined as someone with the knowledge, skills, willingness, ability, and experience to do what needs to be done. In this case, we are talking about planning for, designing, and developing measurement systems. Deming points out, and we agree, that without masters your efforts to improve quality and productivity will fail. No amount of championing by top management will overcome the lack of "know how" in the specific techniques necessary for measurement or any other type of intervention.

In our experience, there are very few measurement masters in American organizations. There are work measurement experts, cost accounting experts, and corporate finance experts, but these are generally too narrowly trained to think about measurement. They also are quite often, if not always, biased towards control-oriented measurement. They have deeply entrenched paradigms that are difficult to break. The fact that measurement masters don't currently exist is not as distressing as the fact that often no one steps forward from an organization with the willingness and ability to become a master. The organization can provide the opportunity but cannot force the willingness or create the ability.

Planning for the design, development, and implementation of measurement systems requires a number of things, the most important of which is to identify or develop a "critical mass" of measurement masters. This group of people will be the architects for the measurement systems throughout your organization. They will need to have in-depth knowledge of conventional measurement systems in addition to in-depth knowledge of the state-of-the-art and practice techniques we identify in this book. They will need to have broad and deep knowledge of measurement, ranging from personnel testing, psychometrics (small units of analysis) to macro-economic analysis and productivity measurement at the industry and national level (large units of analysis). They will need to have a solid foundation in math and statistics (both parametric and nonparametric). They will need to understand the many types of research. They will require excellent problem solving skills, interpersonal skills, exploratory data analysis skills, and professional communication skills. They will need to have good, ongoing relations with your comptroller, personnel department (selection and placement, testing, and performance appraisal), compensation administration department (gainsharing systems), quality assurance department (measurement for quality checkpoints 1 through 5), computer information system department (decision support systems and data base), and the appropriate operations management in order to understand prime user measurement needs. These are the major specifications for measurement masters, and as you can see, your organization probably has not home grown these individuals in the past. They may exist, but it is likely you will have to develop these persons.

Self-study is one way to develop these masters. Sufficient literature does exist for this

External Audiences for Measurement Data	Why They Need It	Data Required	Frequency
Internal Audiences for Measurement Data	Why They Need It	Data Required	Frequency

Figure 6-14. Audience Analysis Form

option to be a possibility; however, the process might be inefficient. Training programs have been developed and are available. It is obvious, however, that many of the specifications cannot be met via a formal training program. The working relationships with the various departments in your organization can only come with time and experience. Much of the knowledge required would hopefully have been obtained in the individual's undergraduate and/or graduate programs. Selection and placement of measurement masters is, therefore, critical. If your organization is large enough to require a team of measurement masters, it might be a good idea to select people from a variety of disciplines (for example, statistics, industrial engineering, industrial psychology, sociology, accounting, finance, and computer and information sciences). This team would make up a multidisciplinary approach to the planning and development of measurement systems. They could work together or as individuals to assist in the development of measurement systems throughout the organization. As a team, they could develop the grand strategy for the overall architecture and strategy for the entire organization.

I'm not sure we are suggesting a new department called the "measurement masters department." This group of masters could be integrated into existing organizational structures. There are many ways for organizing such an effort. I am suggesting that measurement systems are too important to leave to chance. In the past, measurement systems development has been differentiated. That is, the accounting department developed the accounting systems for managers to use — often with little user input. The MIS department has been swamped trying to keep up with changes in hardware and software, exponentially increasing demands on systems, and "pain-in-the-neck" users who think they are the only ones who are important. The industrial engineers developed standards that were used to control behavior, not necessarily improve it. The personnel people developed measurement systems to conveniently determine how to uniformly distribute X dollars among Y people. The managers in operations have inherited measurement systems from the managers before them, who inherited theirs from the managers before them. At best, operating managers have taken band-aid approaches to improving measurement systems. Many end up creating parallel systems: their own, which is often informal, and the last manager's, which they ignore.

Measurement systems are some of the most important management processes in your organization. They deserve better engineering, design, development, preventive maintenance, and attention than we have given them in the past. Our efforts have been piecemeal and fragmented. Our efforts have produced low-quality results because myopic masters have developed pieces of the measurement system ignorant of the total-picture system requirements. The development of a team of measurement masters who will plan and assist with the development and implementation of measurement systems throughout the organization is called for in the 1980s and beyond.

Guiding Principles

There are many principles that support the theory and practice of measurement that we are developing in these three chapters. Four specific principles undergird our proposed methodology for developing performance improvement oriented measurement systems. We believe that these principles are compatible with the need expressed in Chapter 3 for organizations to move toward the Organization of the Future by changing certain management processes and practices. In fact, we believe that measurement, evaluation, and control systems based upon these principles are essential if organizations are to respond effectively to The New Competition.

1. *Measurement cannot be used to drive performance improvement—the driver must be the business strategy and the performance improvement plan* . In developing a measurement system, it is necessary to clearly understand the function, purpose, and limitations of performance measurement. A measurement system cannot convince a manager or a management team member that performance improvement is necessary. This awareness must come from an understanding of the types of information gathered and shared in the first step of the PIPP — the organizational systems analysis. Once managers and management team members have accepted the competitive necessity of continuous performance improvement, then measurement becomes an integral and essential tool for guiding decision making and directing action toward successful performance

improvement.

Note in both the management systems analysis and the performance improvement planning process that measurement system development follows development of improvement plans. Management teams that have previously resisted measurement "do a 180" when the sequence is strategies for improvement leading measurement. Measurement is seen as a valuable tool rather than a "forced upon us" evil.

2. *Acceptance of the measurement process is essential to its success as a performance improvement tool.* Measurement techniques that are not acceptable to those being measured are unlikely to stimulate performance improvement or satisfy information needs. Measurement systems for improvement must be viewed as tools to help those who want to make improvements be able to do so. This acceptance can be enhanced by having those whose performance is being measured involved in developing the measures and the measurement systems. Involvement will enhance acceptance and create measurement systems that are more relevant than if they were designed by outside experts or consultants.

The goal is to effectively implement a successful improvement process supported by effective measurement. One must balance the quality of the measurement process with the acceptance of the process in order to achieve effective implementation. A high-quality measurement approach/system that has no acceptance will not likely be implemented or support improvement needs. Conversely, a low-quality measurement system with high acceptance will not likely achieve desired results. Matching measurement masters with managed participative approaches for developing measurement systems has been found to be the highest-quality solution.

3. *Measure what's important—not what's easy to measure.* Measurement tends to steer performance and resource allocation toward those things that are measured. As a result, if organizations fail to ensure that their measurement systems measure the "right" things, they will drive performance in the wrong direction. A corollary to this principle is that it is better to have a crude measure of something important than a precise measure of something trivial. For example, in some work conducted by the Maryland Center for Quality and Productivity, a group of food-service managers were attempting to develop performance measures for dining halls. A considerable debate ensued about the importance of measuring customer satisfaction. One participant stated that if they didn't measure how customers felt about their meals, nothing else mattered. Others agreed, but felt that customer satisfaction was not feasible to measure, so they argued that the measure should be dismissed. Through his persistence, the manager convinced the others that it was possible to measure customer service, and he described a crude system. The plan was to build a box with seven slots in the top of seven compartments. On the front of each slot a face would be painted. The faces would have expressions ranging from a strong frown to a strong smile. When diners left the dining hall they would be given a token. They would indicate their satisfaction with the meal by dropping the token into one of the seven slots corresponding to how they felt about the meal.

While this measure is crude, it is still vital and creative. One might not want to use this as the only measure of dining hall performance, yet a measurement system without some measure of customer satisfaction, no matter how simple, would be deficient at best.

4. *Adopt an experimental approach to measurement systems for improvement.* Peters and Waterman (1982) pointed out that excellent organizations have a bias for action. Their dictum "ready, fire, aim" is quite appropriate for developing measurement systems for improvement. Using the techniques described in this book, develop the best measures you can and then try them out. If they don't give you what you need, you'll be smarter then and you can change them. Don't wait until you feel the measures are perfect before you start using them. If you do, you may never have a measurement system in place.

Some of you may be uncomfortable with this principle. The perceived lack of precision may make you nervous, especially if you have been shaped to think about measurement from an industrial engineering/work measurement perspective, an accounting perspective, a corporate finance perspective, or a psychometric perspective to psychology or sociology. However, you must consider what we are saying in light of the improvement focus. First, the simplicity of the systems we propose make them easy to change and improve over time. Second, much of the precision implied in other measurement systems is often illusory. We are not recommending abandonment of traditional control-oriented measurement systems. We do recommend improved balance between the improvement-oriented measurement efforts and the control-oriented efforts.

As we said at the outset of this section, the four principles reviewed are not exhaustive. We list a number of others for your consideration but do not elaborate upon them.

5. *Eliminate the use of numerical goals, work standards, and quotas* (Deming 1986).

6.*What is needed is not a standard set of measurements created by experts and imposed on organizations, but rather a method by which management teams and their various clienteles can create performance measurement systems suited to their own inevitably special needs and circumstances* (Morris 1975).

7. *The greater the participation in the process in creating a performance measurement system, the greater the resulting performance change, and the greater the ease of implementation of future changes based upon performance measurement.*

8. *Any system should result in a vector of performance measures, not attempting to achieve a single measure. Much of the controversy and lack of acceptance stems from attempts to make a very complex problem appear too simple.*

9. *A performance measurement system must not appear to those involved as simply a passing fad.*

10. *The measurement system must clearly fit into the management process and be acknowledged as a decision-making and problem-solving support.*

11. *The behavioral consequences, the unintended and potentially dysfunctional consequences of performance measurement, must be anticipated and reflected in system design.*

12. *A useful system must be seen by those whose behaviors are being assessed as being non-manipulative, not gamed.*

13. *An effective measurement system must build upon consistent and well understood operational definitions for the seven performance criteria.*

14. *The unit of analysis/target system must be clearly defined and delimited in order for measurement to succeed. An input/output analysis is a necessary precondition.*

15. *One must create visibility and ownership for the resulting measurement systems in order to ensure effective longer-term utilization.*

16. *One must clearly separate the process of measurement from the process of evaluation. The difference between a control chart and specifications/requirements and standards must be understood.*

We leave you with this list of guiding principles to consider as you develop improved measurement systems for your organization. We turn our attention now to the issue of knowing what techniques for measurement are available.

Knowing What's Available

We have discussed to this point important aspects associated with the process of planning for the development and implementation of improved measurement systems. Management systems analysis, the eight-step planning process, defining target systems, measurement systems audits, audience analysis, the identification of or development of measurement masters, and principles

Table 6-2. Performance/Productivity Measurement Tools and Techniques

Techniques/Tools	Description
MFPMM - Multi-Factor Productivity Measurement Model	The MFPMM is a dynamic, aggregated, indexed, and computerized approach to measuring productivity. MFPMM partials out the effects of price recovery for each input factor. Information is provided on quantity and price change ratios, cost drivers, percent change in productivity and price recovery, and the dollar effects on profits due to changes in productivity and price recovery.
MCP/PMT - Multi-Criteria Performance/Productivity Measurement Technique	The MCP/PMT is an innovative, widely applicable, and reasonably simple approach to measuring group performance. The MCP/PMT is particularly useful in measuring the performance of white-collar groups. The technique integrates nicely with the NPMM and the Objectives Matrix to make more effective use of the measures obtained.
NPMM - Normative Performance Measurement Model	The NPMM is an important component of a performance process so that work groups can design measurement systems suited to their own needs. The NPMM considers the behavioral consequences of measurement so that the measurement effort is accepted and not considered manipulative or a passing fad by those being measured.
CSS - Common Staffing Study	CSS is an approach to indirect labor measurement developed by IBM. Measures are developed using input/output activity indicators for each major work group. The major purposes of CSS are to highlight areas for improvement, provide a measure of indirect productivity improvement, and provide a relative measure of indirect productivity across locations.
CDEF - Cost Definition Methodology	Price Waterhouse has developed CDEF as an approach for preparing cost baseline data in support of factory modernization efforts. CDEF utilizes a top down analysis technique which facilitates the identification of appropriate efficiency and cost measurement criteria, selection of improvement opportunities, and economic justification of identified investments.
DCF/SSA - Discounted Cash Flow/ Share Savings	The DCF/SSA model is a time-phased model of cash receipts (or savings) and cash disbursements over a particular planning horizon. The model consists of (1) a time-phased model of cash receipts/disbursements over a finite planning horizon, with a portion of the receipts being shared savings, and (2) a calculated Internal Rate of Return (IRR) measure of economic effectiveness.
SPerfC - Statistical Performance Control	SPerfC is based on the same principles as used in Statistical Process Control. The difference is that SperfC is used for monitoring all seven performance criteria. SPerfC defines a management process for effectively controlling the variance and shifting the mean performance in each of the seven criteria.

Table 6-2. Performance/Productivity Measurement Tools and Techniques

Techniques/ Tools	Description
TOPS - The One Page Management System	TOPS is a measurement system useful in white-collar settings. TOPS is designed to overcome the data-rich information poor (DRIP) problem often associated with white-collar measurement by providing management and staff with visibility target areas in need of improvement. Three one-page reports - focus, feedback, and management - combine to provide a total overview of an individual's performance.
Work Measurement	Work Measurement includes motion and time studies necessary to determine standards (standard time and labor costs) so that the efficiency of workers is improved. Work standards can be used for one worker or for a team. Work Measurements are used to measure how well a worker performs relative to a predetermined standard.
Cost/Benefit Analysis	This is used for the analysis of the public project. It attempts to evaluate the benefits for the users of a project coming from a government agency.
Variance Analysis	Accounting technique used to determine sources of variations of profitability of an organization or division (profit center).
	(Adapted from Sink and Rossler, 1987)

to guide the development of measurement systems have been discussed. Measurement is both an art and a science. As such, measurement masters need to understand the theory of measurement as well as the techniques for measurement. Knowing what is available is an ongoing quest for information. Knowing what is available requires that your measurement masters adopt a continual learning approach. The literature is filled with new concepts, approaches, case studies, and theoretical issues, and your measurement masters have to keep current.

The half-life of an engineer is reported to be in the neighborhood of five to seven years. The half-life of a quality and productivity master, a measurement master, is probably less. This is a tremendously dynamic period in terms of new technique development and application testing. The rapid change is being caused by environmental and technological changes that are putting pressures on your organization to adapt. If you just cater to crises during these periods, you're going to be behind everybody else and lose the game. Your measurement masters, like other masters in other areas, have to stay ahead of the game; they have to proactively search for new approaches, methodologies, techniques, and implementation tips. They have to constantly search for ways to move up existing S-shaped curves and for entirely new S-shaped curves.

Table 6-2 depicts a partial listing of measurement techniques and approaches that are presently available and ought to be investigated by your measurement masters. Some of the techniques presented are conventional, some are state-of-the-art and practice techniques. Some are worthy of application in your organization, some not. All are worthy of study by your measurement masters. We source the approaches so that your measurement masters can begin their investigation.

It is important to keep one of our suggested guiding principles in mind during this phase of planning for measurement system improvement: that of measurement systems quality improvement being a continual improvement process, not a series of programmatic interventions. Your measurement-master team should be charged with the continual evolution process. This process should appear much more like a constant, smooth evolution rather than a series of jerky, false starts and programs. Quality checkpoint 1 calls for thoughtful design up front, which should help to ensure that our efforts to improve measurement systems are not simply a trial-and-error process. You ought not plan to fail, and you should not fail to plan.

Selecting the Approaches, Methodologies, Models or Techniques

It is difficult to prescribe how to select appropriate techniques for measurement since there are so many variables that must be considered. Existing measurement systems, organizational culture, management style, type of business, where an organizational system is relative to "the cube," resistance to measurement, stage of evolution of present systems, and the level of awareness of the need for and importance of improved measurement systems are all factors that must be considered by your measurement masters as they decide where to begin. We have given some thought to guidance that we could provide in the area of deciding which techniques to employ and have come up with the beginnings of an expert system. Seung-il Shin and Phillipe Riel (1988) have adopted decision-tree methodology and developed a decision contour map approach to answering the question of which techniques to employ. We present these approaches in this section and hope it is beneficial. Please feel free to provide feedback as to its utility.

General methodology

The Vroom and Yetton (1974) methodology of contingency theory goes as follows:

1. List the possible solution to the problem to be tackled;
2. Determine the problem's attributes or situational characteristics;
3. From these attributes formulate diagnostic questions about the problem;
4. Build decision rules that will allocate the proper technique to the given situation determined by the particular attribute;
5. Formalize the decision rules with a systematic decision process that will lead to the solution (decision tree construction).

Set of measurement techniques. The types of measurement systems that were retained as possible prescriptive solutions for the system to be considered are described in Table 6-2. This is not an exhaustive list of measurement tools available. However, the list features the most important and widely used techniques developed in the past ten years or so.

Problem attributes. Nine attributes were found to be pertinent to the problem of choosing the proper performance measurement system. These attributes refer to the system in terms of the process involved and the management setting that prevails and attempts to encompass the socio-technical dimensions of the situation within which the system is embedded.

The first attribute (measurement criteria) refers to the performance criteria that is dominant over the others and which determines in a large proportion the overall performance of the system. The second criteria is the unit of analysis of the system under consideration. The third one is the available frequency of measurement provided by the system: How often can the system be assessed? The fourth one refers to the sense of urgency associated by the problem experienced which calls for the proper planning horizon (how quickly after its implementation do results of the measurement system arrive?) The type of data made available by the system constitute the fifth problem attribute. A sixth attribute is the prevailing management style. A seventh attribute is the purpose of the measurement system to be implemented. The type of employees involved in the organization who will use the measurement system is the eighth attribute. Finally, the last problem attribute refers to the structure of the problem to which the organization is confronted.

Again, these attributes specified above are not exhaustive. Oftentimes, you might find other problem attributes relevant to your situation.

Diagnostic questions. The diagnostic questions pertinent to the decision were found to be the following:

- Is the primary purpose of the measurement system for control or improvement?
- Is the measurement system to be of the aggregated or disaggregated type?
- Is the unit of analysis at the individual, work group, divisional, or the organizational level?
- Is the system centralized or decentralized?
- Is the system mainly composed of a blue- or a white-collar work force?
- Is the task actually performed in the system very well structured or not?
- Is there a short-term or a long-term requirement relative to the urgency for rapid results of the measurement system?
- Is there any significant performance criteria (effectiveness, efficiency, quality, productivity, quality of work life, innovation, profitability/budgetability) that dominates the others in such a way that this criteria is determinant in the overall performance of the system?
- Is the management style actually prevailing in the system an autocratic, consultative, or participative type?
- What type of data is available? Current or past, quantitative or qualitative?
- Is the data available on a daily, weekly, monthly, quarterly, or only on a yearly basis?

Decision rules. The next step of this methodology encompasses building decision rules that will actually allocate the proper techniques to the given situation characterized by the diagnostic question. The decision rules associated with these diagnostic questions are the following (with the feasible set of prescriptions for each case):

1. **The purpose rule**. For control: MFPMM, MCP/PMT, DCF/SSA, CDEF, SPerfC, TOPS, WM, C/B Analysis, Variance Analysis (VA). For improvement: NPMM, CSS, SPerfC, TOPS, WM.
2. **The aggregation rule**. For aggregated systems: MFPMM, MCP/PMT, NPMM, CSS, SPerfC, TOPS. For disaggregated systems: CDEF, DCF/SSA.
3. **The unit of analysis rule**. For the individual level: TOPS, WM. For the work group level: MCP/PMT, SPerfC, WM. For the functional or departmental level: MCP/PMT, NPMM, DCF/SSA, CDEF, C/B Analysis, VA. For the firm or divisional level: MFPMM, NPMM, CSS, DCF/SSA, CDEF, C/B Analysis, VA.
4. **The work-force-type-rule**. For blue-collar setting: MFPMM, MCP/PMT, NPMM, CSS, SPerfC, CDEF, DCF/SSA. For white-collar setting: MFPMM, MCP/PMT, NPMM, CSS, CDEF, DCF/SSA, SPerfC, TOPS, WM, C/B Analysis, VA.
5. **The task rule**. For structured work: MFPMM, NPMM, DCF/SSA, CDEF, SPerfC, WM.

217

For unstructured work: MCP/PMT, NPMM, DCF/SSA, CDEF, C/B Analysis, VA.

6. **The measurement horizon rule**. For long-term horizon: MFPMM, MCP/PMT, NPMM, CSS, CDEF, DCF/SSA, C/B Analysis, VA. For intermediate term: MCP/PMT, NPMM, CSS, CDEF, DCF/SSA, SPerfC, TOPS, WM, C/B Analysis. For short term: TOPS, WM.

7. **Performance criteria rule**. For the effectiveness: MFPMM, MCP/PMT, NPMM, SPerfC, TOPS. For efficiency: MCP/PMT, NPMM, CSS, SPerfC, DCF/SSA, TOPS, WM, VA, C/B Analysis. For quality: MCP/PMT, SPerfC. For productivity: MFPMM, MCP/PMT, NPMM, CSS, SPerfC, WM. For quality of work life: MCP/PMT, TOPS, SPerfC. For innovation: SPerfC, MCP/PMT, TOPS. For profitability/budgetability: MFPMM, MCP/PMT, DCF/SSA, CDEF, VA, C/B Analysis.

8. **Data type rule**. For the case of past and current data available: MFPMM, SPerfC. For the case of unavailable past data: MCP/PMT, TOPS.

9. **Data timeliness rule**. For data available on a weekly basis: TOPS, WM. On a monthly and quarterly basis: TOPS, SPerfC, C/B Analysis. On a yearly basis: MFPMM, MCP/PMT, NPMM, CSS, DCF/SSA, CDEF, VA.

The decision tree construction. The next step would be to construct a decision tree that would lead the management to the proper measurement technique. A sample decision tree is constructed using retained decision rules (see Figure 6-15). The tree incorporates the decision rules and diagnostic questions for each attribute identified here. Because of the complexity of the decision process and the number of variables involved in the diagnostic questions, only a limited number of decision rules have been retained for this sample decision tree: the purpose rule, the unit-of-analysis rule, and the performance criteria rule. Those three rules are thought to be critical in the decision process of a productivity/performance system. However, the six other rules developed here are not necessarily trivial. The decision maker is likely to use them to make sure that the solution or prescription he or she chooses is compatible with the overall situation of the system under consideration. The sample decision tree is thus a three-stage decision process where the purpose of the measurement system is determined, and the unit of analysis and the dominant performance criteria to measure are determined according to the decision rules.

The decision "contour map" approach

As is shown in Figure 6-15, the decision tree approach is complex, even in the case where only three decision rules are adopted. The complexity of the tree in terms of all possible outcomes makes the construction of such a tree virtually impossible. This is especially true when we have a large combination of problem attributes and decision rules. Instead of this device, another visual representation is proposed—the "contour map"—which is thought of as meeting the following design criteria:

- Flexible—it can incorporate as many problem attributes as possible simultaneously;
- Easily combines diagnostic questions and decision rules;
- Easy to construct and modify;
- Reduces complexity and time to construct the whole decision tree;
- Gives a good visual representation of what is going on; and
- Can alleviate or reinforce decision rules.

Figure 6-16 depicts the decision contour map for selecting a productivity measurement tool incorporating six decision rules, plus diagnostic questions, as well as the problem attributes.

How do you use the contour map to find the tools suitable for your situation? First, go over each decision rule and circle the diagnostic question in each rule suitable for a given situation. After circling all the diagnostic questions suitable for a given situation, trace the lines toward the center of the concentric circles along with the lines. The dots on each line represent measurement techniques that meet the diagnostic questions for the decision rule. If dots are found on all the lines for a specific measurement tool after tracing each and every diagnostic question selected, the tool is supposed to be the most suitable measurement technique appropriate for the situation. There could be cases in which more than two tools are found. In that case, any one of the measurement techniques can be used; or by adding one or two relevant diagnostic questions, the number of feasible solutions (here, they are measurement techniques) can be reduced. On the other hand, if no tools are found while tracing the lines, alleviating one or two of the most unimportant decision rules could lead to a possible solution.

Overcoming Resistance to Change

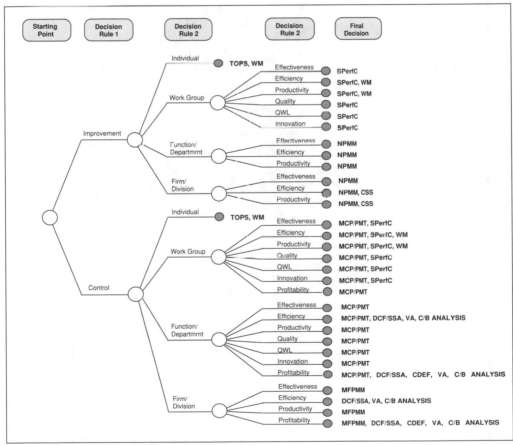

Figure 6-15. A Sample Decision Tree

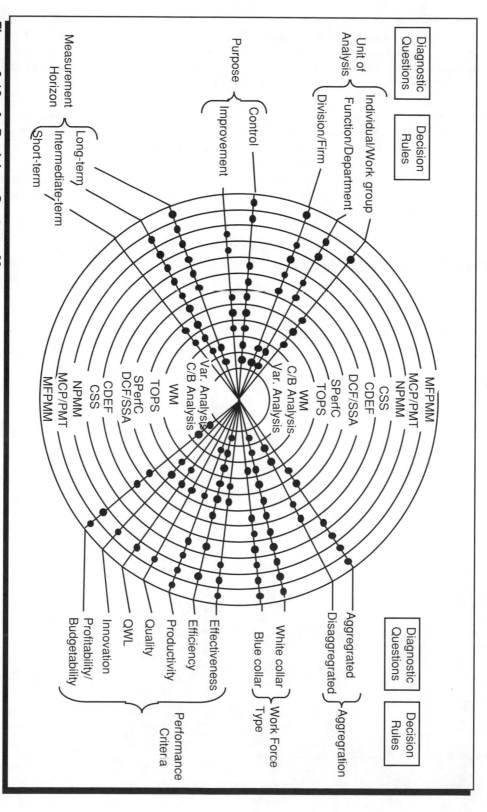

Figure 6-16. A Decision Contour Map

Force-field analysis

Developing a performance measurement system is a complex organizational intervention. As such, it must be carefully planned to ensure that it will have the desired impact. A useful analytic tool to employ, prior to the development of the measurement system implementation plan, is a technique known as force-field analysis (Lewin 1938).

The technique is based on the idea that for any proposed action (e.g., successful implementation of a performance measurement system) there are driving forces and restraining forces. Driving forces act like tailwinds and are a positive force in favor of the proposed action. Restraining forces act like headwinds to block or slow down the proposed action. To the extent that these forces can be identified and their relative strengths assessed, you can better decide how to proceed in implementing the proposed action. In its most sophisticated application, once the driving and restraining forces are defined, psychological scaling techniques should be utilized to quantify the strength of the forces. These might then be arrayed in a diagram such as that shown in Figure 6-17.

Even if the scaling is not done, the thought process to arrive at the driving and restraining

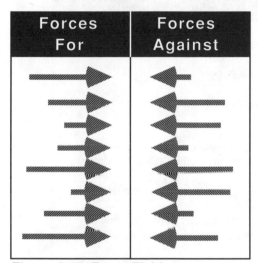

Figure 6-17. Force-Field Analysis Diagram

forces is a useful process. A force-field analysis conducted for the implementation of a performance measurement system in one organization is shown in Figure 6-18. In this example, the management team that served as the measurement development team also developed this diagram.

To use this as a tool for implementation planning, it is necessary to define strategies that will increase the "forces for" and decrease the "forces against." While it is possible for management to implement an action simply by increasing the driving forces, such a strategy is often counterproductive. It may appear that the implementation succeeds in the short run, but there will be resistance, possible gaming, and conceivably, even sabotage. The negative forces generated by imposition of a strategy against the will of a group will show up in other ways, and the performance of the group will suffer.

Using the example in Figure 6-18, a communication program might be designed that would attempt to build on the "forces for" by giving examples of communication with the public, increased ability to compete for resources, and better focus. This same opportunity could be designed to try to remove or reduce the "forces against." For example, the fear of more paperwork might be reduced by a manager pointing out that, "Every effort will be made to make use of data that is already in the performance tracking system. Furthermore, there may be opportunities, due to better output control made possible by the measurement system, to eliminate some of the current measurement systems and thereby reduce the net paperwork."

Thus, in using the force-field analysis as a planning for effective implementation tool there are three generic strategies. First, we try to increase the "forces for" the implementation. Second, we try to eliminate or reduce the "forces against" the implementation. Third, for those "forces against" that we cannot impact, we acknowledge their presence and encourage the management team to find creative ways to work around them.

Traditionally, the forces against development of improved measurement systems are:

Forces For	Forces Against
Better communication with public	More time
We're a goal-oriented organization	More paperwork
Personnel evaluation system requires performance targets	Computer won't give us the data
Provides ability to spotlight good performance	Can't control our destiny due to personnel, purchasing, budget, etc.
Necessary to achieve excellence	Resistance to being measured
Help us focus on "right things" to measure	Outside support does not allow us to move as quickly as we can
Better ability to compete for resources	Information overload -- Lot of data, not much information
Where we stand with other organizations	

Figure 6-18. Complete Force-Field Analysis Diagram

1. Fear of exposing poor performance;
2. Fear of exposing good performance;
3. Perception of more time, effort, and/or paperwork;
4. Fear of loss of autonomy;
5. Information overload (data rich information poor)—perception that this will worsen;
6. Previous misuse and abuse of measurement;
7. Fear of failure;

8. Lack of skill and/or lack of measurement masters;
9. Fear of unknown outcomes and consequences of measurement;
10. Paradigms regarding measurement, measurement techniques, and measurement uses and abuses; and
11. Incompatible reward systems—no incentive.

For more detail on overcoming the resistance to measurement, see Tuttle and Sink (1984). We now turn our attention to a discussion of the components of the measurement system development and implementation plan.

Components of the Measurement System Development and Implementation Plan

The resulting plan that can be developed by tailoring the eight-step planning process or by other means should contain certain essential components. Management systems analysis, as we have discussed earlier, contains five basic steps of which the last three focus specifically on the development and implementation of measurement systems. Preparatory steps need to be taken to set the stage for and/or lay the foundation for measurement system development. These preparatory steps are:

1. Organizational system analysis for the target system, specifically focusing on and including input/output analysis;
2. Force-field analysis, to include the design and development of a communication plan designed to increase driving forces and reduce or eliminate restraining forces we are trying to ensure that there is a cultural support system for measurement to succeed;
3. Educational and awareness-oriented interventions aimed at sharing information and knowledge about measurement theory, principles and strategies; and
4. We highly recommend that measurement system development be viewed as Step 7, an integral part of a performance improvement planning process.

In short, we are recommending that a measurement system not be developed in the absence of a focus on continual performance improvement. It is difficult to perform Steps 3 through 5 of management systems analysis without having done Step 2—Identification of Performance Improvement Interventions. Your measurement system development and implementation plan must incorporate these four elements (see Figure 6-19).

Your measurement system development and implementation plan must also incorporate your plans of action for actually building the measurement system. Step 3 of MSA calls for determining what to measure. We address specific prescriptions for how to do this in the next chapter. Basically, we recommend that the management team of the target system utilize the Nominal Group Technique to develop a prioritized list of performance measures for their organizational system.

Step 4 of MSA calls for determining what data is required to create the measures identified in Step 3. The team or the measurement master must identify data requirements, sources, retrieval procedures, storage and re-retrieval methods, and typically even new data capturing systems development. This step can be described in a short paragraph; however, it is an exceedingly difficult step in the process. We find that management teams often suffer under the illusion that central, easily accessible, automated data bases exist for much of the required information. Reality suggests that this is not the case and that data accessibility, availability, quality, and reliability are not what they might appear to be.

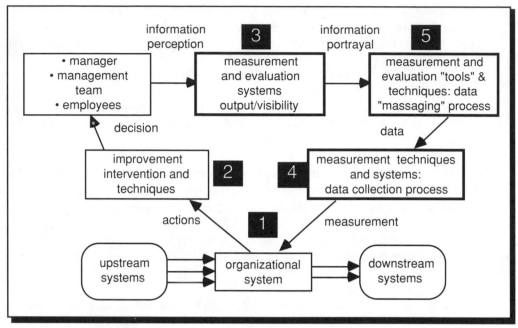

Figure 6-19. Design and Development is a Clockwise Process

The final step associated with designing and developing a measurement system is that of addressing techniques, tools, and methods for converting data into information. How will we store and retrieve the data? How will we process or massage the data? How will we portray the data/information? What procedures will we follow in terms of: who sees the information? in what format? at what frequency? Who will maintain the data base and the data-to-information conversion process? What software, if any, will we use to assist us with this process?

You have any number of tools to assist with this step of data processing and portrayal. New, state-of-the-art and practice measurement techniques, complete with software support, spreadsheets of increasing flexibility and complexity, increasingly sophisticated and user-friendly computer systems, and improved knowledge of how to apply statistical process control techniques are all available to assist a management team and measurement master with this critical last step. We will devote considerable attention to this step in the next chapter.

The last step in the measurement development process and the last component of your planning document focuses on real-time implementation of the systems. A constant improvement orientation — a "ready, fire, aim" — attitude is a must. A bias for action at this stage is critical. Visibility and ownership for the measures and the measurement system must be created. We recommend the development of a "visibility room or rooms" for the management team and other users. If you strive to make it perfect the first time you get the charts and graphs up in the room, you will likely never get the room completed. If you start with a satisfactory measurement system and recognize and expect that it will be modified and improved over time, then you will likely succeed. However, our experience suggests that this step is a get-over-the-hump step. It takes a lot of patience, persistence, and prodding from the master in order to get the visibility room off the ground and running. Visibility rooms, like babies, initially take a lot of care and feeding.

Note that once the measurement system has been designed and developed, the flow in the management systems model goes from clockwise during design to counterclockwise during implementation. (See Figure 6-20.)

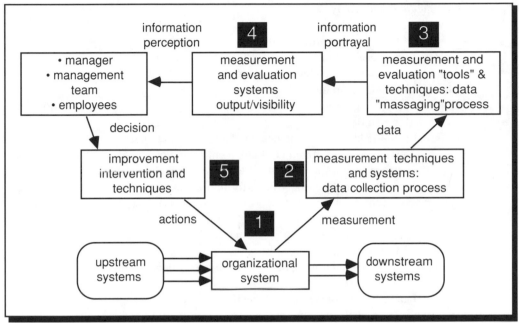

Figure 6-20. Design and Development is a Clockwise Process

CLOSURE

We have attempted to help you better understand the major issues that must be addressed as your organization begins to plan for improving the design and development of your measurement systems. You have multiple measurement systems that have been independently developed, and this is causing problems as you strive to become the Organization of the Future. The eight-step performance improvement planning process can be adapted specifically to develop a plan for the improvement of your measurement systems. The participants in that session might be the masters you have selected— say a group of seven masters in addition to another group of seven users of measurement systems, providers of measurement systems, and top managers. This group of fourteen could, in a two- to three-day period, develop the skeleton for a grand strategy for the continuing development of your organization's measurement systems. During that planning session, the group will have to consider the issues raised in this section.

We have provided a grand strategy, of sorts, for getting started. We used the management systems model as our conceptual model, our roadmap. The interrelationship and integration between management systems analysis and the eight-step performance improvement planning process was again highlighted in this chapter. The strategy we are suggesting for designing and developing measurement systems is much more systematic and disciplined than most management teams and organizations are used to and perhaps will be comfortable with. We believe that measurement is such a vital management process that it deserves to be better engineered and designed. We have found that this general approach works well in the real world.

Let's summarize the steps we have suggested in measurement systems design:

1. Organizational Systems Analysis
   - Define the target system;
   - Define the purpose of measurement;
   - Conduct audience analysis;
   - Review of upline strategic plans;
   - Review of target system strategic plans;
   - Define, operationally, performance for the target system;
   - Conduct an existing measurement system audit;
   - Identify and/or develop measurement master;
   - Confirm accepted guiding principles for measurement within the organization and target system; and
   - Conduct force-field analysis and design communication plan.
2. From the Performance Improvement Plan, identify and/or revisit the strategies developed for performance improvement for the target system and upline systems.
3. Decide what to measure. Identify what information the management team of the target system need/want to confirm that (a) the target system is performing, and (b) the target system is improving.
   - Develop consensus measures for performance;
   - Apply AIM to those measures; and
   - "Operationalize" the measures, determine the operational definitions (identify indicators and attributes) for the measures.
4. Identify data required, sources, and collection devices.
5. Identify how to convert the data into the needed information, address the storage, retrieval, processing, and portrayal questions. Select approaches, methods, tools, and techniques for processing data.
6. Finalize and document your measurement system development plan.
7. Develop and maintain the visibility system for the measurement system, and recycle the design and development process as an integral part of the PIPP, Step 7, each year. Note that this recycle process will not be zero-based each year.
8. Constantly and continually improve the measurement systems.

We recognize that no two people (masters) or organizations will implement this procedure in exactly the same way we describe it in this chapter. Certain steps or substeps may be paid little attention to or even deleted. You may find that the sequence of steps doesn't make sense for your specific application. You will very likely find that you will have to simplify the description and/or change the language. All of this is natural and to be expected. We encourage you to be chefs and not just cooks.

Let's now move from the design and development of measurement systems to the continued development and implementation of measurement and evaluation systems in the Organization of the Future.

REFERENCES AND SUGGESTED READINGS

A & D's Future and You: A Performance Improvement Guide. 1986. Honeywell Aerospace and Defense Management Development Center. Bloomington, Minnesota.

Deming, W. E. 1986. *Out of the Crisis.* Massachusetts Institute of Technology. Center for Advanced Engineering Study. Cambridge, Massachusetts.

Kurstedt, H. A. 1985a. The management system model helps your tools work for you. MSM Working Draft Articles and Responsive Systems Article. Management Systems Laboratory. Virginia Tech. Blacksburg, Virginia.

_____. 1985b. The industrial engineer's systematic approach to management. MSM Working Draft Articles and Responsive Systems Article. Management Systems Laboratory. Virginia Tech. Blacksburg, Virginia.

Lewin, K. 1938. *The Conceptual Representation and the Measurement of Psychological Forces.* Duke University Press. Durham, North Carolina.

Morris, W. T. 1975. *Work and Your Future: Living Poorer, Working Harder.* Reston Publishing Co. Reston, Virginia.

_____. 1979. *Implementation Strategies for Industrial Engineers.* Grid Publishing, Inc. Columbus, Ohio. (Currently out of print, being rewritten under new title by D. S. Sink.)

Peters, T. J., and R. H. Waterman Jr. 1982. *In Search of Excellence.* Harper & Row. New York.

Porter, M. 1985. *Competitive Advantage Creating and Sustaining Superior Performance.* The Free Press. New York.

Shin, S., P. F. Riel, and D. S. Sink. 1988. Productivity measurement: A situational approach. *Proceedings of the International Industrial Engineering Conference.* Institute of Industrial Engineers. Norcross, Georgia.

Sink, D. S., and P. Rossler. 1987. Performance measurement and evaluation: Who for, what for, tools and techniques. *Proceedings of the International Industrial Engineering Conference.* Institute of Industrial Engineers. Norcross, Georgia.

Thompson, J. D. 1967. *Organizations in Action.* McGraw-Hill. New York.

Vroom, V. H., and P. W. Yetton. 1973. *Leadership and Decision Making.* University of Pittsburgh Press. Pittsburgh, Pennsylvania.

7. DEVELOPING AND IMPLEMENTING MEASUREMENT AND EVALUATION SYSTEMS FOR THE ORGANIZATION OF THE FUTURE

MANAGEMENT SYSTEMS ANALYSIS REVISITED

In the last chapter, we reviewed the management systems model and the five-step management systems analysis (MSA). We discussed the interrelationship between the performance improvement planning process (PIPP) discussed in detail in Chapter 4 and the five steps of the MSA. In particular, we demonstrated the overlap between Step 1 of the PIPP (OSA) and Step 1 of MSA (gain a better understanding of the system). The reason for the redundancy is that preparing a management team to plan requires some of the same steps as does preparing a management team to measure. The first steps of both processes require preparation and foundation laying. We pointed out that Step 7 of the PIPP, measurement and evaluation, focuses on developing systems to determine the impact of our efforts to implement our performance improvement plans. We compared Steps 3 through 5 of the MSA as being the details of Step 7 of the PIPP; MSA really attempts to begin to specify how you do Step 7 of the planning process. The interrelationship between MSA and PIPP is depicted in Figure 7-1.

We also mentioned that Step 2 of the MSA—Performance Improvement Interventions —is accomplished in Steps 3 through 5 of the PIPP. So, the planning process details performance improvement planning while the management systems analysis details measurement. In one process, PIPP, the focus is on plan development; in the other, MSA, the focus is on measurement system development. Yet, both processes have the other one embedded within them. It is like looking at the same object—a complex, holographic image—from two different angles. The holographic image we are looking at is called performance management (see Figure 7-2).

When we look at it from the performance improvement planning perspective, we get the PIPP model. The PIPP model helps us describe what we see. When we look at it from the measurement system perspective, we get the MSA model. The MSA model helps us describe what we see in the performance management process that relates to measurement. Both models focus on and explain performance management; one focuses on planning, the other on measurement. The issue here is purpose and point of entry: if you are in a planning mode, we utilize the strategic performance improvement planning process; if you are in the measurement mode, then you must connect your effort to the planning process. Some argue that this unnecessarily complicates things —too many steps to remember and too many models to understand. Others appreciate the multiple perspectives and see the interrelationships. We believe the performance management process needs to be described and understood in as simple a fashion as possible, but not simpler lest we lose rigor and validity. The trick has been to balance relevance with rigor. We trust that we've done that.

Management systems analysis is merely a structuring device to assist you in the process of systematically developing measurement systems. It has been designed and developed to ensure that measurement systems are not developed in the absence of planning. It has been designed and developed to ensure that measurement systems incorporate strategic issues and balance control with improvement orientation. If you learn to operationalize MSA within your organization, it can

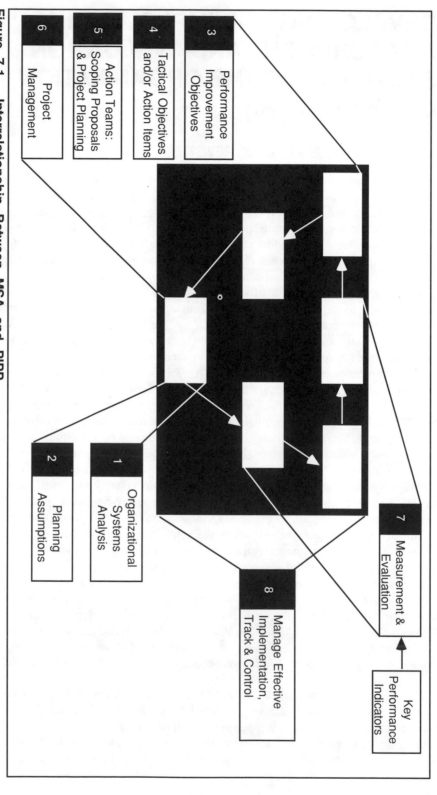

Figure 7-1. Interrelationship Between MSA and PIPP

3 Performance Improvement Objectives

4 Tactical Objectives and/or Action Items

5 Action Teams: Scoping Proposals & Project Planning

6 Project Management

2 Planning Assumptions

1 Organizational Systems Analysis

8 Manage Effective Implementation, Track & Control

7 Measurement & Evaluation

Key Performance Indicators

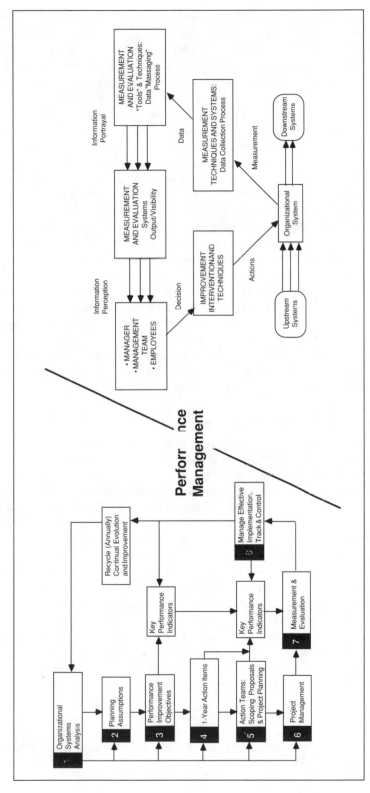

Figure 7-2. Performance Management

help you ensure that the quality of your measurement systems will improve. Remember that the guiding principle of establishing the process, controlling the variance, and then focusing on shifting the mean holds for measurement system design and development. Measurement systems are processes that can be designed, engineered, and managed. The ordering of steps in MSA ensures that you won't let tools drive your developments (i.e., you won't be a hammer looking for a nail to pound). The steps force you to gain an improved understanding of the target system, identify the improvement needs of the target system, identify the information/measurement needs of the management team, develop the data requirements to satisfy the information needs, and then to select tools that will convert data into information. The sequencing of these steps reflect the sound conventional wisdom of management support system theory and practice.

The purpose of this chapter is to go beyond design and planning for measurement systems. This chapter is intended to be a logical extension of Chapter 6 in that it focuses on how to develop and implement measurement and evaluation systems. We outline a step-by-step procedure for building successful measurement systems for any type of target system. This procedure, with minor modifications, can work for the largest of target systems (the company, plant, or division) or the smallest of systems (the work group, the section, or the department). The procedure, again with minor modifications/tailoring, can work with any type of target system (i.e., white collar or blue, professional and technical, line/direct or indirect, and service or product oriented). Our desired outcome for this chapter is that it would provide you with enough guidance so that you could implement the procedure and develop improved measurement systems. To do that we will now walk you through Steps 3 through 5 of MSA: identify what the information needs of the management team are and determine what to measure; determine the data requirements for the information needs identified in Step 3—what data is needed, where to get it, and how to store it; and, select specific tools for data storage, retrieval, processing, and portrayal.

Form Measurement Development Teams

An early step in the process is the formation of the teams of people who will be completing various steps of the process. We use the word teams because we believe that measurement systems cannot be successfully designed, developed, and implemented by individual measurement analysts. A major source of failure and frustration of measurement systems development in the past has been the involvement of too few people. The industrial engineer, the cost accountant, the systems analyst, or programmer developing measurement and evaluation systems independent of significant user or management team involvement is widely recognized as being ineffective in the longer term. In the early Ohio State Productivity Research Group studies back in the late 1970s, I involved users of the system, providers of the services, and top management in the development of productivity measurement systems for ADP services (Morris 1977). We found that we ended up with high-quality measurement systems, greater acceptance of the results, and a better foundation for moving through to implementation of the measurement systems. We (Tuttle and Sink) have consistently confirmed the validity of the design principles identified by Morris (1975). These design principles support the importance of involving teams of people in the measurement systems design process.

A measurement development team might be:

1. The entire management team for the target system identified;
2. A subset of the management team for the target system;
3. A team of measurement masters tasked with the assignment of developing measurement systems for multiple target systems;

4. A combination of measurement masters with members of the management team for a given target system; or

5. Managers of the "parent system" and even key customers (internal or external).

Keep in mind that we define a management team to be the entire group of managers, staff, and other employees that make up a target system. For example, in a department of twenty-five people, you could define the management team to be the entire twenty-five people. This is not frequently the case in American organizations. However, as we evolve from manager-led, control-oriented organizations through self-managed organizations and toward self-governing and self-directing, our conceptualizations of what the management team is will have to change. You can be sure that the concept of management team is different in a traditional American organization than it is in a company such as M&M Mars, General Foods, Procter and Gamble, or others that are organized as semiautonomous or autonomous work/performing teams (Lawler 1986; Hackman 1986; Walton 1985; Davidson 1982; Kanter 1983).

The concept of who is a part of a management team for organizational systems is changing by necessity. Who should plan? Who should make selected decisions or solve specific problems? Who should be involved in the various steps of problem solving? Who should develop an organizational systems measurement system? These questions need to be re-examined as your organization attempts to respond to the challenges of The New Competition and become the Organization of the Future. Traditionally, the answer to who should design and develop measurement systems has been answered by the experts. The experts have designed and developed them, often with little input from the customer. Morris (1979), in a book entitled *Implementation Strategies for Industrial Engineers*, suggests that there are various "professional modes of functioning" (i.e., expert, challenger, collaborator, acceptant listener, facilitator, and teacher) and that it is important to know when to use these different modes. If the goal is effective implementation of a measurement system, as we think it should be, then tradeoffs between quality of the design and acceptance of the design may be appropriate. This requires that we re-examine our conventional answer to the question: "Who should design and develop measurement systems?"

We suggest that for smaller organizational systems (i.e., approximately six to twenty) that most, if not all, of the members of those organizational systems be involved in many of the steps of the process that we are about to describe. In larger organizational systems, target units of analysis—the management team in charge of that system plus representatives from subsystems within the larger target system—can make up the measurement development team. Ideally, we are looking for approximately six to ten people to make up a measurement development team. The people would represent various viewpoints on what constitutes performance for the target system. A sampling of measurement masters would ensure that technical quality is maintained but not at the expense of relevance. As you move this process lower in the organization, you need people with experience, verbal ability, the ability to think abstractly, and the ability to deal with ambiguity.

Let's now turn our attention to what you do with these measurement development teams once they are formed.

Review and/or Develop Results from the Performance Improvement Planning Process

At this stage in the process, the measurement master, coordinator, facilitator, or manager will likely have completed Steps 1 through 6 of the performance improvement planning process. If that is the case, then the first thing you must do with the newly formed measurement development team

233

is to review the results of the planning process. This requires review of upline plans (plans for organizational systems upstream, downstream, or upline of the target system) with the measurement development teams. It may have been some time since the plans were developed, and we need to ensure that the measurement development team is current as to progress with the planning process. You would be reviewing the results of Steps 1 through 6 with the team.

Obviously, we are recommending that a performance improvement plan exist for the target system. If the target system has not developed a plan, then we recommend that a first step is the development of such as plan. Is it possible to develop measurement systems without going through the planning process? The answer is obviously yes. However, our experience and the theory and research we have reviewed suggests that this is not advisable. We run the risk, for example, of ending up measuring A while hoping for B, of ending up with measurement systems that are not compatible with our strategies, and of ending up with measurement systems that do not link to improvement. Measurement systems development taken out of the context of strategic planning and performance improvement planning is very likely to be ineffective, inefficient, and produce low-quality results.

Target System and Downstream, Upstream, and Upline System Strategic and Performance Improvement Plans Review

In his recent book, *Thriving on Chaos: Handbook for a Management Revolution*, Tom Peters argues strongly for a revamping of measurement systems in organizations. His guiding principle for this revamping is "measure what's important" (Peters 1988). The problem in organizations today is not lack of measurement but the lack of focus on those few measures that are really important. How is that focus developed? How do people in the organization know what to value? How do foremen and team leaders in the operational areas of the organization know how to prioritize the multiple options competing for time and resources?

On a very personal level this is the role of leadership. The second author recently discussed these issues with Israel "Izzy" Cohen, the chairman of Giant Foods, one of the industry leaders in the supermarket business. "This is a very simple business," said Cohen. "We must provide clean stores, good stock, and courtesy to the customer." On his twice-per-year visits to every one of Giant Foods' 141 stores, Cohen checks for these three performance indicators. In particular, he recognizes "staffers" (Giant has no employees, only staffers or associates) who have excelled in courtesy to the customer. Giant's customer service values are continually reinforced through courtesy training and courtesy committees.

At an organizational systems level, the focus is provided by an organization's planning process and its business strategy. At Giant Foods, the business strategy hinges around customer service. Giant differentiates itself from its competition by superior customer service. This business strategy has helped it capture 37 percent of the market in the very competitive Baltimore-Washington area. This is almost double the market share of its nearest competitor.

The effectiveness of Giant's strategy is illustrated by its impact on customers. As a personal aside, I attended a spring management conference for the Virginia Department of Transportation. At that conference, five employees were singled out as being innovative and were asked to brief the 125-plus other managers on their local initiatives. One of the managers asked to speak began by talking about core business values and customer service. She spent considerable time talking about Giant Foods' philosophy and about how it impressed her and has influenced her management approach. I found that impressive to have a customer bragging about how you run a business based upon the experience of being a customer!

Organizations typically have very little alignment between their core business strategy and what they measure two or three levels down in the organization. Tuttle had an experience that illustrated this point. He was conducting a measurement workshop leading up to the second NASA productivity and quality conference. The room was filled with productivity and quality specialists from major aerospace firms. The participants were asked to audit their present measurement systems by applying a logic similar to that described in Chapter 6 (AIM). They were asked to write down the sources of competitive advantage for their organizations (e.g., quality, cost, responsiveness to unique customer requirements, and technological superiority). They were then asked to list the performance indicators that they currently track as productivity and quality specialists. Finally, they were asked to raise their hands if they felt there was a close match between the strategic performance dimensions and their currently tracked indicators. Out of a room of forty people, only two hands were raised. People from the leading aerospace firms were essentially saying that there was little relationship between what they were measuring and the strategic direction of the organization. We believe that a similar analysis could be done for other organizational control systems (e.g., pay, promotion, budgeting, etc.). If that were done in your organization, would there be a clear relationship between your business strategy and the criteria, measures, and indicators used for decision making and problem solving?

If the answer to that question is no, it points out a serious problem. With respect to measurement, our current focus, this is a problem because measurement systems have a powerful influence over performance. Resources tend to flow from unmeasured to measured aspects of performance. If our measurement systems are not aligned with the strategy, we are actively driving performance and resource allocation decisions in directions that reduce, rather than enhance, our organization's competitiveness.

We've previously used the example of the Honeywell A&D measurement system. There, three measures that were of strategic importance to the firm were consistently measured for all Honeywell locations. These related to inventory reduction, value added, and scrap/rework. A Senate Productivity Award-winning organization in Maryland illustrates the same point in a business that is very different from Honeywell or Giant Foods. This organization is the water and sewer department of Anne Arundel County in the Anne Arundel Department of Utilities. Management has clearly articulated the three aspects of performance that are strategically important to the Department as QCI—quality, cost, and image. These three dimensions are continually reinforced. They appear on posters, people wear buttons with QCI on them, managers are evaluated on their success with respect to improving QCI, and measures at all levels of the organization from data processing to water pumping stations are being developed to enable people to operationalize what QCI means at each level of the organization. This organization has clearly linked its strategic direction with day-to-day actions—the essence of strategy implementation.

We have attempted to continually reinforce the criticality of the linkage between planning and measurement. The performance improvement planning process has key steps that focus on linking measures to long-range objectives and strategic and tactical objectives. Strategic direction at all organizational levels is essential to success. Whether this is done via defining and publicizing the guiding principles—the strategic plan—or having it imbedded in the communications from leaders on an ongoing basis isn't really important. The goal is to clearly articulate and obtain commitment to critical success factors. Measurement must be a component of this process. The critical success factors that make up strategic direction must be clearly communicated and must be imbedded in the measurement systems throughout the organization.

The target systems that attempt to develop improved measurement and evaluation systems must review the strategic plans from upline organizational systems to ensure that target system strategy and measures are consistent and compatible with overall organization direction. We all don't live and work in an organization like Giant Foods or Honeywell A&D. Most of us live in organizations where there is ambiguity with respect to strategic direction and critical

235

success factors. Most of us live in organizations where upline plans may not even exist. Target systems must strive to develop their measurement systems with as much relevant data as possible. The relevant data needed to build a quality measurement system may not be easily accessible. Collection of and analysis of the target systems strategic plan and relevant upline systems plans is an important step in this methodology.

KEY RESULT AREAS, CRITICAL SUCCESS FACTORS, LONG-RANGE OBJECTIVES, STRATEGIC THRUSTS, AND SOURCES OF COMPETITIVE ADVANTAGE

The jargon associated with planning and measurement is, at times, overwhelming and confusing. As we have said, with respect to measurement system development, organizations (target systems) must translate their business strategy into the right stuff for measurement. The terms or dimensions that are used to define and describe strategic plans and business strategy have many different labels — key results areas (KRAs), critical success factors (CSFs), long-range objectives (LROs), strategic thrusts and factors, and sources of competitive advantage. This list of terms is probably not comprehensive, although it is representative of the more common terms employed. What term or terms you choose to utilize in your organization's planning and measurement process isn't really important. Pick one or a couple that you feel comfortable with, operationally define them, and then use them consistently. When you bring in outsiders, as consultants or guest speakers, force them to translate their concepts into your dictionary of terms rather than the reverse. If you don't do this, you will confuse your people and undermine your process by allowing outsiders to sell their model complete with terms in opposition of what is working for you. The purpose of these terms is to focus the organization on what's important in terms of planning, action, and measurement. The use of terms is, in effect, simply the development of a common vocabulary so that the organizational members can consistently and efficiently communicate with one another. This set of terms represents those used in planning to communicate those things that are of strategic importance to the organization.

An anecdote illustrates the point. A tourist was walking down the street in Washington, D.C., one night and saw a drunk up ahead on his hands and knees under a street light. Curious, the tourist walked up to the inebriated individual and inquired, "What are you doing?" The drunk, a bit surprised, said in slurred speech, "I'm looking for my car keys." The tourist, trying to be helpful said, "Where did you lose them?" "Over there," the drunk replied, pointing to the dark alley a few yards away. Again, puzzled by the logic, the tourist asked, "Why are you looking for your keys here then?" The drunk replied, "Because the light is better here."

Based upon our experience, without a model to guide them organizational systems tend to be like the drunk; they look for measures where the light is. They tend to measure what is easiest to measure rather than measure what is really important to measure. It does not necessarily follow that what is important to measure is always hard to measure. However, our experience suggests that many of the important measures are not as easy to measure as is return on investment or getting the product out the door on time or tracking the budget. In fact, Deming asserts that the really important things organizations need to know (e.g., the cost of an unhappy customer) are unknown and unknowable.

Why do organizations tend to measure what's easy to measure? First of all, because measurement consumes valuable resources. Unless the organization (all organizational systems and people within them) understands and is committed to what is important from a strategic viewpoint, one measure is as good as any other. In fact, since measurement can be threatening, measurement of easy to measure and/or trivial aspects of performance that can easily be manipulated often makes good political sense. Measuring where the light is is a way to stay out of trouble. In most organizations, managers rarely get beat up because they are measuring the wrong things; they are much more likely to suffer negative consequences from creating visibility for some of the right things. They suffer negative consequences as a result of performance drops in indicators that are reported upline, even if they are trivial from a strategic viewpoint.

The mechanisms for focusing measurement development activities on those strategically important aspects of performance can be referred to under many labels. In this discussion, we prefer a label that is clearly different from the business-as-usual labels many organizations currently use. The terms "objectives and goals," although frequently used in conjunction with strategic planning, often only reflect an illusion that there is a strategic focus. We believe that the terms "key results areas," "critical success factors," or "strategic thrusts/factors" emphasize the points we are trying to make in this section. Therefore, we prefer the use of these terms to the more conventional term "goals." It is a refinement you may elect to adopt as your planning processes mature.

In developing the measurement system, an organization must define these dimensions. If the organization has followed the planning process described in Chapter 4 and elsewhere in this book, the strategic dimensions would have been addressed and developed in Step 1 — organizational systems analysis. If this planning process has not been followed and the organization has not clearly specified the strategic performance dimensions, then the target system must strive to obtain them. Note that the target system may be an suborganizational system within a larger organization. We are suggesting that the strategic performance dimensions for the parent organization be identified and analyzed in the context of performance improvement planning and measurement system development for the various sub-organizational systems throughout the larger organization.

The strategic performance dimensions for the parent organization should exist as an integral part of the strategic plan for the organization. They would exist if the parent organization employed the eight-step planning process described earlier. If they do not exist, they should be developed. There are many ways to develop strategic performance dimensions; a process we have found effective is described in Appendix C (Tuttle and Weaver 1986; Tuttle, Wilkinson, and Matthews 1985).

Key Performance Indicators Versus Step 7 of the Performance Improvement Planning Process

In the performance improvement planning process model, we presented key performance indicators (KPIs) as they associate with Step 3, strategic objectives, and Step 4, tactical objectives/action items. We mentioned that KPIs focus on whether or not the management team is:

1. Doing what they said they would do—the effectiveness question;
2. Doing what they said they would do efficiently—the efficiency/resource consumption question; and,
3. Doing what they said they would do in a "quality fashion."

There may be other measurement issues that KPIs should focus on, however, it seems to us, that these represent the major concerns.

We also discussed Step 7 of the performance improvement planning process, which focuses on impact assessment on the organizational system (target system). Step 7 focuses on determining how well the organizational system is performing and on the impact of our performance improvement interventions on the performance of the system. It is this step in the planning process model that we are addressing in Chapters 5 through 7 of this book. In a sense, the management systems analysis model is a detailed look at Step 7 of the planning process. If we "burst out" Step 7 of the PIPP, we see the management systems analysis model.

Step 7 of the PIPP focuses on assessing the impact of our performance improvement efforts on the total performance of the organizational system. Are the things we said would improve performance actually doing that? Where the KPIs focus on project management measures for specific objectives and action items, Step 7 focuses on the impact of those interventions on the total performance of the target system.

Determine What To Measure (Step 3 of MSA)

Once an organization has identified or developed its strategic performance dimensions, the decision regarding what to measure can be addressed by answering the following question: "What criterion, measures, attributes, and indicators should the management team of the target system track on a periodic basis to determine if the strategic performance dimensions are being accomplished?" As shown in the management systems analysis, this question relates to information needed to manage the system.

This appears quite straightforward. In practice, it is a bit more complex. The complexity arises from the translations that must be made of the strategic performance dimensions for the various units of analysis within your organization.

To illustrate this point, let's consider an auto plant. Assume that three strategic performance dimensions have been identified— cost, quality, and availability. From the perspective of the plant manager, where the unit of analysis is the total plant, the strategic performance dimension of quality could have several operational definitions: e.g., total number of defects per vehicle, number of customer complaints or warranty claims in the first ninety days of ownership, and more. The materials manager for the plant, a different unit of analysis, might operationalize quality in a very different way: e.g., the number of parts from vendors that must be reworked. The accounts payable manager has still another unit of analysis perspective and might operationalize quality in terms of errors on check requests. Note that each of these managers have different units of analysis for which they and their management teams are responsible. Note also that each should operationalize quality at each of the five quality checkpoints for their individual domains. Our examples don't reflect this. The same translation process of determining how to operationalize each strategic performance dimension at each unit of analysis must take place.

Thus the decision of what to measure becomes a decision that is influenced by what the organization's strategic performance dimensions are. The information that a management team looks at to tell them how the organizational system is performing should be influenced by, but not constrained by, the organization's strategic performance dimensions.

In the methodology proposed here, that decision should be made by a knowledgeable team of individuals drawn from the target system. Other alternatives to a participative or consultative process of arriving at the decision of what to measure include having the manager decide unilaterally, having the parent system impose measures, or having an outside expert recommend measures. Since we are emphasizing measurement for the purpose of improvement, we believe that the members of the target system should develop their own scorecard measures. We feel that this will lead to measures and indicators that are the most acceptable, understandable, and credible to members of the target system. This should lead to more effective utilization of the measurement system.

The Process To Decide What To Measure

Based on the authors' experience, we recommend using the Nominal Group Technique (NGT) as the process to bring the members of the measurement development team to consensus. In situations where bringing the measurement development team together, face to face, is difficult, you might consider use of a similar technique called the Delphi Technique (Delbecq, Van de Ven, and Gustafson 1986). Research and experience has proven them both to be effective and efficient at producing consensus measures of performance.

The task statements we most frequently use to generate the list of measures are: "How will we know how well we are doing?""What measures and/or indicators should the management team of this organizational system monitor on a periodic basis to determine how well the system is performing?" and "What can/should we measure to help us know where we need to improve, how well we are doing, and if we are improving?" Your range of questions that you might ask is large and not limited to the three examples we have given.

In Tuttle's experience, the NGT process should be carried out separately for each strategic performance dimension, key result area, and so on. Generally this will lead to three to five indicators per dimension. In Sink's experience, the NGT process should focus broadly on measures of performance for the organizational system, not constraining the thought process with strategic performance dimensions. The group should simply identify those measures that should be used to help improve the performance of the system. Once this is done, an audit procedure called AIM would be applied to ensure that the resultant list of measures meet our requirements in terms of comprehensiveness; AIM is discussed in the next section.

While the measurement team is developing this set of measures, it should not constrain its thoughts due to feasibility issues. Their focus should be more on the importance of the management team having the information than the feasibility of generating it. The output of this process will be a prioritized list of measures. Once the session has produced this output, an initial discussion regarding the output can take place to set the stage for AIM.

The initial screen involves a review by the management team of the organizational system. Some or even all of the management team might have been in the measurement development session. The entire management team would need to review the resultant set of prioritized measures. Certain issues need to be addressed:

- Is the measure or indicator properly worded?
- If it is in ratio form, is the ratio properly formed?
- Is the measure important to the management team?
- Is it worth the cost required to collect, store, retrieve, and portray the data? Is it feasible?

Once this initial screen has taken place, the measurement development team can perform a more detailed audit of the measures called audit to improve measurement (AIM).

Apply the Audit To Improve Measurement (AIM) Technique

The next major step in the general measurement methodology we are describing is to analyze the results of Step 3 of MSA. Step 3 has identified, in a structured, participative fashion from the views of the management team or the measurement development team, the performance information needs/requirements/desires of the management team. The last section described how to obtain consensus from the management team or the measurement development team relative to measures of performance for the target system. Examples were provided to illustrate the types of results that have been obtained from a variety of types of organizational systems. As you saw, the technique for generating consensus and prioritized measures of performance was the Nominal Group Technique. There are certainly other ways to develop measures of performance for organizational systems. The Delphi Technique, for example, would be an approach similar to the NGT. The major difference would be that the Delphi Technique moves information only, not the people, too (Sink 1985; Delbecq, et. al. 1986). We could also use a less participative approach, perhaps relying on experts or the upper managers in the system. As we indicated in the last section, if the goal is to link measurement to improvement—the development of "red-loop" measurement systems—then we recommend the approach described.

Once a list of measures is obtained, they must be analyzed and AIM has been developed to assist in this process. An example of AIM is provided in Table 7-1.

A structured way to audit the results from Step 3 of MSA is AIM. The top-priority measures are inserted in the columns of the AIM table. The rows of the AIM table are a variety of factors against which we are auditing the specific measures. These factors are:

1. The seven performance criteria;
2. The strategic factors of the organizational system;
3. The long-range objectives of the organizational system;
4. The strategic objectives (Step 3 from the PIPP) for the organizational system;
5. The tactical objectives/action items (Step 4 from the PIPP) for the organizational system;
6. The stages of the I/O process (i.e., upstream, input, transformation process, output, outcome);
7. The type/intent (i.e., "red-loop" control or "blue-loop" improvement); and
8. The intended user(s).

We provide a completed AIM matrix for your review and to help you better understand how the matrix is developed.

Once the AIM matrix is completed, a visual inspection provides the opportunity to evaluate the quality of the resulting top-\priority measures. For instance, we can begin to identify where we have too much or too little coverage. We can identify where we need to develop new measures or where we need to combine like measures to avoid redundancy. The principle we are trying to operationalize here is the one that suggests that "you get what you inspect, not what you expect." If you don't measure it, you can't assume you will get it. We are trying to assure that our instrument panel is complete and well designed.

We suggest, based upon past experience, that the measurement development team take a first cut at completing the AIM matrix and then review the results and implications with the management team of the target system. It may even require that one person—a master from the measurement development team do the analysis first and then have the rest of the team review and critique the straw-man analysis. The objective of AIM is to improve the quality of the measures comprising the instrument panel. The process of completing AIM is most critical. The process of completing the matrix is educational and forces those involved to carefully think through what it is they really want to see regarding the performance of their organization. We suspect that a lot of informal AIM type work took place as the test pilots and engineers developed instrument panels in the aircraft of the past and present. It is critical—imperative—that the measurement development team and the management team stop to analyze the results of Step 3 of MSA. You can accomplish this step in a structured fashion using AIM.

Table 7-1. AIM Worksheet

Audit Factor \ Measures and/or Measurement Systems	No. New Programs / No. Rewritten Programs (1)	Percent Time Spent on Priority Projects (2)	New Products (3)	No. Task Loading Changes (4)	Quality of Cost Estimates (5)	"Time Sharing" (6)	ENC/DRO Turnover (7)	Capital Equipment Requests (8)	Letters of Recognition (9)	(10)
Key Performance Dimensions										
1. Complete Projects in a Timely Manner										
2. Reduce New Product Intro Lead Time										
3. Improve Accuracy on Cost Estimating										
4. Improve the Effectiveness of Sustaining Functions										
Performance Criteria										
Efficiency										
Effectiveness										
Quality Checkpoint 1										
Quality Checkpoint 2										
Quality Checkpoint 3										
Quality Checkpoint 4										
Quality Checkpoint 5										
Productivity										
Quality of Work Life										
Innovation										
Profitability/Budgetability										
Organizational System										
Inputs: Labor										
Material										
Capital										
Energy										
Data/Information										
Transformation Processes										
Outputs										
Outcomes										

Table 7-2. Final AIM Worksheet

Audit Factor / Measures and/or Measurement Systems	No. New Programs No. Rewritten Programs (1)	Percent Time Spent on Priority Projects (2)	New Products (3)	No. Task Loading Changes (4)	Quality of Cost Estimates (5)	"TimeSharing" (6)	ENC/DROTurnover (7)	Capital Equipment Requests (8)	Letters of Recognition (9)	(10)
Key Performance Dimensions										
1. Complete Projects in a Timely Manner		√	√	√			√			
2. Reduce New Product Intro Lead Time			√		√					
3. Improve Accuracy on Cost Estimating					√			√		
4. Improve the Effectiveness of Sustaining Functions	√					√				
Performance Criteria										
Efficiency		√								
Effectiveness	√									
Quality Checkpoint 1										
Quality Checkpoint 2										
Quality Checkpoint 3				√						
Quality Checkpoint 4										
Quality Checkpoint 5										
Productivity							√			
Quality of Work Life						√				
Innovation					•				√	
Profitability/Budgetability								√		
Organizational System										
Inputs: Labor										
Material									√	
Capital										
Energy										
Data/Information										
Transformation Processes										
Outputs										
Outcomes										

Operationalizing the Measures

The next step in the overall methodology is broadly described as operationalizing the measures. We hesitate using a made up word like "operationalize." There is perhaps too much "ize" and "izing" of words. However, the word operationalize does succinctly capture the next step and has appeared to clearly communicate this to real world managers and measurement masters. The point is that one now has to take specific measures and determine how to:

1. Collect data necessary for the measure;
2. Decide what the "countable" is for the measure, what scale will be used, and what attribute;
3. Decide/determine how to store and retrieve the data effectively and efficiently; and
4. Determine how to process, "massage," and transform data into information, and portray the information.

It appears to us that Steps 4 and 5 of the MSA and the measurement process in general are where people have the most trouble. Usually, management teams do not have a great deal of difficulty with Step 3 of the process— the development of measures or desired/needed information. Use of the NGT seems to help management teams reach a consensus as to what information they need/want relative to performance measurement for their organizational systems. It is interesting to note that the consensus measures that they arrive at in Step 3 often are not being provided by existing measurement and information systems. Our experience suggests that the real difficulties with building improvement-oriented measurement systems begins when the team starts to think through the design process of operationalizing the selected measures. Further, it doesn't appear to be any easier a task for the staff support people—the intended measurement masters—in the organization.

So, we will devote the next several subsections to discussion surrounding the operationalization of measures developed from Step 3 of the MSA.

Criterion, Measures, Indicators, Surrogates or Proxy Indicators, and Attributes

We spoke earlier of operational definitions and quoted Deming's thoughts on the subject. It is frequent and predictable that the results of Step 3 of MSA and the NGT session will not produce operational measures. That is, some of the measures identified in the NGT session will not reflect things that are countable. For example, a data center within an organization might identify customer satisfaction as being a top priority measure of center performance. The question we then ask data center management teams is, what to count? The answers are frequentl, number of complaints, amount of repeat business, number of positive letters received, and results from a customer survey. Some measures are directly measurable and others are not.

The words measure, indicator, criterion, surrogate, proxy measure, attribute, key result area, key performance indicator, and variable are often used interchangeably and with little precision. It does not appear to us that the field of measurement (consisting of practitioners, quality assurance, statisticians, industrial psychologists, sociologists, accountants, industrial engineers, human factors engineering, and other professions and disciplines) is consistent in use of terms. Different disciplines tend to use different sets of terms in different fashions. This isn't necessarily bad and we aren't going to try to change that; however, we do hope to establish some consistency in use of terms within the field of performance measurement for organizational systems.

The measurement terms that we believe need to be used and operationally defined for developing measurement systems for organizational systems are the following: strategic performance dimension, criterion, key performance indicator, measure, indicators and attributes, and surrogate or proxy indicators. We have already exposed you to planning terms such as strategic factor, key result areas, critical success factors, long-range objectives, strategic and tactical objectives, and action items. The field of planning and measurement is filled with terms and jargon that is confusing even to the serious student and master. We two authors even tend to use different terms in our practice and writing. For the purpose of this book we have attempted to agree upon a standard convention of terms for planning and measurement. In this respect, we have failed to completely come to consensus as to terms and relationships. We have had healthy discussions, and as a result, each has crystallized his own views.

What follows is largely Sink's thoughts; however, in many respects both authors are not that far apart in their thinking. We both use many of the same terms and, in general, use them in the same way. Tuttle views these terms in hierarchy. This hierarchy is presented in Table 7-3.

Table 7-3. Hierarchy of Measurement Terms

Level	Terms	Example
Construct	Dimension, Criteria	Quality
Subconstruct	Attribute	Reliability, Vendor Quality Checkpoints 1-5
Measure	Indicator, Key Performance Indicator Proxy/Surrogate Indicators	No. of defectives/ Total no. of items
Measurement	Operational indicator, data	6/100 or 6%

(Note: Measurement = rules for assigning numbers to objects to represent quantities of attributes (Nunally, J. 1967. *Psychometric Theory*. McGraw-Hill. New York.)

Both authors agree with the concept of the hierarchy and with the levels in the hierarchy. The terms are generally agreed upon. What follows is a description of a number of the key terms that we believe you will be utilizing as you develop measurement systems.

Strategic performance dimension

We discussed strategic performance dimensions several sections ago, along with the various alternative terms that can be used as labels for SPDs—critical success factors, strategic thrusts/ factors, and key results areas. As we said, a strategic performance dimension reflects the strategic factors for a business. What will be the basis of our competitive edge? What things must we do to succeed? What businesses are we in and how will we differentiate ourselves? One way to think of these is as superordinate performance criteria. They reflect those things we must do and are to be accompanied by measures and/or key performance indicators. The term *strategic performance dimension* is a Step 1 of the performance improvement planning process issue. By what measures of performance will our organization be known? What measures of performance will determine whether we will succeed? How will we be judged, and how do we want to be judged from a strategic point of view? The linkage between the plan and effective implementation is critically dependent upon the development of measures and indicators for these strategic performance dimensions. We discuss strategic performance dimensions in the planning process context and in the measurement system development context because they are developed in the planning process and operationalized in the measurement system.

Criterion

We have presented seven fundamental measurement criteria for organizational systems. For units of analysis ranging from the work group to the firm we believe these seven criteria constitute performance. According to Webster's dictionary, criterion is a means of judging—a standard, rule or test—by which a judgment of something can be formed. In this case, we are suggesting that there are seven major categories of performance measures for organizational systems.

Key performance indicators

Key performance indicators, as we have discussed earlier, are measures of effectiveness, efficiency, and quality for the objectives resulting from the Performance Improvement planning process. Effectiveness—have we done what we said we would do? Efficiency—how much resource have we consumed in relation to how much we said we would consume? Quality—have we done the things we said we would do as well as we should have? As we indicated, key performance indicators are developed for each objective in Step 1, organizational systems analysis (long-range objectives); Step 3, strategic objectives; and Step 4, tactical objectives/ action items.

Measure

A measure is an operationalization of a criterion in our taxonomy. Again, according to Webster's dictionary, a measure is the extent, dimension, or capacity of anything. A performance measure, in conventional terms, tends to be a subset of the seven criteria we have identified. If you read the literature on productivity measurement, you will find examples of measures of performance for all sorts of units of analysis and for all of the seven criteria. Measures reflect an attempt to take the seven criteria one step closer to operationalization. Measures are an attempt to develop a countable for a criterion. An example for the criterion effectiveness would be the number of objectives accomplished, on time, and within specifications.

It is not uncommon for a criterion to have a measure that is not directly operationalizable or countable. For example, for the criterion *effectiveness* customer satisfaction might be an identified measure. There is no one best way—no one most common way—of measuring customer satisfaction. Further, you could argue that customer satisfaction as a measure is, in fact, also a quality measure. Sometimes measures identified for criterion are directly countable and sometimes they are not. When identified measures are not directly measurable/countable, then you must proceed one level lower and look for indicators or attributes.

Indicators or attributes

The measurement literature, particularly measurement of productivity, quality, and performance at the organizational system level, uses the terms indicators and attributes extensively. Our interpretation of how these terms fit into the hierarchy of measurement terms is that indicators and attributes are synonyms from a usage standpoint. Webster defines an indicator as any device, as a gauge, dial, register, or pointer that measures or records and visibly indicates. Webster defines an attribute as a characteristic or quality of a thing. In our taxonomy of terms, we use indicator and attribute as terms that represent a further attempt to identify something that is countable relative to a criterion or measure. When the identification of a measure for a criterion has not provided a countable, then the measurement development team must proceed to another level of detail. An example would be the development of measures of quality for a service or product: Is it acceptable or unacceptable? This is a Quality Checkpoint 4 question. The measure is acceptability: How do we operationally define/measure acceptability? This question leads us to search for indicators or attributes. Did the service or product meet the specifications? What were the specifications?

It becomes obvious that the design and development of a measurement system requires a great deal of logic development. The logic behind the relationship between criterion, measures, and indicator/attributes is often difficult to develop. It takes time and practice. The consistent use of terms in the area of organizational systems performance measurement is important to progress in this field.

It is not infrequently the case that a given measure is not directly measured. There are no direct indicators or attributes. The measure is so complex that we must use proxy or surrogate measures.

Proxy or surrogate indicators

A proxy or surrogate indicator is something that we use to get at a given measure indirectly, and it is related or correlated to the measure we are trying to operationalize. We use proxy or surrogate indicators when we cannot directly measure a given measure. The difference between an indicator or attribute and a proxy or surrogate indicator is the extent of directness in the relationship between the indicator and the measure. In many cases, in the real world the distinction between indicators and attributes and proxy or surrogate indicators may be unnecessary. A proxy or surrogate indicator is something we use in place of something we can't use, identify, or find. Webster defines the word proxy as the authority to act for another. The word surrogate is defined as, something used in another's place as a substitute. In psychology, there are well-known experiments with the use of surrogate mothers and their impact on chimpanzee behavior.

These five concepts represent our taxonomy of necessary measurement terms. The consistent use of terms in the area of planning and measurement is necessary for progress to take place. It is not necessarily important that you accept and adopt our taxonomy; it is necessary that you adopt one and use it consistently within your organization.

A picture might help to crystallize the terms employed in planning and in measurement and how they interrelate. Figure 7-3 depicts the points that we have been trying to make in the past several sections. Progress in any discipline or endeavor is, in part, marked by the development of effective and efficient communication systems. The development of a language for planning and measurement is critical to progress in the area of performance management.

Examples of Measures and Indicators for Each of the Seven Criteria

Examples of measures and indicators for each of the seven criteria are tabulated in Table 7-4 . Most of the measures and indicators are derived from Sloma (1980) and Harrington (1987). It is not uncommon for a criterion to have a measure that is not directly operationalizable or countable. Furthermore, different units of analysis, time frame, functions and/or departments complicate the identification of measures and indicators. The terms shown in Table 7-4 are an attempt to draw generic measures and indicators for each criterion.

Measurement and data (Step 4 of MSA)

Figure 7-4 depicts the MSA again, with Step 4 highlighted. The interface that Step 4 represents is the measurement to data interface. We indicated how to determine what to measure in Step 3. This step focuses on information needs/ requirements of the management team to support their role of managing continual performance improvement. Step 4 focuses on the creation of necessary

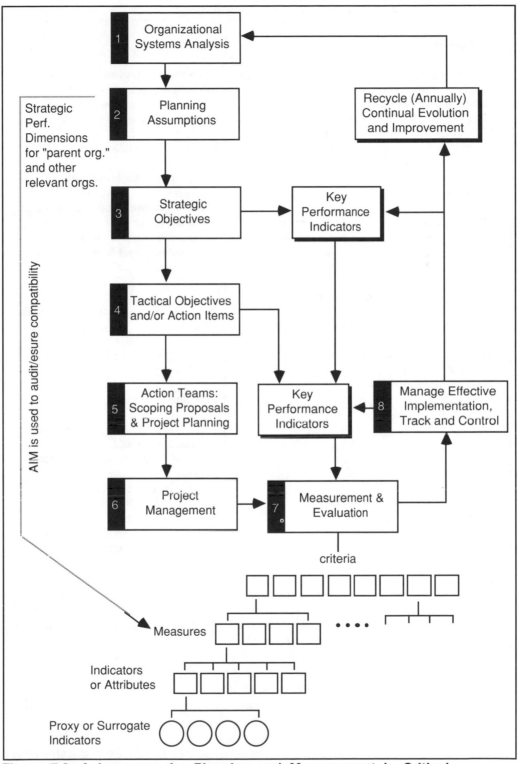

Figure 7-3. A Language for Planning and Measurement is Critical

Table 7-4. Examples of Measures and Indicators

Effectiveness	Productivity
• Percentage of sales quota met by salesperson • Customer turnover per district and product • Slippage of schedules • Market share (actual and potential percentage) • Reputation level from customers • Number of plans achieved/total number of plans • Percentage of goods shipped on time	• Sales per employee • Production rate per employee • Production lead time from raw material to finished product
Efficiency	**Quality of Work Life**
• Maximum, minimum, or low-limit target levels • Percentages of shortages of scheduled material for production • Change in the average total costs of handling a requisition • Inventory reports of items below minimum point • High rates of spoilage or waste • Machine downtime • Labor (direct and indirect) ratios • Average lead time • Machine utilization ratio • Space utilization	• Employee absenteeism and turnover rates • Number of employee grievances • Number of accidents • Employee hours worked exceeding target levels
	Innovation
	• Number of new production methods adopted • Time and cost savings by employing new methods, technology
Quality	**Profitability/Budgetability**
• Ratio of percentage of rejects in items received • Rejection rates • Quantities of corrective work • Rate of customer complaints	• Actual product sales, as opposed to budgeted sales • Budget variances exceeding target levels • Profits as percent of capital employed (ROI) • Profits as percent of sales (ROS) • Profits per employee • Percentage of increase in dividends • Debt ratios to total assets

data to support or provide the information required. The following list of questions represent the issues that need to be addressed in this step of MSA.

1. What data is required in order to provide the information and support the measures identified in Step 3 of MSA? What do we need to count? What are the indicators?
2. Where will we get the data necessary to support the measures identified in Step 3 of MSA? Does it exist? Will we have to create it?
3. How will we obtain and retrieve the needed data?
4. How will we store the data so that it can be retrieved later effectively and efficiently?
5. Who will be responsible and accountable for collecting the data on a timely and periodic basis?

These are the major issues and questions that must be addressed at this stage of management systems analysis and development.

It is a deceptively complex step. We often assume that data is easily accessible and readily available. The illusion of an automated, centralized data base that you can efficiently tap into to support the measurement needs of the management team is apparent in many organizations.

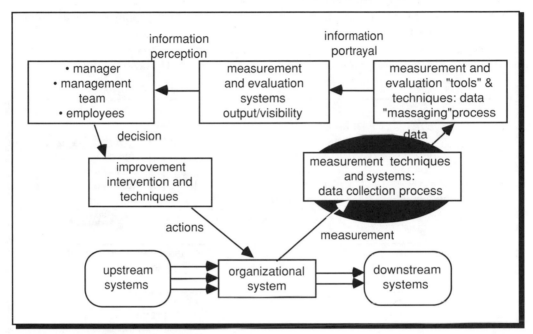

Figure 7-4. Step 4 of the MSA

The type of data required to support improvement-oriented measurement is often not available or it is scattered throughout the organization in multiple files, both hard and soft. Our experience suggests that Step 3 of the MSA and measurement system development process is fairly straightforward and relatively simply to do—as we have described it. The operationalization of what the management team comes up with in Step 3 of MSA is the stumbling block. This is where the guidance of and energies of the measurement master, the comptroller, or the management information specialist come to play. Someone must provide the necessary guidance and support to push through Step 4, the measuremen- to-data interface. It is a painful step, particularly in cases where management support systems, data bases, and accounting systems are not well developed. This will be the case in most small businesses and even smaller organizational systems within larger organizations.

Methods, procedures, and forms need to be developed in order for this step to become effective and efficient. The collection of data to support measurement and information require- ments and needs is, in itself, a process that can be designed, established, and controlled. We can and should apply the concepts imbedded in statistical process control and methods engineering to this step in MSA as in others. We don't have any magic or quick fixes to pass on relative to this step. Measurement systems development, as we are describing it in this methodology, is inherently a design process. As in all design processes, there is an element of creativity and innovation involved. Successful turn-key measurement systems are not common. Turn-key, off-the-shelf data massaging tools are common. However, the logic as to what you use these tools to do and how you utilize what they give you is inherently a design process. This is why we have stressed the importance of the measurement master. We now turn our attention to the last developmental step in MSA, what we call the measurement toolbox.

Data storage, processing, retrieval, and portrayal (Step 5 of MSA)

Figure 7-5 depicts the MSA again and highlights Step 5. We have to this point in the measurement methodology developed information requirements in Step 3 and data requirements for this information in Step 4. We now must determine how to store, retrieve, process, and portray the data. We are looking at the data to information transformation process. How do we convert the data we

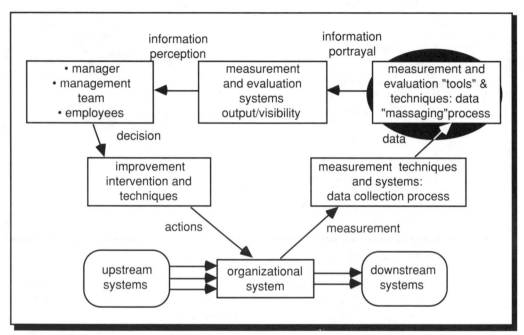

Figure 7-5. Step 5 of the MSA

collect in Step 4 into the information requirement identified in Step 3? What tools or techniques can be used to store, retrieve, process data, and eventually portray information? What is the best way to portray the needed information so as to enhance decision making, problem solving, and best support the continual improvement process? These are the type of questions and issues that must be dealt with in this step of MSA. There are conventional methods for portraying data and information that must be considered; control charts, run charts, graphs, tables, histograms, frequency distributions, pie charts, bar charts, the objectives matrix, and three dimensional graphs are a few examples. We find that many information systems do not reflect enough creativity and variety in terms of how the output is portrayed. We find that the user of the information is not considered when the portrayal format is determined. We find that the user is not involved in the maintenance of the output, which tends to hinder moving from information portrayal to the decision-to-action interface.

The fact that this is the last step in MSA highlights a point. Too often we find that would-be measurement masters look like "hammers looking for a nail to pound." We find people armed with tools and techniques, determined to use them no matter what. Software packages looking for applications, measurement techniques looking for places to happen, and accounting systems looking for homes; tools that look for applications don't usually end up being effectively applied. Tools misapplied gain undeserved bad reputations; we condemn the tool when the application and applier were the problem. Measurement tool and technique application must also be user-driven. We begin the measurement methodology with an effective understanding of what the management team needs/requires in the way of measurement information to support continual performance improvement move to data requirements and finally end up with data transformation questions.

There are many tools and techniques that can support performance measurement systems—techniques and approaches that support gaining information about each of the seven performance criterion. In the next two sections, we will provide a review of both conventional measurement and evaluation approaches, as well as state-of-the-art and practice approaches. We will provide an executive overview of the conventional approaches (e.g., work measurement, cost accounting, corporate finance, and performance appraisal), and give current references for further and more detailed reading for each of these. The approaches will be described in the context of the measurement methodology we have been describing for you.

CONVENTIONAL MEASUREMENT APPROACHES IN THE CONTEXT OF THE GENERAL MEASUREMENT METHODOLOGY

We will begin our discussion of tools for converting measurement data into measurement information by reviewing the methodology that we have developed. We repeat that the word "tools" in Kurstedt's terminology is broadly used to mean models, techniques, software, hardware, methodologies, experience, MIS, MSS, DSS, and intuition. In this section, we will be examining models, methodologies, and techniques that can be used to collect, store, process, retrieve, and portray data about the performance of various types of organizational systems and, in some cases, individuals and work centers.

The General Measurement Methodology — A Review

We felt that it would be beneficial to review, in outline fashion, the methodology we have been describing. We first insert another copy of the MSA process (see Figure 7-6). You will recall that MSA is a three-step process of:

1. Improving the management teams or measurement development teams understanding of the target system;
2. Identifying specific performance improvement interventions that can be made; and
3. Developing a measurement system to tell the management team if performance is improving.

The order of these steps does not infer that the identification of performance improvement interventions occurs in the absence of measurement. This is an ongoing process. We differentiate between the design and development of a management system and the synthesis and use of a management system. During the design and development of a management system, in this case a measurement system, we believe you proceed in a clockwise fashion relative to the management system model beginning with gaining a better understanding of the organizational system. Once the measurement system has been designed and developed, the sequence of actions changes. Measurement begins to be the driver, in that we are using our measurement system to control our processes. Once you establish the measurement system, where you start in the process becomes almost a moot issue. The management process is a cyclical process, an open system with closed loops. Notice that we broke the third step of MSA down into three substeps:

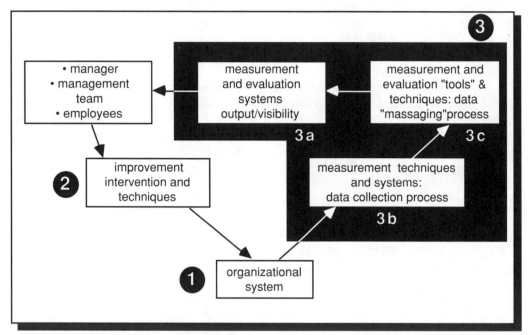

Figure 7-6. Three Steps of the MSA

3a. Identify information needs/requirements;
3b. Identify data requirements for needed information; and
3c. Determine how to collect, store, retrieve, process, and portray the information.

This methodology drives measurement from an improvement focus. The management team first develops their performance improvement plan and then identifies how to determine if the plan is being implemented effectively, efficiently, and in a quality fashion. They also determine how to measure the impact of the plan. Note that we have attempted to make the point that if the performance improvement plan and the measures of an organizational system are incompatible with the strategic performance dimensions and the strategic plan of the larger parent organization, then we might have a case where the subteam wins at the expense of the overall team. This is why Tuttle stresses the linkage of measures for the organizational systems to the strategic performance dimensions for the larger organization.

Also recall that Step 2 of MSA is, in effect, operationalized in our methodology by Steps 3 through 8 of the performance improvement planning process. Steps 3 through 8 of the PIPP simply "burst out" the process of determining how to improve the performance of the organizational system. Step 1 of MSA and Step 1 of the PIPP overlap; they examine the same issue of how to gain a better understanding of the organizational system. You should not develop improvement or measurement strategies without a good understanding of the target system and the larger system

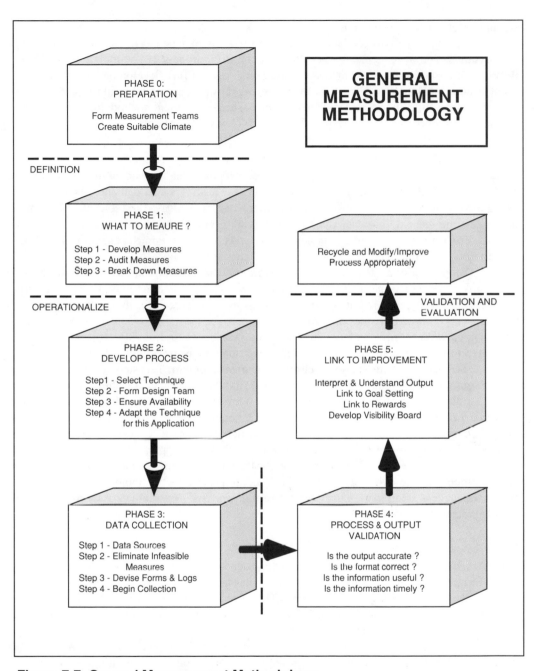

Figure 7-7. General Measurement Methodology

within which the target system resides.

So, we have two conceptual models to help us understand this complex process of improvement and measurement—the MSA and the PIPP models. If you took Step 3 of MSA, development of the measurement system, and Step 7 of the PIPP, development of the measurement system, and burst out these steps, the following flow process model would appear. We have attempted to outline, in process flow fashion, the basic measurement methodology we have been describing in this chapter and Chapter 6. Figure 7-7 shows this attempt.

Phase 0 — preparation

Preparing a management team, a measurement development team, or an entire organization to develop improved measurement systems is not an easy task; it is a critical one. Most of us exist in organizations that don't understand measurement, that have misused and abused measurement, and over time these deficiencies must be dealt with. Some of the preparatory steps are rather straightforward; others are more complex and will take significant time to accomplish. The first step in Phase 0 is relatively more straightforward than the second.

Step 0-1. Form measurement development team. We have already discussed this step and won't repeat the issues and tasks involved. We will reinforce the importance of selecting masters of measurement in addition to persons knowledgeable regarding the target system. Sink's bias (Sink) is to try to have the entire management team be the measurement development team. This is not always feasible, and may in some circumstances be undesirable. However, when it is possible, it makes later steps and final implementation much simpler and effective.

Step 0-2: Create a suitable climate for measurement. This step of Phase 0 is, as you can imagine, more complex and difficult than the first. How to create a culture and climate that understands and promotes measurement for improvement is a challenge. How to operationalize Deming's challenge to throw out all standards is tough. How to overcome the resistance to measurement and take the threat out of measurement requires patience, persistence, knowledge, and skill. How to develop guiding principles that will model appropriate behaviors related to measurement will be something to be thought through. Creating a climate that will support measurement for improvement is a critical step in our general methodology, and will play a big role in the success or failure of your attempts to build improved measurement systems and become the Organization of the Future.

Phase 1 — What to measure

We have spent considerable time in this chapter discussing how to decide what to measure. This phase of our general measurement methodology has three basic steps.

Step 1-1. Develop the measures. The measurement development team or the entire management team utilizes the NGT or DT to develop a prioritized list of measures of performance for the target (their) organizational system.

Step 1-2. Audit the measures. The measurement development team, the management team, or a select group of measurement masters utilize AIM to audit the resulting list of measures obtained from Step 1-1. The objective of this step is to improve the quality of the set of measures to be used by the management team.

Step 1-3. Breakdown the measures. Many of the measures that come out of the NGT or DT sessions will not be directly operationalizable. That is, the measures will not be countable in the form in which they are written. As we discussed earlier, some measures (often many) will need to be further broken down into attributes, indicators, subattributes, and surrogates and/or proxy measures. We are looking for things we can count. An example Deming uses in his chapter on operational definitions is "What is round? What is safe?" How will we operationally define round or safe? What will we count to tell us if it is round enough or safe enough? If a measure of performance for a data center is customer satisfaction, what will we count to tell us if we are achieving it? The purpose of this third step in Phase 1 of our general measurement methodology is to operationalize the definitions of the measures identified. For some this takes a lot of work, for others it is relatively straightforward.

Phase 2 — Develop the measurement process

The second phase of the general measurement methodology focuses on the process of capturing, storing, retrieving, processing, and portraying the data necessary to create the information required by the management team. We are in the toolbox of MSA in this phase. What measurement techniques will we use to process data and create information needed?

Step 2-1. Select the technique. The first step in this phase is to have measurement masters select the appropriate techniques for the particular application. This step obviously requires good familiarity with existing techniques. Of course, this is a requirement for a measurement master.

Step 2-2. Form a design team. At this point a technique design, development, and application team needs to be formed. This may be the existing measurement development team or a subset of it. The purpose of this design team is to develop the application of the selected technique(s) for the organizational system application.

Step 2-3. Ensure availability of model requirements. The third step of Phase 2 focuses on having the design team determine whether or not the model/technique they have selected can in fact be implemented. Model requirements are reviewed in detail at this stage and it is determined whether they can be met. If they cannot, then another technique/model may be needed. If some are questionable, then the team will need to determine how to adapt to meet the requirements. We may find that we need to design our own technique due to requirement incompatibilities. Modification to existing techniques/models is almost always required, and these would be discussed and developed in this step.

Step 2-4. Adapt the technique(s)/model(s). As mentioned in the last step, modification of existing techniques and models is almost always a reality. The design team would have to think through how to adapt the selected model or models to ensure success in their target application. This can range from a portrayal issue, modifying report generators, to actually altering the model itself in terms of how data is processed. The ultimate adaptation, of course, is when a new model is designed specifically for the target application.

Phase 3 — Collect the required data

This third phase focuses on Step 3c of MSA—what data to collect and how to get it. Data requirements for the models will have to be determined, which sets up the five steps of this phase.

Step 3-1. Identify data sources. Once data requirements have been determined, sources for the data need to be identified. Where can we get the data? Is it currently collected? By whom? How is it stored? How will we retrieve it efficiently? If it is in a data base, how do we tap the data base and move it to ours? What will it cost to get the data? Is it worth it? These are examples of the types of questions that need to be resolved in this step.

Step 3-2. Eliminate infeasible measures. At this stage, it may become apparent that certain measures are infeasible. They may be unoperationalizable for any number of reasons. It may be necessary for the design team to get back to the management team and discuss their findings at this point. Other measures that get at the same issues may be available and might be used as a substitute for one that is difficult to operationalize. The results of AIM must be consulted at this point to ensure that the elimination of a measure doesn't sacrifice the overall validity and quality of the measurement system.

Step 3-3. Devise forms and logistics. In some cases, the data may not be readily available and a procedure for collecting, storing, and retrieving it may be necessary. This is done in this step.

Step 3-4. Check accountabilities. Measurement systems require discipline like other management processes. We discussed accountabilities in the planning process and how Steps 5 through 8 were designed to ensure effective implementation. This step in the general measurement methodology focuses on the same issues. Who will continue to reliably, accurately, and in a timely fashion collect the required data? Who will continue to ensure that the measurement system is portrayed in a timely and effective fashion? Who will be accountable for keeping the visibility rooms, boards, and charts current? Unless this step is done effectively, the measurement system is doomed to failure.

Step 3-5. Begin data collection. The measurement development team would at this stage be ready to turn the system on. We would begin to collect data, process it, portray it, and monitor its use by the management team. This step signals the beginning of an ongoing debugging, evolution, and improvement process.

Phase 4 — Process output validation

The measurement system is up and running. The management team is getting reports, charts, and graphs. A visibility system is beginning to emerge. Critical questions and concerns will begin to emerge. Is this all there is? I thought there would be more. This isn't as helpful as I thought it would be. How do we use this information? Was this worth all the cost? I don't believe the results — we're not that bad, or we're not that good. I don't like the way the output is formatted. The information is not timely; by the time I get it it's too late. I'm still data rich and information poor (DRIP). How do we link the results to decisions and actions?

All these questions and many more will arise once you turn your system on. They are predictable, understandable, and manageable. Don't panic and don't give up; press on! Every system goes through a shakedown period; measurement systems are no different. Your measurement development team will have to work out the bugs with the management team. I've worked with clients that have developed beautiful measurement systems and sophisticated reports. They've had them for three to four years and one day they wake up and realize that they aren't using the information; they aren't linking the information to action and decisions. The measurement development team must make the evolutionary improvement process happen. You can't force it to happen too fast, but it can be managed.

Phase 5 — Link to improvement

Unless this final phase in the general measurement methodology happens successfully, the effort will be a failure. The key to success is to link measurement to improvement. A number of things are built into this methodology to try to ensure that this happens. The use of measurement masters, the involvement of the management team, and the focus on improvement first and measurement second are all designed into the methodology in an attempt to ensure measurement is linked to improvement.

The design of the PIPP and the general measurement methodology are such that ownership for the resulting measurement systems should be high. Our hypothesis, supported by our experience, is that the process utilized to develop the measurement system will go a long way toward ensuring that measurement is linked to improvement. There are ways to specifically ensure that measurement is linked to improvement. For example:

1. Control charts that tell a self-managed team when to take action to improve a process;
2. Measures that promote cooperation through linkage to group gainsharing systems;
3. Measures that guide problem solving by a performance action team, etc.;
4. Measures that truly are linked to the reward system;
5. Visibility rooms/systems that are developed, maintained, and effectively utilized by management teams as an integral part of their performance management process.

There are, of course, countless other examples of how to ensure that measurement is effectively linked to improvement. We believe that the key is to ensure that the management team views measurement and understands measurement in the context of the strategic Performance Improvement Planning Process. Our experience suggests that if management teams understand measurement as an integral part of the performance improvement process, they will embrace it rather than resist it. Overcoming resistance to measurement begins by ensuring that management teams understand the role that measurement plays in the continuous performance improvement process.

Our intent in the remainder of this section is to review conventional measurement approaches in the context of the General Measurement Methodology we have been describing. Our intent is not to provide a detailed treatise on how these approaches are done. We simply want to help the reader better understand how these conventional approaches fit into the methodology we are describing. We are intentionally not providing enough detail for someone to fully understand and implement these approaches and techniques. We will provide references for each approach so that the interested reader, perhaps the measurement master, could obtain in-depth knowledge of how to implement each of these.

Work Measurement (Contributed by Paul Rossler)

The purpose of work measurement is to determine how long it should and does take to perform tasks. Work measurement has tended to be broken into two major areas: the actual measurement of work and the methods engineering portion. The measurement of work has focused on determining how long tasks do or should take—both the descriptive and the prescriptive. The methods engineering component has focused on how work is done and how it should be done— again the descriptive and the prescriptive.

Back when we defined the seven performance criteria, we operationally defined efficiency as resources expected to be consumed/resources actually consumed. One of the purposes of work measurement is to determine the numerator of the efficiency equation (resources expected to be consumed, or REC). The primary criterion of the seven that work measurement focuses on is efficiency.

When we look closely at the methods engineering portion of work measurement, we see that effectiveness and quality are also considered in that we are looking at how should work be done. Traditionally, I believe that the primary focus has been on prescribing how work should be done to optimize efficiency. The term "efficiency expert" confirms a perception that this is the primary focus. I believe that increasingly, work measurement and methods engineering will need to focus on prescribing or assisting teams to discover how work should be done in consideration of effectiveness, quality, efficiency, innovation, and quality of work life. If we don't do this the efficiency expert might not have a job in the future.

Table 7-5. Work Measurement and Methods Engineering Techniques

Focus on Resource Consumption	Focus on Methods Analys and Prescription
Direct Time Study	Possibility Guides
Mathematical Techniques Using Historical Data	Work Activity Analysis
Predetermined Time Systems	Work Unit Analysis
Standard Data Systems	Work Sampling
Technical Estimate	Motion Analysis
Time Standards by Fiat	Process Analysis
Self-Reporting	Operation Analysis
	Multiple Activity Analysis Chart

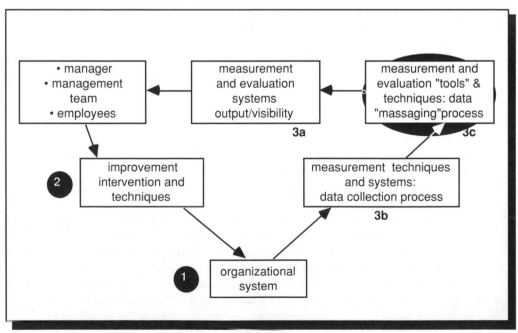

Figure 7-8. Tool Box in the MSA

There are numerous techniques associated with the field of work measurement and methods engineering. We won't review those techniques; we will simply list them (see Table 7-5) and provide references where you might go to gain an understanding of how to do them.

Work measurement techniques are tools that can be used to collect, store, process, retrieve, and even portray data and information regarding how much resource should be consumed and how much resource is consumed on given tasks. Note that the specific resource that has been the focus of work measurement has been labor. In other words, how long it does or should take to do something has been the primary focus of work measurement. Note also that the primary unit of analysis for work measurement has been the individual or the work center. Work measurement techniques were not designed for larger units of analysis.

Work measurement techniques fall into the toolbox of MSA, Step 3c, while methods engineering falls into the Steps 1 and 2 box of MSA (see Figure 7-8). In descriptive form, method engineering describes how work is being performed and, therefore, is describing the transformation processes. In prescriptive form, methods engineering prescribes how work should be performed, how we can improve, and, therefore, is an example of a technique in Step 2 of MSA.

Work measurement and methods engineering are compatible with our general methodology. There will be situations where these approaches are necessary to satisfy an information requirement of a management team. The measurement master must be well-versed in work measurement approaches. This conclusion is not at all inconsistent with the guiding principles for measurement systems that Deming has provided or that we provided earlier. As we have said repeatedly, measurement must be separated from evaluation. Work measurement does not in and of itself create dysfunctional consequences such as those enumerated by Deming. Standards, knowledge of how long something should take, how much resource will be consumed, and what it will cost to do something are important for forecasting, estimating, and making bids. It is the misapplication of standards that Deming and others are opposed to, not the techniques of work measurement. We refer you to the following two references for further elaboration of this important point (Smith 1978, 1988).

Cost Accounting (Contributed by Paul Rossler)

There are two types of accounting: financial accounting and managerial accounting (see Table 7-6). Financial accounting and managerial accounting would be better labeled as external accounting and internal accounting, respectively. Financial accounting emphasizes the preparation of reports for external users such as government and regulatory agencies, financial institutions, and the investing public. The purpose of financial accounting, then, is to provide information to other audiences. Managerial accounting (often referred to as cost accounting), on the other hand, is primarily for the management team accountable and responsible for system performance. The purpose of managerial accounting is to create information to facilitate planning and control of operations.

Within the framework of MSA, managerial accounting falls in Steps 3a, 3b, and 3c. An effective managerial accounting system requires that the information needs of the management team be identified; measurement, accumulation, and preparation of the data needed to produce this information; and, portraying this data as information. The management accounting system then is very compatible with our general measurement methodology.

A problem with our managerial accounting systems today is that they have been designed using the financial accounting model. Johnson and Kaplan, in their excellent book entitled *Relevance Lost: The Rise and Fall of Managerial Accounting*, state that by 1925 virtually all management accounting practices used today had been developed: cost accounts for labor,

Table 7-6. The Distinctions Between Management Accounting and Financial Accounting

	MANAGERIAL ACCOUNTING	FINANCIAL ACCOUNTING
1. Primary Users	Organization managers at various levels.	Outside parties such as investors and government agencies, but also organization managers.
2. Constraints	No constraints other than costs in relation to benefits of improved decision-making.	Constrained by generally accepted accounting principles (GAAP).
3. Behavioral Implications	Concern about how measurements and reports will influence managers' daily behavior.	Concern about how to measure and communicate economic phenomena. Behavioral impact is secondary.
4. Measurement Frequency	Flexible, varying from hourly to multiple-years.	Less flexible. Usually annual or quarterly.
5. Evaluation Focus	Future orientation: formal use of budgets as well as historical records (e.g., 1988 budget vs. 1988 actual costs).	Past orientation: historical evaluation (e.g., 1988 actual performance versus 1987 actual performance).
6. Reports	Detailed reports on plant, department, product, process.	Summary reports.

(Horngren and Sundem 1987)

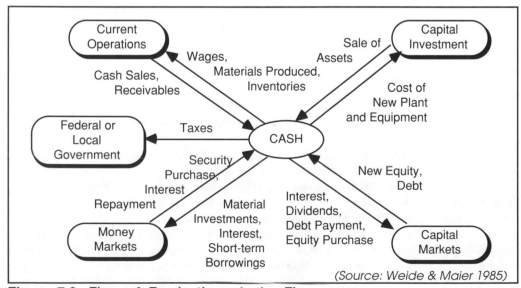

(Source: Weide & Maier 1985)

Figure 7-9. Flow of Funds through the Firm

material, and overhead; budgets for cash, income, and capital; flexible budgets, sales forecasts, standard costs, variance analysis, transfer prices, and divisional performance measures. These practices had evolved to serve the information needs of managers who were faced with managing increasingly complex and diverse organizations. At that point, the pace of innovation seemed to stop (Johnson and Kaplan 1987). The failure of our managerial accounting systems to keep pace with the evolution of product and process technologies has eventually led to distorted product costs, delayed and overly aggregated process control information, and short-term performance measures that do not reflect increases or decreases in the organization's economic position.

Recently, managerial accounting systems have received increased attention. Managers have been asked whether their cost accounting is up to date. There is an increasing awareness on the part of managers that their accounting systems are not providing them with the information they need to better manage and improve performance. Fortunately, there are innovative managers, practitioners, academicians, and consultants beginning to address these problems and offer alternatives. (See for example, Bruns and Kaplan 1987). Price Waterhouse's cost definition methodology and the CAM-I Study on cost accounting systems are just two examples.

Corporate Finance (Contributed by Paul Rossler)

Financial management is concerned with managing the flow of funds through the firm (see Figure 7-9). The purpose of financial ratios is to provide managers with information concerning the flow of funds through the firm. Most financial statements and financial ratios were developed by financial managers and analysts who discovered that studying certain relationships conveyed useful information for decision making. The practice of assessing and evaluating financial ratios is a well-developed and evolving measurement discipline. Financial managers use ratio analysis to provide them with information on the flow of funds so that investment decisions can be made; future financial conditions and possible results can be forecasted; profitability of operating areas can be assessed and evaluated; and, the firm's performance relative to profitability issues can be assessed and evaluated. Using MSA as our framework, financial ratios and statements are located in Box 3a of MSA. Note the unit of analysis is the firm level (typically plant, division, or corporation).

There are a number of financial ratios used. We won't review all of these ratios here; instead, we list the four major categories of ratios and provide references for your further study:

1. Liquidity ratios help determine if the firm can pay its current liabilities when due.
2. Financial leverage ratios provide insight into the extent to which the firm is relying on debt financing. They also help to determine the firm's ability to raise additional debt and its capacity to pay the debt when due.
3. Turnover ratios help management judge how well the firm is managing and controlling its assets. They also assist in evaluating the amount of capital needed to generate sales.
4. Profitability ratios help evaluate performance in controlling expenses and earning a return on resources committed.

Financial management is a part of Step 2 of MSA. Financial ratios fall into Step 3c of MSA. The process of calculating financial ratios from financial statements falls into Step 3b. Note that the financial statement can be considered the data base for financial ratios; however, the financial statement itself can be considered as part of Step 3a. This highlights the fact that information is user-defined and driven by user needs.

Table 7-7. Contrasts Between Traditional Management and MBO

Traditional Management	MBO
Boss sets goals and delegates responsibility	Boss and subordinate set goals mutually
Planning, organizing, staffing, directing, and controlling interwoven with in-process planning	Processes of management executed in planning period (sophisticated planning); everything is laid out before activity begins
Evaluation at the end of implementation	Evaluation during planning period, during operation, and at end
Accountability centralized	Accountability decentralized
Decision making done with nebulous alternatives	Decision making done with alternatives listed in priority array ;consequences of alternatives clear
Focus is on activities	Focus is on results and achievements
Problem solving has past orientation	Problem solving has future orientation
Management system coordinated with people	Management system coordinated through objectives and people
Leadership by personality and charm	Leadership by style, process, and goals
Improvements a random process (luck factor high)	Improvements a way of life (central sense of mission)
Objectives generated from top management	Objectives generated from all levels of management
Forms and rules are basis of control of human resources	Strategic annual plans are basis of control of human resources
Only few management persons interact	Entire organization interacts
System aimed primarily at operations or productions	System aimed at all functions and departments, including operations and productions
Employee participation is source of ideas and solutions	Participative management style allows shared decision making
Problem solving during implementation	Problem solving as much as possible during planning
Responsibility for planning with top management	Responsibility for planning with every manager
Day-to-day managing	Results-to-results managing

(Mali 1986)

**Example Productivity
Gainsharing Calculation**

Example Productivity Gainsharing Calculation	$1,000,000
Output	$800,000
Allowed Input (80% of Output)	$780,000
Actual Input	$20,000
Gain (Loss)	$10,000
Company's Share (Assume 50%)	$10,000
To Reserve Pool (Assume 25%)	$2,500
Available for Distribution	$7,500
Bonus as Percent of Participation Payroll (Assume $100,000 Payroll)	7.5%

**Figure 7-10. Example of a
Gainsharing Calculation**

Management by Objectives (Contributed by Paul Rossler)

Management by Objectives (MBO) is the major method or approach used by managers to operationalize goal setting. It is a participative system of managing in which managers look ahead for improvements, think strategically, set performance-stretch objectives at the beginning of a time period, develop action and supporting plans, and ensure accountability for results at the end of the time period (Mali 1986). Table 7-7 compares and contrasts traditional management practices with those of MBO.

As practiced and applied, MBO has gone through at least three distinct phases over the past twenty years. During the first phase, it was used primarily as a performance appraisal technique. Emphasis was placed on jointly developing objective criteria and standards for individuals in a given job. The second phase of development of MBO focused on its use in planning and control. In this application, MBO was used to tie objectives to plans and, in turn, was a basis for budget control and used performance appraisal as a central component. The third phase involved using MBO as an integrative management process. The emphasis was on a more participative approach, with a focus on action planning, action research, dynamic performance review and evaluation, and a more flexible system that focused on individual and group growth and development. Mali (1978) presents such an MBO hybrid termed "managing productivity by objectives." This is essentially an MBO process with a focus on productivity.

MBO falls in the improvement interventions and techniques box of MSA (Step 2) and the toolbox of MSA (Step 3). The MBO process involves the identification of performance improvement goals and objectives and measures of performance. Progress relative to these goals is tracked, and appropriate control and improvement interventions are made. In this way, MBO attempts to link improvement to measurement.

Recently, MBO has come under attack. Deming (1986) tells us to eliminate management by objectives. However, we believe Deming is referring to how MBO is used for control, rather than for constant improvement. If applied with a focus on constant improvement, goal-setting techniques like MBO represent a potentially significant source of productivity improvement in U.S. organizations. Goal-setting theory tells us that goals which are specific, difficult (yet achievable), and accepted by those that must implement the goals drives improved performance.

Gainsharing (Contributed by Paul Rossler)

The idea of pay for performance is one that has a long history. Sharing the gains of improved productivity through gainsharing has been around for some fifty years. The purpose of gainsharing is to reward group level performance improvement (typically at the plant level). In a gainsharing plan, a benchmark level of productivity is established using historical data, standards, and/or goals. Current period productivity is then measured and compared to this benchmark. If productivity in the current period improved relative to the benchmark, the dollar value of the productivity gain is shared between the company and employees. Figure 7-10 depicts an example of a gainsharing calculation.

Gainsharing falls into the improvement interventions and techniques box of MSA (Step 2) and the tools box of MSA (Step 3). As an improvement intervention and technique gainsharing is used to:

1. Promote coordination, communication, and teamwork;
2. Focus attention on cost savings;
3. Reward innovation and increase acceptance of change;
4. Encourage people to work smart;
5. Encourage people to provide ideas as well as effort;
6. Create a sense of ownership; and
7. Encourage more flexible management-labor relations.

Table 7-8. Various Approaches to Gainsharing

Productivity Measures Used in Common Productivity Gainsharing Plans				
Simple Scanlon	Split Ratio Scanlon	Multi-Cost Scanlon	Rucker	Improshare
$\frac{\text{Labor Costs}}{\text{Sales Value of Production}}$ where SVP equals sales less returns and allowances change in inventory.	$\frac{\text{Labor Costs by Product}}{\text{Sales Value of Production}}$	$\frac{\text{Labor, materials, and overhead}}{\text{Sales Value of Production}}$	$\frac{\text{Labor Costs}}{\text{Value Added}}$ where value added equals SVP less materials, supplies, and purchased services.	$\frac{\text{Actual Hours}}{\text{Total Standard Hours Produced}}$ Uses a Base Productivity Factor to adjust standards past actual output.

Gainsharing as an improvement intervention is best implemented in organizations that have mature performance management efforts (Kilmann 1985; Sink and Rossler 1988).

The measurement models associated with gainsharing are located in the toolbox of MSA. The original and perhaps best known form of gainsharing model is the Scanlon Plan. Other popular conventional approaches to gainsharing are the Rucker Plan and Improshare®. Table 7-8 shows the Scanlon, Rucker, and Improshare® measurement models.

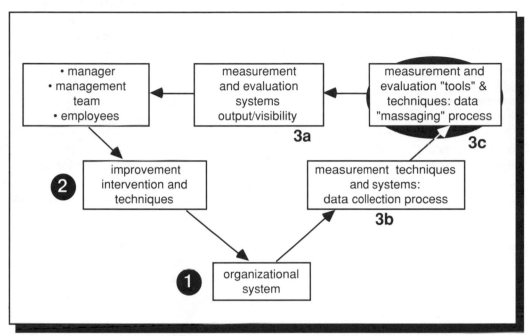

Figure 7-11. Step 3c of MSM

The design of a gainsharing system is compatible with our general measurement methodology. Measurement is a critical component of gainsharing for four reasons. First, to establish and communicate a strong link between rewards and performance, the measures used for gainsharing must capture and reflect the variables, factors, and relationships people have control over. Second, if a company is basing rewards on performance improvement, it should be able to verify whether the improvement has, in fact, actually occurred. Third, properly designed measurement systems motivate, promote, and encourage proactive performance improvement interventions. Fourth, measurement is needed to help target improvement interventions and ensure effective and efficient execution of these improvement interventions. For gainsharing to be fully integrated in the overall performance management process of planning, measurement and evaluation, control, and improvement, valid performance measurement must be incorporated.

STATE-OF-THE-ART AND PRACTICE MEASUREMENT METHODOLOGIES, MODELS, AND TECHNIQUES IN THE CONTEXT OF THE GENERAL MEASUREMENT METHODOLOGY

We have now examined how conventional approaches to measurement relate to the measurement methodology we have been presenting. We now turn our attention to state-of-the-art measurement approaches in the context of the General Measurement Methodology. Within the past ten to twenty years there has been increased interest in productivity and quality and, in particular, in measurement, among other things. This increased interest in measurement has led to attempts to develop new measurement techniques and approaches. A general trend has been a change in the unit of analysis as a focus of measurement. Whereas in the past the unit of analysis for a number of conventional approaches was the individual or work center, the unit of analysis for a number of the state-of-the-art approaches is the work group, function, department, plant, or even firm. Another trend has been to focus more on the seven performance criteria than in the past.

Some of the techniques that have been and are being developed represent real progress. Others represent attempts by opportunists to capitalize on market need and immaturity on the part of much of that market. The measurement master plays a vital role in sorting out the sound measurement approaches from the unsound.

We are just now completing a study for the Department of Defense that looks at defense contractor productivity and quality management. Early in that project, we conducted a comprehensive survey of the literature and the field to identify available measurement techniques (Sink, Tuttle, and Devries 1984). We came away believing that the major productivity measurement models were the TFPMM and the Multi-Criteria Measurement Methodology (Objectives Matrix is a version). There were other measurement approaches we identified, such as the IBM Common Staffing Study, the Cost Definition Model (CDEF) by Price Waterhouse, statistical quality and process control, gainsharing models, and family of measures approach; however, we knew they did not operationally measure productivity as it is properly defined.

Our focus in this section is not just to review productivity measurement approaches, but to also review approaches that focus on other performance criteria. This is clearly an ambitious, perhaps impossible, task. We have selected those techniques that we feel have the most promise and visibility today. You must keep in mind that with most of these techniques we are very early in their developmental history and evolution. Consider what the field of aircraft instrumentation looked like in the early part of this century. We are in exactly that kind of an era with respect to performance measurement. It's exciting, challenging, and also frustrating.

We have chosen to look at the following models, techniques, and methodologies in the context of our measurement methodology:

1. The Total-Factor Productivity Measurement Model;
2. Family of measures approach;
3. Statistical performance control;
4. Common Staffing Study; and
5. Productivity Map.

We show the MSM again to remind you where we will be focusing during this next section (see Figure 7-11).

We stress that your measurement masters must carefully select the right tools for specific situations. We, again, encourage you to consider the concept of contingency measurement technique selection. We will not provide detailed theoretical background or how-to instructions for these models. Our goal is to help you understand how each model fits into the overall measurement strategy we have been describing. We provide comprehensive references for each approach so that your measurement masters may obtain more in-depth knowledge.

Total-Factor Productivity Measurement (Contributed by Tony Pineda)

Total-factor productivity measurement is an area of measurement that attempts to quantify, in local currency and constant value terms, all of the outputs of an organization and divide them by the total value of all of the inputs that were used to create those outputs. There are a number of variations on this theme in terms of operational models and definitions. All seem to have been derived from the early work of Hiram Davis (1955). The conceptual foundation of all current operational models, including software support, is the same. Definitionally, some argue there is a difference between total productivity measurement (TPM) and total-factor productivity measurement (TFPM). Their argument is that one looks at all output divided by all input and the other looks at value added (sales, inventory adjustments, and cost of goods sold) divided by labor and capital (cost of materials consumed is removed from the numerator and denominator). Nevertheless, total-factor productivity measurement is definitely a state-of-the-art and practice performance measurement approach. Organizational systems productivity measurement has only been around since the mid-1950s. In practice, organizational systems productivity measurement is rare in most organizations. We have no real way of knowing, but an insignificant number of organizations in the world truly measure productivity in an operational sense. Far fewer organizations are using productivity information to make decisions, solve problems, formulate and/or evaluate strategy.

The point that seems important to me is that productivity is one of the seven performance criteria for an organizational system. Productivity is inextricably related to effectiveness, efficiency, and quality. Management teams need information about productivity in order to better manage their organizational systems. Furthermore, most of the TFPM models relate profitability to productivity and price changes. This should make it more useful to managers.

The field of productivity measurement, if you dare call it a field, is made up of economists, business types, practitioners, industrial engineers, accountants, industrial psychologists, and others. For about twenty to thirty years now the field has been attempting to improve operationalizations of productivity measurement. The first estimates of total-factor productivity prepared in the United States were those of Tinbergen (1942), Stigler (1947), and Barton and Cooper (1948) [(National Research Council 1979; Kendrick and Vaccara 1980)]. Davis (1955), Kendrick and Creamer (1965), Craig and Harris (1973), the American Productivity Center (as it was called then, 1978), Sumanth (1979), Loggerenberg and Cucchiaro (1982), Miller and Rao (1987), Sink (1985), and LTV/Aircraft Products Group (then called Vought Aero Products, 1985) have made conceptual or operational contributions to the TFPM field. Economists such as Solow (1950s), Denison (1962), Griliches and Jorgenson (1966), and Gollop and Jorgenson (1975) (National Research Council 1979) have also developed econometric models for TFPM.

There are model and methodology developments ongoing. Refinements to the formulation of the equations that make up the model are being investigated (Gollop 1982; Miller and Rao 1987; Sink 1988; Loggerenberg 1986; and Sumanth 1984). Gollop uses logarithmic derivatives of production functions and defines total-factor productivity as the growth rate of physical output (or deflated value of output) less the weighted average of the growth rates of physical inputs (or deflated value of inputs) so as to avoid confounding price and productivity effects and to ensure that the TFP measure is not sensitive to the choice of the base period. His model can also aggregate measures into the next higher level unit of analysis. Loggerenberg (1986), on the other hand, uses functions with finite and discrete differences or intervals instead of continuous functions. He breaks down productivity into capacity utilization and efficiency; capacity utilization deals with fixed inputs such as equipment and facilities, while efficiency deals with variable inputs such as materials. Strategic options are also suggested depending on productivity, pricing, and profitability figures obtained. Miller and Rao (1987) deflate current dollars to each preceding period down to the base period, unlike APCs model which deflates current dollars direct to its base period equivalent, disregarding any intermediate periods. Thus, they consider all dollar fluctuations

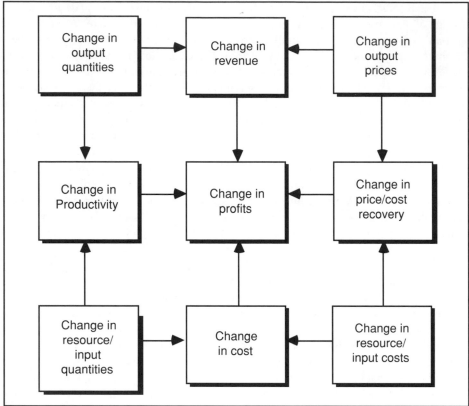

Figure 7-12. Conceptual Framework for TFPMM

between the base and the current periods. Sumanth (1984) developed another model computing total productivity of a firm as the sum of total productivities of each of the products. The total productivity of a product is the ratio of the constant dollar value of total output over the total constant dollar value of all inputs used for that product. Through his break-even concept, he relates total productivity to profit. Sumanth has also presented a model at the International Conference on Productivity Research in 1987 relating productivity to other performance criteria such as efficiency, quality, and innovation. Virginia Productivity Center has recently isolated the joint dollar effects of productivity and pricing on profitability from dollar effects purely attributable to productivity and pricing, respectively. The Center at Virginia Tech is also doing research on the theoretical and methodological differences of the available TFPM models.

There are software developments that are ongoing. The National Productivity Institute of South Africa has the software called REsource ALlocation STrategist (REALST) and VPC has SCORBORD. The intent is to try to create software that will facilitate the storage, retrieval, processing, and portrayal of productivity information. Both the model and methodology developments and the software developments are refinements to the total-factor productivity measurement tools. The effort is focusing on Step 3c of the MSA.

This work is important, as productivity is an important criterion. However, the literature and our experience reveals a fixation on the toolbox (Step 3c). Unless productivity measurement models and software are viewed in the larger context of building improved management systems for management teams, we run the risk of becoming "hammers looking for nails to pound."

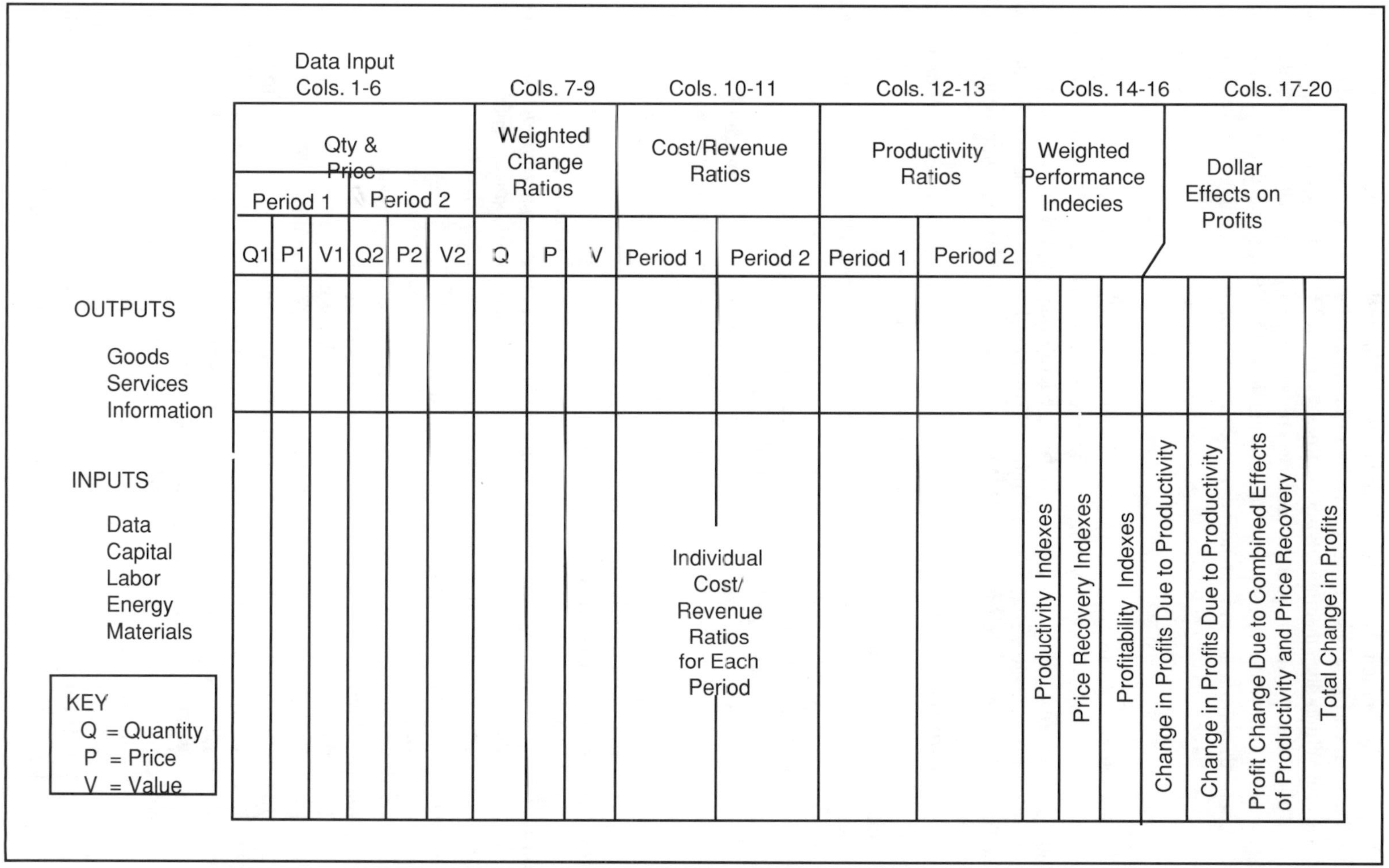

Data Input
Cols. 1-6

		Cols. 7-9	Cols. 10-11	Cols. 12-13	Cols. 14-16	Cols. 17-20

OUTPUTS
Goods
Services
Information

INPUTS
Data
Capital
Labor
Energy
Materials

Qty & Price

Period 1: Q1 P1 V1
Period 2: Q2 P2 V2

Weighted Change Ratios: Q P V

Cost/Revenue Ratios: Period 1, Period 2

Productivity Ratios: Period 1, Period 2

Individual Cost/ Revenue Ratios for Each Period

Weighted Performance Indecies
Productivity Indexes
Price Recovery Indexes
Profitability Indexes

Dollar Effects on Profits
Change in Profits Due to Productivity
Change in Profits Due to Productivity
Profit Change Due to Combined Effects of Productivity and Price Recovery
Total Change in Profits

KEY
Q = Quantity
P = Price
V = Value

Figure 7-13. TFPMM and its SCORBORD Format

Productivity measurement is critical to having a well-balanced and effective measurement system. There are a lot of types of productivity information that can be looked at. The critical questions are: Which does the management team want to see? How do they want it portrayed? How will they use the information? Before we pursue implementation issues further, we'll quickly review the model in its most fundamental form. We'll assume that the masters of measurement that want to understand advanced nuances of the model will investigate the references we have provided at the end of the section.

The model

The Total-Factor Productivity Measurement Model (TFPMM) is a dynamic, aggregated, indexed, and computerized approach to measuring productivity. The TFPMM can be utilized to measure productivity change in labor, materials, energy, and capital. It also measures the corresponding effect each one has on profitability. With essentially the same accounting data that are used to track revenue and costs, the TFPMM can provide additional insight into the individual factors that are most significantly affecting profits.

The TFPMM is based on the premise that profitability is a function of productivity and price recovery; that is, an organizational system can generate profit growth from productivity improvement and/or from price recovery. Productivity relates to quantities of output and quantities of inputs, while price recovery relates to prices of output and costs of inputs. Price recovery can be thought of as the degree to which input cost increases are passed on to the customers in the form of higher output prices. The relationship between productivity, profitability, and price recovery are depicted in Figure 7-12.

The data required for the TFPMM are periodic data (i.e., monthly, quarterly, annually or more) for quantity, price, and value of each output and input of the organizational system being analyzed. Since value equals quantity times price, having two of the quantity, price, and value variables obviously yields the third algebraically. Quantity, price, and/or value of the various outputs produced and most of the inputs consumed are straightforward and should be provided by most basic accounting systems.

The TFPMM compares data from one period (base period) with data from a second period (current period). This comparison forms the basis of the productivity/price recovery/ profitability analysis. The choice of a base period is a critical decision, since it establishes the period against which the current period will be compared. Therefore, the base period should be as representative of normal business conditions as possible. If the data exists, the budget or standards could be used as the base period data. Depending on the needs of the user, the availability of data, product cycle time, and so forth, period length could be a week, a quarter, a year, or any other period for which input data can be matched to output data.

From the base and current period data, the TFPMM generates a series of ratios and indexes, each communicating different information about the system under study. Figure 7-13 depicts, from left to right, the data input and then the ratios and indexes derived from them: weighted change ratios, cost/revenue ratios, productivity ratios, weighted performance indexes, and total dollar effects on profits. Note that this is VPC's model. Other models use different formats and processes but the same data and basic information. Weighted change ratios depict the percentage increase (or decrease) of an output or input item from the base to current period. Price, quantity, and value-weighted change ratios are generated by the model to show the percentage changes from period to period. Cost/revenue ratios reflect the percentages of reported revenue consumed by a particular input in a given period. This information provides the user with insights as to where leverage exists. The most common method of productivity improvement is cost reduction, and these ratios show exactly where cost reductions will pay the biggest dividends. Productivity ratios— the ratios of total output value to the various input values — depict absolute productivity values in the base and current period. These ratios show the absolute increase or decrease of productivity for each of the inputs. The weighted performance indexes are actually output over input change ratios from Period 1 to Period 2. The final set of indexes are the dollar effects on profits. In other words, these indexes indicate what impact (in dollars) are caused by changes in productivity, price recovery, and profitability. The ratios and indexes identify areas that need improvement, and they also identify areas that are operating at an acceptable level. If the information is used correctly, productivity can improve, which in turn should increase profits.

The TFPMM is most appropriate at the firm and plant levels and would be most useful to senior management. It could be used at the cost center level as a separate accounting system for an assembly line or an individual product line; however, at lower levels of organizations, managers do not normally need the kind of detail offered by the model. The TFPMM has been most often applied in manufacturing settings, but it can be used anywhere the necessary data exists.

It is estimated that somewhere between fifty and 100 organizations in the United States are utilizing this approach. Among these are: Phillips Petroleum Company, Anderson Clayton, General Foods, Hershey Foods, Sentry Insurance, John Deere, Federal Express, Xaloy and Glaxo Pharmaceuticals, and at least twenty industry, government, and business users in South Africa.

Case example

Figure 7-14 depicts an actual case example. The figure represents the computer output or tableau for SCORBORD. Only a portion of the output is presented here, but it will suffice to serve as an example by which to clarify the model. We will briefly describe what the output tells us regarding the performance of this fiberglass boat manufacturing firm in Periods 1 and 2.

Columns 1 through 6 are data input to the model. Columns 1 through 3 present Period 1 data regarding output and input quantity, price unit costs, and revenues/costs. Columns 4 through 6 present equivalent Period 2 data.

As can be seen, comparing Period 2 to Period 1 shows that this company: sold more boats and raised prices; used less labor and had an increase in labor rates; used more fiberglass and paid more for it; and used more wood and electricity while unit cost for both remained the same. Also, the data columns show that the company did not choose to capture its capital consumption in the data for the model.

Columns 7 through 9 represent weighted change ratios. Column 7 tells us the period price and cost-weighted change ratios for outputs and inputs. For example, the company:

1. Produced 27.27 percent more boats in Period 2 than Period 1;
2. Consumed or paid for 5 percent less labor in Period 2 than Period 1; and
3. Consumed 36.36 percent more fiberglass in Period 2 than Period 1.

Column 8 tells us the Period 2 quantity weighted change ratios for outputs and inputs. For example:

1. Boat prices increased 15 percent from Period 1 to Period 2;
2. Labor unit costs or salaries and wages increased 13.11 percent from Period 1 to Period 2; and
3. Fiberglass unit costs increased 70 percent from Period 1 to Period 2.

271

	PERIOD 1			PERIOD 2		
	(1) QUANTITY	(2) PRICE	(3) VALUE	(4) QUANTITY	(5) PRICE	(6) VALUE
BOAT A	50.0	500.00	250000.00	70.0	5500.00	385000.00
BOAT B	30.0	10000.00	300000.00	35.0	12000.00	420000.00
TOTAL OUTPUTS			550000.00			805000.00
LABOR MANAGEMENT	320.0	20.00	6400.00	304.0	22.00	6688.00
LABOR GLASS	800.0	8.00	6400.00	760.0	9.00	6840.00
LABOR ASSEMBLY	1120.0	6.00	6720.00	1064.0	7.00	7448.00
TOTAL LABOR			19520.00			20976.00
FIBERGLASS	2200.0	50.00	110000.00	3000.0	85.0	255000.00
WOOD	750.0	3.00	2250.00	1000.0	3.0	3000.00
TOTAL MATERIALS			112250.00			258000.00
ELECTRICITY	8000.0	0.10	800.0	8200.0	0.10	820.00
NATURAL GAS	100.0	4.00	400.0	90.0	4.00	360.00
TOTAL ENERGY			1200.00			1180.00
TOTAL INPUTS			132970.00			280156.00

	WEIGHTED CHANGED RATIOS			COST/REVENUE RATIOS		PRODUCTIVITY RATIOS	
	(7) QUANTITY	(8) PRICE	(9) VALUE	(10) PERIOD 1	(11) PERIOD 2	(12) PERIOD 1	(13) PERIOD 2
BOAT A	1.4000	1.1000	1.540				
BOAT B	1.1667	1.2000	1.400				
TOTAL OUTPUTS	1.2727	1.1545	1.464				
LABOR MANAGEMENT	0.9500	1.1000	1.045	0.0116	0.0083	85.94	115.13
LABOR GLASS	0.9500	1.1250	1.069	0.0116	0.0085	85.94	115.13
LABOR ASSEMBLY	0.9500	1.1667	1.108	0.0122	0.0093	81.85	109.65
TOTAL LABOR	0.9500	1.1311	1.075	0.0355	0.0261	28.18	37.75
FIBERGLASS	1.3535	1.7000	2.318	0.2000	0.3168	5.00	4.67
WOOD	1.3333	1.0000	1.333	0.0041	0.0037	244.44	233.33
TOTAL MATERIALS	1.3630	1.6860	2.298	0.2041	0.3205	4.90	4.58
ELECTRICITY	1.0250	1.0000	1.025	0.0015	0.0010	687.50	853.66
NATURAL GAS	0.9000	1.0000	0.900	0.0007	0.0004	1375.00	1944.44
TOTAL ENERGY	0.9833	1.0000	0.983	0.0022	0.0015	458.33	593.22
TOTAL INPUTS	1.2990	1.5983	2.107	0.2418	0.3480	4.14	4.05

	WEIGHTED PERFORMANCE INDEXES			DOLLAR EFFECTS ON PROFITS			
	(14) CHANGE IN PRODUCTIVITY	(15) CHANGE IN PRICE RECOVERY	(16) CHANGE IN PROFITABIL-ITY	(17) CHANGE IN PRODUCTIV-ITY	(18) CHANGE IN PRICE RECOV-ERY	(19) JOINT CHANGE EFFECT	(20) CHANGE IN PROFITABIL-ITY
BOAT A							
BOAT B							
TOTAL OUTPUTS							
LABOR MANAGEMENT	1.340	1.050	1.401	2065.45	349.09	264.73	2679.27
LABOR GLASS	1.340	1.026	1.369	2065.45	189.09	272.73	2527.27
LABOR ASSEMBLY	1.340	0.989	1.321	2168.73	-81.45	300.36	2387.64
TOTAL LABOR	1.340	1.021	1.362	6299.64	456.72	837.82	7594.18
FIBERGLASS	0.933	0.679	0.631	-10000.00	-60000.00	-24000.00	-94000.00
WOOD	0.955	1.155	1.098	-136.00	347.73	81.82	293.18
TOTAL MATERIALS	0.934	0.685	0.637	-10136.36	-59652.20	-23918.10	-93706.81
ELECTRICITY	1.242	1.155	1.428	198.18	123.64	29.09	350.91
NATURAL GAS	1.414	1.155	1.626	149.09	61.81	14.55	225.45
TOTAL ENERGY	1.294	1.155	1.488	347.27	185.45	43.64	576.36
TOTAL INPUTS	0.980	0.722	0.695	-3489.45	-59010.00	-23036.70	-85536.27

Figure 7-14. Total-Factor Productivity Measurement Model VPI/VPC

Column 9 tells us the simultaneous effect of changes in prices/costs and quantities sold/used. Column 9 for output rows tells us the increase in revenues from Period 1 to Period 2 (e.g., material costs up 129.8 percent; total costs up 110.7 percent).

Columns 10 and 11 depict cost/revenues ratios and assist in invoking Pareto's principle with respect to focusing in on where our costs drivers are. For example, material costs in Period 1, Column 10, were 20.41 percent of total revenues, while material costs in Period 2, Column 11, were 32.05 percent of total revenues.

Columns 12 and 13 are the absolute productivity ratios for Periods 1 and 2, respectively. Labor productivity was 28.18 in Period 1 and 37.75 in Period 2. These numbers will only have meaning once they are tracked over time and interpreted in the context of what is or has happened to the company.

Columns 14 through 16 represent the weighted performance indexes. Column 14 tells us the rate of change of productivity from Period 1 to Period 2. Labor productivity is up 34 percent, material productivity is down 6.66 percent, and overall productivity is down 2 percent. Column 15 tells us the rate of change of price-recovery or prices over costs from Period 1 to Period 2. We can see that material price recovery is down 31.5 percent; that is, suppliers increased their costs to the company faster than it raised its prices to its customers. Column 16 depicts the simultaneous change in prices/costs and quantities sold/used. Profits increased 36 percent from Period 1 to Period 2 due to productivity and price recovery gains in the labor area. Overall, profits decreased by 31 percent due to a slight decline in overall productivity and a significant decline in overall price recovery.

Columns 17 through 20 depict the dollar effect on profit changes from Period 1 to Period 2 from productivity and price recovery. The bottom line is that this company became $85,536.27 less profitable from Period 1 to Period 2.

This brief discussion of this case application of the TFPMM should suffice to at least clarify the basic characteristics of this technique for measuring productivity and other elements of performance.

Family of Measures

There are a range of measurement methods that result in a family of performance measures designed to explain performance in an organizational system. Two theoretical models were proposed by Sink et. al. (1984): the Multi-Criteria Productivity/Performance Measurement Technique (MCP/PMT) and the Normative Performance/Productivity Measurement Methodology (NP/PMM). Tuttle and his associates have developed two methodologies that lay the organizational groundwork for and operationalize the family of measures concept. These are the Methodology for Generating Efficiency and Effectiveness Measures (Tuttle and Weaver 1986) and the Strategic Performance Measurement Process (Tuttle and Ross 1988). Thor, of the American Productivity and Quality Center, has spoken to the "family of measures" approach for a number of years and has utilized the Nominal Group Technique approach developed at The Ohio State University in 1976 to operationalize this concept. Other approaches focus on the reporting formats for portraying family of measures data and for aggregating them into a single composite indicator. These include the Objectives Matrix (Felix and Riggs 1983; Riggs and Felix 1983) and the Product-to-Contingencies Approach (Weaver in a personal communication 1988). Finally, at least two software packages have been developed that help organizations operationalize the family of measures approach. Notable among these are the VPC's PRFORM package and Pacesetter Software's Productivity Map.

It seems clear from the wide-ranging interest shown this approach, that family of measures is probably the most widely used approach to performance measurement. However, it

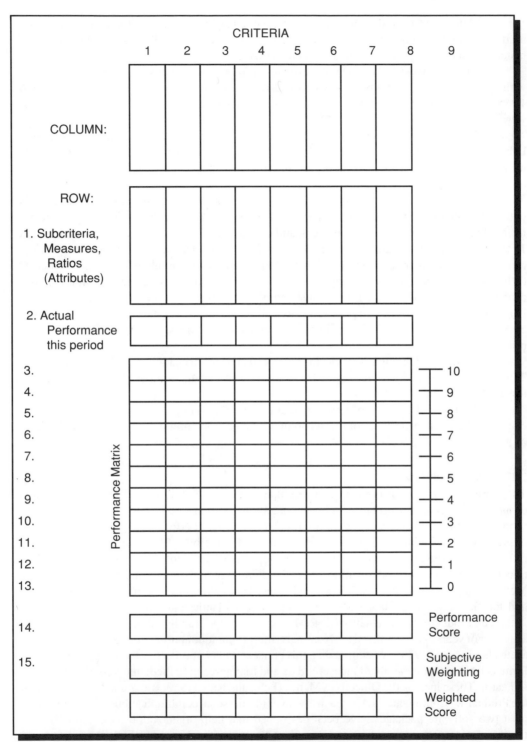

Figure 7-15. The Objectives Matrix Reporting Form

appears that there are as many ways of doing this approach as there are applications. Herein lies one of the problems with this approach, in our opinion. There is a tendency to have an "any road will get us there" mentality. We have argued for a slightly more systematic approach to the development of a family of measures system. In fact, the general measurement methodology we have presented in Chapters 6 and 7 is really a very specific family of measures approach.

When people begin to build a family of measures approach, they have preferences for how they want the information from the system portrayed. Some prefer what we call the instrument panel approach. They prefer to see the disaggregated measures and to "aggregate" in their minds. Other managers and management teams prefer to be able to "collapse" the vector of measures into one number or dial. Still others prefer to see both the disaggregated measures and the one dial itself.

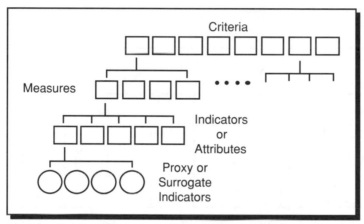

Figure 7-16. Development of Countables

The literature in the area of multicriteria/attribute decision making has addressed the issue of aggregation for a number of years. Stewart (1978), Felix and Riggs (1983), and more recently Sink (1985) and Tuttle and Weaver (1986) have focused on the development of multiattribute decision making applications for performance measurement situations.

We have discussed in detail how to develop the family of measures that a management team desires to monitor (i.e., Step 3a of MSA, Step 7 of the PIPP, and the Key Performance Indicators associated with Steps 3-5 of the PIPP). We would like to focus our attention in this section on Step 3c of the MSA and on the issue of how to aggregate the set of measures into one dial that tells you whether the performance of the organization has gone up or down. We'll assume that you understand, by now, how to identify, obtain consensus for, and develop a prioritized list of performance measures for an organizational system. We will also assume you know how to audit to improve the measures (AIM) you obtain from the NGT session. We assume you may not know how to aggregate these measures and so we will focus on that portion of the family of measures process.

We should note that there are only slight operational differences between the Multi-Criteria Measurement Methodology of Stewart and Sink and the Objectives Matrix of Riggs and Felix. We'll provide an abbreviated description of the Objectives Matrix and assume the measurement master will read further in the list of suggested references at the end of this chapter.

OBJECTIVES MATRIX—A WAY TO AGGREGATE YOUR FAMILY OF MEASURES

The Objectives Matrix was originally proposed by Felix and Riggs (1983) and draws on multiattribute decision theory concepts that have been around for years. Our description herein will depart somewhat from the Felix and Riggs description of the matrix to make it compatible with the methodology described in this book. We will also present a version used by the Maryland Center for Quality and Productivity, and which incorporates the concept of goals for the measures/indicators, and the revised version, which has been labeled the Objectives Matrix with Goals. Basically the matrix (see Figure 7-15) is a reporting form that allows a management team to track their performance against a family of measures. It also permits weighting and aggregation of measures into a composite index of performance for the organizational system as a whole. The matrix can be used as a feedback device to members, or different portrayal formats may be designed and utilized. PRFORM, for example, has a report generator that allows the management team to view the information in various formats.

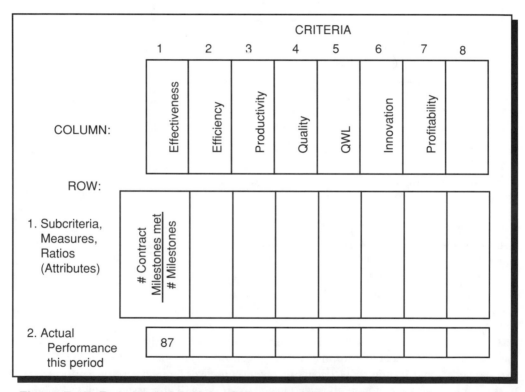

Figure 7-17. Rows 1 and 2 of the Objectives Matrix

Developing the Matrix

Step 1. Target system/unit of analysis and major performance dimension/ criterion identification. The first step in developing the matrix involves determining its scope. Most likely, the matrix will be developed for the target system/organizational system you have selected. If the target system were your total organization, then the columns of the matrix might be the strategic performance dimensions and the measures/indicators associated with the dimensions. An alternative approach would be to develop a single matrix for each strategic performance dimension. This would be recommended if there are several different facets of the dimension that need to be measured. One example would be a strategic performance dimension, e.g. quality. As we have indicated, quality must be operationally defined and measured at at least five checkpoints, and there will undoubtedly be multiple attributes of quality at each checkpoint. You might have the columns in the matrix represent the eight quality attributes suggested by Garvin (1988) of performance, features, reliability, conformance, durability, serviceability, aesthetics, and perceived quality. You might also develop your own attributes for each of the five checkpoints. The point is that you have to determine what to put in the columns of the matrix. You might put the results of your NGT session and have a mixed set of various performance measures. You might have multiple matrices, each focusing on a different strategic performance dimension. This is where your measurement masters are going to come in handy in terms of design of the application.

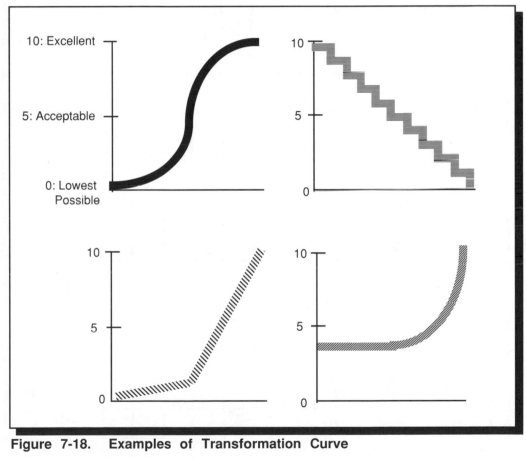

Figure 7-18.   Examples of Transformation Curve

Step 2. Development of countables (measures, indicators, and attributes for each dimension and/or criterion). The next step in developing the matrix involves identification of the countable for each of the columns. You will recall that we developed a taxonomy and hierarchy of terms earlier in this chapter: strategic performance dimension, criterion, key performance indicators, indicators/surrogates/proxy measures, and attributes. Once you have identified the

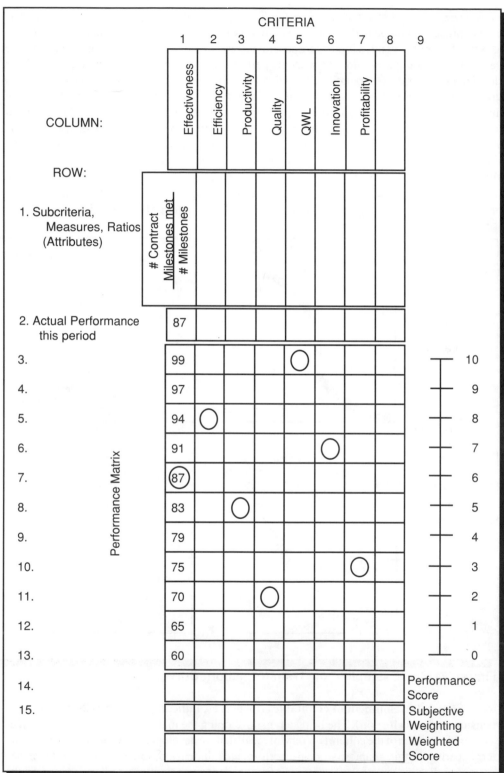

Figure 7-19. The Objectives Matrix with Performance Scores

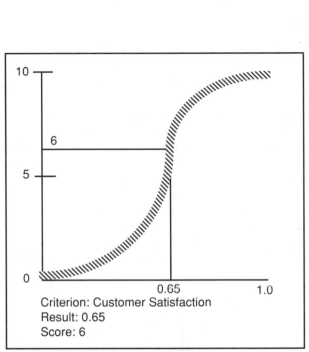

Criterion: Customer Satisfaction
Result: 0.65
Score: 6

**Figure 7-20. Scoring the Criterion
by the Transformation Curve**

unit of analysis and what to measure, you have to develop countables for the columns of your matrix. Some "higher order" measures are directly measurable; others are not and must be broken down into "lower order" measures. For example, a strategic performance dimension of quality will very likely need to be broken down into specific measures; perhaps even indicators or attributes in order to be operationalized. Figure 7-16 depicts this concept.

Line/Row 2 of the matrix then lists the various measures and perhaps even indicators/ attributes or subattributes for each of the strategic performance dimensions or seven criterion that have been identified in Line/Row 1 (see Figure 7-17). For example, effectiveness is the criterion, customer satisfaction was identified as a measure of that, and warranty costs, number of complaints, and return business were identified as indicators for that measure. Note that you may have to go to the subattribute level before finding a countable for the measure identified in Rows 1 or 2. This may mean that your matrix has three or even four rows for the measurement hierarchy. For the purpose of simplicity, we will demonstrate a two-row measurement hierarchy example and assume that your measurement masters can extrapolate the example to a more complex case.

The number of columns for Row 1 and Row 2 are user-specified. The example we are depicting is for illustration purposes only.

Step 3. Development of transformation/preference curves. The next step in matrix development involves establishing preference curves/transformation curves for each of the indicators/attributes in Row 2. In the Total-Factor Productivity Measurement Model, the common denominator used to aggregate results and identify dollar impact of productivity on profits is local currency (i.e., dollars in the United States, yen in Japan, and deutsche marks in Germany). In the Objectives Matrix case, where we are often dealing with white-collar situations and in situations where there is no obvious common denominator to use for aggregation purposes, we have to invent a common denominator. In graph form, we have a y-axis that has a scale ranging from zero to ten. We call this the common performance scale. The x-axis represents the specific scale associated with the countable in Row 2 in our example. This scale ranges from the lowest value to the highest value possible for the specific measure, indicator, attribute, or subattribute. The x-axis scales will vary considerably. For example: number of complaints, productivity ratios, sales, profits, warranty costs, return business, papers written, students graduated, cost of poor quality, and mean time between failure.

The transformation or preference curve simply transforms a scaled level of performance on the natural scale (i.e., the final countable for the measure, indicator/attribute, such as number of complaints, number of scratches, and perceived user friendliness) to a scaled level of performance on the common scale. Figure 7-18 shows several examples of transformation curves. We show these transformation curves as graphs at this point because it is easier for some to understand the concept graphically rather than in matrix form.

The Objectives Matrix represents these transformation curves in tabular form. We present the next stage of development of the matrix in Figure 7-19. Note that the body of the matrix —shaded— contains the x-axis or natural scales for each of the measures and indicators/attributes. In this example, Column 9 represents the y-axis of all the transformation curves, which is the

#	Criterion	Ranking/ Priority
1.	Reports/projects completed and accepted _____ Constant value budget $	1
2.	Customer satisfaction	2
3.	Quality of decision support from systems developed	3
4.	Meeting user flexibility requirements	4
5.	Existence of and use of work scheduling/project managment	5
6.	Projects completed on time _____ Total projects completed	6
7.	Number of requests for rework/ redoing a project	7
8.	Existence of and quality of strategic planning for vacilitied, equipment staffing, manage- ment, processes, and systems	8

Figure 7-21 Ranking Procedure for Performance Measures

common scale and ranges from zero to ten. The numbers in the body of the matrix represent discrete points on the transformation curve itself. Note that the graphic representation allows us to portray more data in that we see a continuous representation of the x-axis to y-axis transformation. The matrix representation allows us to capture and portray a finite set of transformation points in the cells. Reconsider what we have talked about in the management systems model, and you will see that this is a Step 3a and 3c issue of MSA—information portrayal. Some of your management team members may want to see the Objectives Matrix in graph form; others may want to see the table format. PRFORM has been programmed to provide either portrayal format.

#	Criterion	Ranking/ Priority	Rating	Weight	
1.	Reports/projects completed <u>and accepted</u> Constant value budget $	1	100	$\frac{100}{730}$	=.137
2.	Customer satisfaction	2	100	$\frac{100}{730}$	=.137
3.	Quality of decision support from systems developed	3	100	$\frac{100}{730}$	=.137
4.	Meeting user flexibility requirements	4	90	$\frac{90}{730}$	=.123
5.	Existence of and use of work scheduling/project managment	5	90	$\frac{90}{730}$	=.123
6.	<u>Projects completed on time</u> Total projects completed	6	85	$\frac{85}{730}$	=.116
7.	Number of requests for rework/ redoing a project	7	85	$\frac{85}{730}$	=.116
8.	Existence of and quality of strategic planning for vacilitied, equipment staffing, manage- ment, processes, and systems	8	80	$\frac{80}{730}$	=.111
			730	1.000	

Figure 7-22. Rating Procedures for Performance Measures

We have referred to the transformation curves also as preference curves. The reason for this is that the process of developing these curves is a subjective one—involving preferences or judgments. In utility theory, decision makers are asked to attempt to combine risk and uncertainty and develop utility curves. In this type of application, we are asking decision makers, members,

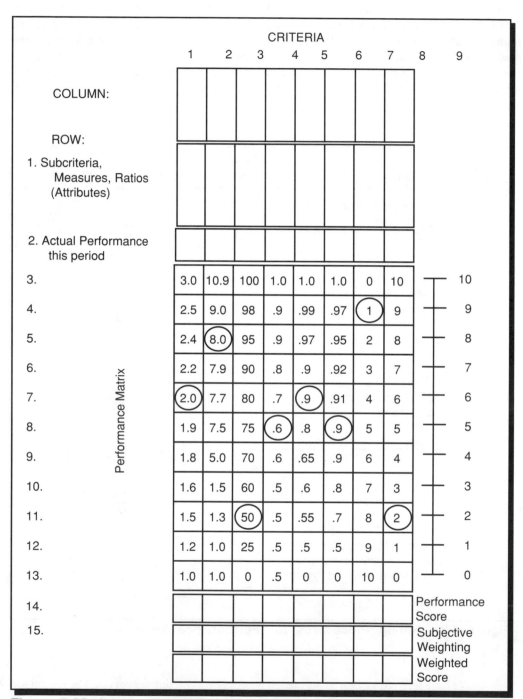

Figure 7-23. Interim Format of the Objectives Matrix

and/or individuals of a management team to transform performance on the natural scale for each attribute to performance on the common scale. For example, on a scale of zero to ten where zero represents the lowest possible level of performance and ten represents excellence, how many points would you give for no customer complaints, ten customer complaints, fifty, or more? Figure 7-20 depicts one management team's answer to this question in the form of a transformation curve.

There are a variety of procedures that can be utilized to develop these transformation curves. You could borrow from utility theory and modify procedures used to develop utility curves. Stewart (1978) used a curve recognition/matching process. He would show managers and management teams different types of curves and ask them which one most closely represented the way they felt that the transformation process for each measure or indicator/attribute would look. Anchoring points on the curve and then connecting these points is probably the most common approach.

However, there are different strategies for how to anchor the curves. Tuttle suggests the following procedure. Establish a baseline performance on the indicator. The baseline is the present level of performance against the specific measure or indicator. This is consistent with most other recommended approaches. The baseline is anchored at Performance Level 3 in the Objective Matrix procedure. Sink (1985) and Archer (1970) use a baseline value anchored at five. Once the baseline is set, then performance levels zero and ten on the common scale can be anchored. Tuttle suggests that level 10 be the target level established in the current planning period. Others (Archer 1970; Sink 1985) suggest that level ten might represent excellence or the best possible level of performance. For example, level ten might represent zero defects and no customer complaints. Both strategies have their merits—be a chef and pick the one that will work best for you. Level zero is the lowest level of performance that can be envisioned.

You now have three points anchored on the transformation curve, and other points may be designated to allow for greater precision of presentation of preferences. We don't have any sure-fire ways to tell you how to complete the curve. Since we are building measurement systems for the primary purpose of improvement, if we end up with curves that we don't like (that are too tough or too easy or don't represent reality) then we can change them. PRFORM incorporates an interactive session in which the manager, measurement master, or management team is paced through the transformation curve development process. The software stores the preferences, presents the final curves and allows the user to then modify them.

Step 4. Development of ranking, rating, and weighting for the measures, indicators/ attributes, and perhaps subattributes. At this stage in the general measurement methodology you will have already generated your list of priority strategic performance dimensions, criteria, and measures. If you have decided to continue the measurement system development process using this approach, you will have developed operational (countable) measures, indicators/ attributes, and perhaps even subattributes for your strategic performance dimensions and criteria. If, as we have suggested, you have utilized the NGT or Delphi Technique, you will have a prioritized, ranked list of measures. These ranked measures appear in Rows 1 and 2 in the Objectives Matrix. Each row of the matrix needs to be ranked. If you have two rows, as we have shown in the example, both rows will need to be ranked. If you had to have three rows (i.e., a case where you had strategic performance dimensions in Row 1, measures in Row 2, and indicators in Row 3, or a case where you had the seven performance criteria in Row 1, measures in Row 2, and indicators/attributes in Row 3), you would need to rank the items in each of the three rows. Figure 7-21 depicts an example.

Now, starting at the lowest level, at the lowest row—in this case Row 2—you begin to rate the items. We want to spread 100 points across the measures in each of Columns 1 through

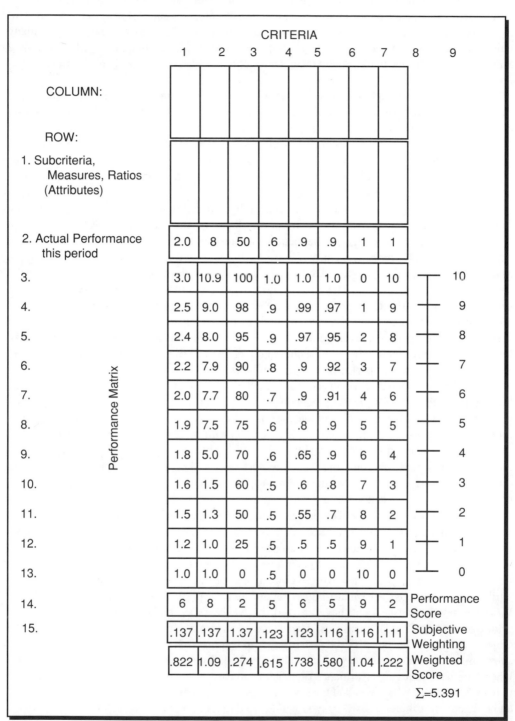

Figure 7-24. Final Format of the Objectives Matrix

8. We give the number one ranked item 100 points. We then compare the second ranked item to the first and ask, "How much less important is the second than the first?" We compare the third ranked item to the second, answering the same question. We continue this until all items within a given column are rated. Figure 7-22 shows this process for the example we have been using. The rating points in a given subcolumn are added up and a total is arrived at. Each rate ranging from zero to 100 is divided by that total and a relative weight is determined. These weights will add to 1.000 for each subcolumn. This same procedure needs to be done for the next higher row. When this procedure is complete, the matrix has reached the next major stage of development and is ready for use. Figure 7-23 shows the matrix in the form it will be in at this point. PRFORM also walks the user through this ranking, rating, and weighting procedure.

      Step 5. Using the matrix. Collecting, storing, retrieving, and processing the data using the matrix is the next step in the Objectives Matrix approach. The length of time between use of the matrix, or the period length, needs to be determined. Frequently, the length of a period for this measurement technique is monthly. The current period performance level (natural scale score or x-axis) is recorded in Row 14 (for our example). The transformed common scale score (y-axis) is recorded in Row 15 (for our example). The weighted score for each measure or indicator/attribute is shown in Row 16 (for our example). If we sum up the weighted scores across Row 16 we arrive at a total performance score for the organizational system. Figure 7-24 shows this completed for one period.

      Essentially we end up with one matrix for each period. We store the matrices and begin to track performance over time. We can portray the total performance scores over time or changes in this score over time. We can plot individual performance scores for strategic performance dimensions and criterion. We can divide the sum of the weighted scores for the current period by the sum of the weighted scores for the a baseline period and obtain a percentage of improvement from base. PRFORM stores matrices and allows the user to generate certain reports that portray information from the Objectives Matrix.

Assessment and evaluation of the Objectives Matrix

The matrix is a convenient way to report/portray performance measurement data. As you can see, it is a nice way to aggregate your family of measures into a total performance score. It is an example of an MSA Step 3c tool that can store, retrieve, process, and portray measurement data and information. It can, when used properly, provide a linkage between the PIPP and measurement; it is a way to do Step 7 of the planning process. The approach, if developed the way we have described it, is philosophically compatible with the concept of continuous improvement of performance. The performance levels can serve as successive hurdles to be attained and should not, as standards often do, act as a ceiling on improvement.

      Matrix applications are often fairly crude, subjective, messy, and from a mathematical, statistical, decision science, purist point-of-view not defensible. You could certainly question the validity of the results and perhaps even the process. The aggregation process treats each of the dimensions as though they are mutually exclusive and independent even though they often may not be. This inherently enters bias and error into the technique.

      Overall, however, the process of developing the matrix is quite valuable and serves to explicitly define performance. Even with the flaws in the approach, it is probably superior to what most managers are currently using. Over time the maturity of the management team and the measurement master with respect to measurement in general and this approach in specific will improve, and the process and product validity should improve.

      Like all of these new measurement techniques, it will take some time to get comfortable with the theory, the concepts, the techniques themselves, and proper application. Abuse and misuse of this technique is, we believe, fairly widespread. People have a tendency to either make this too complex or too simple. They jump into using this technique on a widespread basis before developing a solid understanding of how it can and should be used. We believe the general approach, when applied in the context of our general measurement methodology, has much promise for your organization, particularly in traditionally hard to measure areas.

For those measurement masters interested in learning more about the technique, we provide a detailed list of references at the end of this chapter.

Statistical Performance Control

It is interesting to stand back and compare and contrast the table of contents of a traditional statistical quality control text used in higher education in the United States with a text focusing on the same topic written by a Japanese; for example, Dr. Kaoru Ishikawa (1976, 1985). They reflect, perhaps, different paradigms about quality in an organization. These different views on quality in the organization may be at the heart of many nations' and organizations' competitiveness problems. In a traditional quality-control textbook you see: an introduction and history of quality; a review of fundamental statistics; large sections on control chart theory, development, and process control theory; a large section on acceptance sampling; and, then, of course, large appendices with numerous tables (Duncan 1986; Grant and Leavenworth 1988; Feigenbaum 1983; Hansen and Ghare 1987; Wadsworth, Stephens, and Godfrey 1986). These are all sound, well-written textbooks; however, let's compare the contents of Ishikawa's books, which have information on how to collect data, histograms, cause-and-effect diagrams, check sheets, Pareto diagrams, graphs, control charts, scatter diagrams, binomial probability paper, sampling, sampling inspection, and practice problems.

Now we admit this is an unfair and perhaps biased comparison of approaches to quality control education. Ishikawa's audience is perhaps different, we haven't done justice to the true content of the American counterpart books, or maybe these books shouldn't be compared. But let's just pursue this comparison on the chance that there might be something here. I (Sink) was educated as an industrial engineer. Industrial engineering has and continues to do most of the formal, higher education training for industrial quality control. Every IE program I know of has at least one solid undergraduate course that is required in quality control. I was taught out of the Duncan text. When I came out of the course, I understood statistics far better than I did after taking statistics courses at Ohio State. I understood the theory behind acceptance sampling, did a lot of homework problems, and had a feeling for the different kinds of plans that exist. I understood control charts, could do homework problems and develop p-charts, c-charts, u-charts, X bar charts, R-charts, and more. We also obtained an initial introduction to experimental design, testing hypotheses, analysis of variance, regression and correlation, and a few other advanced statistical techniques and refinements to basic SQC. When I arrived at Eastman Kodak, it began to be clear "what they did teach me at Ohio State" and " what they did not teach me." They did teach me how to think analytically and they introduced me to fields of study—quality control being one of them. I quickly began to understand that my education had just begun.

Over the years, I have concluded that we are teaching our young IEs how to construct X bar charts, R-charts, p-charts, and so forth, but are not developing an understanding as to why this is important or how you put them to use. I have witnessed young IEs who believe that their job is done when they get the standard set or develop the control chart. I have tried to convince them that their job has just begun and that the easy part was the math, the technique, and the statistics, but all too often the paradigm of undergraduate education and American organizational culture is too strong to break.

Ishikawa's approach to communicating in a *Guide to Quality Control* reminds me of Tukey's (1977) approach to communicating about exploring data. Tukey goes to the heart of data collection and analysis and develops new approaches to understanding data and exploring it, prior to confirming what it may or may not be telling you. In a similar fashion, Ishikawa begins his book with a fundamental issue—how to collect data and the purpose of collecting data. If you reflect back on the management systems model and analysis, you will see a similarity: Step 3a of MSA (what information do you need?), Step 3b (what data do you need to create the information?), and Step 3c (how do you store, retrieve, process, and portray the information and data?). Most American texts on quality control begin in the toolbox of MSM, Step 3c of MSA, and end there. The students do not spend enough time gaining an appreciation for the management system for which quality control techniques are being developed. Most students don't know what to do with the data once they have it. We have not been communicating the context within which statistical quality/process control will be used. It is in vogue today to push SPC and to do this by aligning with one of the "three wise men" (Deming, Juran, or Crosby) [Author's note: We believe there are more than three, but Americans have always tended to be somewhat parochial in their view of the world] and giving everybody a course in SPC. Our view, and I suspect others would agree, is that this is unwise.

First, the best view of total quality management is an integrated and comprehensive one. The wisest and ultimately most successful organizations will develop a TQM philosophy and approach that integrates the best of Crosby, Deming, Juran, Ishikawa, Garvin, and others. Second, as Deming has said, rushing out to train everyone in SQ/PC is not the answer. The tools and techniques of SP/QC are not universally applicable, and they are not the only way to process/ analyze data. Not all improvement projects will require SQ/PC, but they provide a very powerful set of tools and techniques if used appropriately.

We have urged our clients to allow the strategic performance improvement planning process direct where to apply training and technique development. The process will identify where in your organization SP/QC can have the most impact, where the people are most ready and in need of it. Garvin (1988) and others have reviewed the history and evolution of the concept of quality. They conclude that we have entered a new stage of maturity/evolution with respect to quality management; Garvin calls it strategic quality management. We're beginning to hear more about new and old concepts, such as cost of quality, quality function deployment, company wide quality management, new paradigms for quality assurance, and Taguchi methods and design of experiments. Every field matures and evolves; the field of quality is obviously no exception.

We are changing paradigms regarding what quality is, how it should be managed, its relative importance, how to employ techniques, and who should manage it. I don't think that the paradigms of how we should teach it in higher education, particularly in IE, are changing rapidly enough. The operational definition we provided for quality—our six quality checkpoint concept—provides a nice, simple conceptual way of thinking about all of these changes. A quick scan of any of the titles of articles, for example, those in *Quality Progress*, show considerable attention being paid to Quality Checkpoints 1, 3, 5, and 6. As we said earlier, Checkpoints 2 and 4 are important, but we must "cease dependence upon them as the sole way to achieve quality" (Deming 1986). Much of our formal education efforts are only focusing on Checkpoints 2 and 4; therefore, it is not surprising that we are going through a revolution in how quality is managed in organizations.

WHAT IS STATISTICAL PERFORMANCE CONTROL AND MANAGEMENT?

Neither of the authors of this book are experts in statistical quality or process control. We are, in fact, Johnny-come-latelys of sorts to the field of quality; it seems we are in good company today.

This is honest, but doesn't necessarily mean we can't contribute to what is taking place in this area. The niche, the contributions we believe we can make, are in the area of total quality management, improved translation, communication, and operationalization of what is being said and how to implement the things being said by the gurus in the field. In particular, we believe that the strategic performance improvement planning process and the general measurement methodology are extremely compatible with and supportive of the things happening in the field of quality. We believe that quality should be viewed as an important and inextricably interwoven element of performance. We think that the concept of six quality checkpoints and the process of operationally defining, measuring, and managing quality at each of these checkpoints is very important. Our research and development work progresses in these areas.

Statistical performance control is the application of the concepts and techniques of statistical quality and process control for attributes and variables of quality to attributes and variables of the other six performance criteria. We believe that it should be obvious that whether the variable or attribute focuses on quality or some other criteria, the same statistical analysis techniques may apply and be useful in helping to solve problems, make decisions, or improve performance. [Note: We use the terms variables and attributes in the statistical sense here to mean: "When a record is made of an actual measured quality characteristic, such as a dimension expressed in thousandths of an inch, the quality is said to be expressed by variables." "When a record shows only the number of articles conforming and the number of articles failing to conform to any specified requirements, it is said to be a record by attributes" (Grant and Leavenworth 1988.)] What we are suggesting then is that the characteristic being measured need not be just quality, that we may be measuring conformance to an effectiveness requirement or an innovation requirement. This is conceptually what we mean by statistical performance control, or SPerfC. The variable or attribute, in our measurement terminology strategic performance dimension, criterion, measure, indicator, proxy measure/indicator, attribute or subattribute, may be related to any of the seven performance criteria.

The design and implementation of an SPerfC system requires some understanding of statistical control from the user, and a brief review is appropriate. System performance is always subject to a certain amount of variation as a result of chance. Some stable "system of chance causes" is inherent in any operation, and variation within this stable pattern is inevitable. The reasons for variation inside/outside this stable pattern may be discovered and corrected. Statistical descriptors are used to describe these patterns of variation. Descriptors used include: frequency distributions or measures of the central tendency of a distribution (i.e., mean) combined with some measure of dispersion of the distribution, such as standard or deviation (Grant and Leavenworth 1988).

Where it is known that a set of numbers (measures) are distributed according to the normal curve, the mean and standard deviation tell us what proportion fall within any specified limits. When a distribution is normal, 95 percent of all values fall within two standard deviations of the mean, and 99 percent within three standard deviations. When the distribution of a set of numbers is not normal, other frequency patterns may apply. The mean and standard deviation of the distributed pattern allow us to determine when a process is in control. For a performance measure approximating the normal, more than 1 percent of values falling outside three standard deviations from the mean tells us it is out of control. This assumes that the process was in control when the mean and standard deviation were calculated. Once a process is out of control, we need to identify the cause of the variation.

Deming (1986) introduces the interesting concept of "common" and "special" causes of system variation. A common cause is one that is inherent in the design of the system and cannot be changed or removed by those who are a part of the system and must be tackled by those who manage or design the system. A special cause is an assignable cause of variation due to certain events occurring within the system. A special cause can be removed by those in the system. To achieve performance improvement, both types of causes must be analyzed.

How Do You Do Statistical Performance Control? (Contributed by Sanchoy K. Das)

There are primarily two phases in the SPerfC methodology. The first stage involves designing and implementing a particular application, while the second stage involves defining rules for interpreting the data and taking appropriate actions. Both stages are executable in a ten-step process. Steps 1 to 6 form the design and implementation stage of SPerfC, while Steps 7 to 10 form the improvement stage. A brief description of each step follows:

Step 1. Identify performance measures. Identification of performance measures is typically the first step in implementing any measurement technique. Processes for identifying measures were discussed earlier in the "determine what to measure" section. Almost any kind of measure may be selected; there is only a single restriction—the measure must be quantifiable.

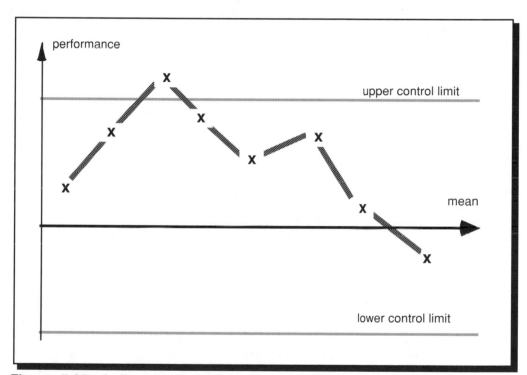

Figure 7-25. A Performance Time Control Chart

Step 2. Determine the mean and variance of each measure. There are two ways of determining the mean performance. The first approach is to set the mean performance level equal to the acceptable performance level or some work standard. The second approach is to set the mean to the actual mean performance generated by the current system under existing conditions. For SPerfC to be successful, it is required that the second approach be used. The practice of using work standards as measures of acceptable performance needs to be critically re-examined. Deming

(1986) strongly preaches the abolition of all standards. In reality, the problem is not so much in the use of standards but more in the process by which they are determined; the work standard typically not being a true reflection of the attainable performance. SPerfC prescribes that the standard be determined from system performance and not vice versa. The mean performance level and variance is computed from historical data. If X_t denotes the measured performance over time and T is the number of measured periods, then the mean and variance are given by:

$$X_{mean} = \text{Sum of all } X_t\text{'s/T}$$

$$X_{Sdev} = \sqrt{(\text{Sum of all } (X_t - X_{mean})^2/T)}$$

Step 3. Compute upper and lower performance limits. Defining the control limits determines the effectiveness of a control chart since, in a sense, the control limits transfer the control chart data into information. The control limits indicate a boundary for the statistical variation of a measure which is in control. Control limits are computed as multiples of the standard deviation from the mean. For a normally distributed measure 99 percent of all data will occur within plus or minus three standard deviations. Thus, the multiple three is typically used to compute the limits for a process in statistical control. The limits are then given by:

$$\text{Upper Control Limit} = X_{mean} + 3(X_{Sdev})$$
$$\text{Lower Control Limit} = X_{mean} - 3(X_{Sdev})$$

Step 4. Set up a control chart visibility board. The information generated by the SPerfC charts needs to be portrayed both to the people who are part of the system and those who are managing the system. Improvement efforts are of two types: system (self) initiated and manager initiated. Unavailability of performance data is the primary cause of lack of system-initiated improvement efforts. The control chart is an effective visual tool. A room (or wall) should be designated for their display; this will ensure both types of improvement efforts. Additionally information, as generated in Steps 7, 8, and 9 should also be displayed.

Step 5. Set up a procedure for data collection and input. We do not propose any particular method for data collection here. The manager must determine the best procedure for his particular application. The procedure must be simple and reliable. Responsibilities for collection and input to SPerfC must be assigned. The shorter the lead time between data collection and display on charts the more effective the results.

Step 6. Track performance over time. SPerfC is designed for performance tracking and continuous comparison. Performance levels should be marked on the control charts continuously since their primary objective is to determine performance trends.

Step 7. Identification of special and common causes. One of the philosophies of a SPerfC system is "control the variance and shift the mean." Identification and removal of special and common causes operationalizes this improvement philosophy. Removal of special causes helps in controlling the variance, while removal of common causes helps in controlling the variance and shifting the mean. There are several approaches for identifying common and special causes. These include: cause and effect diagrams (Ishikawa 1985); roadblock identification analysis and removal technique (Sink, Das, and Tuttle 1987); and analysis of control charts.

Step 8. Removal of special and common causes. Step 8 complements Step 7 and involves removal of the causes identified in the earlier step. An appropriate procedure for ensuring that the removal process is executed needs to be set up. The actual removal process will depend on the nature of the cause. The process can be scoped out either individually or as a team. Steps 7 and 8 are the most critical steps of SPerfC; if they are not executed correctly, SPerfC will fail.

Steps 9 and 10. Analyze and review interventions and the process. These steps are geared towards improvement of the system. SPerfC is a dynamic system and must grow and change with the system it measures. If improvement interventions are successful, then increase the mean performance level or adjust the high and low performance levels. Add and remove measures as necessary. Consider integration with other measurement systems.

We have presented here, briefly, the concept and technique of SPerfC, which requires a lot of design input from the manager and cannot be just applied off the shelf. Several procedures within SPerfC have to be designed by the manager in consultation with the people who will be evaluated by the system. A sample SPerfC control chart is displayed in Figure 7-25. Whenever performance crosses the low or high levels, the cause must be determined and either removed or reinforced.

Common Staffing Study

[Author's note: Most of the material in this section is based on information provided by Mr. Louis Sportelli, former operations manager, IBM Federal Systems Division. We provide references at the end of this section that the interested reader may pursue in order to better understand this approach.]

The Common Staffing Study (CSS) was initiated in IBM in 1968 as an attempt to measure and improve "productivity" in indirect labor areas. We put productivity in quotes because the technique does not actually measure productivity as we have operationally defined it in this book; however, we believe that the measurement approach can help to improve productivity. It has been applied in thirty-five plants in about thirteen countries within the IBM corporation. IBM manufacturing uses many of the traditional indicators to gauge manufacturing performance. Some of these include:

- Product cost targets—actual manufacturing cost/planned product cost (note that this is similar to our operational definition of efficiency);
- Announcement program cost commitment—actual manufacturing cost/estimated cost at time product was announced that remains in effect throughout life of product (note this is also an efficiency measure);
- Burden rate—manufacturing overhead cost/number of direct (touch labor) manufacturing hours (note that this is an input index; that is it is one type of input divided by another type of input);
- Cost per point—total manufacturing cost/number of points shipped (note that this is an input over output measure and, as such, is a type of partial factor productivity measure); and
- Indirect/direct ratio—a common input index used to assess the number of "support" people (indirect) per "build" (direct) people.

While each of these and many other indicators used have specific values, they provide little value to a manager in directing him/her "how" or "where" to improve productivity, particularly among indirect or white-collar employees. Predetermined time systems have been used at IBM for over twenty years to assess productivity in direct manufacturing departments and also as a basis for cost estimating, scheduling, and layout. However, in most cases, these tools do not apply to the work of indirect employees, which is highly variable and requires discretion and judgment on the part of incumbents.

Model Functions (14)	Activities	Indicator (Cause)
General Services	(8) Secretarial Services	Indir. Manpower
Personnel	(15) Salary Administration	Total Manpower
Finance	(14) Vendor Billing	Purchasing $
Plant Eng. & Maint.	(10) Facility Maintenance	Square Feet
I/S & DP	(9) Computer Operations	Installed Equip.
Production Control	(10) Production Scheduling	# Machine/Models
Procurement	(4) Production Buying	Prod. Purch. $
Mfg. Indirect	(4) Technicians	Direct Manpower
Mfg. Engineering	(16) Tool Design	Tool Dollars
Quality Assurance	(17) Inspection	Inplant Dir. Work
Industrial Engineering	(10) Cost Estimating	Value Add $
Materials Distribution	(9) Warehousing	Transactions
Facility Services	(9) Safety	Total Manpower
Product Engineer. (WTC)	(5) Product Support	Part Numbers

Figure 7-26. Model Functions, Sample Activities, and Indicators

FACILITY SERVICES	
ACTIVITY	INDICATOR
FAC CLEANLINESS	TOT GOSF
SAFETY	TOT MANPOWER
FAC SECURITY & PROTECTION	TOT GOSF
CAPITAL EQPT CONTROL	BRASS TAG/TOOLS CONTROLLED
MAIL SERVICE	INDIRECT MANPOWER
RECORDS MGMT	INDIRECT MANPOWER
REPRO SERVICES (MANUALS)	MACHINE SHIP $
REPRO SERVICES (NON-MANUALS)	INDIRECT MANPOWER
WIRE & TELE SERVICES	INDIRECT MANPOWER

Figure 7-27. Facility Service Function with Activities and Indicators

What CSS is

CSS is a methodology that allows management to assess the level of staffing of indirect manufacturing functions in relation to an "average" or "typical" level. It is based on the assumption that it is not feasible or economical to measure most indirect manufacturing jobs in terms of outputs. Thus, the CSS technique was developed to focus on indirect work from an input-to-activity perspective.

Essentially, CSS involves developing regression curves/lines for indirect staffing as it relates to certain other variables. For example, you might correlate secretarial support to plant population and develop a regression line for the relationship. Simplistically put, if a plant were above the line, they would be expected to justify or bring their secretarial support in line with other plants of that size. Coupled with a continuous improvement culture and orientation this could be, if applied properly, a very powerful indirect cost control and improvement procedure. It becomes obvious by now that this approach is an interplant comparison technique, which means that you need multiple plants or access to multiple plant data. The CSS approach is much more complex than this initial description reveals.

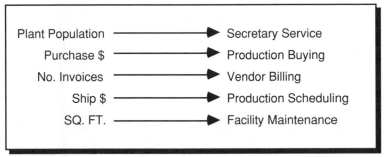

Figure 7-28. Examples of Indicators in IBM Manufacturing

What CSS is not

CSS is not productivity measurement. In our terminology, it is an efficiency measurement technique. It relates certain types of inputs to other types of inputs or inputs to types of activities and functions. This does not mean that CSS is not a productivity improvement technique. In fact, we believe that this measurement approach has tremendous potential for cost control and improvement.

The CSS methodology

There are four basic steps to the CSS technique:

1. Define activities;
2. Identify causes;
3. Survey locations; and
4. Data analysis.

Step 1. Define activities. Activities are commonly performed tasks that cut across all manufacturing locations. They are common denominators of indirect manufacturing work. For example, procurement engineering— the task of identifying manufacturing requirements, maintaining cost estimates, and more for parts purchased from a vendor.

These activities are standardized by assigning them to a "model function" (e.g., facility engineering and maintenance, personnel, manufacturing engineering, or industrial engineering). The CSS system has approximately 140 activities assigned to fourteen model functions. Figure 7-26 presents the fourteen model functions along with a sample activity and indicator.

Step 2. Identify causes (indicators). Causes are factors in a manufacturing environment that cause indirect work. These causes are called indicators. There are approximately sixty of these indicators. For example, plant population is an indicator (cause), and we would expect that as it changes, the need for secretarial services (an activity) will change according to some functional relationship. The statisticians in the reading audience will identify this process as the

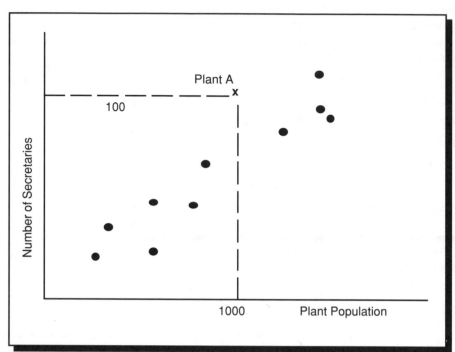

Figure 7-29. Ratio - All Plant

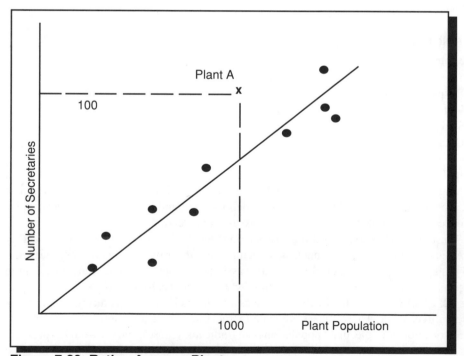

Figure 7-30. Ratio - Average Plant

regression analysis application process. You probably will cringe a little bit at the use of terminology, but should be encouraged by the application.

Figure 7-27 lists some sample indicators and their associated activities. Indicators are used in the CSS to help compensate for the differences that may exist because of plant size, product, or mission.

Appendix C provides the total listing of model functions, activities, and indicators. Figure 7-28 is an example for the facility services function.

Table 7-9.   Norm Index - Procurement Function

Activity	Location A	Location B	Etc.	Total
Production Buying	1.14	0.96		1.00
Document Processing and Control	0.77	1.34		1.00
Etc.				
Total	0.83	1.20		1.00

Table 7-10. Norm Index - By Plant

Function	Location A	Location B	Etc.	Total
Industrial Engineering	1.02	0.91		1.00
Procurement	0.83	1.20		1.00
Etc.				
Total	1.14	.96		1.00

Step 3. Survey locations. Once per year each manufacturing location inputs, via terminal, to a computer data base the number of people in each activity and the quantities of each indicator at their location.

Step 4. Data analysis. Productivity ratios, as they are called in CSS terminology, are computed in the form of:

No. of people in the activity
No. of units in the indicator

For example, for the activity "secretarial services" for which the indicator was "plant population" the ratio might be:

$$\text{Productivity ratio} = \frac{\text{No. of people in secretarial services for Plant A}}{\text{Plant population}}$$

$$= \frac{100}{1000}$$

$$= 0.1$$

If this ratio were plotted on a graph with those of other plants, we would obtain the chart shown in Figure 7-29. From this figure, we see that there is a trend to the data and that Plant A is an exception to this trend. The average plant can be depicted by a line passing through zero and providing the best fit to the other points. The slope of this line can be determined statistically using lincar regression techniques. Such a line is shown in Figure 7-30.

From this figure it can be observed that the average plant with a population of 1,000 would have ninety secretaries, or a "productivity ratio" of 90/1,000 or 0.09. (Note: We continue to put the term productivity ratio in quotes so that the reader will know that this is a misnomer. These numbers are actually input indexes of efficiency ratios.) The relative "productivity index" for Plant A would be:

$$\text{Relative productivity index} = \frac{100/1,000 = 0.10}{90/1,000 = 0.09}$$

$$= 1.11$$

Thus, Plant A is 11 percent above average for a plant of its size. Then a plant manager could see whether his "productivity ratio" is high or low and have some idea as to how much improvement would be required to bring Plant A to an average level.

Other types of questions could also be answered by consolidating the data in different ways. Table 7-9 shows how the norm indices might be shown for a model function, e.g., procurement.

The next level of aggregation is the norm index by function by plant (see Table 7-10). Higher levels of aggregation are also possible (e.g., plant to plant, division to division, and country to country).

In practice, the most useful comparison for an individual manager is the productivity performance of an individual plant over time. By comparing a plant with itself, a manager can tell if productivity is improving or declining.

Assessment of CSS

CSS is a surrogate productivity measurement technique. If you accept the underlying assumption that the outputs of white-collar, indirect employees are not feasible to measure, then this technique is a valuable tool. Even if the outputs of indirect employees are measurable, this tool provides a means of assessing the appropriateness of relative staff levels. In many organizations, the technique would be valuable if only for its ability to insert some discipline into the indirect cost control process.

In our opinion, the major flaws with CSS should be obvious to most readers at this point. In certain aspects, it violates a number of the guiding principles of measurement system development. It has been difficult, in some cases, to obtain the acceptance of plant managers in certain locations. These managers argue that if their numbers are out of line with the norm that their facility is different and the differences can be explained. The regression line violates, to some extent, the "throw out all standards" principle. Unless a continuous improvement orientation is adopted with the application of CSS, the line may peg or constrain performance. We believe that CSS was designed primarily as a control device and, as such, we believe it does this very well. Coupled with an improvement-oriented strategy, this could be a very powerful measurement and improvement approach for larger organizations. We suspect that smaller organizations would have difficulty obtaining the data to drive the technique unless an industry association facilitated the process.

Clearly, the CSS is another new tool to put in the Step 3c portion of MSA. It provides a disciplined taxonomy of terms to describe and analyze indirect support activities. As indirect and support activities increase as a proportion of our labor costs, this tool and others will be welcome, if not necessary, additions to the tools available for storing, retrieving, processing, and portraying performance data and information.

CLOSURE

We have attempted to, and we believe against some measures have succeeded in, helping you understand how to develop and implement a measurement system for your Organization of the Future. We have stressed the importance of viewing this process in the context of the strategic performance improvement planning process. We highlighted the third step in management systems analysis as being the measurement step and discussed, in detail, all three steps (3a, 3b, and 3c).

The general steps outlined in this chapter were:

1. Form measurement development teams;
2. Review results of the Strategic PIPP;
3. Determine what to measure (Step 3a of MSA);
4. Apply AIM;
5. Operationalize the measures; and
6. Determine what techniques to utilize to process the data, portray results, and assist in evaluation.

We reviewed the general measurement methodology in more detail than the outline here provides in our introduction to the conventional measurement approaches. Rather than provide a detailed "how to" for various techniques, both conventional or state-of-the-art and practice, we attempted to explain the purpose of the techniques, general approaches taken, application problems, and most importantly, how the techniques can be used in the context of our general measurement methodology. We provided detailed references for each specific technique so that the masters in the reading audience would have guidance as to where to go for more detailed technique instruction. Our purpose was to help you better understand the forest of measurement rather than focus on specific trees.

Our approach has been: to present the theory, philosophy, principles, and concepts; then to focus on how to design your approach, and how to get started; and to end with a specific methodology for actually developing and implementing improved measurement systems. We believe that Chapters 5, 6, and 7 represent the essence of measurement for the Organization of the

Future. If your management teams understand this methodology and apply it in the context of the strategic performance improvement planning process and your measurement masters support the methodology with specific tool and technique knowledge, you will successfully respond to The New Competition and become an Organization of the Future.

REFERENCES AND SUGGESTED READINGS

American Productivity Center. 1978. *Productivity Measurement*. A notebook and reference manual. Houston, Texas.

Archer, B. L. 1970. Technological innovation: A methodology. Royal College of Art (unpublished working paper). London, England.

Bruns, W. J., and Kaplan, R. S. (Eds.) 1987. *Accounting and Management Field Study Perspectives.* Harvard Business School Press.

Craig, C. E. and R. C. Harris. 1973. Total productivity measurement at the firm level. *Sloan Management Review.* 14(3). Spring, 13-29.

Davidson, W. H. 1982. Small group activity at Musashi Semiconductor Works. *Sloan Management Review.* Spring, 3-14.

Davis, H. 1955, reprinted 1978. *Productivity Accounting.* University of Pennsylvania.

Delbecq, A. L., A. H. Van de Ven, and D. H. Gustafson. 1986. *Group Techniques for Program Planning.* Green Briar Press. Middleton, Wisconsin.

Deming, W. E. 1986. *Out of the Crisis.* Massachusetts Institute of Technology, Center for Advanced Engineering Study. Cambridge, Massachusetts.

Duncan, A. J. 1986. *Quality Control and Industrial Statistics.* Richard D. Irwin, Inc. Homewood, Illinois.

Feigenbaum, A. V. 1983. *Total Quality Control* (3rd ed.). McGraw-Hill Co. New York.

Felix, G. H. and J. L. Riggs. 1983. Productivity measurement by objectives. *National Productivity Review.* 2(4): 386-393.

Garvin, D. A. 1988. *Managing Quality: The Strategic and Competitive Edge.* The Free Press. New York.

Gollop, F. M. 1982. Evidence for a sector-biased or sector-neutral industrial policy: Analysis of the productivity slowdown. Working Paper No. 115. Boston College.

Grant, E. L. and R. S. Leavenworth. 1988. *Statistical Quality Control* (6th ed.). McGraw-Hill. New York.

Hackman, J. R. 1986. The psychology of self-management in organizations. *Psychology and Work: Productivity, Change and Employment.* Edited by Pallack, M. S., and R. O. Perloff. American Psychological Association. Washington, D.C.

Hansen, B. L. and P. M. Ghare. 1987. *Quality Control and Application.* Prentice-Hall. Englewood Cliffs, New Jersey.

Harrington, H. J. 1987. *Poor Quality Cost.* Marcel Dekker, Inc. ASQC Quality Press.

Horngrem, C. T. & Sundem, G. L. 1987. *Introduction to Management Accounting.* Prentice-Hall. Englewood Cliffs, New Jersey.

Ishikawa, K. 1968. *Guide to Quality Control.* JUSE Press, Ltd. Tokyo, Japan.

_____. 1985. *What is Total Quality Control? The Japanese Way.* Prentice-Hall. Englewood Cliffs, New Jersey.

Kanter, R. M. 1983. *The Change Masters.* Simon and Schuster. New York.

Johnson, H. T. and R. S. Kaplan. 1987. *Relevance Lost: The Rise and Fall of Managerial Accounting.* Harvard Business School Press. Boston, Massachusetts.

Kendrick, J. W. and D. Creamer. 1965. *Measuring Company Productivity: A Handbook with Case Studies.* The National Industrial Conference Board. Studies in Business Economics. No. 89.

Kendrick, J. W. and B. N. Vacarra. 1980. *New Developments in Productivity Measurement and Analysis.* The University of Chicago Press. Chicago, Illinois.

Kilmann, R. H. 1984. *Beyond The Quick Fix.* Jossey-Bass, Inc. San Francisco, California.

Lawler, E. E., III. 1986. *High Involvement Management.* Jossey-Bass, Inc. San Francisco, California.

Mali, P. 1986. *MBO Updated.* John Wiley & Sons, Inc.

Miller, D. M. and P. M. Rao. 1987. Analysis of profit-linked total-factor productivity measurement models at the firm level. Working Paper, No. 87-001. University of Alabama.

Morris, W. T. 1975. *Work and Your Future: Living Poorer, Working Harder.* Reston Publishing Co. Reston, Virginia.

_____. 1977. *Productivity Measurement Systems for Administrative Computing and Information Services: An Executive Summary.* The Productivity Research Group at Ohio State University, OSU Research Foundation. Columbus, Ohio.

_____. 1979. *Implementation Strategies for Industrial Engineers.* Grid Publishing Co. Columbus, Ohio.

National Research Council. 1979. *Measurement and Interpretation of Productivity.* National Academy of Sciences. Washington, D.C.

Nunally, J. 1967. Rules for assigning numbers to objects to represent quantities of attributes. *Psychometric Theory.* McGraw-Hill. New York.

Peters, T. 1988. *Thriving on Chaos: Handbook for a Management Revolution.* Alfred A. Knopf. New York. 483.

Riggs, J. L. and G. H. Felix. 1983. *Productivity by Objectives.* Prentice-Hall. Englewood Cliffs, New Jersey.

Sink, D. S., T. C. Tuttle, and S. K. Das. 1987. Measuring and improving white-collar productivity: A NASA case study. *Proceedings. 1st International Conference on Productivity Research.* Miami, Florida.

Sink, D. S., T. C. Tuttle, and S. J. DeVries. 1984. Productivity measurement and evaluation: What is available? *National Productivity Review.* Summer, 265-287.

Sink, D. S. 1985. *Productivity Measurement: Planning, Measurement and Evaluation, Control and Improvement.* John Wiley & Sons. New York.

Sink and Archer. 1985.

Sink, D. S., and P. E. Rossler. 1988. Compensation management systems in the organization of the future. *Proceedings of International Industrial Engineering Conference.* Institute of Industrial Engineers. Norcross, Georgia.

Sink, D. S. 1988. Essentials of Quality, Productivity, and Performance Management. Short course. LINPRIM, Inc. Blacksburg, Virginia.

Sloma, R. S. 1980. *How to Measure Managerial Performance.* Macmillan Publishing Co, Inc. New York.

Smith, G. L. 1978. *Work Measurement: A Systems Approach.* Grid Publishing Co. Columbus, Ohio.

_____. 1988. Work measurement under attack: The IE's response. *Quality and Productivity Management.* (4):11-14.

Stewart, W. T. 1978. A yardstick for measuring productivity. *Industrial Engineering.* Institute of Industrial Engineers. Norcross, Georgia. 10(2).

Sumanth, D. J. 1979. *Productivity Measurement and Evaluation Models for Manufacturing Companies.* University Microfilms International. Chicago, Illinois.

_____. 1984. *Productivity Engineering and Management.* McGraw-Hill. New York.

Tukey, J. W. 1977. *Exploratory Data Analysis.* Addison-Wesley. Reading, Massachusetts.

Tuttle, T. C. and C. N. Weaver. 1986. *Methodology for Generating Efficiency and Effectiveness Measures (MGEEM): A Guide for Air Force Measurement Facilitators, AFHRL-TP-86-36.* Air Force Human Resources Laboratory. Brooks AFB, Texas.

Tuttle, T. C. and D. Ross. 1988. Measuring the right stuff. Working paper. Maryland Center for Quality and Productivity. College Park, Maryland.

van Loggerenberg, B. J. and S. J. Cucchiaro. 1982. Productivity measurement and the bottom line. *National Productivity Review.* Winter.

van Loggerenberg, B. J. 1986. The deterministic nexus between productivity and price change. *South African Journal of Science*, vol. 82. January.

299

Wadsworth, H. M., K. S. Stephens, and A. B. Godfrey. 1986. *Modern Methods for Quality Control and Improvement*. John Wiley & Sons. New York.

Walton, R. 1985. From control to commitment in the work place. *Harvard Business Review*. March-April, 77-84.

Weaver, C. N. 1988. Personal communication to T. C. Tuttle. Air Force Human Resource Laboratory. Brooks AFB, Texas.

Weide, J. V. and S. F. Meier. 1985. *Managing Corporate Liquidity: An Introduction to Working Capital Management*. John Wiley & Sons. New York.

8. MAINTAINING EXCELLENCE

We have decided to close the first edition of this book with a chapter on maintaining excellence. There's a lot more we would like to tell you about the Organization of the Future, and we will do so in future editions of this book. We feel good about the progress we've made in getting our thoughts and experiences down on paper to this point. So we'll end by explaining what you do once you've successfully implemented the strategic performance improvement planning process and general measurement methodology and, as a result, achieved a measure of excellence. We, quite frankly, know a lot less about maintaining excellence than we do about achieving it. We do know they are both difficult to accomplish, yet we have a suspicion that it is a little easier to become number one than to stay number one.

We have just completed a guide of best practices for quality and productivity management for defense contractors. We struggled with the decision of how to end the guide. We decided to end it the same way we'll end this book—by looking at wisdom in regard to maintaining excellence. We use the word "wisdom" because maintaining excellence is not something for which someone can necessarily prescribe specific techniques or simple solutions. Maintaining excellence, we suspect, is made up of profound knowledge, leadership, intuition, instinct, guiding principles, values, visions, lessons from religious and philosophical thinking on leadership and quality, "whole brain thinking," risk and uncertainty, and many other cerebral and perhaps even spiritual issues. We believe that maintaining excellence is tough and complex and that understanding it requires being able to manage the challenge holistically—focusing on both the objective and the subjective, rational and irrational, explicit and implicit, qualitative and quantitative, pragmatic and not so pragmatic, as well as the soft and the hard. What it takes to motivate and manage an organization to become excellent may be quite different from what it takes to maintain organizational excellence.

We have selected some favorite thoughts and concepts of others on the subject of maintaining excellence that we will share with you as a closure to this book. The logical flow of this chapter may not be as tight as you or we would like, but that perhaps reflects the topic and its complexity. Some of the thoughts are new, some not so new—all, we believe, are relevant to the topic of this last chapter. For example, we wrote to head coaches, professional and collegiate, from baseball, basketball, and football teams that had won a Super Bowl, World Series, or national championship and asked them to share their thoughts on how to maintain excellence. Many responded; most agreed that it was difficult and that they had not succeeded as well as they would have liked. We will intersperse these quotes throughout the last chapter as "food for thought."

Denny Crum, Head Basketball Coach, University of Louisville
On Maintaining Excellence

We thrive on the theory that you either get better or worse, you never stay the same. If you are not working hard to improve, then you are forming bad habits that make you worse. We try to show some improvement every week and do something better this week than we did last week—both as individuals and as a team. We feel while this doesn't guarantee victory, it gives us our best chance to be playing best come year end.

Jacob's Ladder

> ....(they're) trying to save me,
> but I'm doin' alright, the best that I can,. . .
> Step by step, one by one, higher and higher,
> Step by step, one be one, climbing Jacob's ladder. . .
> All I want from tomorrow is to get. . . better than today.

These lyrics from Jacob's Ladder, a song written by Bruce Hornsby, convey the theme of this last chapter. They may reflect how managers and employees in American organizations feel as they are bombarded with a seemingly endless stream of consults and programs, each promising a simple solution to their complex problems. They reflect a continuous and constant improvement orientation. They are at the core of a total quality management effort. They must reflect attitudes, beliefs, and values of the organization. They must be guiding principles. Most importantly, they must be translated into behaviors in the organization.

> Don't come in here and tell us these things! We're doing our best. You make it sound like we don't care about quality and productivity. We're doing our best. In fact, we're pretty damn good! If you think you could do better, then have at it. Don't come in here with all these fancy theories and concepts and tell us we're bad—it's an insult. We're good, maybe even excellent! Can we get better? Sure we can, and we are! You can't convince me we should change. Screw the Japanese, who won the war anyway?"

This quote is a condensation of the kinds of comments we hear quite often in American organizations. Quite a contrast between "climbing Jacob's ladder" and "we're doing our very best," isn't it?

"Everyone doing their very best isn't good enough" (Deming 1986).

We suspect there is a widely held belief in your organization that maintaining the *status quo* will be sufficient for survival and success in the near future. We suspect many of you are vehemently disagreeing with the statement we just made. "Not true in our organization," you're saying. We hope you are right. But is your level of commitment and activity directed at continual improvement up to New Competition standards? Are you proactively concentrating on key process establishment, control, and improvement? Are you getting better fast enough? And how would you know?

Staying a Leader Is More Difficult Than Becoming One

The continuing challenges your organization has faced and will face during the next two decades prompt numerous reactions ranging from "denial and disbelief, anger and blaming, buying time and testing, retreat to acceptance and adjustment" (Grayson and O'Dell 1988). We have found that most organizations—the people in them—would prefer to view the challenge ahead of them as one of building on excellence. In *The Two-Minute Warning*, (Grayson and O'Dell 1988) examine why it is so hard to remain a leader. They provide an historical analysis at the national level of "leaders' perceptions and the way of the challengers."

The Two-Minute Warning and Lessons From History

There are observable and repeated trends in the process by which a world leader slowly but surely loses its leadership in productivity, economic vitality, and eventually, economic power and influence in the world. For example, there are remarkable similarities between the era from 1785 to 1890 as England wrested power from the Netherlands, rose to the number one position, and then slowly lost their leadership to Germany, the United States, and others. Arnold Toynbee, the historian, viewed maintaining excellence as a series of "challenges and responses." England, like nations before her, failed to adjust to new competition and respond appropriately. Over the past thirteen years, the United States is last in growth rates for productivity of all industrialized nations. Can we turn this trend around? Will we be willing to pay the price? Grayson and O'Dell pose a thought-provoking question and defend their answer brilliantly: "America is at a turning point, the two-minute whistle has blown, we have less than two decades to adjust lest we lose our leadership. Can we, will we successfully adjust?"

Joel Barker, a futurist we have referred to before, summarizes his film about change and the future, *Discovering the Future: The Business of Paradigms*, with six points. His last point, and his most important, is that we have the ability to change our paradigms. That is to say, we can change the way we look at things. He suggests we must change the way we look at and think about things if we are to successfully cope with the challenges posed by the future. Toynbee concluded, after an exhaustive study of civilizations, that the rise and fall of nations is a matter of choice, not a locked-in repeating pattern. These are obviously very "internal locus of control" views of the world. They presume, perhaps implicitly believe, that there are more strategic controllable factors than strategic uncontrollable factors. We support this view and have embedded it in the roadmap for change we have outlined in this book.

Grayson and O'Dell list ten lessons from history; factors that caused leaders to decline and challengers to rise to take their place. We will review them briefly. You are encouraged to read their book for elaboration.

Lessons from history: Leaders' perceptions

Lesson 1. Complacency is the cancer of leadership. Five factors tend to contribute to a growing sense of complacency. We urge you to consider them as your organization begins to systematically think about maintaining excellence.

1. *Affluence*. Success is often listed as one of the major roadblocks to quality and productivity improvement by managers and employees. A softening sets in, a belief that maintaining the *status quo* is sufficient for survival and success. Thurow in the *Zero-Sum Solution* (1985) and Reich in *Tales of a New America* (1987) speak to this dilemma and its consequences. America benefitted from almost twenty years (1947 to 1967) of little worldwide competition in a number of key industries and businesses. America has benefitted from more than thirty years of relative affluence. It may be killing us.

2. *Lack of competition*. The United States, like Britain, Rome, and many others, has experienced a relatively long period of low competition. In 1950, most of the major industrial bases of the world had been decimated by World War II. For a period of a little over seventeen years, many U.S. firms operated relative monopolies in the world marketplace. Lack of competition causes skills to atrophy.

3. *Belief of invincibility and immortality*. History is filled with sports teams that won game after game or, after a long period of dominance, began to read their own press. The 1968-69 Ohio State Buckeye football team comes to mind. The week before the last game of the season with archrival Michigan, *Sports Illustrated* published an article about the Buckeye team, the 1967-68

National Champions. The article suggested that the undefeated Buckeyes (they had won something like twenty-four straight games) was the best team of the decade, perhaps ever. At that time the Big Ten had a no-repeat rule for the Rose Bowl, and only one team could go to a bowl game from the conference. *Sports Illustrated* suggested that the best team, the number one team, in the nation would be sitting at home on New Year's day watching lesser teams play their bowl games. Despite Woody Hayes' best efforts to fight off complacency, the belief in invincibility, the Buckeyes went to Ann Arbor the next weekend and lost to a 6-3 Michigan squad with a rookie coach named Bo Schembechler, 24-12. This same phenomena may be every bit as real at Harvard, IBM, GM, Eastman Kodak, and elsewhere.

4. *New challenges, old responses.* Toynbee stressed the theme of "challenges and responses" repeatedly in his study of history. The illusion that what worked once will necessarily work again is a trap that many have fallen into. "Those who will not accept new remedies are doomed to repeat past mistakes." There is a back-to-basics movement in this country that is simultaneously being followed with a smorgasbord of programs. There is a tendency on the part of U.S. managers to simultaneously work harder at old responses while randomly sampling from the infinitely large collection of new programs being peddled by an endless stream of experts. As Deming points out, these practices are taking us "off to the Milky Way" and "down the tube."

5. *Disregard.* "The British were warned of the German economic threat as early as 1840, and again, repeatedly over the next decades, especially near the end of the 19th Century. These warnings were, as we know, not heeded. U.S. managers and employees have shown great tendency to respond to the warnings provided over the past twenty years with 'excuses for doing nothing'" (Thurow 1984).

This complacency factor is more than just a signal detection theory problem. It is possible for the right signal to be detected and nothing done about it. This is what disregard means. The data is present; it is disregarded. Coaches frequently plead with their teams to prepare for every opponent. Coaches of teams that are number one have to work doubly hard because everybody is shooting for you. Players often disregard the data; the result is an upset.

Lesson 2. Leaders overlook relative growth rates of their challengers. Assuming that the 1973 to 1986 productivity growth rate trends continue, by the year 2003 the U.S. will rank seventh in absolute productivity as measured by Gross Domestic Product per employee. Canada (1994), France (1996), Norway (1998), Germany (1999), Belgium (2000), and Japan (2003) will all, in the years indicated in parentheses, overtake the U.S. Differences in productivity growth rates, competitive benchmarking, must be paid close attention to if you hope to maintain excellence.

Lesson 3. Changes are so slow that leaders fail to sense challengers. "History assures us that civilizations decay quite leisurely" (Durant as quoted in Grayson and O'Dell 1988). In psychology there is a concept called "threshold" and "just noticeable difference." The concept has been studied, and it has been found that human beings have certain thresholds for noticing differences, or changes. Competitors often, particularly at the national or industrial level, creep up on you at relatively slow rates, such that leaders fail to detect and respond to those challenges. Questionable and frequently changing statistics on growth rates have confounded this factor. U.S. managers are bombarded with confusing and often apparently contradictory statistics, leading to a disbelief on their part that there really is a problem.

Lesson 4. Initial size is not a predictor of winners. As many sports teams know, size, or initial size, is not a good predictor of winners. The NCAA basketball playoffs are constantly riddled with upsets of major proportions; little guys knocking off the big guys. Rome, the Netherlands, England, the Thirteen Colonies, and Japan have all at one time been disregarded as being too small to worry about. Consider Japan as an example. In 1950, Japan's economic strength was negligible. Now,

- Japan is the second-largest economy in the Free World. It produces 10 percent of the world's GNP and it's predicted it will produce 20 percent by the year 2000.
- Japan's long-term foreign assets at the end of 1986 totaled nearly $397 billion, higher than OPEC's peak holdings of $380 billion in 1983.
- Nomura Securities is the world's largest securities firm, and it alone is responsible for financing nearly one-third of the entire 1986 U.S. federal deficit.
- Seven of the top ten banks in the world in terms of deposits are Japanese. Japanese banks have 36 percent of the deposits of the world's top 500 banks; the U.S. 11 percent.
- Japan is the largest passenger car producer in the world, and by 1988, 17 percent of the cars sold by Detroit under U.S. labels will have been made by the Japanese (Grayson and O'Dell 1988).

The lesson: A leader tends to overlook small challengers as insignificant at first. When they grow larger and begin to enter domestic and foreign markets, the leaders tend to think the challenger must be engaged in 'unfair' competition, based on 'unsound or immoral principles.' If we are losing, it must be an unfair fight (Grayson and O'Dell).

The world is not a safe place for leaders. Challengers often have everything to gain and nothing to lose. They are burdened with fewer paradigms. They can motivate and inspire progress differently than can leaders. They have advantages. It is easier to become number one than to stay number one.

Lesson 5. Gainers have drive. Gainers—challengers—often have "the eye of the tiger." Their visions are clear and crystallized, and it is often easier to gain widespread acceptance of those visions. Motivation of those aspiring to become number one is different than motivation of those who are number one. Note throughout these ten lessons from Grayson's and O'Dell's book the relevance of the wisdom and lessons to the organizational system unit of analysis.

Lesson 6. Challengers stress education. Emphasis on education—how much is done, what type is done, and how it is done—is stronger in challengers than in leaders. Differences in performance of the U.S. educational systems and those of Japan and other countries is significant and apparently growing. As Thurow points out, the quality of an organization's performance is highly dictated by the quality of its inputs. One of the most valuable inputs for any organization is its people. We tend to view training and development as expenses rather than investments; as a result our objective is to minimize it, to get it as cheap as possible. Japanese students in elementary and secondary education go to school six days a week, 240 days per year, and average about six to seven contact hours per day. American counterpart students go to school five days a week, 180 days per year, and average about four to five contact hours per day. When I reveal these data, a number of Americans respond by saying that we can do more with less. I suggest that this is American—leader—arrogance and it's dangerous. Thurow points out in *Zero-Sum Solution* that the quality of our labor input in terms of educational preparation is not world-class. Is your organization's selection, placement, training, and development process world-class?

Lesson 7. Gainers copy leaders. We have a paradigm about copying. We have gotten the impression that we didn't do it in our rise to economic power. "The record of history is clear;

all nations copy from one another, directly and indirectly." Followers don't simply copy the leaders' ideas; they

1. Adapt them to their nation and other nations;
2. Improve upon them (sometimes called "creative imitation"); and,
3. Most importantly, put the ideas to work in the marketplace speedily (Grayson and O'Dell 1988).

As an old Japanese saying has it, "The highest compliment a student can pay his teacher is to surpass him."

The wishbone formation was developed at the University of Texas, and Oklahoma University has used it many times to beat U of T. History is filled with "unsuccessful" invention. Innovation is the creative process of changing whatever it takes to successfully respond to challenges, threats, problems, opportunities. Innovation is successful invention. Becoming number one is a relatively easier job than staying number one because challengers have drive, stress continual education, and understand the role of copying.

Lessons from history: The challengers close in

Lesson 8. Quality improvement and customer focus have historically been key strategies of challengers. Challengers tend to focus, by necessity, more on the strategic factors of quality and customer focus. Leaders (for many reasons) tend to be unable to maintain focus on critical strategic factors. Successful organizations become arrogant and begin to neglect those things that made them successful. Challengers attack these deficiencies in the performance of the leaders and use them to win. The process by which leaders maintain quality and customer focus changes over time and slowly, but almost surely, becomes ineffective. We see this trend with internal as well as external customers.

Lesson 9. The paradox of protection; it helps challengers and hurts leaders. In the early stages of growth, England, the United States and Japan all used protection to help their "infant" industries get started and to catch up to the leaders. After reaching maturity and facing competition, leading nations tend to use protectionism not for growth but to reduce competition, to save jobs in inefficient industries, and to prevent change. This presents a Catch-22 situation. The right response is to adjust, but this is not easy for a leader.

Lesson 10. The leader's ability to adjust diminishes over time. The longer a leader is a leader, the more difficult it becomes to adapt. This is largely a cultural and attitudinal phenomenon; however, it is very real. Can the United States still adjust given the number of built-in habits, traditions, laws, and vested interests? Has the United States reached a climacteric? (A climacteric, as described by Grayson and O'Dell, is a turning point for an economy, a critical stage of the economic aging process.)

These ten lessons represent challenges preventing maintenance of excellence. They are insidious and quite pervasive. Even the best managers, coaches, and leaders struggle to overcome the tendency for their organizations to succumb to entropy. The strategic factors, those things that you must manage and control to succeed, change over time. Managers and leaders must constantly assess, with an open mind, these factors and levels of performance against them. We think these ten lessons from history provide valuable insight into the question and answer of how to maintain excellence. We have talked about why becoming a leader is different from staying a leader and examined ten specific lessons from history about leaders. We now want to focus on the way of The New Competition.

The Way of The New Competition

We devoted an entire chapter to a description of The Challenge and The New Competition. We attempted to instill upon you and your organization the notion that the ways of The New Competition are dramatic departures from past practices. These ways of The New Competition reflect changes in paradigms regarding management and leadership. We highlighted that levels of performance in The New Competition, in some cases, are orders of magnitude greater than traditional perceptions and standards in the United States. Xerox has gone beyond our analysis and comparative sampling by performing competitive benchmarking studies. They identified "key performance indicators" or "strategic performance dimensions" against which their organization would be assessed. They then searched to identify who was performing best in each category. For example, in the category of inventory management, they found L. L. Bean Company. This confirms the point we made earlier about The New Competition knowing no one nationality. Competitive benchmarking, when tied to strategic planning for an organization, is a very powerful tool for overcoming many of the problems of leaders discussed in the last section.

> The toughest part of competitive benchmarking is communicating to your people just how tough the competition is.
>
> *Paul Regensburger*
> *Manager of Benchmarking for the Copier Division of Xerox*
> *(American Samurai 1986)*

Constant improvement, maintaining the excellence achieved while constantly striving to improve other aspects of your performance; this is a recurring message among great organizations. It requires recognition that this must happen along with the discipline to make it happen. It requires patience, persistence, consistency, establishing processes, controlling their variances, and shifting their means.

> There is no simple, single way to describe what it takes to sustain 22 consecutive years of increased earnings and 36 consecutive years of increased dividends...there isn't any single action that accounts for what we are accomplishing—it's thousands of actions being made daily—some large, some small—but each vitally important to our performance.
>
> We are facing more competition than ever before....I accept the fact of competition but I reject the notion of its inevitable intrusion at our expense! Competition is not an abstract concept—not a faceless organization. Competition is another human being—just as you are—who is saying: 'I can offer customers greater value than the human beings at Dun and Bradstreet. I can work smarter and faster to understand what benefits the customer is looking for. I have a greater ability than the men and women at D&B to understand and correctly match my costs to those benefits. I have a greater resolve than D&B people to effectively manage my costs; and in so doing my ratio of benefits to price will constitute customer value at a level which will compel the customer to leave D&B and come with me.' In short, competition is an individual human being who is personally challenging each of us as human beings for the most important turf of all—the business of a customer...And if the customer does prove the competitor right, we will have no one to blame but ourselves.... Our ability to prevail in the face of competition rests on the men and women of D&B...who understand that to effectively compete requires that one be customer focused in the broadest sense—

and that to be customer focused requires a taste and resolve for change; a taste and resolve for action with a sense of urgency; a taste and resolve for a relentless focus on quality.

Charles Moritz
Chairman and CEO
The Dun and Bradstreet Corporation

I was so impressed with the talk from which this quote came that I wrote and asked Moritz if we (the VPC) could use the talk, in written form, in an issue of *Quality and Productivity Management* (QPM), the journal of the VPC. (We published his remarks in Volume 6, Number 3 of QPM.) The Way of The New Competition will clearly be different. Leadership, visions, communication, customer focus, bias for action, orders of magnitude higher levels of performance, constant and continual performance improvement cultures, a relentless focus on quality—all these things, and more, are the critical dimensions of the Organization of the Future. These things will not come easy; there is no quick fix; there is a price to pay for excellence.

Winning is the most misunderstood phenomenon today. Winning isn't the most important thing, preparing to win is. Being willing to pay the price to prepare to win ensures you will give your very best. You don't want to pay the price to prepare to win—go somewhere else!

Bobby Knight
Head Basketball Coach
Indiana University

I know that Bobby Knight is a controversial person. I also know that, like many other outspoken people, there are many truths hidden in the way he coaches and leads. This quote may seem harsh in its style, however, I think it makes a very important point. Excellence comes at a price. Preparing to perform, in any endeavor, is critical. There is, in my opinion, a belief or perhaps a hope that improvement might be attained via an easy path. When we describe our views of the roadmap to change for American organizations we are often challenged to suggest an easier way, a quicker way. I think management of performance is a very difficult, highly technical task that requires patience, persistence, and consistency. Managing is very hard work. It is physically and psychologically demanding and draining. It is insidiously consuming. It requires constant attention to details while simultaneously being able to stand back and grasp situations in the "gestalt." It is a skill and yet there is an increasing need to have managers systematically study and understand the technology of management.

We recently lost a job at an organization because top management felt that strategic planning wasn't a technology, that strategic planning is just the process of throwing people in a room and tasking them to develop a strategic plan. We argued that there is a science to planning; just like there is a science to engineering a job, installing a piece of equipment, or writing software. We suggested that the process by which you plan is as important as the plan itself. We lost the argument and the job because top management failed to understand that management processes must be continually improved and can be engineered.

The Way of The New Competition may be a dramatic departure from the past for many of you and your organizations. For others, the Way of The New Competition may be a natural evolution. However, we suggest that for most American managers and for most managers of globally competing organizations, the Way of The New Competition will require at least an introspective examination of management processes and practices. In doing this, we suspect that you will find that personal style, cognitive style, how we collect information, how we process information, and how we solve problems all need to be assessed in light of new demands on management and leadership.

Lessons from Zen, Tao, and Whole-Brain Thinking

Work on personality types, cognitive styles, problem-solving styles and preferences is not pervasive in the popular literature, but it does exist and is relevant to the task of responding to the challenges posed by The New Competition. Gareth Morgan suggests that effective leaders and managers develop a skill, usually an intuitive process, for "reading" the situations they are attempting to manage (Morgan 1986). They develop comprehensive, often very holistic, views of situations. His outstanding book entitled *Images of the Organization* builds on a premise that our theories, explanations, and ensuing behaviors are based on metaphors about organizations. Metaphors imply a way of thinking and a way of seeing our world; in this case the world of complex organizations. He goes on to describe various metaphors or images of organizations that are prevalent. The metaphors he examines are:

1. Organizations as machines;
2. Organizations as organisms;
3. Organizations as brains;
4. Organizations as cultures;
5. Organizations as political systems;
6. Organizations as psychic prisons;
7. Organizations as flux and transformation; and
8. Organizations as instruments of domination.

Most of these ways of thinking about organizations have implications for the task of continually improving quality and productivity. For example, our conceptualization of organizations strongly influences our strategies and tactics for quality and productivity improvement. If you ask seven different managers, all with different educational and experiential backgrounds, all working in the same organization, how to best improve quality and productivity, you almost always get unique and often divergent answers. Some of the differences are due to the different data bases upon which answers are being developed, but much of the difference is based upon their preferred ways of thinking about how to change behaviors in the organization. These preferred ways of thinking about things are a reflection of the metaphors they have developed for organizations and organizational behavior.

Morgan summarizes by saying that as our world becomes increasingly complex our styles of thinking must attempt to match the levels of complexity. He argues, as does Killman (1984), for the need to "go beyond quick fixes." He suggests that organizational analysis, problem solving that is driven by well-rounded thinking, and broader images of the organization are critical to progress. We believe that the strategic performance improvement planning process helps management teams to begin to do what Morgan and others call for.

However, our ability to analyze organizational situations, such as productivity and quality improvement efforts, is dominated by cognitive style (how we prefer to or are trained to think). Numerous authors have suggested that improved "whole-brain thinking" will improve management and leadership performance (Wonder and Donovan 1984; Pirsig 1974; Morris 1979; Hampden-Turner 1981). Most suggest that self-awareness regarding your preferences and style is an important first step to positive change.

We suggest that there are some lessons from religion and philosophy that will be valuable to the manager, leader, and organization attempting to become the Organization of the Future.

Garvin speaks about five definitions of quality; for example, one of them being transcendent. "Quality is neither mind nor matter, but a third entity independent of the two...even though quality cannot be defined, you know what it is" (Pirsig 1974, 185 and 213). It seems to us that there are transcendent aspects to management and leadership. The transcendent aspects, we believe, are the stuff of which maintaining excellence and the Organization of the Future are made. It goes beyond the processes and approaches to planning and measurement that we have spoken about to this point. It may, for many organizations, require an "inquiry into values," such as the one Pirsig describes in *Zen and the Art of Motorcycle Maintenance*. It may require the development of guiding principles using the procedure described in Chapter 6. The performance improvement planning process is designed to develop teams, but you may require a deeper, more intensive organizational systems analysis step to begin to change the true problem-solving style and culture of your organization.

I want to take a slight departure at this point to elaborate upon the "you will know it when you see it," transcendental aspect of quality. I'll make my points using an example that I have experimented with in the classroom. Pirsig talks about defining quality and presents a story about a professor who asks a class of students to write an essay on quality. The students struggle with the assignment, and so to make a point, the professor provides a copy of the complete set of papers to all the students in class and then asks them to read them and to rank them from best to worst. Once the students have done this, he presents the data, from all the students. There was a reasonable degree of consensus as to which were the better papers and which were the poorer-quality papers. I do this same exercise the first several weeks of my class. I ask the students to write a professional, quality paper on a topic I have assigned. I do not tell them what "quality" or "professional" means. My students have consistently been able to rank the papers with high levels of agreement in terms of quality and professionalism.

Pirsig concluded that there are aspects of quality that are transcendent. Deming suggests that some of the most important aspects of organizational system performance are unknown/ unmeasured and unknowable/unmeasurable—"we'll know it when we see it" type of stuff.

I agree with these points in principle; however, you must be careful not to extrapolate too far with them. Let me continue the classroom example to clarify the issue. Once my students have written their papers, with little guidance other than the specifications for them to be "quality" and "professional," and they have ranked the papers as a class, I ask them to talk about what they used to determine the ranks. I do a short NGT with them, asking them individually and silently to list the things (factors and criteria) that caused them to rank papers the way they did. After about a five- to ten-minute period of silent, individual writing, I go around the room and ask each student for one of the items on their list. We do this until we have exhausted all their items. We then clarify the items on the list, ensuring that every student understands the item and ensuring that like items are combined. We want to end up with a collectively exhaustive list and a mutually exclusive list of things that caused the students to rank the papers the way they did.

Once this is done each student is given seven three-by-five index cards and asked to rank the seven most important items on the resulting list that has been posted in front of them (I use standard NGT ranking procedures at this point). I pick up the cards from each student and tabulate the results. An example of the results is shown in Figure 8-1.

Note that each item (criteria) is ranked and rated. I use these sheets to grade the students' papers with the rest of the term. I believe that my students' professional writing skills are improved because they are forced to make them explicit, to think about things that previously had been left to the professor. I have never felt the need to reject or even modify the resulting evaluation forms. My point is that the students do know quality writing when they see it and, most importantly, they can explicate what it is they see. This process of explicating criteria is inherently a critical step

EVALUATION CRITERIA	RANK	RATE	WEIGHT	SCORE	WEIGHTED SCORE
FOLLOW ASSIGNMENT/ EFFECTIVENESS Meet assigned objectives Define and meet author's objectives	#1	100	0.190		
COMMUNICATION QUALITY Logical flow Style of writing Clarity	#2	95	0.181		
RESEARCH QUALITY/ CONTENT Technical accuracy Depth Integration, assimilation of course materials & outside materials	#3	90	0.171		
ORIGINALITY/INNOVATION Insightfulness Original ideas/presentation Convincing points	#4	85	0.162		
PROFESSIONALISM Grammar Overall appearance Citation & Referencing Figure & table use	#5	80	0.152		
ORGANIZATION QUALITY Structure between ¶s and within ¶s Heading logic & hierarchy logic	#6	75	0.144		
TOTAL WEIGHTED SCORE		525	1.000		

Figure 8-1. Position Paper Evaluation Sheet

in the measurement process regardless of whether the criterion is quality or any of the other six. "You know it when you see it" doesn't, in my opinion, mean it has to be left unmeasured or undefined. On the other hand, I would be the first to admit that there are elements of the students' papers that they and I are influenced by when we rank them that don't end up as criterion.

The same point could be made for white-collar performance measurement, management performance assessment, leadership evaluation, product performance, and so forth. Aspects of performance will be explicable and measurable while certain aspects will not be. The important thing is to make explicit and visible those aspects that we can put our fingers on and then to use them as a system of performance measurement focused on improvement.

Another excellent book entitled *The Tao of Leadership: Leadership Strategies for a New Age* has caused a number of our clients' top management teams to reflect on leadership and management style issues as they relate to quality and productivity improvement. The book is filled with philosophical tidbits that may yield improved understanding of how to enhance progress towards the Organization of the Future. A few examples are:

- At birth, a person is flexible and flowing—the rigid group leader may be able to lead repetitions and structured exercises but can't cope with living group process. Whatever is living and flexible and flowing will tend to grow. Whatever is rigid and blocked will atrophy and die.
- The wise leader is like water— the leader works in any setting without complaint, with any person, cover, or issue that comes on the floor; the leader acts so that all will benefit and serves well regardless of the rate of pay; the leader speaks simply and honestly and intervenes in order to shed light and create harmony. Like water, the leader is yielding. Because the leader does not push, the group does not resent or resist.
- Endless drama in a group clouds consciousness—too much noise overwhelms the senses. Continual input obscures genuine insight. Allow regular time for silent reflection. When group members have time to reflect, they can see more clearly what is essential in themselves and others.

There are a total of eighty-one chapters/lessons in this book by Heider (1985). Those philosophical views on effective leadership, combined with the wisdom of leadership shared by Bennis and Nanus in *Leaders*, provide a glimpse of leadership as it must exist in the future.

Beyond sharing information, knowledge, power, and rewards; searching for excellence; changing how you plan and measure and solve problems; training everyone in SPC techniques; the one-minute manager on everything; developing change masters; gainsharing and employee involvement and automation; and all the other popular fixes of the day, are some deeper and more complex issues. They are the issues of values, beliefs, and leadership. Our leadership and managerial behaviors reflect how we prefer to and have been shaped to think about the world around us. The world around us has changed dramatically and we must re-examine our principles and our practices. Maintaining excellence requires that you successfully deal with these issues.

Leaders

". . .the only thing of real importance that leaders do is to create and manage culture. . ." (Schein 1985)

Bennis and Nanus (1985) suggest that many popular authors who are describing (and prescribing) the challenge and response neglect a very important issue—power. They define power as the basic energy to initiate and sustain action translating intention into reality. Barnard addressed this issue in 1939 in his classic, *The Functions of the Executive*, when he identified and described the functions of the executive to be:

1. Providing a system of communication;
2. Maintaining the willingness to cooperate;
3. Ensuring the continuing integrity of organizational purpose; and
4. Leading to affirm decisions that lend quality and morality to the coordination of organized\activity and formulation of purpose.

Kanter also addresses this issue effectively in her two classics *Men and Women of the Corporation* (1977) and *The Change Masters* (1983). Many authors today really don't have the insight and intuition necessary to understand this aspect of organizational behavior. Hence, their descriptions and prescriptions are incomplete and ineffective.

Bennis and Nanus go on to state that leadership is the wise use of power. They, like Burns (1978) and Bass (1985), speak to a special type of leadership called "transformative" or "transformational" leadership. They identified four types of "human handling skills" that the leaders they studied exhibited:

1. Attention through vision;
2. Meaning through communication;
3. Trust through positioning; and
4. Deployment of self through (a) positive self-regard and (b) the Wallenda factor.

They contrast transformational leadership with transactional leadership. The transformational leader is creating visions, sharing information and knowledge, building trust and commitment, and has positive self-regard and is an eternal optimist focusing on strengths, making them decisive rather than dwelling on weaknesses. Their positive self-regard rubs off on the members of their organizational system. They feel good about themselves and their people feel good about themselves. Perhaps most importantly, transformational leaders are proactive.

The strategic performance improvement planning process, if managed properly, is an excellent device for transformational leaders to utilize to move the organizational system forward. We understand the difference between a transactional leader and a transformational leader but struggle with the "how to." We have been fortunate to have found a number of leaders and managers who want to be transformational but are struggling with the process of doing so. The desire to do so coupled with the process we have described in this book has worked well in numerous situations over the past ten years.

As we move toward new patterns of management and leadership, practices and processes of management will have to change. Moving from manager-led and dominated organizational systems to self-managed organizations will not be easy. Hackman has conceptualized this transition, even beyond the self-managed stage. Figure 8-2 depicts this transition. As we attempt to move from left to right on the x-axis, critical issues will need to be successfully addressed.

For example:

1. What does "shove the responsibility and accountability for planning, problem solving, and decision making to the lowest appropriate level" mean? How do you do that? What constitutes the lowest appropriate level? How often do you do it?
2. What factors determine when sharing power is appropriate and will be successful? When is participation appropriate? (We think that there are at least four factors that must be considered: need for acceptance, need for quality, availability of time, and maturity of the followers [Sink 1985].)
3. What happens if we take this too far, we share too much power? How does the situation affect what is appropriate in terms of participation and leadership style?
4. How do you have strong leadership and still move towards a self-managed work team concept?
5. Can this process be self-managing; can we expect that the management team can lead this process, or will we need outside help? Do we need an "honest broker" for the process? Can the leader be the process facilitator?

6. How do we do this in the face of intense pressures to perform and improve performance now? Will performance go down early in this process? If so, how do we justify this?
7. How do we fight off the tremendous number of Theory X oriented managers in positions of power throughout the organizations?
8. How do we overcome the "dilemmas of managing participation" that Kanter talks about in her book *The Change Masters*?
9. How do we strategize this so that we have a vision of where we are going and a roadmap for change and so we will be consistent and persistent?

These questions reflect concerns and issues that organizations that are in the process of becoming Organizations of the Future are asking themselves. They are questions that have no one right answer. We believe that if you follow the roadmap for change we have outlined in this book that the answers will become self-evident over time. The capacity to deal with the concerns and issues identified here exists in your organization. All you have to do is tap that capability.

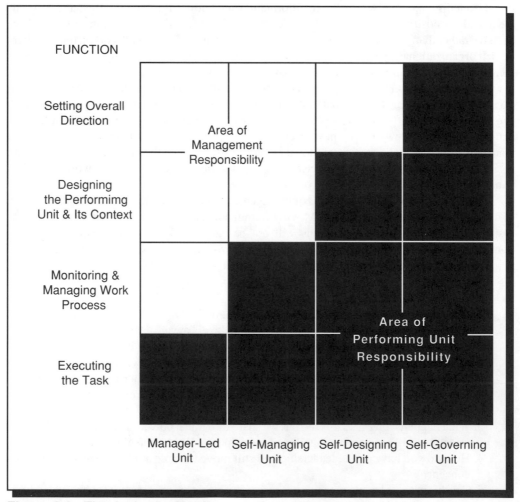

Figure 8-2. The Authority Matrix (Adapted from Hackman 1986)

Future Perfect

We had a client from Brazil with us the other day. At the end of the session with them, we asked when they wanted the final report from our two-day meeting (suspecting they would ask for it in two weeks, we were prepared to send it to them in a week). To our surprise, they asked to have it before they left. It was 3:00 PM and they were leaving at 5:00 PM, so we had a challenge in front of us. I went to my staff and told them we had to have the clients' final report for this meeting by 5:00; to which they responded that it was an impossible and unrealistic request. They informed me that the process we use to prepare final reports like this was well established and that the best they could do was one week.

> We critically need new management theory to explain and to further the transformations that we are witnessing yet only dimly understand because we are too much in their midst. In the industrial economy, our models helped us to manage aftermath, the consequences of events that had already happened. In this new economy, however, we must learn to manage the beforemath; that is, the consequences of events that have not yet occurred. This is managing in the future perfect tense. By 2001, when the new economy probably will have matured, we will observe our holistic approach to management and wonder how it ever could have been otherwise (Davis 1987).

Davis' book, entitled *Future Perfect*, reflects the theme of how we have chosen to end this book. He speaks about the life cycle—the conception to consumption— of products and services. He stresses the concept of making ideas acts; instantaneous satisfaction of customer needs, future perfect. My staff couldn't meet our Brazilian customer's needs because of a production process. They had a process that has a cycle time of five days; our customer wanted a cycle time of less than two hours. My staff assumed, incorrectly so, that the process or the specs for the output couldn't change and were willing to not satisfy the customer rather than change the process or investigate flexibility in the specifications for the report.

> The only way an organization's leaders can get there (the objectives of the strategy) from here (the current organization) is to lead from a place in time that assumes you are already there, and that is determined even though it hasn't happened yet (Davis 1987).

"The present is the past of the future, and organization can be used to push the strategy toward its realization rather than be pulled along by it" (Davis 1987). Increasingly, organizations will have to respond more quickly to their environment, opportunities, and New Competition. Flexibility, proactivity, and responsiveness will be key issues. Individuals in the organization when asked to produce a report in two hours will have to adopt a "can do" attitude and figure out how to comply, rather than defending why they can't.

White-collar just-in-time applications will become more prevalent in the near future. We have a client whose top manager—a technical director—has set a goal to "turn over" the in-basket three times a day. He reviews his in-basket and either processes the item, sends it back to the originator because he doesn't understand why he got the item, or throws the item away. The concept of future perfect is not prevalent in white-collar settings, and it may take just-in-time applications to things like in-baskets to force the concept to become a reality.

You cannot implement the concept of future perfect without a process that operationalizes continuous improvement and that builds commitment and self-management in the organization. My staff has to accept the "can do" philosophy, be innovative, and be in a self-management mode

315

in order for us to continue to respond to changing customer needs and requirements. On the other hand, it seems to me that Quality Checkpoints 1 and 5 are critical and essential to the success of implementing the concept of future perfect. It is critical to ensure that customers' expectations and specifications and satisfaction with your performance are continually monitored.

The concept of anticipating the future, of being responsive to changing customers' needs and requirements, and of building an organization that can continually improve cycle times and quality of products and services is critical to becoming the Organization of the Future. As we have said repeatedly, The New Competition is aggressively improving everything they do. You must develop a strategy to respond to the challenge posed by The New Competition and to become the Organization of the Future.

The organization, the management team, that follows the crowd will usually get no further than the crowd. The organization that walks alone is likely to find itself in places where no one has ever been. Creativity in managing and performing is not without its attendant difficulties, for peculiarity breeds contempt. The unfortunate thing about being ahead of your time, is that when people finally realize you were right, they will say it was obvious all along.

Your organization, your management team, has two choices with respect to what to do about this book and the concepts within it: You can dissolve into the mainstream, do nothing, or you can become distinct and do something.

To be distinct, you must be different. To be different, you must strive to be what no one else but you, your organization, your management team can be: **Your Organization of the Future.**

REFERENCES AND SUGGESTED READINGS

Bass, B. M. 1985. *Leadership and Performance Beyond Expectation.* The Free Press. New York.

Bennis, W., and B. Nanus. 1985. *Leaders: The Strategies for Taking Charge.* Harper & Row. New York.

Davis, S. M. 1987. *Future Perfect.* Addison-Wesley. Reading, Massachusetts.

Grayson, J., and C. O'Dell. 1988. *The Two-Minute Warning.* The Free Press. New York.

Hackman, J. R. 1986. The psychology of self-management in organizations. *Psychology and Work: Productivity, Change and Employment.* Edited by Pallack, M. S., and R. O. Perloff. American Psychological Association. Washington, D.C.

Hampden-Turner, C. 1981. *Maps of the Mind.* Collier Books. New York.

Heider, J. 1985. *The Tao of Leadership: Leadership Strategies for a New Age.* Bantam Books. New York.

Jacobson, G., and J. Hillkirk. 1986. *Xerox: American Samurai.* Collier Books. New York.

Kanter, R. M. 1977. *Men and Women of the Corporation.* Basic Books, Inc. New York.

_____. 1983. *The Change Masters.* Simon and Schuster. New York.

Kilmann, R. H. 1984. *Beyond the Quick Fix.* Jossey-Bass, Inc. San Francisco, California.

Morgan, G. 1986. *Images of the Organization.* Sage Publications. Beverly Hills, California.

Moritz, C. W. 1987. Quality means a customer focus. *Quality and Productivity Management.* 6(3). VPC, Virginia Tech. Blacksburg, Virginia.

Morris, W. T. 1979. *Implementation Strategies for Industrial Engineers.* Grid Publishing Co. Columbus, Ohio.

Pirsig, R. M. 1974. *Zen and the Art of Motorcycle Maintenance.* Bantam Books. New York.

Reich, R. B. 1987. *Tales of a New America.* Times Books. New York.

Schein, E. H. 1985. *Organizational Culture and Leadership.* Jossey-Bass, Inc. San Francisco, California.

Thurow, L. C. 1984. Revitalizing american industry: Managing in a competitive world economy. *California Management Review.* 27(1). Fall, 9-41.

_____. 1985. *Zero Sum Solution: Building a World-Class American Economy*. Simon and Schuster, New York.

Wonder, J., and P. Donovan. 1984. *Whole-Brain Thinking*. William Morrow.

APPENDIX A

A Partial List of Organizations We Have Worked
With Over the Last Ten Years

Ore-Ida Foods
U.S. Dept. of Navy
Honeywell Aerospace and Defense Company
U.S. Dept. of Defense
Tennessee Valley Authority
Burlington Industries
U.S. Senate Productivity Award Board (VA)
Naval Air Systems Command
VA Dept. of Transportafion
Naval Ordnance Station - Indian Head
Venezuelan Productivity Commission
Hubble Lighting
Kal-Kan
Norfolk Naval Shipyard
AIRLANT (U.S. Navy) Aircraft Maintenance
Eastern Envelope
Institute of Industrial Engineers (IIE)
National Fruit Product Co.
Institute of Industrial Engineers
National Fruit Product Co.

Naval Training Systems Center
U.S. Dept. of Energy
Naval Aircraft Maintenance Office
San Diego Gas & Electric
State Mutual Companies
United Illuminating
Military Traffic Management Command
Rhodia, S.A.
XALOY
NASA-Goddard and Marshall Space
  Flight Centers
VA Tech College of Engineering
Blue Cross of Washington
M&M Mars
LTV-Vought Aero Products
AIRPAC (U.S. Navy) Aircraft
  Maintenance
Beatrice Foods
Auditor Gemeral of Canada

APPENDIX B

Process for Developing Key Result Areas

The measurement development process we are about to undertake tries to accomplish this linkage through the concept of key result areas (KRA). Key result areas are the areas of performance that the organization must attempt to carry out if it is to achieve its strategic aims. Once the Key Result Areas are defined, then the process proceeds to the development of performance indicators for these strategically defined performance areas. We will now turn to a description of this process. It was developed under support from the Air Force Human Resources Laboratory, and was referred to as MGEEM the methodology for generating efficiency and effectiveness measures. A modified version of the process has been called the strategic performance measurement process [(SPMP Tuttle and Ross 1988)]. In this discussion we will maintain the label MGEEM for the process. The steps to be discussed are: forming the measurement development teams, generating Key Result Areas, generating indicators, reviewing indicators, and pitfalls to avoid.

   1. Participant knowledge—Do the participants have sufficient knowledge of the organization and its primary work processes to contribute ideas and make meaningful judgments. This knowledge is usually assured through obtaining a balance of experienced individuals at a range of grade levels.

   2. Participant communication skills—Because the MGEEM is a verbal process, the communication skills of participants are important. Not only must participants have knowledge, they must be able to communicate that knowledge. On the other hand, inexperienced individuals who are immature but are highly verbal create different problems for the process. Such individuals, unless carefully managed by the facilitator, can steer the process in inappropriate directions. In addition to these concerns, the facilitator should stress to the management team the need to have a cross-section of the organization and to include people who will "speak their mind" in constructive ways. Management should have the final word in selecting participants, however, because they, and not the facilitator, must live with the results.

   3. Position/influence in the organization - A basic assumption underlying MGEEM is that participation in the development of a solution will increase the acceptability of that solution. Therefore, the facilitator should seek to ensure— all else being equal—that key opinion leaders in the organization are included in the measurement development team (MDT). Individuals may be opinion leaders by virtue of formal or informal power. It is important to identify key individuals and consider them for participation. A key opinion leader who is left out might jeopardize acceptance of the resulting MGEEM products.

   4. Comprehensiveness—The solution resulting from MGEEM will be best if the participants have the widest possible information base to consider. Therefore, the best situation is to include representation from multiple points of view (e.g., all facets of the target organization, next higher level organization, and significant "customer."

One Team or Two

In most cases, it will be desirable to form two MDTs in order to broaden the participation. Generally, a management team called Team A is used to define the measurable facets of a unit's mission, which have been labeled "key result areas." A second MDT, a worker-level team, called Team B, is recommended to develop the indicators or measures for the Key Result Areas. There are exceptions to this guideline. If the organization is small (e.g., ten to fifteen people), then forming two teams is probably not feasible. Also, if the organization is comprised of professionals[1] who operate in a very participative manner (e.g., researchers, engineers, social workers, and so forth), they may be uncomfortable with the idea of only managers involved in developing KRAs. In this case, one MDT might be utilized that is comprised of both managers and non-managers, and which develops both KRAs and indicators.

The key result areas development process takes place in a meeting that typically takes about three hours. The meeting is run by the measurement facilitator. A key factor in the ability of the measurement facilitator to function effectively is the physical space arrangement. Ideally, the room will be a well-ventilated one with adequate lighting for people to work effectively and be comfortable. The room shape is important from the point of view of the available wall space for use in hanging newsprint sheets. There should be at least twenty linear feet of wall space which is free of pictures, windows, doors, and other obstructions. The room size should be sufficient to accommodate a long conference table, or a U-shaped arrangement of tables which face the long wall. The room set-up should have, in addition to the conference table, at least one easel with a newsprint pad, markers, and masking tape. Three different-colored markers are helpful to assist in highlighting subsequent rounds of editing the items generated in group sessions.

Assuming that the steps recommended in the communications plan have been carried out, participants should be aware of the purposes of the measurement process in the organization. Therefore, this initial briefing should have the following objectives:

1. to explain the steps in the measurement development process;
2. to create the proper mental set for KRA development; and
3. to explain what KRA are and their role in the measurement development process.

The facilitator initiates the process by writing the question to be answered on a sheet of newsprint and hanging it on the wall where all participants can see it. In posing this question the facilitator should say: "This is the question I would like you to answer." (At this point, write the following question on the newsprint pad.)

What categories of results is this organization (name the target organization) expected to accomplish?

"As you think about this question, all of you should put yourselves in the position of the manager of the target organization. In other words, today you are the boss!"

Participants are asked to "silently generate" answers to the question posed by the facilitator. This process is very important since ideas generated serve as the primary content for the remainder of the process. Allow sufficient time so that participants do not feel rushed but have time to reflect on their task. Usually ten to fifteen minutes is sufficient. To begin this process, the facilitator should say:

"On a sheet of paper write a list your answers to this question. Please do this individually without discussion. Take as much time as you need to fully answer the question. Does anyone have any problems with the question as it is stated?" (At this point, some participants may want to change a word or discuss the question. Minor changes in wording can be made in order to help the participants accept the question. It is important that participants "buy in" to the task at this point.) "If there are no questions then begin."

The next step in the process is the round-robin listing of the participants' ideas. The purpose of this activity is to move the ideas generated by participants from their papers to a newsprint pad as quickly as possible. This process is conducted without comment or discussion, except for clarification in order to accurately and legibly record ideas. The facilitator moves around the group in round-robin fashion getting one idea from each participant. This process continues until all participants say "pass," indicating that all of their ideas have been recorded.

To begin this process, the facilitator should say, "Now we would like to have you read your items one at a time so that we can record them on the newsprint pad. The objective is to write your items as quickly as possible, therefore, we will not have any discussion of items as they are written except to correct inaccuracies. I will start with ('name a participant'). Then I will proceed around the table in round-robin fashion untill all items on your lists have been transferred to the newsprint." (Name a participant) "Will you give me one item off your list?" (Once the item is written, ask the participant if the item is O.K. If not, then make any corrections necessary. If it is O.K., then proceed to the next person and write his/her item. If not, correct the item on the newsprint until the participant is satisfied that it has been written correctly.) A sample listing of original KRAs from a food service organization is shown in Table B-1.

Once all the ideas are listed, the facilitator leads the group through a review process. The purpose of the review process is to modify the statement of items to improve clarity and accuracy, as well as to reduce overlap. Participants may ask questions to have the meaning of an item explained. A third purpose is to make combinations of items as appropriate to remove redundancy or to achieve a consistent level of item specificity. This can be achieved by taking items that are too broad and spreading the content across two or more items. Conversely, items may be combined if they are too narrow or specific in order to achieve an appropriate level of specificity. As a guide, the initial KRA list might contain from thirty to fifty items. Following discussion and clarification this number should be reduced by approximately twenty to forty percent.

Participants are then asked to select the items from the list which they feel are the most important KRAs for the unit. The facilitator establishes the number to be selected. Generally, having the group select five to seven items is recommended. While this is difficult, it helps the group focus on an appropriate level of specificity for the KRAs. It also serves to clearly highlight areas of agreement or disagreement among the group with respect to the priorities of the organization.

The facilitator can run the voting process as follows:

"Now that you have had an opportunity to discuss the items, it is time to prioritize the key result areas. Please bear with me because the voting process is a bit tedious. However, it is important that you follow the process exactly. You will be using the index cards that are on the table. Each person should have five index cards.

First, look at the items that remain."(At this point, the facilitator might circle in red the numbers of items that remain — or use some other means to point out the items eligible for the voting process.) "From this list of items, select the five that you feel are most important in terms of answering the question we initially posed. Remember, as you make this selection you should be viewing this process from the point of view of the unit commander. Once you have selected the five items, write them one at a time on the index cards you have been given. Write the item number in the upper left corner of the card and the item itself in the middle of the card." (It is helpful for the facilitator to draw a sample card and illustrate where to write the item and the number [see Figure B-1].)

"When you have completed this step, place all five cards on the table in front of you. Consider only the five cards that are in front of you. Of these five, which item is most important? Select the item and write the number '5' on the lower right corner of the card. Turn that card over." (The facilitator should illustrate this by writing the number in the lower right corner of the card diagrammed on the newsprint pad (see Figure B-2). "Of the four remaining items, which is least

Table B-1. Original Key Result Areas: Food Service

1. Provide quality meals to customers.
2. Best possible variety of food.
3. Ensure effective training programs.
4. Quality facilities.
5. Equipment turnover — 5 year plan for replacement of equipment.
6. Organize and manage supervisors to operate facilities.
7. Maintain acceptable sanitary/housekeeping conditions.
8. Maintain effective relationships with other base agencies.
9. Satisfy customers through consistent quality, variety, service, and quality facilities.
10. Maintain adequate manpower to reach objectives.
11. Effective quality assurance evaluation.
12. Controls and safeguards inventory — food and supplies.
13. Provide sufficient personnel to satisfy deployment needs without sacrificing production at home or exceeding normal work hours.
14. Set good example for people to follow -support the people, maintain standards, reward and recognize people, morale, esprit, job satisfaction, and maintain quality facility for staff.
15. Meet the required set schedule and respond to emergency needs.
16. Support the wing/base mission and maintain effective relationships with other agencies.
17. Make productive/efficient use of available resources. Obtain adequate funding for equipment/ supplies.
18. Maintain fiscal accountability.
19. Continue to improve operations rather than stagnate.
20. Compliance with regulations (e.g., fiscal accountability, meet suspenses, inventory control, sanitation, budgeting, and obtain funding).
21. Satisfy your wing commander.
22. Be versatile, creative, innovative, imaginative.
23. Support his/her people.
24. Food service long-range planning.
25. Maintain required documentation.
26. Be able to tell your boss "like it is."
27. Manage the gray areas.
28. Identify, report, and follow-up on equipment maintenance.
29. Develop realistic budgets and obtain funding.
30. Provide satisfactory workplace for our people .
31. Provide quality food at correct selling price.
32. Zero defects on fraud, waste, and abuse.

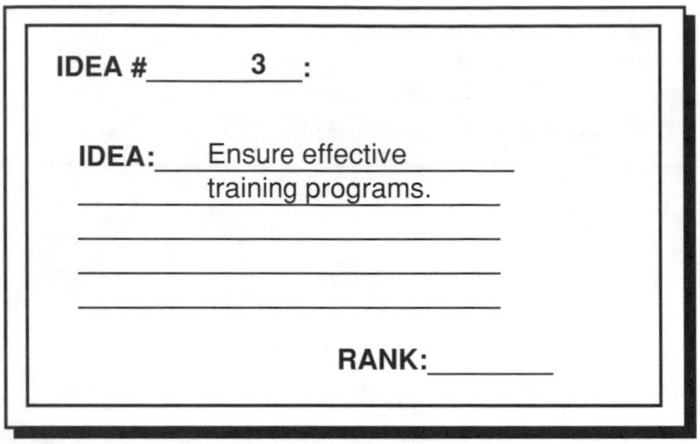

```
IDEA #_____3___:


   IDEA:___Ensure effective_____
   _____training programs._____
   _____
   _____
   _____

                    RANK:_____
```

**Figure B-1. Sample Voting Card
With an Idea Written On It**

important? Write the number '1' on the lower right corner of the card. Turn the card over. Of the remaining items, select the one that is most imporant and write a '4' in the lower right corner o fthe card. Turn the card over.

Of the two remaining cards, select the one that is least important and write a '2' in the lower right corner. Write a '3' in the lower right corner of the remaining card. This completes the voting process. Please give me your cards." (As the votes are tallied, it is a convenient time to give the group a break. The vote tally can be recorded as shown in Table B-2.)

Perhaps the most important step in the process with respect to the quality of the resulting product and the degree of participant commitment to the result is the discussion that follows the first vote. If there is complete consensus following vote 1, this discussion is unnecessary. However, complete consensus is rare at this point. Therefore, the purpose of this discussion is to bring out additional information that will promote consensus and modify items in ways that will promote better consensus. The facilitator's role in this step is to guide the group through this discussion, always focusing on the items and on ways to make the items more meaningful, less ambiguous, or more accurately stated. The facilitator should use the voting pattern from vote 1 as the starting point for this discussion. The discussion should center around items for which more than one participant voted, but which show a reasonably wide spread in the voting pattern. For example, in discussing the voting pattern shown in Table B-2, the facilitator might say:

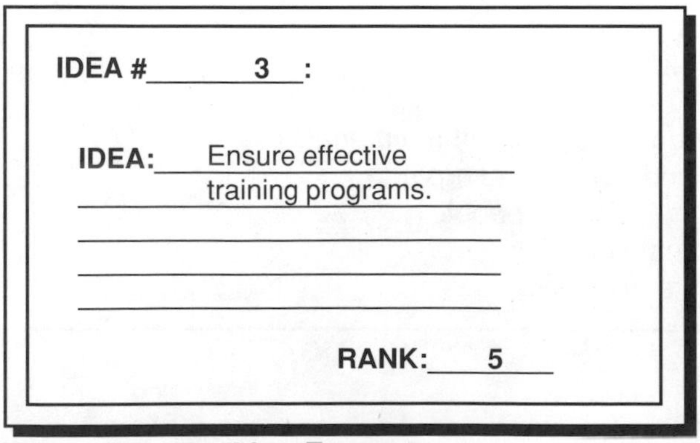

```
IDEA #_____3___:


   IDEA:___Ensure effective_____
   _____training programs._____
   _____
   _____
   _____

                    RANK:____5_____
```

Figure B-2. Ranking Example

Table B-2. Food Service Key Result Areas: Vote 1 Results

Task statement: Select the seven (7) items that you feel are most important.

1.		
2.		
3.	5-2-4-4-4	5/19
4.	1-3-4-1	4/10
5.	4-1-5-1-3	5/14
6.		
7.	2-5	2/7
8.	4	1/4
9.	7-7-6-6-1-7-5-7	8/46
10.		
11.	3-2	2/5
12.	3	1/3
13.	2-2	2/4
14.	6-4-7-6-2-6	6/31
15.		
16.	6-5-7-7-7	5/32
17.	3-5-2-6-6	5/22
18.	3-1-3	3/7
19.	3	1/3
20.	2-4-1	3/7
21.		
22.	1-5-5	3/11

"Now we are going to discuss this voting pattern that resulted from your first vote. As you can see, the group does not see things exactly the same way. In this discussion, we are attempting to make the items better, not 'twist your arms' to get you to vote in a certain way. However, it is our goal to achieve as much agreement among group members as possible.

Let's look first at item number 3. Five people voted for this item and three people did not. Those who selected it rated it 5-2-4-4-4. Would someone who felt that this item was important please tell us what caused you to select it?" (Now allow time for this person to point out the strengths one to two minutes is sufficient — don't allow long speeches.) "Would anyone else like to say why they voted for this item?" (Continue until anyone who wants to talk has had the opportunity to briefly argue for the item.)

"Now, could someone who did not select this item tell why you did not feel this was one of the top items?" (Continue the discussion as before until all issues are aired.)

"Now that we have heard this discussion, what changes should we make in the item? Should it be combined with another item?"(The facilitator is guided by the group to either make no changes to the item, to modify it, to delete it, or to combine it with another item. If it is combined, the number of the item should be written as a subscript below the number of the item it is being combined with, as shown in Table B-3.) The discussion can attempt to create consensus by making sure everyone has the same interpretation of what items mean and by allowing participants to attempt to influence values through adding information not available to all members (e.g., history of the organization, future trends that may influence priorities, customer or higher headquarters views, and so forth). This is an open information-sharing and clarification session, however, and not a coercive, arm-twisting discussion.

Table B-3. Food Service Key Result Areas: Vote 2

3.	2-4-1-6-3-2-3-3	8/24	5
5.	1-5-6-3-2-3-2-2	8/24	5
9.	6-7-7-7-4-6-6-7	8/50	1
13.*	3-4-4-1	4/12	7
14.	4-6-3-7-5-5-6	7/36	2
16.	3-1-5-5-1-7-7-5	8/34	3
17.	7-1-6-4-4-4	6/26	4
20.	5-2-2-2-5-1-1	7/18	6

*Item dropped by consensus following vote 2.

The voting process is repeated for the items that remain. Five to seven items should be selected as most important. If the facilitator believes that there are strong unresolvable disagreements among participants, the number of items might be increased to seven to nine. However, this is usually unnecessary, and the number voted on is not necessarily the number of items that will eventually be retained and recommended to management.

Following the second vote, sufficient consensus is normally achieved and the process can be ended. If not, the facilitator should repeat the steps explained above until sufficient consensus is obtained.

Once the process is terminated, the facilitator must document the process. A format for reporting the final results of the session is shown in Table B-4.

Table B-4. Food Service: Final Key Result Areas

(max =8/64)

8/50 1. Customer Satisfaction. Satisfy customers through consistent quality and variety of food and service and through providing and maintaining quality facilities.

7/36 2. Human Resource Management/Leadership. Maintain a motivated work force with high morale, esprit and job satisfaction; involves workforce in decision making; implements creative and innovative practices; encourages high performance through recognizing and rewarding personnel; and provides leadership by example.

8/34 3. Support. Maintain productive relationships with other base agencies that you support and on whom you depend for support.

6/26 4. Productivity of resources. Make productive /efficient use of all available resources.

8/24 5. Equipment Availability. Provide the equipment required to accomplish the food servicemission.

8/24 6. Training Effectiveness. Ensure that personnel are effectively trained.

7/18 7. Administrative Compliance. Comply with Air Force MajCom regulations and requirements.

Appendix C

Model Functions, Activities, and Indicators for
Common Staffing Study (CSS)

1. FACILITY ENGINEERING & MAINTENANCE

ACTIVITY	INDICATOR
FACILITY ENG COORD + CONTROL	BLDNG + EQPT $ PLANNED
FACILITY INST + REARRANGE	INDIRECT MANPOWER
FACILITY MAINT LESS CLN RM	GOSF LESS CLEAN RM
FACILITY MAINT FOR CLN RM	NSF OF CLEAN RM
UTILITIES OPER, MAINT + CONTROL	GOSF SVD BY UTILITY OPER
MFG + PROC EQPT TECH SUPPORT	REPL VAL MFG EQPT INST
POLLUTION/ENVIRON CONTROL	CHEMICAL EXPENDITURES
CHEMICAL CONTROL	CHEMICAL EXPENDITURES
MAINT OF MFG + PROD EQPT	PROC + NON-PROC EQPT INST
TEST EQPT MAINTENANCE	REPL VAL TEST EQPT INST

2. FINANCE

ACTIVITY	INDICATOR
BUSINESS CONTROLS	REG MANPOWER
PAYROLL	REG MANPOWER
CASH CONTROL	REG MANPOWER
FIXED ASSETS	BRASS TAG/TOOLS CONTROLLED
LABOR ACCOUNTING	REG MANPOWER
INVENTORY CONTROL	TOT ACTIVE PART NUMBER
GEN ACCOUNT MISC	REG MANPOWER
BUDGET	REG MANPOWER
MACH/PARTS/COMP COSTING	TOT OUTPUT $
MFG FINANCIAL PLANNING	TOT OUTPUT $
VENDOR INVOICING + BILLING	PURCHASE $
IPT/ID/IC INVOICING + BILLING	TOT IPT/ID/IC $
FINANCIAL PLG SYSTEMS LAB/DEV	TOT GROSS DEV $ BUDGETED
CAPITAL PLANNING	CAPITAL COMMITMENT $

3. GENERAL SERVICES

ACTIVITY	INDICATOR
COMMUNITY RELATION & LEGAL	REG MANPOWER
NEW PRODUCTS	NEW PRODUCT VALUE ADD $
GRAPHIC SERVICES	INDIRECT REG MANPOWER
LOC REPRO/MANUALS	INDIRECT REG MANPOWER
MANAGEMENT SUPPORT	TOT REG MANPOWER
ADMINISTRATIVE SUPPORT	INDIRECT REG MANPOWER
DIRECT MFG MANAGEMENT	REGULAR MANPOWER
INDIRECT MFG MANAGEMENT	REGULAR MANPOWER

4. INDUSTRIAL ENGINEERING

ACTIVITY	INDICATOR
LAB COST EST	TOT GROSS DEV $ BUDGETED
MFG COST ENG	VAL ADD $
PROC COST EST	PROD PUCH $
DIRECT MP PLANNING	TOT DIRECT WORKLOAD
INDIRECT MP PLANNING	TOT INDIRECT MANPOWER
MATL HANDLING/PKG ENG	TOT OUTPUT $
COST REDUCT COORD	VAL ADD $
ADV IND ENG	VAL ADD $
WORKLOAD TRANS COORD	DIRECT WORKLOAD TRANS
SPACE & LAYOUT PLAN	TOT GOSF

5. I/S & DP

ACTIVITY	INDICATOR
IS ADMIN LOCAL	ADMIN FUNCTION WL
IS MATL MGMT LOCAL	MATL MGMT FUNCTION WL
IS TECH LOCAL	TECH FUNCTION WL
NON - IS ADMIN	ADMIN FUNCTION WL
NON - IS MATL MGMT	MATL MGMT FUNCTION WL
COMP OPERATIONS IS	INST IS - DP POINTS W/O TERM
COMP OPERATIONS NON - IS	INST NON - IS - DP POINTS W/O
OPERATIONS SUPPORT	INST IS - DPO POINTS W/O TERM

6. MANUFACTURING ENGINEERING

ACTIVITY	INDICATOR
UNANN/NEW PROC/COMP SUPPORT	NEW PROD VAL ADD + CAP $
UNANN/NEW PAT SUPPORT	NEW PROD VAL ADD + CAP $
CURRENT PROC/COMP SUPPORT	CURRENT PROD VAL ADD + CAP $
CURRENT PAT SUPPORT	CURRENT PROD VAL ADD + CAP $
ME DESIGN + DEBUG PROC/COMP	TOOLS/TEST EQPT/MACH COM $
ME DESIGN + DEBUG PAT	TOOLS/TEST EQPT/MACH COM $
ME PROC ENG + VEND SUP PRO/COM	TOT ACT PURCH P/N
ME PROC ENG + VEND SUPPORT PAT	TOT ACT PURCH P/N
ME PROD TEST CAPITAL EQPT BUILD	TOOLS/TEST EQPT/MACH COM $
PROD LINE SUPPORT - FSD	TOT SITE FSD $
ME RECORDS	ME EQUIVALENT WORKLOAD
ME CLERICAL	ME EQUIVALENT WORKLOAD

7. MANUFACTURING INDIRECT

ACTIVITY	INDICATOR
TRAFFIC	TRAFFIC DOCUMENTS PROCESSED
RETURNED MACH & PARTS CONTROL	RETURNED MACHINE & PARTS
STATIONERY STORES	INDIRECT MANPOWER
RECEIVING	INITIAL RECEIPT TRANS
WAREHOUSING	STORAGE & DISBURSING TRANS
MATLS MOVEMENT INTERNAL	RECEIVING & DISBURSING TRANS
PARTS PACKING & SHIPPING	SHIPMENTS
MACHINE SHIPPING	MACHINE SHIPMENTS
KITTING FOR INPLANT ASSY	PARTS KITTED

8. PROCUREMENT

ACTIVITY	INDICATOR
PRODUCTION BUYING	PROD PURCH $
NON PROD + LAB + CAP BUYING	NON PROD DOC + PURCH $
PROCUREMENT REC PROC + CONTROL	PROD + NON PROD DOC + PUR $
PURCHASING PLANS + CONTROLS	TOT PURCH $

9. PRODUCTION CONTROL

ACTIVITY	INDICATOR
MACHINE LEVEL CONTROL	FCSI + EC RELEASES
CUSTOMER ORDER PROC CONTROL	TOT ORDER ACTIVITY
PARTS ANALYZING	TOT ACTIVE PI PART NUMBERS
ENG CHANGE + RELEASE ANALYSIS	PART NUMBERS REL + CHANGED
MES + AUTOSHIP ORDER CONTROL	MES + AUTOSHIP TRANS
BOX PROD SCHEDULING	NUMBER OF MACH + MOD TYPES
PARTS/PROD SCHEDULE + CONTROL	ACTIVE INPLANT MFG PART NUMBERS
CONSIGNED INVENTORY CONTROL	NO. OF CONS MATL SHPM TO VENDOR
INPLANT PRODUCTION EXPEDITING	TOT ACTIVE PI PART NUMBERS
PLANS + CONTROLS	PROD CTL EQUIVALENT WORKLOAD

10. PERSONNEL

ACTIVITY	INDICATOR
EMPLOYMENT	NUMBER OF INTERVIEWS
TRANSFERS, SEP & LEAVES	REG MANPOWER
EMPLOYMENT REC/APPRAISAL PRG	TOT MANPOWER
EMPLOYEE RELATIONS	TOT MANPOWER
SALARY ADMIN + JOB EVAL	TOT MANPOWER
BENEFITS	REG MANPOWER
SUGGESTIONS	NUMBER SUGGEST PROC
MEDICAL - US/CANADA	TOT MANPOWER
MEDICAL - WTC	TOT MANPOWER
EDUCATION & MGMT DEV	REG MANPOWER
IBM CLUB	TOT MANPOWER
IBM COUNTRY CLUB	COUNTRY CLUB MEMBERSHIP
CAFE SERVICES - US & CANADA	TOT MANPOWER
CAFE SERVICES - WTC	TOT MANPOWER
EQUAL OPPORTUNITY PROGRAM	TOT MANPOWER

11. QUALITY ASSURANCE

ACTIVITY	INDICATOR
INT INSP OF UNANN/NEW	INPLANT DIR WORKLOAD
INT INSP OF CURRENT	INPLANT DIR WORKLOAD
INT INSP OF UNANN/NEW PROC/COMP	INPLANT DIR WORKLOAD
INT INSP OF CURRENT PROC/COMP	INPLANT DIR WORKLOAD
RECEIVING INSPECT	PROD PURCH $
QA RESEARCH & TECH SUPPORT	VALUE ADD $
QUAL SUPPL SUPPORT	PROD PURCH $
TOOL GA & TEST EQUIP EVAL	TOT MANPOWER
REL TESTING	VALUE ADD $
QA AUDITS	TOT DIRECT MANPOWER
NON CONF/FAIL ANALYSIS	VALUE ADD $
QE UNANN/NEW PAT	NEW PROD VAL ADD + CAP $
QE UNANN/NEW PROC/COMP	NEW PROD VAL ADD + CAP $
QE CURRENT PAT	CURRENT PROD VAL ADD + CAP $
QE CURRENT PROC/COMP	CURRENT PROD VAL ADD + CAP $
ANALYSIS CHEMICAL LAB	CHEMICAL EXPENDITURES
MECH & ELEC LAB ANALYSIS	VALUE ADD $